WANTED
DEAD
OR ALIVE

MANHUNTS FROM
GERONIMO TO
BIN LADEN

BENJAMIN RUNKLE

palgrave
macmillan

Maps by Philip Schwartzberg, Meridian Mapping, Minneapolis

First published in 2011 by PALGRAVE MACMILLAN® in the U.S.—a division
of St. Martin's Press LLC, 175 Fifth Avenue, New York, NY 10010.

Where this book is distributed in the UK, Europe and the rest of the world,
this is by Palgrave Macmillan, a division of Macmillan Publishers Limited,
registered in England, company number 785998, of Houndmills, Basingstoke,
Hampshire RG21 6XS.

Palgrave Macmillan is the global academic imprint of the above companies
and has companies and representatives throughout the world.

Palgrave® and Macmillan® are registered trademarks in the United States, the
United Kingdom, Europe and other countries.

ISBN: 978-0-230-10485-3

Runkle, Benjamin.
   Wanted dead or alive : manhunts from Geronimo to Bin Laden / by
Benjamin Runkle.
      p.   cm.
   ISBN 978-0-230-10485-3
      1. United States—Armed Forces—History.   2. Intervention (International
law)—History.   3. Fugitives from justice—History.   4. Geronimo,
1829–1909.   5. Aguinaldo, Emilio, 1869–1964.   6. Villa, Pancho,
1878–1923.   7. Sandino, Augusto Cesar, 1895–1934.   8. Noriega, Manuel
Antonio, 1934-   9. Aidid, Mohammed Farah, 1934-   10. Hussein, Saddam,
1937–2006.   11. Bin Laden, Osama, 1957-   12. Zarqawi, Abu Mus'ab,
1966–2006.   I. Title.
E181.R86   2011
355'.00973—dc22

                                                          2011005470

A catalogue record of the book is available from the British Library.

Design by Letra Libre, Inc.

First edition: August 2011

10   9   8   7   6   5   4   3   2   1

Printed in the United States of America.

CONTENTS

ACKNOWLEDGMENTS

It is said that victory has a thousand fathers, while defeat is an orphan. I don't know if finishing this book represents "victory," but I owe a debt of gratitude to countless individuals for their assistance.

I owe a special thanks to three people who helped start the transition of this book from a vague idea in my head to something tangible. To Roger Pardo-Maurer, for the bottle of Portuguese wine and the challenge that got this project started; to my agent E. J. McCarthy, for taking a chance on an unproven author, and whose dedication and even temper were the perfect antidote to the moments of doubt that (hopefully) visit all authors at some point; and to Alessandra Bastagli for having the vision to see what this book could become.

I am incredibly appreciative of those former military officers and policymakers who consented to be interviewed for this book, including but not limited to: Elliot Abrams, LG (Ret.) David Barno, "Dalton Fury," MG (Ret.) Geoffrey Lambert, Arturo Munoz, and Gen. (Ret.) Joseph Ralston. I also am indebted to the nearly dozen past and present members of the Joint Special Operations Command and other government agencies who participated in the task forces that executed the past two decades' strategic manhunts. These "quiet professionals" agreed to review the chapters in which they participated to ensure that I didn't embarrass myself with any gross inaccuracies.

This book would not have been able to take shape without Stephen Herman of the Library of Congress, who tirelessly helped procure long-forgotten histories of the Geronimo, Aguinaldo, and Pancho Villa manhunts. Similarly, my mother Deborah Runkle provided invaluable proofreading assistance and advice from the perspective of a general audience reader. The maps provided by Philip Schwartzberg of Meridian Mapping exceed my most optimistic expectations and vividly brought the campaigns I'd obsessed over for years to life. I am grateful to my former RAND colleagues Ben Connable, Jessica Hart, David Orletsky, and Rebecca Zimmerman for helping to refine the presentation of this book's findings. I am also grateful to everybody at Palgrave Macmillan who helped guide this book to publication, including: Airié Stuart, Colleen Lawrie, Isobel Scott, Erica Warren, Victoria Wallis, Siobhan Paganelli, and Christine Catarino.

Finally, I would like to thank my wife Marya for her support over the past three years. Although she could never understand my obsession with this project, she was always a source of encouragement and, when necessary, a stern task master keeping me moving forward. More importantly, I'm indebted to her for the countless hours she spent taking care of the house and our sons David and Ari—who provided me with inestimable joy when my head was not buried in a book—while I spent weekends and late hours at the office or my mind was lost somewhere in the jungles of the Philippines rather than at home.

This book is dedicated to the men whom David—in his five-year-old's version of this book—refers to as "Super Soldiers." George Orwell supposedly said that "people sleep peaceably in their beds at night only because rough men stand ready to do violence on their behalf." Even with the death of Osama bin Laden, this has never been truer than in the age in which we live. It is ironic and tragic that, although the individuals targeted by US forces are often sanitized and romanticized by history, the "quiet professionals" who protect us are just as often forgotten. Although they embrace this anonymity, we all owe a debt of gratitude to these warriors' courage and sacrifice.

WHEN THE MAN IS THE MISSION

It is both a cliché and an understatement to say that Tuesday, September 11, 2001, is a day that will forever be etched into the memory of all Americans who lived through it.

That day, a sunny, temperate morning on the East Coast turned into a nightmare of inconceivable proportions. The images remain both vivid and horrifying: the fireballs sprouting from midair as American Flight 11 and United Flight 175 crashed into the towers of the World Trade Center; the streets of downtown Manhattan transformed into an apocalyptic landscape of dust and debris; and the austere façade of the Pentagon, that formidable symbol of American power, scarred by a gaping wound one hundred feet wide and five stories high.

Before that terrible day was over, 2,974 people were killed in the deadliest attack on American soil since the calm of another beautiful morning was shattered at Pearl Harbor sixty years earlier. It is impossible to read the opening pages of *The 9/11 Commission Report,* which intensely depicts the hours leading to those fatal moments, without feeling your pulse quicken and a lump form in your throat as that morning's tragic events inexorably unfold.

Fast-forward a week.

In comparison to the previous Tuesday's events, September 18 seems relatively inconsequential. America was still in a state of shock and mourning, yet it was also desperate to regain some small measure of normalcy. That morning, less than five miles from where rescue crews still searched for signs of life amid the wreckage of the World Trade Center, the New York Stock Exchange reopened for business. Later, the cry of "Play ball!" would replace the morbid silence that had settled over empty Major League baseball stadiums across the country.

The Bush administration's senior officials and defense planners had spent the previous week developing the nation's diplomatic and military response to the 9/11 attacks. Within twenty-four hours, the Central Intelligence Agency and federal investigators had determined that the nineteen hijackers were members of al-Qaeda (Arabic for "the base"), acting under the direction of exiled Saudi millionaire Osama bin Laden. Bin Laden had declared war on the United States in 1998, claiming that killing Americans was the "individual duty of every Muslim," and had funded attacks on the US embassies in Kenya and Tanzania in 1998 and on the USS *Cole* as it docked in Yemen in 2000.

As President George W. Bush arrived at the Pentagon that morning, the smell of smoke still lingered in the air, wafting over from where American Airlines Flight 77 had slammed into the building's outer ring. The president had visited the Pentagon the day after the attacks to survey the damage, but this trip had a very different purpose. He was there to meet with Secretary of Defense Donald Rumsfeld and senior military leaders to review the decision to activate thirty-five thousand reservists.

After the meeting, the president attended a gathering with some survivors of the 188 killed at the Pentagon, joined in a spontaneous rendition of "God Bless America" in the Pentagon cafeteria, and then spoke to reporters. One member of the press corps asked the simple question that was on every American's mind: "Do you want bin Laden dead?"

Whereas the president's initial public statement on the attack was hesitant and uncertain—reflecting the nation's bewilderment, perhaps—the ensuing week of reassuring the American people had restored his confidence and determination.

"I want justice," President Bush replied in his Texas drawl. "There's an old poster out West, as I recall, that said, 'Wanted: Dead or Alive.'"[1]

It was an iconic moment in the nascent "War on Terror." With those four words, President Bush inextricably linked the coming struggle in the public's mind with one man, Osama bin Laden. For nearly a decade, until bin Laden's death at the hands of US Navy SEALs on May 2, 2011, statements attributed to bin Laden generated headlines and speculation as to his whereabouts or possible demise. For many Americans, the statement was a symbol of American resilience and swagger in the face of unimaginable tragedy. But for the president's critics—whose ranks would swell as the War on Terror dragged on in Afghanistan and especially Iraq—the remark would come to epitomize Bush's simplistic "cowboy diplomacy." Even President Bush himself would eventually express regret over his choice of words that day.[2]

In reality, Bush's statement was not as dramatic as it seemed at the time. Although he signed a document that day authorizing covert and overt operations designed to capture or kill Osama bin Laden, he was not the first US president to do so. In response to the August 7, 1998, bombings of the American embassies in Kenya and Tanzania that killed 223 people and wounded more than four thousand, Bill Clinton signed a top secret memorandum authorizing the CIA or its agents to use lethal force if necessary in an attempt to capture bin Laden, Ayman al-Zawahiri, and several other top al-Qaeda lieutenants. On August 20, seventy-five Tomahawk cruise missiles slammed into al-Qaeda training camps in Zawhar Kili, Afghanistan, killing at least twenty-one Pakistani jihadist volunteers and wounding dozens more. Although bin Laden was not present at the time of the attack, there was no doubt from President Clinton on down that the objective of the attack was to kill him. Later, Clinton signed another memorandum, authorizing the CIA or Pentagon to shoot down bin Laden's helicopters or airplanes with no pretense that he would be captured for trial.[3]

Osama bin Laden was not even the first individual to be singled out as the objective of a US military campaign. On May 3, 1886, more than a century before a $25 million reward was offered for information on bin Laden's whereabouts, the US House of Representatives introduced a joint resolution "authorizing the President to offer a reward of twenty-five thousand dollars for the killing or capture of Geronimo."[4] In response to Pancho Villa's deadly raid across the Mexican border into Columbus, New Mexico, President Woodrow Wilson announced on March 10, 1916: "An adequate force will be sent at once in pursuit of Villa with the single object of capturing him and putting a stop to his forays."[5] And within hours of the 1989 invasion of Panama, the administration of George H. W. Bush declared that the capture of General Manuel Noriega was its "ultimate objective."[6] In fact, the United States has deployed military forces with the objective of killing or capturing one man nearly a dozen times since 1885.

This book is a history of those strategic manhunts and the lessons we as a country need to learn from them.

✳

WHAT IS A STRATEGIC MANHUNT? Despite the recurrence of such missions over the last 125 years, the term itself does not appear in any military manual or international relations textbook. Perhaps this is because each manhunt has been unique in its operational challenges and strategic consequences, masking the commonalities shared by these campaigns. Despite differences from case to case, strategic manhunts can be broadly defined as the deployment of American military forces abroad for a campaign in which the operational objective is to capture or kill one man. Of course, there are variations on this basic definition: in some cases, other strategic assets—including covert operators or standoff weapons such as missiles or unmanned systems—may also be used; the military forces deployed might pursue additional strategic objectives; and US forces may not be the ones to finally kill or capture their man (if in the end he is caught). But each of the strategic manhunts in this book follows this basic definition.

It is perhaps easier to establish a definition by clarifying what a strategic manhunt is *not*.

First, manhunts are not *coups*, in which the United States provides some form of material support to assist a group of individuals to depose a foreign leader. While coups, like manhunts, target an individual believed to threaten US strategic interests, by design they strictly avoid the deployment of US forces in order to avoid American culpability in the violation of another state's right to self-determination. And coups target heads of state, while in a strategic manhunt forces may be deployed to capture or kill nonstate actors such as rebel leaders, international terrorists, or transnational criminals.

Strategic manhunts are also distinct from a strategy of *decapitation*, which directs air strikes against key leadership and telecommunications nodes during a conflict under the assumption that these are a modern state's Achilles' heel.[7] One prominent form of decapitation strategy is a campaign of *targeted killings,* such as those employed by US forces against the Viet Cong in the Phoenix Program; by Israeli forces against Palestinian terrorists in the Second Intifada; by US special forces against al-Qaeda and Mahdi Army operatives in Iraq; and the current "Drone War" against al-Qaeda and Taliban leaders in Afghanistan and Pakistan.[8] Although these campaigns all targeted individuals, these leaders were targeted because of their specific roles in broader organizations rather than the unique threat they posed. In other words, decapitation strikes targeting individuals are a *means* to achieve the *end* of battlefield victory. In a strategic manhunt, the neutralization of the individual is an end in itself. Simply put, the man *is* the mission. Similarly, some attacks against enemy leaders during the course of an ongoing conflict are *targets of opportunity* rather than strategic manhunts. The classic example of this operation is the shoot-down of Admiral Yamamoto during World War II, when US intelligence intercepted a radio message indicating his flight schedule on a series of visits to frontline bases in April 1943. Although American naval air forces subsequently ambushed Yamamoto and destroyed his aircraft, his elimination was never a specific strategic objective of US forces.[9]

Strategic manhunts are also distinct from *retaliatory attacks,* or attacks whose primary purpose is to deter an enemy leader rather than capture or kill him. The purpose of the April 1986 air strikes against Libya was not to capture or kill Muammar Qaddafi, but rather to retaliate for the deaths of the American servicemen in the April 5 bombing of a West Berlin disco and to deter Qaddafi from further support of international terrorism. Unlike strategic manhunts, the Libya raid was a discrete operation rather than a sustained campaign. Finally, and perhaps most important, strategic manhunts are not *assassinations.* Although assassinations are directed at individuals, by definition they exclude the possibility of capture. Additionally, the essence of assassination is its treacherous nature, which includes the use of violent force during peacetime by covert personnel. Conversely, strategic manhunts use at least some overt deployment of uniformed forces acting under an established chain of command.

✳

IN THE NEXT SEVEN CHAPTERS, I recount the stories of eight strategic manhunts from US history. In Chapter Eight I reexamine the hunt for

Osama bin Laden in light of the lessons learned from 125 years of American manhunts. I find that, contrary to the conventional wisdom that the Bush administration "botched" the operation by not deploying enough troops at Tora Bora, the history of strategic manhunts suggests troop strength is not a decisive factor in whether US forces capture or kill their quarry. Instead, most manhunts are determined by the *human terrain*— the attitudes of the local population that allow US forces to gain intelligence on their target, to work with indigenous forces, and to secure borders and prevent the targeted individual's escape. In the case of the hunt for Osama bin Laden, all these variables were working against US forces, and no amount of troops deployed or technology applied would have changed the unsuccessful outcome. These findings appear to be supported by the details of the Abbottabad raid that finally killed bin Laden and ended the thirteen-year manhunt.

Ultimately, I look past the search for bin Laden to the future of manhunting. Although the failed manhunts, such as those for Pancho Villa and Aideed tend to linger in our collective memory, more often than not US forces have gotten their man. Yet this success seldom correlates with achieving our broader strategic objective. Pursuing an individual and forcing him to go to ground renders him strategically ineffective and create space for other actors to step to the fore in the absence of a comprehensive strategy.

Despite the apparent strategic futility of manhunts, I examine why strategic manhunts will be increasingly attractive to future policymakers. American sensitivity to noncombatant casualties and the ability of individual leaders to threaten US interests have been magnified by the evolution of technology, especially the growth of the international media and the diffusion of weapons of mass destruction and dual-use technology. At the same time, the ability of US forces to lethally target individuals through precision-guided munitions makes such operations increasingly tempting. I conclude by offering policy recommendations for both US civilian decision makers and military commanders. In the end, I argue that how the manhunt affects the targeted individual's broader support network ultimately determines the campaign's strategic outcome, and that the most important tools to capturing or killing US forces' quarry—obtaining human intelligence, developing indigenous forces, and denying safe havens—are not coincidentally the same principles that undergird modern counterinsurgency doctrine.

CHAPTER ONE

THE GERONIMO CAMPAIGN

The American Southwest, in the words of an army officer stationed there in the nineteenth century, is "a region in which not only purgatory and hell, but heaven likewise, had combined to produce a bewildering kaleidoscope of all that is wonderful, weird, terrible, and awe-inspiring, with not a little that was beautiful and romantic."[1]

The sun had barely risen over this Dantesque landscape on May 15, 1885, when Lieutenant Britton Davis realized his day would be closer to the inferno than to paradise.

As he stepped out of his tent at Turkey Creek on the San Carlos Reservation, home to five thousand Apache Indians, the dawn illuminated the stern faces of all the major Chiricahua and Warm Springs Apache chieftains: Naiche—son of the legendary Cochise—Mangus, Chihuahua, Loco, and the aged Nana. Most ominously, Davis saw Geronimo, whom he knew as "a thoroughly vicious, intractable, and treacherous man" whose "word, no matter how earnestly pledged, was worthless." Geronimo stood only five foot eight but was still powerfully built at age sixty-one, and his countenance bespoke "a look of unspeakable savagery, or fierceness." Thirty warriors, all armed, stood behind the chiefs. Worse, not a single woman or child was in sight, "a sure sign of something serious in the air."[2]

They said they wanted to talk. Davis sent for his interpreter, then invited the leaders into his tent. Once inside, the chiefs squatted in a semicircle. Loco began to speak, but he was interrupted by a visibly agitated Chihuahua.

We are not children, Chihuahua said. When the Apaches had agreed to return to the reservation after the last outbreak in 1883, he argued: We agreed on a peace with Americans, Mexicans, and other Indian tribes. We said nothing about conduct among ourselves.[3]

The Apaches had many reasons to be discontented with their life at San Carlos. No Apaches were more independent or warlike than the Chiricahuas and Warm Springs under Davis's supervision. While some Apaches made great strides in their new life as farmers, none of the Chiricahua "were making anything more than a bluff at farming," letting their women tend the fields while the warriors scoffed at performing such unmanly tasks. San Carlos itself was a perpetually hot and dry, gravelly flat between the Gila and San Carlos rivers that earned the appellation of "Hell's Forty Acres" from the officers who served there.[4] In addition to facing the slow encroachment upon their lands by miners and farmers, the Apaches were subjected to an extraordinary level of corruption at the hands of the civilian Indian agents assigned to San Carlos through patronage politics. Davis noted that the weekly ration of flour "would hardly suffice for one day," and the beef cows issued to the Indians were little more than walking skeletons.[5]

On this day, however, Chihuahua was referring to the regulations regarding the treatment of women and the consumption of *tizwin* (a fermented corn mash). The Apaches claimed the right of a husband to beat his wife as an ancient and accepted tribal custom, as well as the right of a husband to cut off the nose of an adulterous squaw, often by biting it off. Among the Indians of the reservation, there were "about a score of women so disfigured," and some of the beatings, typically with a heavy stick, were too brutal for the US Army officers in charge of the reservation to ignore. Consequently, General Crook had prohibited these practices.[6]

Additionally, the brewing and drinking of tizwin was banned due to the Apaches' proclivity for violence when intoxicated. One such drinking spree the previous year had led to a failed ambush of Lieutenant Davis. The leader of the assassination plot, the warrior-chief Kaytennae, was subsequently arrested, exiled, and imprisoned in Alcatraz.

Davis had served in the Arizona Territory for seven years and understood his wards as well as any American officer. He tried to placate the chiefs, but they responded with jeers and veiled threats. Chihuahua taunted Davis through the interpreter: "Tell Fat Boy that I and all the other chiefs and their men have been drinking tizwin the night before and now we want to know what he is going to do about it—whether or not he is going to put us all in jail."[7] He added that he did not think the soldiers had a jail big enough to hold all the Indians who violated the prohibition.

Davis had no option but to play for time. He explained that a problem this serious must be submitted to General Crook for a decision and that he would telegram Crook and notify them as soon as he received a reply. Davis made sure they understood an answer might take several days before riding to Fort Apache to send the message.[8]

The telegram from Fort Apache to Crook's headquarters at Fort Bowie had to pass through civilian hands. In order to avoid leaks, messages were kept simple and cryptic. Moreover, before reaching the general, Davis's telegram also had to pass through Captain Francis E. Pierce. Pierce had been in Arizona for only two months and so decided to wake the veteran Chief of Scouts Al Sieber for advice. Unfortunately, Sieber was sleeping off his own whiskey drunk. Through bleary eyes and an addled mind, he read the telegram.

"It's nothing but a tizwin drink," Sieber muttered. "Don't pay any attention to it. Davis will handle it."[9]

As Sieber returned to sleeping off his hangover, Pierce filed away the seemingly inconsequential note.

The next two days went by without word from Crook. The Apaches grew increasingly apprehensive, assuming the worst as each hour passed.

On Sunday, May 17, Lieutenant Davis was umpiring a baseball game at Fort Apache while awaiting Crook's response. At about four PM, his interpreter and a scout interrupted to report that Geronimo and an unknown number of Chiricahua and Warm Springs Apaches had fled the reservation in the middle of the night. Davis again attempted to contact Crook but was unable to get a message through. It was not until noon the next day that a break in the line was discovered—the fleeing Apaches had cut the line where it passed through the foliage of a tree and cleverly tied the ends tautly together with a leather thong to hide the break.

Once higher headquarters was informed of the Apaches' flight, Davis began preparing his scouts for the pursuit. Speed was essential, for if Geronimo and his band made it to the Mexican frontier, he would be nearly impossible to corner. They left with a detachment of regular troops from Fort Apache in the afternoon, but as daylight faded and dusk transformed the desert sky into darkness, the advance slowed to a crawl lest they stumble into an ambush while following an uncertain trail.

They marched through the night. At dawn the detachment reached a ridge above the valley of Eagle Creek. The scouts pointed to the opposite side of the valley, and looking through their field glasses, Davis and the other officers could see the dust raised by the fugitives' ponies ascending a ridge some fifteen to twenty miles ahead.

Geronimo had escaped.

Realizing that further pursuit was useless, Lieutenant Davis turned back. Another long campaign in Mexico lay ahead, and he needed to wire General Crook for instructions.

✳

AS NEWS SPREAD THAT 120 APACHES under Geronimo were on the loose, "something like mass hysteria gripped the citizens of Arizona and New Mexico." This reaction was not wholly irrational. As one American officer who was sympathetic to the Indians noted, "Contact with others meant war, for war was [the Apaches'] business."[10] The traditional Apache economy was partially dependent upon the periodic raid of settlements, for which they were trained with Spartan-like severity from childhood. The first major Apache rebellion against the settlement of the Southwest in 1870 prompted as hardened a soldier as General William Tecumseh Sherman to recommend abandoning Arizona altogether. In the 1880 outbreak, warriors led by Victorio—seldom more than seventy-five strong—had "fairly deluged New Mexico and Chihuahua [province] with blood," killing more than one thousand Americans and Mexicans over a fourteen-month period, all while being unsuccessfully pursued by three American cavalry regiments, two infantry regiments, a substantial number of Mexican troops, and a contingent of Texas Rangers.[11]

That Geronimo was leading this outbreak only heightened the sense of fear in the Southwest. Geronimo was neither a chief nor subchief, and until the 1880s had been overshadowed by more prominent Apache leaders such as Cochise, Mangus Colorado, and Victorio. However, he had risen to the leadership of a significant faction of warriors through his courage, determination, and skill as a war captain, as well as his mysterious talent as a medicine man.[12] Geronimo's previous outbreaks in 1876 and 1881 established his reputation for brutal savagery. During the 1881 breakout, his biographer Angie Debo notes, "the fugitives killed everyone they encountered" en route to the Mexican border while evading a posse that included Wyatt Earp and his brothers. Another historian notes that Geronimo's path in April 1882 "seems to have been strewn in blood." One officer recorded that "the greatest terror prevailed in Chihuahua at the mere mention of the name 'Hieronymo,' whom the peasantry believed to be the devil sent to punish them for their sins."[13]

The citizenry's panic appeared justified by the renegades' actions as they fled to the border in May 1885. Before reaching Mexico, they killed at least seventeen settlers and stole about 150 horses. Near Silver City, New Mexico, shocked civilians came upon the carnage of a raid they attributed to Geronimo in which the Apaches had killed a rancher, his wife, and their three-year-old daughter. A five-year-old girl was found still alive but hanging from a meat hook that entered the back of her head. She died a few hours later.[14]

✳

IF NO INDIAN TERRIFIED AMERICANS and Mexicans more than Geronimo, no American inspired greater respect in the Apaches than General George Crook. Although his visage was "manly and strong," Crook was not physically imposing. He stood just over six feet tall, with a stocky, powerful frame. His blue-gray eyes were framed by his light brown hair and beard, the latter of which appeared to part in the middle due to his enormous, bushy sideburns.[15] In uniform, Crook "looked the soldier to the very core," but rarely wore one when in the field, disdaining the dash and ostentation that garnered many of his military peers more public attention.[16] Moreover, "there was no private soldier, no packer, no teamster, who could 'down the ole man' in any work, or outlast him on a march or a climb over the rugged peaks of Arizona; they knew that, and they also knew that in the hour of danger Crook would be found on the skirmish line, and not in the telegraph offices."[17]

Crook was Commander of the Department of Arizona from 1871 to 1875, and had established himself as arguably the army's most brilliant Indian fighter. He planned and led the devastating Tonto Basin campaign against the Apaches in 1872–73, which successfully ended the first major round of the Apache Wars. In the face of another catastrophic Apache outbreak, Crook was returned to command of the department in September 1882. Again, he led an expedition into the previously unassailable Apache fortress in the Sierra Madres Mountains and was able to harry the Apaches into surrender, returning more than four hundred Chiricahua men, women, and children to the San Carlos reservation.[18]

✳

"I AM FIRMLY CONVINCED." Crook would later write, "that, had I known of the occurrences reported in Lieutenant Davis's telegram of May 15, 1885, which I did not see until months afterwards, the outbreak of Mangus and Geronimo a few days later would not have occurred."[19] Having missed the chance to deter the outbreak, Crook set in motion a three-tier strategy to track down Geronimo. First, acting under the provisions of the July 1882 agreement between the United States and Mexico that allowed the troops of one country to cross into the other "if in close pursuit of a band of savage Indians," he deployed two columns south of the border. The first, a combined force of ninety-two scouts and Troop A of the Sixth Cavalry under Captain Emmet Crawford, was to go down the western flank of the Sierra Madres in Sonora province. This force would be paralleled on the eastern flank in Chihuahua by a troop of the Fourth Cavalry under Major Wirt Davis. While these commanders were flushing out the hostiles, another hundred scouts were sent eastward to patrol the Mogollon and Black Mountains, after which they were to report to Fort Apache.

Once it was clear there were no Chiricahuas lagging behind north of the border, Crook intended to seal the border to catch any renegades trying to return to the United States. Altogether, roughly three thousand soldiers, three-quarters of them cavalry, patrolled the border region. To monitor the campaign, Crook moved his own headquarters forward to Fort Bowie in strategic Apache Pass at the northern end of the Chiricahua Mountains.

Although Crook's strategy centered on the pursuit of the renegades into their sanctuaries in Mexico, the campaign's initial clashes occurred north of the border. As two companies of the Fourth Cavalry approached the settlements near the San Francisco River and the New Mexico border, they found signs that Geronimo had begun killing settlers. On May 22, the scouts found a trail believed to be Geronimo's and followed it twenty-five miles to Devil's River, where they were ambushed. A swift counterattack into the hail of fire from the steep canyon walls, led by First Lieutenants Charles B. Gatewood and James Parker, quickly dispersed the Apaches. Gatewood and Parker captured the enemy position at the crest of the canyon, and five hundred yards farther they took the renegades' now-abandoned camp. Seventeen fires were still either burning or filled with live or hot coals, and the hostiles left behind horses, various items of clothing and equipment, and a lot of beef. These possessions were gained at the cost of two soldiers and an Indian scout wounded.[20]

Less than a month later, on June 8, another company of the Fourth Cavalry was camped in Guadalupe Canyon when a courier arrived with news that the Apaches were heading in the direction of Cloverdale and Skeleton Canyon, and with instructions to proceed at once to intercept them. As the nine-man detail left behind to guard the camp and supply train gathered for lunch, they "were surprised by a thundering volley from the hills nearby." One sergeant was immediately felled by a bullet in his forehead as he ate his biscuit and bacon. Four more soldiers were killed, their bodies desecrated, and the Apaches made off with the camp stores the soldiers were guarding.[21]

On June 11, Crook ordered Crawford's command to enter Mexico, to be followed a month later by Major Davis's expedition. The two detachments endured extreme conditions as they combed the Sierra Madres for the hostile Apaches. One officer recalled: "The command had been subject to every possible hardship . . . excessive heat, very little water, poor rations, bacon made rancid by unusual heat, and at night were pestered not only by mosquitos [sic], but by ants, large and small, with an occasional centipede," some up to eight inches long.[22] Major Davis's surgeon recorded 128 degrees in the shade one afternoon.

In addition to the blazing heat, it rained almost constantly throughout July and into August. This hindered the campaign by making travel an ordeal, impeding the mobility of the US forces, making "the country through which we passed . . . so soft that our mules with even their light loads sank to their knees in mud, and riding at times was out of the question."[23] It also made Geronimo's band almost impossible to track, as the rain obliterated their trail almost as soon as they made it.

Despite struggling through these conditions, Crawford's and Wirt Davis's commands managed to score some limited successes. At about nine AM on June 23, Crawford's scouts found Chihuahua's camp in the Bavispe Mountains northeast of Opunto. The leader of his scouts deemed it impossible to surround the camp without being seen, thus making it impossible to capture any of the hostiles. Once the scouts moved into the best position possible, they opened fire. Again, rather than hold their position to defend their supplies, the renegades fled, escaping with their women and children through several deep canyons that joined near the camp. The scouts pursued them as quickly as the rough terrain would allow, and for several miles a running battle continued between the scouts and the fleeing braves. Although all eight warriors of the hostile band escaped—along with four boys and three women—Crawford's scouts returned to camp with fifteen women and children captured, including Chihuahua's entire family.[24]

Major Davis's command enjoyed similar tactical successes. On August 7, his scouts attacked Geronimo's camp west of Casas Grandes, Chihuahua. The renegades were caught by surprise, and the warriors were forced to jump over a steep bluff in order to avoid capture. Although Geronimo personally escaped, he lost thirteen horses and mules—along with saddles, blankets, and dried meat—in the attack. More devastatingly for the old warrior, two of his wives and five children from his family were among those captured. A month later, on September 22, Davis's scouts killed another Chiricahua in the mountains near Bavispe.[25]

While these skirmishes undoubtedly took a psychological toll on Geronimo and his warriors, they were strategically inconclusive. As Lieutenant Gatewood wrote his wife: "We are still aimlessly wandering around these mountains hunting for Indians that are not. . . . Up one hill and down another would sum up the whole thing."[26]

North of the border, US forces suffered from a critical dearth of intelligence due to the duplicity of the very people they were charged with protecting.[27] South of the border, the Chiricahuas' mobility and intimate knowledge of the terrain frustrated even the most experienced Indian campaigners. Recognizing the futility of hunting the Apaches with cavalry and a pack train, in August Crawford ordered Lieutenant Davis and Sieber to pursue Geronimo with about forty handpicked scouts. Geronimo led this detachment on a long chase, crossing the Sierras into Chihuahua before turning north to slip across the boundary into New Mexico, eluding the soldiers stationed there and disappearing into the interior of the Territory. Davis and the scouts had to pursue every lead while avoiding the natural barriers ripe for ambush in the mountainous terrain and thus traveled "a hundred and forty or fifty miles to cover a hundred as the crow flies." Davis's detachment was given provisions for three days, which they made last for six. When their rations gave out, they kept on Geronimo's trail, living "on the flesh of the ponies the hostiles had killed and such roots, berries, etc., as the country afforded and the scouts knew to be edible."[28] Lieutenant Davis's men rode and walked five hundred miles through the mountains and deserts before finally limping back across the border at Texas and reaching Fort Bliss on September 5.

Filthy, exhausted, and sick of the war, Davis resigned his commission and set off to manage the ranch of a family friend in Mexico.

✳

EVEN CROOK'S INTEGRATED NETWORK of defenses—at the time the most thorough attempt in American history to guard the Mexican border—proved futile in preventing the fugitives from raiding into US territory at will. After literally running Britton Davis out of the army, Geronimo and four warriors set out on foot to recapture their families. The war party crossed the border and, on the night of September 22, slipped into their camp on the White Mountain Indian Reservation and rescued one of Geronimo's wives and a three-year-old daughter. Then, "like a famished wolf amidst a flock of sheep," Geronimo struck swiftly and frequently as he raced eastward, "puddles of White Mountain blood marked his passing." The war party eventually turned south and rode for the Chiricahua Mountains. With the Apaches' horses giving out, it appeared that the pursuing troopers of the Tenth Cavalry finally had them cornered. But ranchers in the vicinity of White Tail Canyon were holding their fall roundup and ignored warnings that Apaches were in the area. They left thirty of their best mounts tied around the ranch house and awoke in the morning to find them gone.[29] Freshly mounted, the Apaches were once again beyond pursuit and fled southward to the border.

As historian Robert Utley summarized it, "The Sierra Madre campaign of 1885 was an exhausting and profitless struggle against heat, insects, hunger, thirst, and fatigue."[30] General Crook had nothing to show for his troops' exertions and decided to give them some much needed rest and the opportunity to prepare for a more extended campaign in Mexico than originally anticipated. In October he summoned

Crawford and Wirt Davis back to Fort Bowie to refit and prepare for another assault on the Sierra Madres.

The army resupplied by making purchases. The Apaches resupplied by making raids. By November 1885, the fugitives were woefully short of cartridges for their Winchester and Springfield rifles, ammunition that could not be found in Mexico. Moreover, the poverty-stricken Mexican peasants in Sonora had little left to steal. Thus, in early November, Josannie, a war leader and Chihuahua's brother, reentered the United States and began a raid in the Florida Mountains of New Mexico with ten to twelve warriors. Newspapers in the East were filled with headlines of the daring raid, as Josannie moved into New Mexico and killed settlers, ranchers, and soldiers with seeming impunity. On December 27 the hostiles were reported in the Chiricahua Mountains of southeastern Arizona, but a blinding snowstorm covered their trail, allowing Josannie's war party to return safely to Mexico. In the six weeks they had been north of the border, they traveled 1,200 miles, killed between thirty-eight and forty-five people, and stole 250 horses and mules while losing only one warrior.[31]

✴

THE UNSUCCESSFUL SUMMER CAMPAIGN and subsequent raid by Josannie led to increasing political pressure on General Crook to produce results. The Commander of the United States Army, Lieutenant General Philip Sheridan, traveled all the way from Washington, DC, to Fort Bowie to review the situation. He wanted Geronimo's band destroyed, and on November 29 told Crook to go on the offensive.

Crook's response to Josannie's raid was to take his own previous innovations, already considered radical by many in the US Army, to their logical conclusion. Although regular troops were supposed to provide rallying points for the scouts and protection for the pack trains, they also severely inhibited the scouts' mobility. Crook was willing to forego the advantages offered by white soldiers and created a force comprised of one hundred Indian scouts, a pack train, and only three officers. The model for this flying column had been suggested to him back in 1883 in the Sierra Madres campaign, when his scouts had begged to be allowed to go ahead of the main expedition.

The critical decision, therefore, was which American officer would lead this experimental unit. But in reality, the choice was obvious from the start. Captain Emmet Crawford had commanded the scouts in Crook's 1883 expedition into Mexico, and upon the successful completion of that campaign was placed in charge of the San Carlos reservation, where he oversaw the renegades now on the warpath until just two months before the outbreak. Six foot one, with gray eyes, a fellow officer said of Crawford: "Mentally, morally, and physically he would have been an ideal knight of King Arthur's Court." The Apaches alternately called him "Tall Chief" because of his height and "Captain Coffee" because of his apparent addiction to the beverage. When reenlisting scouts in October and November for the expedition, Crawford chose only White Mountain and friendly Chiricahua Apaches—mountain Indians who he knew were ideally suited for the arduous task of trailing Geronimo in the difficult Sierra Madres. These Indians joined the expedition not only because they hated the renegades, but also because they trusted Crawford, who was known for his concern for the scouts serving under him.[32]

Crawford's company crossed the border once more on December 11. They moved steadily south in Sonora for three weeks, finding nothing, before establishing a base camp in Nacori, on the western edge of the Sierra Madres, and from there deploying scouting parties. Finally, in early January, one of these parties came across a Chiricahua trail near the Aros River. The scouts reported that it led to Geronimo's band, holed up in a range known to the Mexicans as *Espina del Diablo,* or "Backbone of the Devil." Upon the discovery of this fresh "sign" on January 8, 1886, Crawford pushed his men forty-eight hours without sleep in a desperate attempt to find and attack the hostile village. His party was now more than 150 miles south of the border, farther south in Mexico than any US command had ever chased Apaches.

Just before daylight on January 10, Crawford's scouts drew near the high, rocky point where Geronimo's camp was suspected to be. Crawford divided his force, hoping to surround the rancheria. Slowly, carefully, the scouts crept forward, "scarcely breathing as we moved."[33]

Suddenly, the braying of the hostiles' burros shook the stillness of the cold, mountain dawn and alerted Geronimo to the scouts' presence. Geronimo jumped up on a rock and yelled: "Look out for the horses!"

Chiricahua warriors ran out and tried to secure their mounts, but the scouts opened fire, shrieking cries of defiance from the surrounding rocks. Geronimo's men took cover and returned fire from a nearby cluster of rocks that formed a stronghold.

After a minute, Geronimo's voice was heard once again: "Let the horses go and break toward the river on foot! Scatter and go as you can!"

Although a rush into the camp would have ensured the capture of at least the women and children, the scouts remained pinned down by the hostiles' fusillade, deaf to the appeals of their officers to advance. The hostiles escaped into the darkness, and daylight revealed they had once again left behind all their stock, provisions, and blankets. The scouts, exhausted by the forced march that made the skirmish possible, collapsed on any level ground they could find to sleep on, unable to exploit their victory.[34]

While the scouts' bullets did not find their marks, the capture of Geronimo's supplies was a terrible blow in the harsh winter conditions of the Sierra Madres. Toward the middle of the afternoon, as Crawford and his men were still recuperating, a squaw came into the camp. She said that Geronimo and his followers were camped a few miles away and wished to talk to Crawford about surrendering. Crawford agreed to meet with Geronimo, Chihuahua, and Naiche the next day, and a place for the conference was arranged. Crawford was overjoyed as the squaw departed, as the message seemed tantamount to an offer of surrender, and everyone in the American camp seemed to collectively exhale, believing the Geronimo campaign was about to end.

✳

A HEAVY FOG SAT upon Crawford's camp the next morning, January 11. Just as the light of dawn made the terrain around them visible, the sentries reported a large body of troops approaching. One scout, believing the oncoming party to be Major Davis and his scouts, called to the approaching force in Apache.

But they were not Apache scouts.

At the sound of Apache voices, the force of 150 Mexican irregulars opened fire on Crawford's camp. Bullets hissed through the air, driving the officers and scouts into the rocks for cover. Crawford ordered his men to hold their fire while he and the other officers shouted in Spanish, identifying themselves as American soldiers and waving handkerchiefs. After about fifteen minutes, there was a lull in the shooting. Crawford climbed atop a prominent rock in plain view of the Mexicans. Although his blue field uniform was in tatters, his brown beard ensured that he looked nothing like an Apache. Waving a handkerchief in each hand, he shouted: "*No tiro! No tiro! Soldados Americanos!*"[35]

Twenty-five yards away, across a small ravine, a Mexican steadied his rifle against a pine tree and took aim. A shot rang out. Lieutenant Marion P. Maus, Crawford's second-in-command, turned and "saw the Captain lying on the rocks with a wound in his head, and some of his brains lying upon the rocks."[36]

Enraged, the scouts immediately unleashed a furious fire upon the *Nacionales*. The battle raged for an hour as the Apaches and Mexicans blazed away at one another, while Crawford lay bleeding in the no-man's-land between the combatants. Finally, the Mexicans raised their own white flag. Four on the American side were wounded, while the scouts killed four Mexicans and wounded five others. Crawford lingered in a coma for seven excruciating days, finally dying on January 18. General Crook maintained that had Crawford lived, the Apache War would have ended there beside the Aros River in January 1886.[37]

On a hillside across the river, the renegades sat and watched the battle rage. A member of the band still recalled seventy years later how "Geronimo watched it and laughed."[38]

✳

THAT AFTERNOON, TWO SQUAWS approached the American camp and reported that Geronimo still wished to hold a council. Maus agreed, and on January 13 he sat down with Geronimo and the other Apache leaders. Geronimo and Naiche said they wanted to talk about surrendering and would meet with General Crook "in two moons," but only on the condition that they choose the site and that Crook come without soldiers. Maus had no option but to agree to these stipulations, and on the sixteenth began the long march north for the border.

Crook could do nothing but wait. Finally, on March 16 Lieutenant Maus—who was encamped near the border—reported that four Chiricahua warriors had visited him and told him that Geronimo and the renegades were ready to meet Crook at Canon de los Embudos, a short distance across the border in Mexico. Crook departed immediately. As agreed, he was escorted only by his aide Captain John G. Bourke, seven men who could serve as interpreters, and the newly reformed Kaytennae, recently released from Alcatraz.

When they arrived at Canon de los Embudos, they found Geronimo had set up his rancheria "in a lava bed, on top of a small conical hill surrounded by steep ravines, not five hundred yards in direct line from

Maus, but having between the two positions two or three steep and rug-ged gulches which served as scarps and counter-scarps." Bourke mar-veled that "[a] full brigade could not drive out that little garrison," and Crook noted that Geronimo had selected such an impregnable defensive position "that a thousand men could not have surrounded them with any possibility of catching them."[39]

On March 25 Geronimo, Chihuahua, Naiche, and a few other Chir-icahua approached the American camp. The rest of the warriors cau-tiously fanned out around them, watching for any sign of treachery. After Crook finished his lunch, they met under a stand of large cotton-wood and sycamore trees, on the bank of a stream just west of the largest funnel. Geronimo sat across from Crook, wearing a simple shirt, vest, and breechcloth, with a bandanna about his head. Twenty-four warriors sat just beyond the inner circle. Crook observed that Geronimo and his men "were in superb physical condition, armed to the teeth, with all the ammunition they could carry."[40]

Crook opened the conference, tersely asking: "What have you to say? I have come all the way down from Bowie." Geronimo responded by stating a long list of grievances to explain why he left the reservation. Crook had decided to assume a hard line in the negotiations and listened quietly. His face betrayed no clue about his thoughts, and throughout Geronimo's hour-long speech he stared at the ground, refusing to even look at the old warrior.[41]

Crook's intransigence was having its intended effect. Bourke ob-served that as Geronimo spoke, "perspiration, in great beads, rolled down his temples and over his hands; and he clutched from time to time at a buckskin thong which he held tightly in one hand."[42] The general and the warrior went over the same topics repeatedly, neither willing to yield, when finally Crook delivered his ultimatum: "You must make up your own mind whether you will stay out on the warpath or surrender unconditionally. If you stay out, I'll keep after you and kill the last one, if it takes fifty years."

In a sense, Crook was bluffing, as he knew Geronimo could escape into the mountains again at any time, and that the Americans would have to pay a high price to catch him by force. Thus, he moderated his terms, shifting from unconditional surrender to confinement in the East with their families for two years, followed by a return to the reservation.

Crook and Geronimo agreed to adjourn for two days so the Apaches could debate the American offer among themselves. Upon returning to his tent, Crook summoned Alchise—another son of Cochise—and Kaytennae to him. Alchise was Crook's staunch friend and supporter, and Kaytennae's incarceration and tour of San Francisco had converted him to a pro-American outlook. No formal session was held the next day, but Crook sent these two men into Geronimo's camp to stir dissent among the renegades and to influence them to thoughts of surrender if possible.

Crook's gambit appeared to have paid off when on the morning of the twenty-seventh he received word from Chihuahua that he was willing to surrender his own band, regardless of what Geronimo did. But Crook wanted to bring in all the Chiricahuas and recognized that Chihuahua's submission could be used to demoralize Geronimo. At last, in the afternoon the conference continued. Sensing a change in mood, Geronimo kept to himself, sitting with another warrior under a mulberry tree, blackening his face with pounded galena while the others once again convened under the sycamores.[43]

Chihuahua, whose speech to Lieutenant Davis ten months earlier harkened the beginning of the outbreak, surrendered by declaring: "If you don't let me go back to the Reservation, I would like you to send my family with me wherever you send me."[44]

Naiche followed: "What Chihuahua says I say. I surrender just the same as he did. . . . I throw myself at your feet. You now order and I obey. What you tell me to do I do."[45]

Finally, Geronimo rose to speak. "Two or three words are enough," he said. "I have little to say. I surrender myself to you." He paused to shake hands with Crook and then continued. "We are all comrades, all one family, all one band. What the others say I say also. I give myself up to you. Do with me what you please. I surrender. Once I moved about like the wind. Now I surrender to you and that is all."[46]

✳

AFTER THE MARCH 27 CONFERENCE, General Crook left the Apaches under Lieutenant Maus's supervision so he could hurry back to Fort Bowie to wire Sheridan the good news. His diary entry for March 28 reads: "Left camp early in the morning for San Bernardino. Met Geronimo and [Naiche] and other Chiricahuas coming from the San Bernardino direction quite drunk."[47]

Crook should have taken this as a sign of trouble, but in an uncharacteristic lapse of judgment, he continued riding north for the border.

Depressed about their surrender and apprehensive regarding their impending exile, Geronimo, Naiche, and most of their band got drunk off mescal purchased from Godfrey Tribolet, a trader contracted to sell beef to the army. From the army camp two ravines away, Crook's soldiers heard gunshots through the night. In the morning, Kaytennae reported that Naiche was so drunk he could not stand, and Bourke found Geronimo and four other warriors riding aimlessly—five men on a pair of mules—"all drunk as lords." In their state of intoxication, the Apaches were able to march only a few miles toward the border on the twenty-eighth.[48]

That night, in a cold, drizzly rain, the Chiricahuas drank again. This time, not only did Tribolet sell them mescal, he filled their heads with horror stories of how they would be murdered as soon as they crossed the border. The Apaches argued among themselves, and when almost everyone else had fallen asleep, Geronimo, Naiche, nineteen warriors, and nineteen women and children quietly slipped away into the night.[49]

Maus did not realize they had fled until the next morning. He immediately set out with his mounted scouts to catch Geronimo, whose band had taken only two horses with them. But the old warrior used his usual tricks, changing direction abruptly when his trail vanished on solid rock. With little food, the fugitives ran and walked sixty miles without stopping. At last, his horses worn out and his rations dwindling, Maus gave up the chase and departed for Fort Bowie with Chihuahua and the seventy-seven Apaches who had refused to join the new outbreak.[50]

✳

ALTHOUGH CROOK WAS DISAPPOINTED by the news of Geronimo's flight, he was confident that as soon as the old warrior's band sobered up he could persuade them to honor their pledge of surrender. This belief appeared to be vindicated when two warriors fell in with Maus's scouts and gave themselves up as soon as their hangovers wore off.

Yet even before word of Geronimo's escape reached Washington, Crook had fallen out of favor with his superiors. President Grover Cleveland refused to approve anything short of an unconditional surrender, and Sheridan was apoplectic. He could barely contain his annoyance and questioned Crook's tactics when he responded on March 31: "Your dispatch of yesterday received. It has occasioned great disappointment. It seems strange that Geronimo and party could have escaped without the knowledge of the scouts."[51] He condescendingly reminded Crook: "You have forty-six companies of infantry and forty companies of cavalry, and ought to be able to do a good deal with such a force."[52]

Crook was tired of the persistent second-guessing of his strategy, and given that the scouts were his special innovation, the suggestion of their disloyalty was a direct reflection on his ability and judgment. On April 1 he requested to be relieved of command of the Department of Arizona.[53] Sheridan waited less than twenty-four hours to call Crook's bluff, and the next day Crook received orders relieving him of command.

On the same day that America's most accomplished Indian-fighter departed from the last Indian war, the surrendered Chiricahuas rode into Fort Bowie.

Crook remained at Fort Bowie until April 11, when he formally relinquished command to his successor, Brigadier General Nelson A. Miles. A journalist who witnessed Miles's arrival described him as "a tall, straight, fine looking man, of 210 pounds weight . . . He has a well-modeled head, high brow, strong eye, clear-cut aquiline nose, and firm mouth. It is an imposing and soldierly figure, all around."[54]

Miles, unlike most of his peers, was not a product of West Point, but rather had volunteered during the Civil War. He was wounded twice, the second time suffering an abdominal wound at Chancellorsville from which he was not expected to recover. Yet Miles survived to rise through the ranks faster than any other officer but George Custer, and after the Civil War, he attained national prominence by marching his troops 160 miles through the bitter cold of December 1877 to corner Chief Joseph and his followers in northern Montana.[55]

Yet whereas Crook was modest and unassuming, Miles was vain, pompous, and unabashedly ambitious to the point of grandstanding. General Sherman, Miles's uncle by marriage, wrote to Sheridan: "I have told [Miles] plainly that I know no way to satisfy ambitions but to surrender to him absolute power over the whole Army, with President & Congress thrown in."[56]

Miles inherited a formidable command. After receiving two thousand additional soldiers he requested, he could deploy five thousand troops—*one-quarter of the entire US Army*—against Geronimo's twenty warriors. On April 20, 1886, he issued instructions to guide the forces serving in the southern portion of Arizona and New Mexico, declaring: "The chief object of the troops will be to capture or destroy any band of hostile Apache Indians found in this section of the country, and to this end the most vigorous and persistent efforts will be required of all officers and soldiers until the object is accomplished." Miles's plan was centered on constant pursuit, "putting in fresh relays and finally wearing [Geronimo and Naiche] down."[57]

To support the offensive operations, Miles divided his area of responsibility into "districts of observation." He directed all commanders to erect heliograph stations on prominent mountain peaks, using the bright sunlight and clear air to transmit messages regarding news of the hostiles. Eventually, thirty of these stations were erected not only in Arizona and New Mexico, but in Sonora as well.[58] Before Miles could set his plans in motion, however, Geronimo once again struck first. On April 27, the Apaches rode out of Mexico into Arizona's Santa Cruz Valley. They killed everybody they encountered, and the raid lasted twenty-three days and claimed fourteen lives. In response, on May 3, the House of Representatives introduced a joint resolution "authorizing the President to offer a reward of twenty-five thousand dollars for the killing or capture of Geronimo."[59]

The next day, Miles issued orders for a punitive expedition into Mexico. Whereas Crook maintained that only an Apache could catch an Apache, Miles believed the cavalry could operate more effectively on its own and retired the scouts. He organized an elite command of specially selected men, "one hundred of the strongest and best soldiers that could be found," for what he declared would be an experiment to "ascertain if the best athletes in our service could not equal in activity and endurance the Apache warriors."[60]

To lead this command, Miles handpicked Captain Henry W. Lawton of the Fourth Cavalry, whom he described as "a resolute, brave officer" and "a man of great energy and endurance."[61] Lawton was six foot five and weighed 230 pounds, "a gigantic Beowulf" with close-cut, raven black hair set over a low and narrow forehead, jet-black eyes, and a large mustache atop "a remarkably fine set of teeth."[62] He had been an eighteen-year-old law student at Harvard when Fort Sumter fell, enlisting four days later. He took part in twenty battles and rose to the rank of lieutenant colonel by the end of the war.

The expedition formed at Fort Huachuca, consisting of Lawton's thirty-five troops from the Fourth Cavalry, twenty infantrymen from the Eighth Regiment, and one hundred pack mules with thirty packers. Despite Miles's distrust of the scouts, the command would be guided by twenty White Mountain and San Carlos Apaches. A young, twenty-five-year-old contract surgeon was assigned to the command as well. Leonard Wood had wanted to enter the army or navy but deferred to his father's wishes and attended Harvard Medical School instead, graduating in 1884 before heading west to seek adventure.

On May 5, Lawton's column proudly marched out of Fort Huachuca while the band played "The Girl I Left Behind." What followed from May to July was a series of skirmishes that looked good on paper but did little to vindicate Miles's strategy. From about May 19 to June 5, Lawton's command was relatively inactive, having lost Geronimo's trail. The only time they did corner any Apaches, on July 13, was due to the efforts of the scouts, who discovered the camp and led the regulars to it. Lawton's command *did* come upon as many as ten dead Mexicans each day as they followed Geronimo. Consequently, one observer concluded: "General Miles has . . . done everything possible; but things in the Territory are a thousand-fold worse than when Crook left them."[63]

In fact, Lawton's expedition quickly degenerated into more of a trial of endurance than a coherent military campaign. After only five days, Lawton's horses all broke down, forcing the cavalry to dismount and join the infantry. The days grew progressively hotter, the wind was "like the breath of a furnace," and the men could not touch their rifles without burning themselves. It was practically impossible to move in the daytime. The troops would start the day's march before four AM, wearing nothing but their "drawers and undershirts," travel until about ten AM, and then lie in whatever meager shade could be found until about five PM, when they would march until nearly ten PM.[64]

When not marching over rocky terrain, the soil was a pulverized dust that covered men and horses and combined with their perspiration to form a solid crust, with no water to spare for washing during the early summer months. The weather changed in July, however, and the rainy season began. Toward evening, the showers would fall, drenching the soldiers to the skin and spoiling what little sleep they had previously enjoyed. Because of the necessity of traveling light, they had no tents, shelters, or overcoats with them—only their saddle blankets. These unsanitary conditions caused them to become carriers for body vermin, suffer from diarrhea and malarial troubles, and develop varicose veins and inflamed joints from the constant climbing.[65] By July 5, Lawton's command had marched 1,396 miles, nearly all over rough, high mountains.[66] Lawton lost forty pounds during the course of the campaign, Wood thirty. Three sets of officers served, and only one-third of the enlisted men made it to the end, surviving "marches that exacted the last ounce of a man's strength, where literally a man had to do or die. For to be left behind on some of those vast stretches of burning sand would have meant . . . a slow, lingering horrible death."[67]

With his campaign failing and his ambitions imperiled, Miles began to contemplate two drastic strategic readjustments. On July 5, after a visit to Fort Apache, he confided to his wife his belief that the reservation Apaches were "to some extent in sympathy with the hostiles and liable to go out at any time. It requires a large force to keep them in check and I am anxious to move them to some other part of the country."[68] Miles formally proposed the relocation of the Apaches through army channels two days later, arguing that even if Geronimo were captured or killed, so long as the Apache tribe remained in the rugged and almost inaccessible mountains of Arizona "Their boys of to-day will become the Geronimos of a few years hence. They are the remnant of a once powerful and warlike tribe that has contended against civilization for three hundred years. All their traditions perpetuate the spirit of war."[69] Miles's proposal was eventually approved, and on August 29 the reservation Chiricahuas were summoned to Fort Apache for what was supposed to be a routine roll call. Instead, they were swiftly surrounded by the cavalry and marched off to the railroad station at Holbrook. There, the 382 Apaches who had kept their word to abandon the warpath were loaded on a train for exile in Florida.

Miles's other readjustment was a peace overture. During his inspection of Fort Apache, Miles encountered the warrior Kayitah, who had been wounded in a May 15 skirmish with US troops. No longer able to keep up with his comrades, he wearily returned to the reservation and surrendered. Kayitah told Miles that some of Geronimo's followers were tired of warfare and that the entire band might be persuaded to surrender if a small party were sent to talk to them. He agreed to serve as one of the emissaries, as did Martine, an influential Chiricahua related to several of the renegades.

Miles wanted an American officer to lead the negotiation so as to convey the proper authority, preferably somebody known to Geronimo and the hostiles. But with Crawford dead and Britton Davis out of the army, Miles did not know whom to select.

In reality, there was only one man for the job.

✳

FIRST LIEUTENANT CHARLES B. GATEWOOD stood about five foot eleven, had gray, melancholy eyes, a dark complexion, and a large, beaklike nose. Upon graduating from West Point in 1877, he was assigned to duty at Fort Apache. In 1882, he was appointed military commandant of the White Mountain Indian Reservation, where he became intimately familiar with—and responsive to—the needs and problems of his wards. Gatewood was held in high esteem by both the White Mountain Apaches and his peers. In 1885, published General Orders in Arizona cited him as having "seen more active duty in the field with the Indian Scouts than any other officer of his length of service in the Army," and one comrade recalled him as "cool, quiet, courageous."[70] When Miles asked Lieutenant Colonel James Wade, commander of Fort Apache, whom he would recommend for the mission, Wade did not hesitate. He declared that Gatewood's "long and varied experience with the [White Mountain and] Chiricahua . . . Apaches" made him the logical choice.[71]

Gatewood was summoned before Miles at Albuquerque on July 13 and issued instructions to accompany Kayitah and Martine "with a message to the hostiles demanding their surrender."[72] Although he suffered from chronic rheumatism in his knee, ankle, hip, and shoulder and doubted his body could handle the rigors of campaigning in the Sierra Madres, he accepted the mission and set out with the two Indians, his interpreter George Wratten, and a packer to handle their three mules, crossing the border on July 19.

On July 21, Gatewood's small command linked up with Lieutenant Parker's troop from the Fourth Cavalry at Carretas, Chihuahua, where Parker had been ordered to wait for him and presumably set him on Geronimo's trail. Yet when Gatewood arrived, Parker reported that "the trail is all a myth—I haven't seen any trail since three weeks ago when it was washed out by the rains."

"Well," Gatewood responded, "if that is so I'll go back and report there is no trail."

Not at all, Parker said. "If General Miles wants you to be put on a trail, I'll find you one and put you on it; if not we'll find Lawton who is surely on a trail."[73]

The journey from Albuquerque to Carretas had aggravated Gatewood's already fragile health. Before they could begin to search for Lawton, he required six days of rest. Finally, on July 27, he was able to travel and set out with Parker's command serving as his escort. After traversing close to two hundred miles of rough terrain in sweltering heat, Gatewood and Parker reached Lawton's camp on the Aros River—some 250 miles south of the border—on August 3.

When they arrived, Lawton had an unpleasant surprise for them: he had no idea where the Chiricahuas were, and claimed to "have heard nothing of the hostiles since the 21st of July." Moreover, Lawton was less than enthused about having Gatewood's mission added to his responsibilities. "I get my orders from President Cleveland direct," Lawton said. "I am ordered to hunt Geronimo down and kill him. I cannot treat with him."[74] He said that he intended to fulfill his mission, but allowed Gatewood to attach himself to the command and try to accomplish his task.

Lawton's command slowly meandered northward. On August 18 they were suddenly blessed with a stroke of good fortune when they encountered some Mexicans packing burros with acorns. They said they knew where Geronimo could be found: near Fronteras, approximately seventy-five miles northwest of their present location, where he was reportedly negotiating with the Mexicans. This was the most credible intelligence Gatewood had heard. That afternoon, after making camp, he and Lawton agreed that Gatewood would leave that night and make a forced march to Fronteras.

As Gatewood packed for the trip, Dr. Wood noted in his diary that Gatewood "was far from well." Nevertheless, at two AM on August 19, Gatewood left Lawton's camp, hoping to ride seventy miles that day.[75]

✳

GATEWOOD'S WORN-OUT DETACHMENT reached the outskirts of Fronteras late that night after riding and walking fifty-five miles. The next day, they learned that two squaws had entered the village and indicated Geronimo's willingness to consider surrender to the Mexicans if acceptable terms were proposed. Gatewood presented himself to the prefect and stated his purposes, but was greeted with surprising hostility. The prefect informed him that he had no intention of accepting an Apache surrender but rather had been secretly deploying some two hundred soldiers in the town with the intent of getting the hostiles drunk and massacring them. He ordered Gatewood to leave Fronteras and not to make any attempt to track the Apache women, lest Gatewood interfere with his carefully conceived treachery.

Gatewood took his entourage in pursuit of the squaws. They headed south to conceal their objective from anybody watching them, and then after dark took advantage of the cover provided by an arroyo to change direction and head for the mountains where Geronimo was believed to be encamped.

The next morning, they found Geronimo's abandoned camp and the trail of the squaws who had been in Fronteras. Gatewood sent a runner back to Lawton with a situation report, requesting that Lawton follow as quickly as possible. After three days of following the squaws' trail, they found signs of the whole band about four miles west of the Bavispe River. Kayitah and Martine told Gatewood that Geronimo was headed north and, more important, that they were much closer to the Chiricahuas than expected.

Gatewood's party now proceeded more cautiously, as every bend of the river offered overlooks ideal for launching an ambush. Gatewood placed a white flag made from a flour sack atop a pole, noting later "but that don't make a man bullet proof."[76] At dusk, Gatewood called a halt. His men had been in the saddle for nearly twenty-four hours. Knowing that the Chiricahuas were close, he ordered a cold camp.

Gatewood's detachment moved out early the morning of the twenty-fourth. Just past noon, Gatewood made camp in a canebrake and ordered Kayitah and Martine to continue by themselves, to locate Geronimo and, if possible, to talk with him. They set out immediately.

After the afternoon dragged on with no word from the two Apaches, Martine appeared at sundown, reporting that he and Kayitah had found Geronimo four miles from their camp. He described the stronghold as "an exceedingly rocky position high up in the Torres Mountains in the bend of the Bavispe." Geronimo had detained Kayitah as a hostage and sent Martine back with the message that he would talk only to Gatewood. As they bedded down, George Wratten recalled: "We lay on our rifles all night, just to be ready in case of need, for we had not yet had our talk with them, and didn't know just what they would do."[77]

They moved out at first light the next morning. Martine led the way, and sometime between eight and nine AM, Gatewood's party arrived at the glade at the river bottom where the conference was to take place. As time slowly passed, everyone nervously scanned the mountainside above them, but there was no visible sign of movement.

Suddenly, armed warriors appeared above them and descended the slope. Martine recalled: "We were very anxious for a few minutes thinking that maybe Geronimo had changed his mind and meant trouble for us." Similarly, Wratten remembered: "We did begin to feel a *little* creepy when we saw we were badly outnumbered and surrounded."[78] But flight was no longer an option.

Geronimo was among the last to arrive. He laid his rifle down twenty feet away before going to Gatewood to shake his hand. He greeted the lieutenant, noted his thinness, and asked about his health. They sat together on a log, with Geronimo moving so close to Gatewood that the officer could feel the Apache's pistol against his hip. Gatewood recalled the tension in the air as the conference began: "[I]magine him looking me square in the eyes & watching my every movement—twenty-four bucks sitting around fully armed . . . & say if you can blame me for feeling chilly twitching movements."[79]

The Apaches asked Gatewood for tobacco and alcohol. Gatewood knew better than to provide them with liquor, but had presciently packed fifteen pounds of tobacco, which he passed around. As every warrior began smoking a hand-rolled cigarette, Geronimo announced his party was ready to hear General Miles's message.

Gatewood was nervous but saw nothing to be gained by stalling. He said: "I am directed by General Miles to ask the surrender of yourself and followers to the United States government."

"On what conditions?" Geronimo asked.

"An unconditional surrender," Gatewood replied. "Surrender and you will be sent to join the rest of your people in Florida, there to await the decision of the President as to your final disposition. Accept these terms or fight it out to the bitter end."[80]

Gatewood recalled that "a silence of several weeks fell on the party, at least so it seemed." After a few moments, Geronimo passed a hand across his eyes and held his arms forward. Both hands trembled badly, and again he asked if Gatewood had something to drink. "We have been on a three days' drunk on the mescal the Mexicans sent us by the squaws who went to Fronteras," he explained. "The Mexicans expected to play their usual trick of getting us drunk & killing us, but we have had the fun; & now I feel a little shaky."[81]

Replying to the question of surrender, Geronimo said they were willing to surrender only if they could return to the reservation, but not if they had to go to Florida. Although Gatewood was sympathetic to Geronimo's demand, he replied that this was out of the question, and that he had no authority to offer terms. Geronimo then gave an impassioned speech repeating the same litany of complaints he had presented to Crook five months earlier. Gatewood remained silent through the tirade, then quietly reiterated Miles's terms. The Apaches withdrew to one side of the clearing to discuss what to do, and after an hour returned to Gatewood.

Geronimo announced that he and his followers decided they would return to their lands at San Carlos or they would fight to the death. He looked Gatewood directly in his eyes, and declared: "Take us to the reservation or fight!"

The two parties were at an apparently insoluble impasse. Unwilling to give up, Gatewood decided to gamble. He informed the hostiles that to return to San Carlos would be a mistake, for all the Chiricahuas and Warm Springs Apaches were to be removed to Florida to join the seventy-seven who had already surrendered under Chihuahua. Naiche's mother and daughter, as well as Geronimo's family, were already in Florida, Gatewood said, and to return to the reservation would be only to live among their traditional enemies, the White Mountain, Aravaipa, and other Apache subgroups.

Geronimo's band was shocked by this news. Again, they withdrew to caucus. Another hour passed before Geronimo announced they had decided to stay on the warpath, but that they wished to discuss it further during the night.

As the sun began to set, Geronimo changed the course of the conversation. He said he knew General Crook well, and might surrender to him, but he knew nothing about Miles. Geronimo asked: "What kind of man was General Miles?" He wanted to know everything about him, from his age to the color of his hair to his experience with Indians to his honesty. Gatewood answered these questions as best he could, pleading ignorance on some points, as the Chiricahuas listened intently to his answers. Finally, Geronimo said, "He must be a good man since the Great Father sent him from Washington, and he sent you all this distance to us."[82]

Before Gatewood left, Geronimo asked him one last question. "We want your advice," Geronimo said. "Consider yourself one of us and not a white man. Remember all that has been said today, and as an Apache, what would you advise us to do under the circumstances?"

Without hesitation, Gatewood replied: "I would trust General Miles and take him at his word."

The Chiricahuas' faces were solemn as his reply was translated. They all knew Gatewood as a man who had never knowingly lied to them. Finally, Geronimo broke the silence and told him he would let him know the result of their council in the morning.[83]

Lawton's command had caught up on the twenty-fifth, and Gatewood and his men arrived in Lawton's camp long after nightfall. Gatewood provided Lawton with a progress report and then went exhaustedly to bed.

His rest was interrupted early the next morning when the pickets passed a call for *Bay-chen-day-sen,* Gatewood's Apache name meaning "Long Nose." The hostiles were approaching the camp and had asked for the lieutenant. With his interpreters, Gatewood went out to meet Geronimo, Naiche, and several of the warriors, who waited a half mile from the American camp. When the Chiricahuas saw him approaching, they dismounted, unsaddled their ponies, and laid their weapons on their saddles—except for Geronimo, who kept a large pistol under his coat beside his left hip.

From a distance, the American camp silently watched and waited as Gatewood and the Apaches seated themselves under an ancient mesquite tree and began to talk.

Geronimo told him the entire band had decided to take his advice to go to the border and surrender to Miles. However, given the dangers they faced traveling through Mexican and American territory, Geronimo asked that his warriors be allowed to keep their arms until they had formally surrendered. He requested that Lawton's command march near them to protect them from other units that might be encountered. Finally, he asked for Gatewood to ride with them and to sleep in their camp.

Gatewood readily agreed to these conditions.

Geronimo then said: "I want to meet the American commander who has followed and fought me so long and once surprised me in my camp."[84]

Gatewood led the Chiricahuas into the American camp and introduced them to Lawton. Geronimo immediately hugged the captain in front of the entire command. Gatewood outlined Geronimo's terms while everyone smoked. Lawton approved Geronimo's requests, and the remaining hostiles entered the American camp.[85]

The Apache wars appeared to be over.

＊

LAWTON, HOWEVER, REALIZED he was still in a precarious position. He remembered that Geronimo had reneged in the past and was more than capable of doing so again. On August 27 he wrote his wife: "I am pretty tired and feel the strain of responsibility weighing on me."[86]

The two groups began the trek north early on the morning of the twenty-eighth. Geronimo, Naiche, and Gatewood kept to the foothills, while Lawton, the regular troops, and scouts maintained a distance of one or two miles along the valley floor. After setting up camp early in the afternoon, a Mexican force of approximately two hundred infantrymen suddenly appeared, coming from the direction of Fronteras. The Apaches nearly panicked, and at Kayitah and Martine's suggestion, they bolted forward in a run for the border. After about an hour with no pursuit in sight, the hostiles halted. If fighting occurred, they wanted to fight alongside the Americans against the Mexicans.

Meanwhile, Lawton held his ground. Leading the Mexican force was the Prefect of Fronteras, who declared he had come to attack the renegades, and even when informed that they had surrendered and were being escorted back to the United States, insisted on a battle. Lawton made it clear that any attack on the Apaches would bring an American attack on the Mexicans. The prefect backed down, and Lawton's intercession helped to avert tragedy.

On August 31 the two parties arrived at Guadalupe Canyon, where they camped while awaiting word from General Miles. Lawton was away for most of the day, trying to find a point from which he could communicate with Miles's headquarters. The Chiricahuas were visibly nervous, as they recognized the location as the site of their deadly ambush of Lawton's troops more than a year earlier. Lieutenant Abiel Smith, left in command in Lawton's absence, wanted to disarm the Indians and make them genuine prisoners of war. He "expressed a desire to pitch in with the troop and have it out right there," an indiscretion of which the warriors caught wind. They began to mount their horses to flee once again. Gatewood also learned that some of the young officers were hatching a plot to lure Geronimo into the American camp on a pretext and murder him.

Lawton hurried back to reestablish control of his command. He hastened to the Chiricahuas' camp, arriving at eight PM, and immediately sought out Geronimo, Naiche, and the other warriors to assure them that everything was all right. Gatewood approached Lawton. "I have been ordered simply to see that the two Indians went to the hostiles and delivered their message," he said. He wanted to take his belongings and leave.[87]

Lawton knew he needed Gatewood to help keep Geronimo and his followers from fleeing once again, and stressed to Gatewood the trouble they would both be in if this happened. When Gatewood persisted, Lawton finally threatened to use force, if necessary, to keep the lieutenant with the command. Gatewood relented and remained.

In addition to the perils of getting the Chiricahuas back to the US border, Lawton had to cajole General Miles to honor his part of the agreement. Unlike Crook, Miles chose to command from the rear, staying in various Arizona forts and never once entering Mexico. Miles sought glory and promotion from the campaign, not a reprise of Crook's fall from grace, and had no intention of going near the hostiles until he was certain they were going to surrender. As Lawton wired one nervous telegram after another, Miles continued to delay. "I do not intend to go down there simply to talk," he wrote Lawton, and sent word that he wanted assurance that Geronimo would surrender.[88]

Lawton was becoming exasperated by Miles's procrastination and on September 2 wrote the general: "I sincerely believed and do yet they wish to surrender. . . . I have followed them four months and know how hard it is to surprise them, and believe that they should not now be driven out again."[89]

Lawton's command and the Chiricahuas arrived at Skeleton Canyon just before nightfall on September 2.[90] Lawton and Geronimo found several commands of regular soldiers already there when they arrived, which triggered the Chiricahuas' fear of treachery. Lawton sent another desperate message through the chain of command, and the next day the Acting Assistant Adjutant General of the Department, William Thompson, heliographed Miles: "Lawton says the hostiles will surrender to you, but if he does not see you today he is afraid they will leave."[91]

Finally, Miles and his entourage arrived at Skeleton Canyon at three PM on September 3. Geronimo immediately rode down from his campsite in the rocks overlooking the stream. He dismounted from his horse and approached the general.[92]

Geronimo shook Miles's hand. The interpreter said, "General Miles is your friend."

Geronimo replied: "I never saw him, but I have been in need of friends. Why has he not been with me?"

The tension broke as everyone within earshot burst into laughter.[93]

As the conference began in earnest, Miles told Geronimo: "Lay down your arms and come with me to Fort Bowie, and in five days you will see your families now in Florida, and no harm will be done to you." Miles became frustrated with the laborious translation procedures that transformed English into Spanish into Apache and back again. He picked up some stones and drew a line in the dirt and said, "This represents the ocean." He placed a stone near the line. "This represents the place where Chihuahua is with his band." He then placed another stone a short distance from the first and said, "This represents you, Geronimo." He picked up a third stone and put it near the second one. "This represents the Indians at Camp Apache. The President wants to take you and put you with Chihuahua." He then picked up the stones representing the Apaches in Arizona and put them beside the one representing Chihuahua in Florida. "This is what the President wants to do, get all of you together."[94]

Miles indicated the stay in the East would be of indefinite duration, but that eventually the Apaches would be returned to Arizona. He concluded: "Tell them I have no more to say. I would like to talk generally with him, but we do not understand each other's tongue."

Geronimo turned to Gatewood and smiled. "Good," he said in Apache, "you told the truth." He shook Miles's hand and said that no matter what the others did, he was surrendering.[95]

The next morning, a formal ceremony was held. On September 5, Geronimo, Naiche, and other warriors were placed in Miles's wagon and set out for Fort Bowie. Looking at the Chiricahua Mountains near the end of their journey, Geronimo said to Miles: "This is the fourth time I have surrendered."

"And I think it is the last time," Miles replied.[96]

Four days later the prisoners were assembled on the parade ground at Fort Bowie and packed into heavily guarded wagons for the trip to the rail station. As they departed, the Fourth Cavalry band played "Auld Lang Syne." Geronimo was left to wonder why the soldiers jeered and laughed as they sang: "*Should auld acquaintance be forgot, and never brought to mind.*"[97]

✳

THE SURRENDER OF GERONIMO and his followers marked the collapse of the last significant Indian resistance to Western settlement. Yet it is far from clear whether Geronimo's capitulation was the key to the successful conclusion of the Apache Wars. Some historians have argued that the end did not come in Skeleton Canyon, but rather in the railroad coaches that shuttled the Chiricahua and Warm Springs Apache from Arizona to Florida. Although Geronimo was in captivity, Mangus was still at large with a small band of followers, and as General Crook himself argued in a letter to Sheridan, "so long as any [Apaches] remain out they will form a nucleus for disaffected Indians from the different agencies in Arizona and New Mexico to join." Although the removal of the reservation Chiricahuas was indisputably cruel and ineptly mishandled, it was effective in draining the swamp that would likely have supported future iterations of guerilla warfare by discontented Apaches. Thus, Robert Utley concludes: "It was the removal of the Chiricahuas, hostile and neutral alike, that brought peace to the Southwest."[98]

Yet the strategic effectiveness of the removal policy is historically underrated because of Miles's dubious treatment of Gatewood and betrayal of the loyal Apache scouts and peaceful Chiricahuas.[99] Although Miles conspicuously attempted to exclude Gatewood from the campaign's honor rolls, several officers deserved credit for the success of the Geronimo Campaign. Gatewood was the only officer remaining in the Department of Arizona with the credibility to convince Geronimo to surrender. Whether or not Lawton's pursuit made Geronimo more receptive to Gatewood's entreaties, the burly captain's deft handling of the nervous Apaches, the vengeful Mexicans, his potentially treacherous subordinates, the ailing Gatewood, and even his overly cautious commanding general prevented Gatewood's fragile accord with Geronimo from falling apart. Finally, even if Miles's initial strategy proved unsuccessful, he demonstrated that most important asset in a commander—flexibility—that led him to seek a negotiated solution when he realized his preferred tactics were failing.

Whereas Lawton eventually rose to the rank of major general, and Miles and Leonard Wood rose to command the entire US Army, Gatewood sank into obscurity, receiving neither a promotion nor a medal for the courage and skill he demonstrated in Mexico. His health broken by the rigors of the Sierra Madres and injuries sustained in a later dynamite explosion, Gatewood entered the post hospital at Fort Monroe, Virginia, on May 11, 1896. Nine days later, still a first lieutenant, he died from a malignant tumor of the liver.

✳

THE HUMILIATING SCENE on the parade ground at Fort Bowie would be the last time Geronimo ever set foot in his native land. Nor would he see his family anytime soon, as Miles had promised him. For eight months the Chiricahua warriors were kept as prisoners 350 miles from their families, with almost no communication between the groups. Worse, as soon as the Apaches arrived in Florida, they began to die in alarming numbers due to the drastic change in climate. They were eventually transferred to Mount Vernon Barracks, Alabama, and later to Fort Sill, Oklahoma.

During his time in limbo, however, Geronimo began the transformation from monster to legend. During the relocation to Fort Sill, crowds gathered at whistle-stops to cheer the celebrated warrior. Geronimo responded with savvy pragmatism, selling his block-lettered autograph for twenty-five cents a copy. With special permission from the War Department, Geronimo was allowed to travel as a sideshow attraction. He attended the Omaha and Buffalo expositions and the 1904 St. Louis World's Fair. He spent a year with a "Wild West" show and cashed in on his reputation by selling souvenir bows and arrows, autographed pictures of himself, and even the buttons off his coat. At the request of Theodore Roosevelt, Geronimo was brought to Washington to ride in the president's inaugural parade of March 1905, along with chieftains from other tribes. As Geronimo galloped down Pennsylvania Avenue, people in the dense crowd yelled "Hooray for Geronimo!" and tossed their hats in the air.[100] When the old warrior finally passed away on February 17, 1909, one writer eulogized him as "the Napoleon of the Indian race."[101]

In time, the settlers, miners, cowboys, and children murdered by Geronimo and his warriors were forgotten, and all that remained was the symbol of heroic resistance, his fame outlasting that of the Americans who pursued him over the hellishly beautiful landscape of the Sierra Madres.

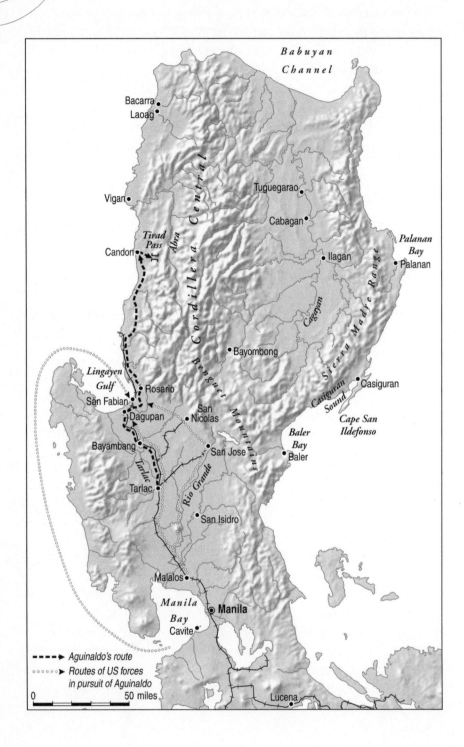

Babuyan Channel

Bacarra
Laoag

Vigan

Tuguegarao

Cabagan

Cordillera Central

Tirad Pass

Candon

Ilagan

Palanan Bay
Palanan

Sierra Madre Range

Abra

Cagayan

Bayombong

Lingayen Gulf

Rosario

San Fabian

Dagupan

San Nicolas

Benguet Mountains

Casiguran Sound

Casiguran

Cape San Ildefonso

Bayambang

San Jose

Baler Bay
Baler

Tarlac

Rio Grande

Tarlac

San Isidro

Malalos

Manila Bay

Manila

Cavite

▬▬▶ Aguinaldo's route
∘∘∘∘∘▶ Routes of US forces
       in pursuit of Aguinaldo

0   50 miles

Lucena

CHAPTER TWO

THE CAPTURE OF EMILIO AGUINALDO

Frederick Funston was no stranger to adversity. Barely four years into his military career, Funston had been shot through both lungs, in his arm, and in his hand; he had taken shrapnel from a Spanish cannon in the chest and had a horse shot out from under him, crushing his legs and impaling his thigh on a dry stick; he had contracted malaria and typhoid fever while fighting in the tropics; and by his wits had narrowly survived being captured by Spanish forces in Cuba.

But on March 22, 1901, he stood on a beach in the Philippines, thinking he was going to die.

A steady rain soaked through his uniform, and he could hear the waves of the Pacific Ocean crashing against the shore. He was leading a ninety-man detachment nearly one hundred miles into uncharted enemy territory on an audacious mission that had rapidly turned desperate. His men were weak with fever. They had survived their arduous journey on quarter rations, and at noon their meager supplies had run out. They were emaciated and could barely stand upright. It seemed impossible that Funston could achieve his objective: capture the rebel leader Emilio Aguinaldo and end the Philippine insurgency with one bold stroke.

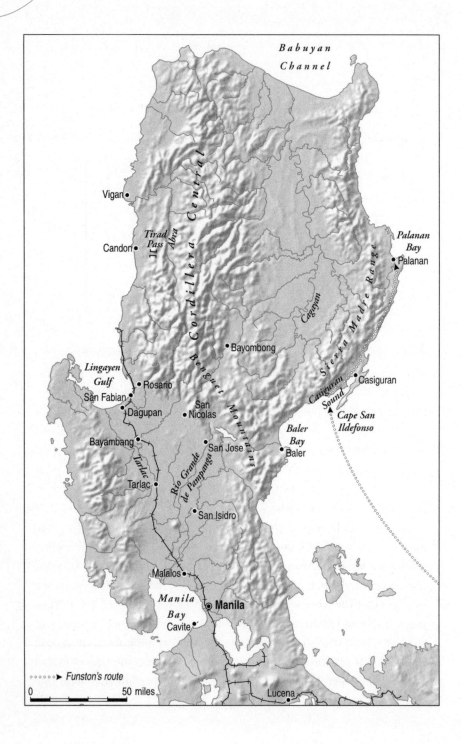

*Babuyan
Channel*

Vigan

*Tirad
Pass*

Candon

Abra

Cordillera Central

Sierra Madre Range

*Palanan
Bay*

Palanan

Cagayan

Bayombong

*Lingayen
Gulf*

Rosario

San Fabian

Dagupan

San
Nicolas

Benguet Mountains

Casiguran

Casiguran

Sound

*Cape San
Ildefonso*

Bayambang

San Jose

*Rio Grande
de Pampanga*

*Baler
Bay*

Baler

Tarlac

Tarlac

San Isidro

Malalos

*Manila
Bay*

Manila

Cavite

Lucena

○○○○○○▶ *Funston's route*

0   50 miles

✳

THREE YEARS EARLIER, few Americans had any knowledge of the Philippines, much less of Emilio Aguinaldo. But as diplomatic relations between the United States and Spain began a downward spiral toward war in Cuba and the Philippines in 1898, American representatives began contacting the twenty-eight-year-old insurgent leader. After the defeat of the Spanish fleet in the Battle of Manila Bay, Aguinaldo spent the night of May 19 aboard Admiral George Dewey's flagship, and the next morning was provided with close to a hundred rifles, some cannons, and ammunition courtesy of Dewey, who encouraged him to "go ashore and start your army."[1] Four days later, on May 24, Dewey allowed a steamer from Hong Kong filled with thousands of rifles and ammunition to reach Aguinaldo because "we had a common enemy, and of course I wanted his help."[2]

Aguinaldo began operations at the end of May, and proceeded to capture much of the Cavite region and lay siege to Manila. By the end of June, Central Luzon was in Filipino hands, and Aguinaldo's army numbered about thirty thousand men. Aguinaldo moved quickly to consolidate his political power, proclaiming himself dictator on May 24 to rule during the initial stages of the renewed insurgency. On June 18 he issued the Philippine Declaration of Independence and established a revolutionary regime.[3]

As Aguinaldo consolidated his position, he was careful to maintain a policy of accommodation toward the United States, allowing US forces to disembark in the suburbs surrounding Manila. Yet as fresh US detachments arrived in the Philippines, reaching twelve thousand troops by late July, Aguinaldo became petulant. Dewey warned Washington that Aguinaldo "has become aggressive and even threatening towards our Army."[4] General Wesley Merritt arrived in the Philippines on July 25 and ordered all correspondence between his command and Aguinaldo stopped until he could "enforce my authority in the event that his pretensions should clash with my designs."[5]

The siege of Manila devolved into two separate campaigns, with both Americans and Filipinos conducting their own operations despite ostensibly cooperating. After a sham battle that contained enough gunfire and casualties to satisfy both Spanish and American honor, the Spanish commander of Manila surrendered to General Merritt on August 13.

The phony battle for Manila aggravated the already tense relations between American and Filipino forces. Unaware of the understanding between the Spanish and the Americans, Filipino forces had joined in the US "attack" and captured several Manila suburbs. The Americans turned them back, and several brief skirmishes erupted. Filipino soldiers hovered at the edge of the front line, furious that the United States had denied them the prize they had fought more than two years to obtain. As darkness fell over the city, Filipinos periodically fired shots into the US lines and threatened to attack. Only a tropical storm that raged most of the night and made the roads in and out of the capital impassable defused the explosive situation. Aguinaldo's forces retreated to the Spanish outer defense network, reversing its direction so that the Filipinos had the Americans trapped inside the city. In effect, a second siege of Manila had begun. General Merritt held the capital, Aguinaldo the rest of Luzon.[6]

As the two armies brushed against each other, incidents began to crop up. From the trenches, the Americans and Filipinos exchanged insults, blows, and occasional gunfire. The strain grew throughout autumn as more US forces arrived, bringing the total US strength in the islands to 15,559 men. Aguinaldo eschewed immediate military action against the Americans while awaiting the results of the Paris Peace Conference. General Elwell S. Otis (Merritt's successor as commander) advised President William McKinley that only the immediate and clearest statement of America's intention to remain in the Philippines would nip Aguinaldo's "political pretensions" in the bud and prevent imminent warfare with the native troops. Instead, the news on December 10, 1898, that the Treaty of Paris formally transferred sovereignty of the Philippines to the United States hit Aguinaldo's loyalists "with the devastating effect of an atomic blast. It was at once disillusioning, disappointing, and tragic."[7]

In response to McKinley's January 1899 proclamation to the Filipinos that America's mission in the Philippines was "one of benevolent assimilation," Aguinaldo issued a manifesto tantamount to a declaration of war.[8] Aguinaldo directed his provincial commanders to stockpile rice and other supplies in preparation for war, encouraged local commanders to forcefully resist American demands, and instructed a fifth column of native commandos inside Manila to plan attacks against the Americans. On January 20 the Philippine Congress voted Aguinaldo authority to declare war whenever he saw fit.[9] Shooting incidents occurred nightly until, on the night of February 4, a firefight between the First Nebraska Volunteers and Filipinos probing their lines brought matters to a head.

The next morning, February 5, General Otis ordered immediate offensive operations. The subsequent battle would be the biggest of the war, fought along a sixteen-mile front and involving all or part of thirteen regiments and thousands of Filipinos. By the afternoon the Americans had overwhelmed the Filipino nationalist forces, taking all the disputed territory between the armies while suffering 238 casualties—of whom 44 were killed in action or died of their wounds—against an estimated four thousand Filipino casualties.[10]

The Philippine War had begun.

✳

AGUINALDO WAS QUICKLY DEMONIZED by Americans. Secretary of War Elihu Root called him "an assassin" and "a Chinese half-breed." Frank Millet wrote in *Harper's Weekly* that "he has the keen cunning of the Chinaman, and the personal vanity and light mental caliber of the Filipino." The *New York Times* declared Aguinaldo was nothing but "a vain popinjay, a wicked liar, and a perfectly incapable leader" whose men were "dupes, a foolish incredulous mob," and that the "mischievous influence of this tricky little man must be broken." Even Admiral Dewey, who had previously spoken fondly of the young Filipino, told anyone who would listen that Aguinaldo was interested only in "revenge, plunder, and pillage."[11]

Otis, whom one historian has described as "the Philippine war's answer to George McClellan, without the latter's good looks," was slow to pursue the battered Filipino forces, and allowed a month to pass before resuming the offensive. In late March he ordered Major General Arthur MacArthur's division to attack along the railway line stretching north out of the capital to capture Malolos, twenty miles up the line. Otis believed the north held the enemy's center of gravity—its army, its capital, and its commander-in-chief, Aguinaldo—and was sure that the capture of this trinity would break the opposition. MacArthur's division pushed the Philippine Army back to the outskirts of Malolos. On the morning of the thirty-first, MacArthur's forces entered the town only to find that Aguinaldo had abandoned his capital during the night.[12]

It was to be the first of many occasions in which US forces narrowly missed their quarry.

US forces pushed into the Central Luzon provinces in April and May, and swept into the southern Tagalog provinces in June when the monsoon arrived. Otis ordered his division commanders to halt and pull back to a more compact line of defense. The army was exhausted, suffering a 60 percent sickness rate, and lacked enough forces to hold the territory it had conquered. With the fall of Malolos, Otis expected the nascent Philippine Republic to collapse, and reported to Washington that the back of the insurrection was broken and that only a few Filipino bandits remained to be dealt with. Thus, the spring campaign ended with a whimper, and US forces hunkered down for the rainy summer, controlling a region that extended only thirty miles north of Manila.[13]

*

IN THE EARLY MONTHS OF 1899. a rumor buzzed through the American barracks and officers' quarters, thrilling even the most battle-hardened veteran. These whispers were confirmed on March 17, when a six-foot-five officer with an iron gray mustache and hair over a ruggedly handsome face stepped off the transport at Manila.

Major General Henry Lawton had arrived in the Philippines.

As one historian noted, "Lawton was America's Lord Kitchener," who enjoyed tremendous popularity with his fellow officers, politicians, and the press. In addition to his reputation as an Indian-fighter, he was a national hero for leading the attack on El Caney in Cuba the previous year. In military bearing, looks, dash, and ability, he was a model officer. He was known as a fighting cavalry man who, unlike the plodding, meticulous Otis, disliked red tape. Whereas Otis jealously husbanded his resources for a repeatedly postponed decisive thrust, Lawton was vigorous and energetic, and was thought to be the ideal commander for the stalled Philippines War. The *New York Times* declared "the puffed-up crack brained egoists of Aguinaldo's had to realize they were no match" for the man who had captured Geronimo. Privately, MacArthur hoped Otis would soon be recalled and be replaced by the more aggressive Lawton.[14]

Yet Lawton carried a dark secret with him across the Pacific. Normally easygoing, Lawton had a drinking problem dating back to the 1880s that produced violent fits of temper when he was intoxicated. Although usually able to control his consumption, he fell into heavy drinking in Cuba and was relieved as military governor of the Santiago

district under the pretense of "ill health." Before leaving for the Philippines, Lawton was summoned to the White House to meet face-to-
face with McKinley for a lecture on temperance. Lawton promised the
president that he would abstain from drinking in his new command,
and deployed to the Philippines with two battalions of the Seventeenth
Infantry and one battalion of the Fourth Infantry.

Lawton honored his promise and set out to live up to the reputation he had earned in nearly forty years of war-fighting. Whereas Otis
seldom left his headquarters, and never left Manila, Lawton led from
the front with little regard for his personal safety. Lawton "looked like
a hero, talked like a hero, and acted like a hero," walking erect even as
he paced back and forth behind his firing line wearing a white pith helmet polished until it shone "like the headlight of an engine" before each
battle. Reporters accompanying Lawton on his excursions observed
that he was able to instill his own tremendous energy into his officers
and enlisted men, whose privations and dangers he shared. On May 17,
Lawton's scouts captured the relocated Philippine capital at San Isidro,
narrowly missing Aguinaldo himself. Yet when he sought permission to
continue on to Aguinaldo's new capital at Tarlac, Otis refused, effectively
terminating Lawton's expedition.[15]

Lawton returned to Manila and stormed into Otis's cluttered office. If Otis "would give him two regiments, would allow him to arm,
equip, and provision them to suit himself, and would turn him loose,
he would stake his reputation as a soldier, and his position in the United
States Army, on the claim that within sixty days he would end the [war]
and would deliver to . . . Otis [Aguinaldo] dead or alive."[16] Otis listened
calmly before giving a rare laugh.

Lawton left Otis's office even more livid than when he arrived.

✳

WITH THE END OF THE RAINY SEASON in October 1899 and the arrival
of sixteen thousand more troops in the Philippines, Otis no longer had
any excuse to delay the decisive offensive that would shatter Aguinaldo's
government and army once and for all. The goal of the fall campaign
was to drive the insurgent army northward, to trap it, and "to capture
Aguinaldo, the head and front of the whole business, the incarnation
of the aspirations of the Filipino people." Otis planned a vast encircling
movement in which each of the divisions under Generals MacArthur,

Lawton, and Loyd Wheaton would act as an independent pincer that together would surround the main body of *insurrectos* in a square some one hundred miles on each side. Behind the newly created Cavalry Brigade commanded by Brigadier General Samuel B. M. Young, Lawton's First Division would move north-northeasterly up the Rio Grande de Pampanga to San Isidro, sixty miles from Manila, and then seventy miles farther north to Lingayen Gulf, simultaneously flanking Aguinaldo's army and sealing off the mountain passes to the east that opened into the valleys of northern Luzon. Once Lawton was well under way, 2,500 men under Wheaton would make an amphibious landing on the southeast corner of Lingayen Gulf at Dagupan, occupy the coast road and western port towns, and link up with Lawton's advance guard.[17]

The third column, composed of MacArthur's Second Division, would follow the railway from Angeles in the south, through the new capital at Tarlac, and drive the Philippine army north into the pocket created by Lawton and Wheaton. MacArthur's forces pushed off on November 8 and captured Tarlac four days later. Once again, however, Aguinaldo and his government had already fled north to Bayambang, about twenty-six miles up the railroad line. Aguinaldo was only a few miles ahead of MacArthur's troops, yet not a man, woman, or child would provide information on his whereabouts. On November 20 the Second Division reached Dagupan, defeated the *insurrectos* there, and occupied the important coastal town of Santa Cruz on schedule.[18]

To the east, Lawton's mission depended upon the ability to move quickly in order to close the mountain passes leading eastward and complete the top loop of the trap to block Aguinaldo's escape into the vast reaches of northern Luzon. But the terrain and weather proved to be a greater foe for the First Division than the Philippine army. The Rio Grande de Pampanga turned out to be either too shallow or too swift for the Division's launches. The roads were morasses, and it took eleven days to advance the initial sixteen miles to San Isidro on October 20, where Lawton's column remained stuck ten days later. On October 27, Lawton dispatched a mobile force under Young north with some artillery, two cavalry squadrons, and a battalion of the Twenty-Second Infantry.[19]

On October 31, MacArthur's scouts intercepted a message from Aguinaldo, declaring that he was shifting his capital 110 miles northeast to Bayombong, a mountain town deep in Neuva Vizcaya province. The document was several days old, raising the alarming possibility that

Aguinaldo would slip through the mountain passes, rendering Lawton's labors in vain. Liberated Spanish prisoners advised Young that Aguinaldo's route would skirt the northern end of his area of operations, taking him east through Umangan to the pass at San Nicholas and then north to Bayombong. The news persuaded Lawton to dispatch the cavalry brigade under Young ahead as a flying column, leaving its wagons behind to live off the country, and try to intercept the Filipino president by a headlong dash into wild country never before seen by a white man.

The ensuing march by Young and his 1,100-man brigade "became celebrated in the annals of the Philippine service, where hard marches were the norm." The unseasonably late rains returned, and bogs spread out from the streams and lagoons so that only the high ground remained above water, and low areas became broad, shallow lakes. The horses became stuck in mud that came up to their bellies, and soldiers had to cut brush and bamboo continually so the primitive sledges used to drag cartridge boxes could pass. The men ate, slept, and marched in the drizzle and downpour. Their perpetually wet clothes rotted on their backs. Rifles rusted, and all the equipment was covered with a thin layer of mildew. When it was not raining, the sun baked the ground and the men gasped for breath in the tropical humidity. They were infected with tropical ulcers, dysentery, fevers, and a variety of other ailments.[20]

Young reached San Jose on November 12 and learned that Aguinaldo—accompanied by his family, members of his cabinet, and an armed guard several hundred strong—was still south of the mountains. His brigade abandoned the sledges and each man carried a bandolier of ammunition and little else. Young set out for Umangan, reaching it the next day, and from there sent his cavalry to Tayug and San Nicholas, closing off two more passes. As Young's brigade pressed northward, his scouts found increasing evidence that Aguinaldo was near. On November 14 the Third Cavalry under Major Samuel M. Swigert encountered the Filipino rear guard outside Pozorrubio. Fatigue, disease, and the debilitation suffered by his men led Swigert to halt his troops on the outskirts of town that night. He rode into Pozorrubio the next morning only to discover that Aguinaldo had passed through the village in the night but had already left. Swigert had to settle for the capture of *el Presidente's* mother and son, his secretary of foreign affairs, and the Filipino's printing press and treasury. Young's main force would have trapped Aguinaldo at Pozorrubio if not for the betrayal of a Tagalog guide who led them to the wrong village.[21]

Young reached the San Nicholas-Tayug area on November 16. Although his forces were isolated, overextended, and suffering from exhaustion, fever, and malnutrition, the general was convinced Aguinaldo had fewer than 150 soldiers remaining and was fleeing north. Young decided he could not wait for orders from higher headquarters, and on November 17 set off after Aguinaldo. If he could only manage to link up with Wheaton's missing force, the trap could be shut and the war ended.[22]

The problem was, where was Wheaton?

With 2,500 men of the Thirty-Third Volunteer and Thirteenth Regular Infantry regiments and detachment of the Sixth Artillery, Wheaton and his transports had sailed from Manila on November 6 and arrived off the Lingayen Gulf port of San Fabian the next day. After a heavy bombardment of insurgent trenches, the troops disembarked within two hours and brushed aside any resistance. Although San Fabian was only twelve miles from the link-up point at Dagupan, it was not occupied by Wheaton's men until nineteen days later. Even when a detachment from Young's Third Cavalry rode into San Fabian on November 14, the normally bold Wheaton continued to act halfheartedly as precious time slipped away.[23] At no time while Young was chasing Aguinaldo northward did Wheaton detect that Aguinaldo and his staff were in the immediate vicinity. Towns such as San Jacinto and Mangalden, through which the Filipinos eventually had to pass, were inspected only cursorily. One battalion came within a mile of Rosario and turned back just as Aguinaldo's party was entering the town from the south.[24]

Meanwhile, of Young's original 1,100-man flying column, only eighty troopers from the Third Cavalry and a battalion of three hundred native Macabebe scouts remained in the chase. Young sent his aide, now–Lieutenant Colonel James Parker, to San Fabian to ask Wheaton to occupy Vigan, a town on the Lingayen Gulf to the north that was a possible destination for Aguinaldo. Convinced he needed all his troops to block the Philippine army, which he still expected in the southwest, Wheaton refused. Similarly, when he learned that some men from the Thirty-Third Infantry had also joined the chase, he recalled them. Young wrote him imploringly: "My forces are much depleted and worn out. Aguinaldo has been playing hide and seek. One day in the mountains, the next . . . on the coast road. . . . If you can assist me in this matter, I don't see how he can escape." Wheaton grudgingly released a battalion under Major Peyton C. March, who proceeded to Namacpacan on the twenty-sixth and immediately put himself under Young's command. Young ordered March's battalion to strike inland toward Candon to block the Tirad Pass.

✳

ON THE MORNING OF DECEMBER 2. March's force of nine hundred men was making its way up the zigzag trail over the pass when "a sharp clatter of Mausers was heard and bullets began singing overhead."[25] The Filipino rear guard—commanded by Aguinaldo's aide and inseparable companion, General Gregario del Pilar—had built a stone barricade at the summit of the pass and held their fire until the Americans were close. The initial volley pinned down March's lead company. Another company attempted to advance under the intense fire, but it too was driven back after sustaining heavy losses.

March dispatched an NCO and ten sharpshooters to an adjoining hill to cover Pilar's rear and to provide suppressive fire should any insurgent raise his head above the parapet. Seeing that the trail led to a wide opening lacking the cover necessary to charge the Filipino trenches, March sent Lieutenant Frank Tompkins and Company H back down the steep hill with instructions to flank the enemy position by scaling the cliffs. Dodging fire from the Mausers, March went up and down the trail reassuring his men. As the engagement on the main trail settled into a stalemate, "an interminable wait which was as trying as active fighting," Company H worked its way up the steep cliffs, with Tompkins and his men hauling one another up by belts, rifles, and ropes cut from their blankets. Shortly before noon, they emerged above Pilar's position, charging down at the same time the rest of the battalion rushed the barricade. The Filipinos attempted to fall back to a second line of defense but were cut down by the marksmen on the hill.[26]

Pilar's role in the "Filipino Thermopylae" was immortalized in Richard Henry Little's account of the battle for the *Chicago Tribune,* and American soldiers buried Pilar with full military honors.[27] Of Pilar's original sixty defenders, only nine survived. Yet their sacrifice allowed Aguinaldo and his remaining forces to safely cross the Benguet Mountains before disappearing into the dark, rocky core of Luzon.

✳

MARCH CONTINUED THE PURSUIT of Aguinaldo, but disease and fatigue were attriting his forces so quickly that two days after the fight at Tirad Pass, he had only one hundred men fit to fight. March pushed deep into the mountains until his entire command collapsed and he had to turn back. Lawton requested permission to cross the mountains into the Cagayan Valley before Aguinaldo got settled and, against Otis's order, sent a three-hundred-man company under Captain Joseph Batchelor on a reduced version of his plan. Batchelor did not find Aguinaldo, but he met with surprising success when Colonel Danilo Tirona surrendered to him with 1,100 men and 800 rifles. Perhaps to discourage further insubordination, Otis recalled Lawton to Manila to take charge of the campaign to mop up the residual resistance around the capital.[28]

On December 18, Lawton led a small patrol to San Mateo, a village eighteen miles northeast of Manila. In a driving rain, the US forces encountered an insurgent force awaiting them in trenches near the Maniquina River. Lawton paced back and forth behind the American firing line, personally exhorting his soldiers onward. The Filipino general, likely searching for a clear reference point by which to direct fire through the downpour, directed his *Tiradores de la Muerte* ("Death Shooters") to concentrate their fire on the tall figure wearing the brilliant white pith helmet and bright yellow rain slicker. One of the aides at Lawton's side was hit shortly thereafter.

Lawton carried his lieutenant to shelter and despite his promise to retire to a safer position, returned to the firing line. Suddenly, he made an awkward motion in front of his face. "What's the matter, General?" asked his remaining aide, Captain E. L. King.

"I'm shot," Lawton replied.

"Where?"

"Through the lungs."

With blood pouring from his mouth, his tall frame slunk to the wet ground. Within minutes the most beloved officer in the Philippines, possibly in the US Army, was dead, his head resting upon the thigh of a staff officer.

In a case of tragic irony, Lawton was struck down by soldiers led by the Filipino General Licerio Geronimo.

＊

AFTER THE FALL OFFENSIVE in 1899, the conventionally minded Otis assumed the war had been won. The destruction of the Republican Army meant that "war in its proper meaning had ceased to exist," and the persistence of rural violence could be ascribed to remnants of the Tagalog military forces and bandits.[29] But what Americans interpreted as the disintegration of the Filipino army in November 1899 was only a change in strategy. Realizing he could no longer confront the superior US forces without sustaining catastrophic losses, Aguinaldo decided to disperse his army and commence guerrilla warfare.

Aguinaldo was aware of the debate the Philippine question had raised in the United States, and calculated that a protracted war with increased US casualties would gradually erode the patience of Americans at home, arouse their opposition to the conflict, and intensify pressure on Washington to reach a settlement. He issued a proclamation explicitly acknowledging his hope to gain a victory through American domestic politics that his forces could not obtain on the battlefield:

> In America there is a great party that insists on the United States government recognizing Filipino independence. They will compel their country to fulfill the promises made to us in all solemnity and faith, though not put in writing. . . . [T]he great Democratic party of the United States will win the next fall election. . . . Imperialism will fail in its mad attempts to subjugate us by force of arms.[30]

Aguinaldo fixed his strategy to the specific objective of getting the American public to repudiate McKinley and elect the anti-imperialist William Jennings Bryan in November 1900. In September and October, the guerrillas launched an offensive against US forces in an effort to influence the presidential elections. They ambushed isolated detachments and supply trains and stepped up their attacks on towns, firing into them at night, burning houses, and otherwise seeking to demonstrate that the army could not protect the populace. Although the guerrillas scored some tactical successes, their offensive failed to prevent McKinley's reelection, thereby ensuring there would be no early American withdrawal.[31]

MacArthur succeeded Otis as commander of the Eighth Army Corps in the Philippines on May 5, 1900. Unlike his predecessor, MacArthur understood that the army was in the midst of a guerrilla war and, assured of his political support, began a more vigorous counterinsurgency campaign. In December, US garrisons were increased by 20 percent and the Philippines were placed under martial law.[32]

Yet Aguinaldo remained as elusive as ever. Since escaping US forces in 1899, Aguinaldo became like a ghost, and rumors of his whereabouts proliferated. Although manifestos appeared above his signature, like Osama bin Laden more than a century later, Aguinaldo was so evasive that some Americans concluded the messages were fakes and that Aguinaldo himself was dead. When Otis departed the Philippines, he claimed the fugitive president was "probably dead," an opinion shared by the head of the Republican government's cabinet, Apolinario Mabini. Filipinos claimed to have seen Aguinaldo's body in various locations, or alternatively, gave credence to rumors that he had fled in disguise to Hong Kong or Singapore. The primitive Igorot mountain dwellers believed Aguinaldo to be a supernatural being capable of flight and usually accompanied by thunder. As one historian remarked, "Aguinaldo had become a bogeyman, a legend, a name with which mothers frightened naughty children." Such was the power of his mystique that McKinley rejected Theodore Roosevelt's request to be appointed civil governor of the Philippines, because Aguinaldo was still at large.[33]

Peeling back the myth growing around Aguinaldo's whereabouts, intelligence gleaned from deserting insurgents suggested he was traveling light, moved his headquarters back and forth across northern Luzon, and used couriers and cooperative civilians to control insurgent operations throughout the archipelago.[34] More significant, however, was Aguinaldo's symbolic importance. He was the personification of the independence movement, and as long as he remained free, his supporters could still claim they fought for a legitimate national government. When MacArthur held an amnesty banquet on July 28, 1900, he found the dining hall decorated with pictures of Emilio Aguinaldo and Philippine flags. As the head of the Civilian Commission on the Philippines, future president William Howard Taft told a friend that unless Aguinaldo and his colleagues were eliminated, they would "overawe the more peaceably inclined inhabitants and the better educated class" in the Philippines.[35]

✳

ONE AMERICAN OFFICER WHO AGREED with Taft's assessment of the strategic problem was Brigadier General Frederick Funston, commander of the Fourth District of the army's Department of Northern Luzon. Funston wrote: "As [Aguinaldo] was insistent that the Filipinos should not accept American rule, and as he was still recognized as the head and front of the insurrection, many of us had long felt that the thing could not end until he was either out of the way or a prisoner in our hands."[36]

Funston, the ruddy-faced, barrel-chested thirty-five-year old "enfant terrible of the Occupying Forces," was a larger-than-life figure despite standing only five foot four. He was born on September 11, 1865, to an artilleryman in the Union Army who moved the family to Kansas after the war and was later elected to Congress. Upon graduating from high school, Funston tried to follow in his father's footsteps by entering the military but was denied an appointment to West Point. He dropped out after two desultory years at Kansas State University, taking a succession of odd jobs until 1890, when he passed a civil service examination and became a government botanist. In this capacity he served on expeditions to such forbidding locations as the newly pacified Bad Lands, the oven-like Death Valley, and the frigid Yukon territory, where he completed a 1,400-mile solo trip down the Yukon River.

Funston happened to be in New York City on a spring evening in 1896 when, out of curiosity, he followed a crowd into Madison Square Garden, where he found a political rally in progress promoting the cause of the Cuban revolution against Spain. The event implanted martial images in Funston's mind that kept him awake with excitement, and before dawn arrived he decided to volunteer for his first war. The Cuban junta needed artillery officers, so although Funston's experience with artillery was limited to once "having seen a salute fired to President Hayes at a county fair in Kansas," he signed on and taught himself the art of gunnery with a Hotchkiss twelve-pounder he found at an arms dealer.[37]

Over the course of a year's fighting in 1897, he was wounded four times. In addition to the persistent hunger he shared with his revolutionary comrades, Funston contracted malaria and was subject to periodic fevers and chills, and contracted typhoid fever during one of his many hospital confinements. On December 12, 1897, while about to go on leave, Funston was captured by a Spanish patrol. Looking directly into the barrel of Spanish rifles, knowing he could be shot at any moment, Funston quickly invented a story of how he was deserting from the *insurrecto* army and was actually looking for Spaniards to whom he could surrender. As he spun his tale, he coolly placed his hand in his pocket, placed the incriminating leave papers in his handkerchief, pulled the handkerchief out to swab the perspiration on his face, and managed to slip the papers into his mouth and swallow them without being noticed. The Spaniards subsequently conveyed Funston to Havana, where he was soon placed upon the first available ship for New York.

The series of wounds and diseases Funston suffered in Cuba would be enough to dissuade the average man from ever again volunteering for war. But such was Funston's passion for adventure—or perhaps his sense of invulnerability—that when the Spanish-American War erupted the following spring, he leapt at the opportunity to serve as the Colonel of the Twentieth Kansas Volunteer Infantry. Thus, on October 27, 1898, Funston sailed for Manila with the Second and Third Battalions of the Twentieth Kansas.

The bantam colonel quickly made a name for himself for his personal courage and aggressive tactics. Funston's Kansans were always in the lead of the American offensives. During the fighting of February 5, 1899, Funston led his regiment up the coast so swiftly that he came under fire from the USS *Charleston* and had to stop. "There goes Kansas," exclaimed MacArthur as the regiment swarmed, yelling and shooting, toward Caloocan during 1899's spring campaign, "and all Hell can't stop her." MacArthur wired back to headquarters: "CALOOCAN TAKEN. KANSAS A MILE IN ADVANCE OF THE LINE. WILL STOP THEM IF I CAN."[38]

On April 27, 1899, MacArthur and Wheaton's combined brigades were halted at the banks of the Rio Grande de la Pampanga by a formidable entrenchment of four thousand Filipinos backed by artillery and a Maxim machine gun. The only way of establishing a beachhead on the enemy bank seemed to be by an artillery barrage to cover the activities of a small unit in the river. After two privates swam across with a coil of rope, Funston personally took seven men across on a raft and, ordering the rest of his troops across in stages, dashed with a half-dozen men into the trenches. Although they found only dead and wounded Filipinos remaining, they soon came under fire from the Maxim gun positioned across a stream three hundred yards away. An American soldier yelled out, "It's the Maxim—we're goners," only to receive a kick from Funston, who told him to be quiet. Funston stood up, saw that the gun was beneath a railroad culvert, and ordered his prone men to rise. "Under that culvert, rapid fire," he yelled, and the gun was silenced.[39] Funston was awarded the Medal of Honor for his part in the crossing of the Rio Grande.

Funston became a favorite of General MacArthur's, who treated Funston like a son and praised him in his official reports. One reason for MacArthur's fondness toward Funston was the latter's indisputable effectiveness as a commander, particularly as the conflict evolved into a grinding counterinsurgency campaign in 1900. Unlike regular army generals, Funston was guided more by pragmatism than by any established theory of warfare. As historian Brian Macallister Linn notes in *The U.S. Army and Counterinsurgency in the Philippine War:* "[Funston] was willing to use whatever means were necessary, and if his solutions were often theatrical, they were also effective." Although a vocal advocate of repression, Funston's actual conduct was characterized by "lenient surrender terms, rewards for collaboration, and personal friendship." He established social contacts with former or captured insurgent leaders in order to gain information on guerrilla organizations, and created a native secret service to provide vital information. Funston also made shrewd use of bribes to revolutionary agents when necessary. His district intelligence service was bolstered by good field intelligence from his garrison commanders.[40]

This adroitness at intelligence would have important ramifications for the course of the war.

*

ON FEBRUARY 4, 1901, Funston was in his headquarters completing paperwork when an orderly entered bearing the yellow slip of a telegram. The message was from Lieutenant James D. Taylor, the company commander of an outpost in the village of Pantabangan, sixty miles northeast of Funston's headquarters in San Isidro. Taylor reported the surrender of several guerrillas, including a courier bearing documents that appeared to be from Aguinaldo himself.

Two days later, a tired, hungry Filipino dressed in rags was brought into Funston's office. Cecilio Segismundo had been a corporal under Major Nazario Alhambra, whose troops were summoned to Aguinaldo's secret location. Segismundo became a courier for Aguinaldo, but after traversing the Sierra Madres and Central Cordilleras with his dispatches, he and his companions were exhausted, footsore, and starving. In desperation, they sought support from the mayor of San Juan, near

Pantabangan, only to discover he had already sworn a loyalty oath to the Americans. This final setback convinced Segismundo that he was through with the revolution. "I am glad to wash my hands of this business," he said to Taylor as he handed over his dispatch pouch.[41] Although most of the documents were ordinary notes from homesick insurgents to their families, Funston noted communications addressed to all the major Filipino commanders in Luzon, each signed by "Colon de Magdalo" or "Colon de Pastor," noms de guerre used by Aguinaldo.

Recognizing the potential significance of these documents, Funston summoned two of his aides to help decipher the encoded documents. One of these was Lazaro de Segovia y Gutierrez, an intelligence officer who was only twenty-two years old but had already been fighting in the Philippines for four years. He initially served with his Spanish regiment, earning seven decorations for gallantry. Once the defeated Castilians were shipped back to Spain, "his love of adventures" and his inability to bring his Filipino wife home with him led him to cast his lot with the *insurrectos* in October 1898. He became a lieutenant and aide to General Marian Llanera, coincidentally coming under fire from Funston's Twentieth Kansas as it swept toward Caloocan. By the spring of 1900, Segovia could see which way the wind was blowing and surrendered directly to Funston that May. Funston recognized a kindred spirit in the gifted and handsome young Spaniard, and made him a translator and aide.[42]

Funston and his aides brewed coffee and prepared to work through the night. After several hours, the discovery of the word "ammunition" in a letter to General Sandico enabled them to break the code, which prompted Funston to break out the whiskey as they translated the dispatches until nearly noon the next day. One document stood out from the piles of mundane correspondence: a letter from Aguinaldo to his cousin Baldomero placing the latter in command of Central Luzon and requesting reinforcements be sent to the president. More important, the letter confirmed the valley Segismundo claimed that Aguinaldo had used to gain access to the Pacific coast. Further interrogation of Segismundo pinpointed Aguinaldo's hideout in the village of Palanan in Isabela province.[43]

With Aguinaldo's exact location finally revealed, Funston quickly decided to personally lead a mission to Palanan to capture Aguinaldo alive and thereby end the war with one bold stroke. Yet it was not immediately clear how this could be accomplished. According to Segismundo, all trails leading to Palanan were guarded by a network of spies, informants, couriers, and watch posts. If an American patrol approached Palanan, Aguinaldo would have sufficient warning to flee deeper into the mountains. Similarly, an amphibious landing on the Pacific coast preceding an overland thrust to Palanan was impossible, as the appearance of smoke from an American steamship would be seen over the horizon and set off the alarm before the Americans could even reach the shore.

As with the night he decided to enlist in the Cuban insurrection, Funston could not sleep as he turned the problem over again and again in his mind. Finally, the answer came to him: if no American patrol could come within miles of Palanan, the only way to capture Aguinaldo would be "to get him under false colors." Aguinaldo had requested his cousin send him reinforcements, but what if the relief troops were not his own? Funston realized he could substitute Macabebes for insurgent forces, as they would be practically indistinguishable from Tagalog insurgents. This relief column would bring some unexpected guests to Aguinaldo—five American officers posing as prisoners of war.

Although Aguinaldo expected this detachment from Baldomero's headquarters somewhere in the Central Plain of Luzon, this trek would be too long and too risky for Funston's purposes. Instead, they would eliminate the two hundred miles of hard marching by planning on sea transport to the point on the Pacific coast where the detachment would have emerged after passing through the mountains. The ideal spot was south of the village of Casiguran, twenty-seven miles north of the last American outpost at Baler, and known to be sympathetic to the insurgents. Between Casiguran and Palanan lay more than one hundred miles of uncharted and unexplored hostile territory where the Americans would be perpetually at risk of betrayal, ambush, and the elements and would be completely cut off from any assistance.

Yet none of Funston's aides wanted to be excluded from the mission.

While in San Isidro, Funston selected the other American officers for the mission. The first, Lieutenant Burton Mitchell, was not only Funston's personal aide, but his first cousin as well. The second, Captain Harry Newton, was chosen because he had once been posted to the garrison at Baler and had traveled as far north as Casiguran, thus giving him some knowledge of the area. The American contingent was rounded out by the addition of the Hazzard brothers, Russell and Oliver, who commanded the detachment of eighty Macabebe scouts assembled for the mission.

In order to deceive the insurgents, however, it was necessary to have Tagalog officers on hand to "lead" the expedition. "The selection of these men was a very delicate manner," Funston noted, "as they would have it in their power to ruin us by disclosing our real character." Given his inventiveness and capacity for leadership, Segovia was an obvious choice to play the part of an insurgent officer. Once the Americans assumed their posture as prisoners, Segovia would command a trio of former insurgents. Hilario Talplacido was a rotund former major in the Republican Army who had been arrested by Funston's forces in May 1900. After several months in jail, he took the loyalty oath and was released to his wife's custody. Talplacido was kept in the dark as to the mission's target, as were two young soldiers: Dionisio Bato, who had been captured, and Gregorio Cadhit, who had tired of the rebellion and surrendered three months earlier. Both had sworn the required oath, as by now had Segismundo, whom Funston pressed into service to guide the column to Aguinaldo. On the day they were to leave for Manila, Bato arranged to be married in the church at San Isidro. The wedding party emerged from the ceremony to see the groom whisked away in a US Army wagon before he even had a chance to kiss his bride.[44]

While in Manila, Funston reviewed the plan with MacArthur, who wanted Aguinaldo taken alive. The Filipinos had created a legend of invincibility around him so that if he were killed, millions of Filipinos would not believe he was dead. Even those who did would merely elevate him to martyrdom status. If he were captured alive, however, his mystique would be dispelled, and the rebellion dealt a fatal blow. The possibility of failure or even disaster was significant. If Funston's deception failed, he and the officers would be killed or captured. But MacArthur proved as bold as Funston and approved the mission. Believing the risks were necessary to end the insurgency, he accepted the possibility of failure, as well as full responsibility for the mission.[45]

At their final meeting, MacArthur somberly remarked: "Funston, this is a desperate undertaking. I fear I shall never see you again."[46]

On March 6, Funston, with the four American officers, Segovia and three Tagalog officers, and eighty Macabebe scouts boarded the gunboat *Vicksburg*. The anchor was raised at 7:30 PM, and the steamer cruised out of Manila Bay into the open sea.

✳

THE NEXT MORNING. Funston and Segovia finally briefed the three Filipinos on the details of the mission. When told of Funston's intention
to capture Aguinaldo alive, they were "thunderstruck" at the audacity
of the plan. Funston and Segovia then went to tell the Macabebes who
had been assembled on the *Vicksburg*'s deck. The revelation of their mission caused disquiet among the Macabebes, who worried whether their
numbers were sufficient for such a dangerous journey. Before any un-
easiness could take hold, the scouts' first sergeant, Pedro Bustas, "a little
shriveled old fellow" who had served in Spanish regiments against the
Moros and later against the Tagalog rebels, spoke up: "I cannot speak for
the others, but I am a soldier of the United States." His speech rallied the
Macabebes, and the rest of the journey was spent drilling them on the
specifics of the mission and memorizing the story they were to repeat
during any contact with the inhabitants of Luzon's eastern coast.[47]

Funston and Segovia retired to the commander's cabin to forge the
letters of introduction necessary to fool Aguinaldo. They drafted two
letters they hoped would appear to be responses from General Lacuna,
whose official stationery Funston's forces had captured the previous November. The first letter, dated February 24, 1901, indicated it had been
written by Lacuna at his mountain hideout in eastern Nueva Ecija province. This letter was intended to provide authenticity for the second letter and acknowledged receipt of Aguinaldo's correspondence of January
13 and 14, and thanked him for confirmation of Lacuna's promotion to
brigadier general. The second letter was dated February 28 and claimed
the receipt of orders from Aguinaldo's cousin Baldomero, who, had he
received the intended message via Segismundo by then, would have assumed command of Central Luzon as per *el presidente*'s instructions.
In this letter, "Lacuna" announced he was sending one of his best companies to join Aguinaldo at Palanan. This group would be under the
command of the heroic Hilario Talplacido, who, in case Aguinaldo had
not heard, had sworn a loyalty oath to the Americans for a time after his
capture, but had since returned to the revolutionary fold.[48]

In addition to the details of the mission, another concern weighed
upon Funston's mind. Before leaving Manila, MacArthur had notified
his subordinate that the War Department had ordered him to muster
Funston out of the army. Because Funston was technically a volunteer

rather than a regular army officer, he was subject to such an order at any time. MacArthur received permission to delay executing the order until Funston had completed an unspecified high-priority task, but unless this desperate venture succeeded, Funston's military career would be finished.

✳

AT ONE AM ON MARCH 14, battered by a thick squall, the *Vicksburg* approached the coast. In total darkness, ninety men quickly and quietly slipped into the gunboat's launches and were lowered into the rough sea. Funston and the other American "prisoners" wore the campaign hats, blue shirts without insignia, khaki breeches, and leggings of army privates. The Macabebe "insurgents" were dressed in ragged clothing. They carried only one day's supply of rice per man. The landing boats pushed through the mist and rain toward the empty shore ahead. With a muffled "Good luck, lads," the sailors shoved the longboats back into the black water of Casiguran Bay and disappeared into the night.[49]

The soldiers on the beach were completely alone.

A steady rain fell through the night, soaking the men as they huddled together beneath the pitiful shelter of palm fronds. Segovia moved from sentry to sentry to remind each of the importance of refraining from firing should anybody approach. Finally, at seven AM they began the march north toward Casiguran with Segovia in the lead. With dawn, Funston underwent the transformation from an audacious general to a dejected army private as the Americans marched in the center of the column, a Macabebe guard on either side of them. Just as the Macabebes were required to speak only in the Tagalog dialect in order to avoid detection, the Americans would have to remain in character day and night until the mission was complete.

Although the column was able to maintain a steady pace, it soon became apparent that the shoreline was far more sinuous than it appeared on the map, and that the march would encompass a greater distance than the anticipated ten miles. In some places, impassable mangrove jungles stretched into the water, forcing the column to wade through the surf for long distances, five miles altogether. When they regained dry land, there were numerous streams to ford. At one point the sandy beach ended abruptly at an expanse of two miles of sharp stones that cut the Macabebes' bare feet like knives.

Several miles into the march, the column came upon their first trace of human habitation along the coast, a small lookout shelter commanding a view of the ocean and beach. Fresh footprints in the moist sand indicated that the shelter's occupant had seen them and run off toward Casiguran to provide warning. At noon they discovered a canoe in the mouth of a small creek. Funston decided the reappearance of Segismundo in the village would alleviate any doubts that their group was insurgents. So the courier, Cadhit, and two Macabebes were sent off in the canoe toward Casiguran. Segismundo was given a message from Talplacido to the head of the village requesting that food and quarters be prepared for the detachment. The Macabebes were given orders to kill the courier and Cadhit should they betray the mission.

After resting for two hours, the column resumed marching shortly after two PM. Around four PM, Segovia saw a lone figure some distance down the beach heading in their direction. He ordered the column into a tangle of shrubs and screw pines to avoid detection. When the man drew close, Segovia hailed him and was informed he had been sent from Casiguran to guide them into the village.

Casiguran was a moderately large settlement of perhaps one hundred board and thatch structures, bounded on three sides by farm plots and groves. An old Spanish stone church and an attached rectory stood next to the town square in its center. "We entered the town in great style," noted Funston, as the lively sounds of the Casiguran municipal bamboo orchestra greeted their arrival at the town's plaza. The Filipinos were welcomed as heroes, while the American "prisoners" were gazed upon with a cold curiosity.[50]

Segovia tried to gain as much information as possible from the villagers. "President Aguinaldo is well content with us," the guide told him, as twice a month they provided his forces with "rice, sweet potatoes, and chickens."

"Has he many soldiers with him?" Segovia asked.

"Yes, sir, very close to a hundred," the village's representatives replied.

The next morning, Segovia set about collecting enough provisions for the long march to Palanan, and under Funston's orders drafted a new set of letters with Talplacido to be sent to Aguinaldo informing him that their column had encountered an American detail making maps, and had killed three, wounded two, and taken the other five prisoner. After preparing the letters and sealing them in bundles, Segovia visited the vice mayor, who dispatched runners to deliver the correspondence and showed Segovia what food had been procured for the journey: a few hundred pounds of rice and Indian corn and "a goodly quantity of sweet potatoes." Despite Segovia's decision to keep one-third of the food they were given to eat in Casiguran in reserve and the vice mayor's pledge to collect what little more the poor village could scrape together, Segovia doubted they would have sufficient provisions to reach Palanan.[51]

Meanwhile, an alarming rumor swept through Casiguran on the fifteenth that General Manuel Tinio had joined Aguinaldo with four hundred reinforcements. This gossip disturbed the Macabebes, who had to be convinced that the element of surprise would be sufficient to overcome the now one-to-five force ratio they faced. That night, Segovia visited the prisoners and updated Funston on the day's events. They agreed the column would leave Casiguran at dawn on the seventeenth. Segovia procured sixteen chickens for the officers and found an old woman willing to sell two carabao yearlings, which were subsequently slaughtered and salted. Yet they still would have enough food for only five and a half days of the seven-day trek. Despite the unresolved logistical problem of how to feed 101 stomachs for a march over one hundred miles of uninhabited wilderness, the Americans held a brief conference and unanimously agreed to take their chances with short rationing and a forced march that *might* get them to Palanan in less than a week.[52]

Although the morning of March 17 was gray and rainy, all of Casiguran's inhabitants turned out to bid farewell to the supposed patriots. At six AM the column was formed in the town square and given the order to march, its chances of success a long shot at best.

✳

THE SOLDIERS PASSED THROUGH muddy rice fields until they reached an immense, ancient forest, which they crossed over a path so narrow they had to march single file. They emerged back out on the beach, where the burning, ankle-deep sand made walking agony for the Macabebes, whose unshod feet throbbed and blistered. Soon, they came up against a sheer mountain face blocking their path where it advanced to the ocean. Harry Newton noted: "Nothing but mountain goats or Filipinos could follow [the path] . . . the slightest misstep would result in instant death."[53] Nevertheless, pulling themselves up by the roots and branches of trees, they managed to ascend to the summit. On the third day, the coastline rose to insurmountable cliffs, forcing them to walk nearly five miles inland. Returning to the coastline, from the high ground they could see that their route northward was littered by a sea of boulders that, according to Funston, "varied in size from that of a watermelon to a freight car. This was the hardest marching of all."[54] Torrents of rain pelted the soldiers throughout their march, drenching their skin through their clothes as they traversed the forbidding terrain.

In addition to the terrain and weather, the column soon faced another problem. During the first meal away from Casiguran, Segovia noticed the Macabebes were broiling large slices of the carabao meat without consideration of the need to conserve their limited supplies. Again, during the evening meal, they seemed to eat without regard for the next day, and Segovia discovered they had eaten more than half their meat supply in the first day. Consequently, the detachment's ration was cut to one-fourth the ordinary daily allowance.[55] Scrounging for food, the scouts spread out and attempted to catch small fish with their hands. A few succeeded while others scraped limpets from rocks or gathered snails. These ingredients were put into a stew with the corn to produce what Funston called "a revolting mess" insufficient to nourish 101 ravenous men.

These hardships quickly took their toll. By the third day, the overweight Talplacido had grown so weak he could no longer walk. Because his presence at Palanan was essential to their deception, he was hoisted and carried by a constant relay of two men. By the fifth day it was necessary to carry him with the combined powers of four men as he increasingly became dead weight while the soldiers grew weaker. Many of the scouts were too fatigued to eat during halts for rest, preferring to immediately collapse to the ground. By the sixth day, some of the scouts were burning with fever, while others were so weak they reeled as they walked. It was necessary for several to clutch their companions' shoulders merely to stay upright and press forward.

The Americans were not in much better shape. The Hazzard brothers and Newton were in the best condition, yet were described by Segovia as "pale and emaciated."[56] Mitchell, unable to hold a meal down for several days, was "weak, emaciated; his sunken eyes stared listlessly out from their sockets, and his clothes hung pitiably from his shoulders."[57] Funston suffered from rheumatism, and even the stalwart Segovia looked on with horror as his foot began to swell and develop an abscess, raising the alarming possibility of a fatal infection. It made the continued march excruciatingly painful.

At noon on March 22, the sixth day, the detachment cooked its last meal.

Funston began to despair. "It was plain that the end was at hand," he would recall. "It seemed impossible that the madcap enterprise could succeed, and I began to regret that I had led all these men to such a finish."[58]

At five PM the general saw two men ahead on the beach watching the column approach. For days, Funston had anticipated hearing the crack of a rifle from a cliff top above, signaling the beginning of the fatal ambush of his column. Segovia went to meet them while the soldiers weakly attempted to close ranks. Funston saw them hand Segovia a letter. He watched as the Spaniard limped back along the line toward the rear. As Segovia passed the captives, he whispered in Spanish: "It's all right. We have them!"

✳

THE TWO MEN WERE FROM Palanan and had been sent to escort the "reinforcements" to Aguinaldo's headquarters. "What a load was lifted from our minds!" Funston recalled. "We were now ten miles from our quarry." At dusk they reached an outpost consisting of a few small sheds, manned by an old Tagalog and a half-dozen Baluga tribesmen. Once again, Segovia waited for everyone to fall asleep before approaching Funston. The Spaniard showed him the letter that had been sent from Aguinaldo's chief of staff at Palanan:

> *Lieutenant-Colonel Hilario Placido*
>
> On account of the circumstances, please arrange to leave the American prisoners which you have at the place called Dinundungan, where this will be delivered to you. Under no circumstances must they be brought here. For a proper guard please leave at Dinundungan until further orders ten armed men under a sergeant or corporal. You should communicate them the orders regarding the prisoners.
>
> This I communicate to you by order of the Honorable Captain General.
>
> May God guard you many years.
>
> SIMEON VILLA
> *Colonel and Chief of Staff*
> PALANAN, March 21, 1901

Segovia had already dispatched a reply, signed by Talplacido, acknowl-edging receipt of the orders and requesting that food be sent in order to complete the last stage of the journey.[59]

While their deception appeared to have been successful, Aguinaldo's order that the Americans be left behind posed several problems. The Macabebes feared their Tagalog officers would once again switch alle-giances and betray them to Aguinaldo's forces. Segovia told Funston that the Macabebes had lost their courage along the route, and without the moral support of the Americans "they will open fire at the sight of the first enemy, and try to take Palanan by assault," thereby spoiling Fun-ston's carefully developed plans. After consultation, Funston and Sego-via decided the Americans would be left behind, but that after an hour's march Segovia would send a scout back to Dinundungan with a letter from Talplacido to the corporal in command of the guard telling him new orders had been received from Palanan for the prisoners to march in their rear. To allay suspicions, these new "orders" would be shown to the genuine insurgents at the outpost, and the prisoners would catch up to the main column.[60]

Although the rice requested from Palanan had not yet arrived, at eight AM on March 23, Segovia ordered his force into formation. Four unfortunate scouts hoisted up the invalid Talplacido as the Spaniard once again painfully limped to the front of the formation. Funston, Mitchell, Newton, and the Hazzard brothers stood nearby and with eleven Macabebes watched the column march inland along a narrow, muddy path that disappeared into a dense forest.

Shortly after nine AM, two villagers from Palanan arrived with the emergency rations, having already provided a share to Segovia's column en route. An hour later the Macabebe scout arrived with the letter stat-ing the prisoners were to come to Palanan after all. Although the elderly Tagalog examined the letter with suspicion and complained that he had constructed the shelters for nothing, he was content to watch as the Ma-cabebes herded the Americans into the woods and out of sight.

Funston and his companions traveled slowly along the muddy path that extended to the northwest from the beach. Although they had eaten all the rice provided, they were still drastically weak. Every few hundred yards, Funston had to lie flat on the ground in order to rest. About two hours after leaving the beach, they heard a furious thumping of feet ahead. Suddenly, a Macabebe sergeant and another scout came rushing down the path, nearly colliding with them in their excitement. Out of breath and unable to speak, they frantically motioned for the party to hide in the undergrowth beside the trail.

As they pressed themselves into the moist earth, the sergeant whispered that the column had met a dozen armed soldiers coming from Palanan to take custody of the American captives they assumed to still be at Dinundungan. Segovia had Talplacido and Cadhit stall them while he went to the rear of the column and told the sergeant to go "as fast as his legs would carry him" until he met the prisoners and told them to go into hiding until the detachment had passed. A few moments later twelve men wearing the clean, blue uniforms of the insurgency passed within thirty feet. Funston and his party held their breath, and watched through a tangle of brush as the group splashed along a creek, unaware of their presence. Once they were out of sight and their laughing voices could no longer be heard, Funston's men breathed a sigh of relief at their narrow escape and returned to the trail.

Funston's party reached the bank of the Palanan River just before three PM. Across a swiftly moving stream about one hundred yards wide, a village was surrounded by a thick wall of jungle. Perhaps eighty thatched houses stood behind the town square in neat rows. A blue, red, and white Filipino nationalist flag flew from a high pole attached to the roof of a one-story building perched on stilts near the river's edge. They arrived in time to see the last boatload of Macabebes forming on the far bank. The boat was sent back for them, but just as they pushed off the sound of gunfire erupted.

Funston's men began shouting and firing their guns into the air to simulate an attacking force. They frantically paddled across the river. Funston stood at the prow and saw his scouts running through the village, yelling and firing wildly in every direction. Segovia emerged from the building splattered with blood. The Spaniard saw the general and ran down to the river bank.

"It is all right," Segovia shouted. "We have him!"

*

A METALLIC GONG HAD GREETED Segovia's column of scouts as they reached the river shore across from Palanan. Segovia saw people gathering in the town square, and from the window of Aguinaldo's quarters he caught the glint of field glasses watching them ferry across the Palanan.

It took fifteen minutes to get all the Macabebes across the river, where-upon Bato and Cadhit organized them into formation. Although the rumors about General Tinio's force turned out to be unfounded, sixty soldiers armed with Mausers were lined up in the square to greet them. Segovia halted the Macabebe formation ten yards from Aguinaldo's honor guard and gave the order to present arms. Leaving Cadhit and Bato in charge of the Macabebes, Segovia and the suddenly ambulatory Talplacido approached Aguinaldo's house, where they were greeted by his physician, Dr. Santiago Barcelona. The physician led them into a sitting room containing only a table and a few benches. They were introduced to the officers gathered in the room and seated. Barcelona said that *el presidente* was in his room dressing and would join them shortly, and provided them with cigarettes and glasses of sugared water. After a few minutes, a door off the entry hall opened. Segovia and Talplacido had both met Aguinaldo while insurgents and quickly recognized the small man in a khaki uniform approaching them. They leapt to their feet and sharply saluted as the fugitive president entered the room.

Although Aguinaldo was not a physically imposing figure, he had an air of command about him. His plain uniform was accentuated by fancy Spanish riding boots, and it fit crisply over his slim build. He wore his dark hair in a pompadour over a wide, high brow that suggested intelligence. His eyes were friendly, clear, and serene.[61] He walked straight up to his guests and greeted them with a handshake. He questioned Segovia about their journey and the situation in Central Luzon, and when he saw the condition of Segovia's foot he implored the Spaniard to sit down.

As they talked, Aguinaldo's officers excused themselves one by one to return to their duties, so that after a half hour only Barcelona, Villa, and Alhambra remained in the room with their president. Segovia noted that two windows and the door afforded the only exit from the room.

It was time to act.

"Lieutenant Colonel," Segovia addressed Talplacido, "the soldiers require rest."

"Very well," the corpulent officer replied. "Ask for permission."

Aguinaldo granted permission. "Before you go," he said, "I congratulate you for your gallantry to have me brought five prisoners."[62]

Segovia limped down the stairs, where his eyes met Cadhit's. Segovia nodded slightly, removed his hat and raised it. "*Now is the time, Macabebes!*" Cadhit shouted. "*Give it to them!*"

The column fired an erratic volley into the troops ahead of them. Segovia turned, and with his revolver drawn ran back up the stairs into the house. The echo of a second volley pierced the air.

Aguinaldo, thinking his troops were firing a welcoming salute, ran to the window and cried out: "Stop that foolishness! Don't waste ammunition!" The scene below was chaotic. His troops were fleeing from the relief column, their cartridges in their belts rather than in their rifles. Some men took cover and frantically tried to load their weapons. A dead body lay on the ground. Amid the shouting, Aguinaldo noticed bullets ricocheting near his window and realized they were under attack.

Aguinaldo turned from the scene and tried to draw his revolver as Segovia rushed into the room, but Barcelona threw both arms around him. Villa and Alhambra had drawn their guns and attempted to shield their leader, while Talplacido had thrown himself to the ground as soon as he heard firing. The standoff seemed like an eternity, but it was only a few seconds before Segovia cried, "We are not insurgents, we are Americans! Surrender or be killed!"[63]

The Spaniard saw an abrupt movement—perhaps Aguinaldo struggling with Barcelona—and opened fire. Alhambra reeled, shot in the face, and fell through a window into the river below, where he was swept away. Villa fell as he was shot in the wrist, but quickly sprang up and jumped through the same window, but was shot in the back as he attempted to escape. Barcelona produced a white handkerchief from his pocket. "We surrender. This is the flag of peace."[64]

Talplacido rose from his spot and seized Aguinaldo just as several Macabebes entered the room. With Aguinaldo and Barcelona under guard, Segovia went outside to settle the situation in the village when he saw Funston's boat reaching the shore. The pain in his foot forgotten in the adrenaline of battle, he excitedly ran to meet his general.

✳

FUNSTON ENTERED THE ROOM where the shooting had occurred. After two years and the extreme hardships of the past week, he was finally face-to-face with his quarry. Aguinaldo was pale and had tears in his eyes. The dazed Filipino asked, "Is this not some joke?"

Funston assured him this was real. "You are a prisoner of war of the Army of the United States of America," he said to Aguinaldo. "I am

General Funston, commander of the expedition. You will be treated with consideration and sent to Manila at the first opportunity in a steamer, which is coming to take us on board in the bay of this village."[65]

Funston stepped outside. The Macabebes were wild with joy and mobbed the American officers to embrace them. Colonel Villa was fished from the river, still bleeding from his wounds. The prisoners were placed in a room under constant supervision from one of the American officers. After clearing the village, the scouts occupied the surrounding trenches to repel the anticipated counterattack from Aguinaldo's forces or any other guerrilla band that might learn of the coup and attempt a rescue.

After spending the twenty-fourth in Palanan to rest and recuperate, all that remained was to traverse the seven miles to the coast the next day to await the rendezvous with the *Vicksburg*.[66]

✳

IT HAD BEEN THREE WEEKS since Funston and his detachment steamed out of Manila harbor, and since then there had been no news of the expedition. General MacArthur waited anxiously for any word from Funston, and began to despair that the mission had failed.

At 6:30 AM on March 28, MacArthur was awakened by a member of his staff. Funston had returned and was waiting downstairs. MacArthur was normally formal, always appearing before his troops immaculately attired and cleanly shaven. On this occasion, however, MacArthur dashed down the palace stairs in his pajamas.[67]

He shook Funston's hand and looked at him quizzically. Funston said, "Sir, I have brought you Don Emilio."

MacArthur skeptically asked, "Where is he?"

"Right in this house," Funston replied.

MacArthur told Funston to remain and ran back up to his quarters while his staff prepared breakfast for the generals and their prisoner, whom he greeted cordially upon his return. Whereas Aguinaldo was taciturn during the meal, MacArthur quickly put the Filipino at ease, treating him as an honored guest and reiterating his earlier promises to guarantee all personal liberties to the Filipino people once the rebellion ended. He ordered quarters prepared for Aguinaldo and directed officers to send immediately for his family, whom Aguinaldo had not seen since the escape from General Young's cavalry sixteen months earlier.[68]

After the meal, MacArthur telegraphed Washington and publicly announced Aguinaldo's capture. As headlines around the world trumpeted the news, the city of Manila exploded with excitement.

Although Admiral Dewey and some imperialist newspapers in the United States called for Aguinaldo's execution, the McKinley administration wanted to avoid creating a martyr. MacArthur hoped to persuade Aguinaldo to issue a proclamation declaring an end to the revolution and request his followers to lay down their arms. Hence, he treated Aguinaldo graciously, quartering him in a large villa near Malacanang Palace and allowing his family and friends to visit. MacArthur visited him daily and explained "the U.S. point of view, the glories and prosperity which would follow as soon as the fighting ended, and the hopelessness of allowing the struggle to continue."[69]

After twenty-three days of vigorous lobbying by his family and a number of prominent Filipinos, Aguinaldo issued his final wartime proclamation on April 19, 1901: "Enough of blood; enough of tears and desolation . . . by acknowledging and accepting the sovereignty of the United States throughout the entire Archipelago, as I do now, without any reservation whatsoever, I believe that I am serving thee, my beloved country. May happiness be thine!"[70]

After issuing his proclamation, Aguinaldo retired to his estate in Kawit, where he lived under house arrest until July 4, 1902. American attitudes toward Aguinaldo evolved once again. The *New York Times* went from vilifying the Filipino to describing him as a "warm, friendly, intelligent, trustworthy, and reasonable person—a man of honor with the best interests of his countrymen at heart." In August 1901, MacArthur acknowledged: "Aguinaldo is a better man than we gave him credit for."[71]

Aguinaldo lived in Kawit for the rest of his life, managing the family plantations and other holdings, growing relatively prosperous, but always wearing a black bow tie of mourning for the republic that was never recognized. Yet he never bore ill feelings toward his former enemy. He acknowledged that had McKinley not decided upon annexation, the Philippines would likely have been partitioned by other great powers.[72]

Aguinaldo's fondness for America was perhaps best illustrated on July 2, 1923, when the new class of plebes arrived at the United States Military Academy at West Point, New York. Among the approximately 350 young men standing in formation for the first time that day was Emilio Aguinaldo Jr. Elsewhere in the formation, Frederick Funston Jr.

also stood at attention. By less than a year they missed studying under Superintendent General Douglas MacArthur.

✳

AGUINALDO'S CAPTURE REMOVED a vital symbol of resistance, and the former president's proclamation acknowledging American sovereignty legitimized the surrender of other insurgent commanders. Over the next several months, an impressive array of Filipino leaders answered Aguinaldo's appeal, as Generals Tinio, Alejandrino, Mescardo, Lucon, Cailles, and Sandico turned over their commands to the Americans and swore the required loyalty oath. Over 20,000 rebels turned themselves in and declared allegiance to the United States. Rebel activity dropped dramatically, and both MacArthur and the War Department trumpeted Aguinaldo's capture as the "most important single military effect of the year," a coup that all but ended the war. Even the most prominent domestic critic of the war, William Jennings Bryan, believed Funston's deed "may end the war for the present."[73]

Yet Aguinaldo's capture was less important to achieving victory in the Philippines than it initially appeared. By the summer of 1901, the defeat of the Philippine insurgency was nearly complete due to the adoption of an effective counterinsurgency strategy. In reality, Aguinaldo's movement had never gained the widespread popular support necessary to conduct an extended insurgency: his government represented only the islands' wealthy classes, governed much as the Spaniards had, was plagued by significant ethnic divisions, and was forced to rely on widespread terrorism and intimidation of Filipinos in order to enforce its writ. Conversely, some infamous cases of brutality aside, the American "policy of attraction" actually offered more in the way self-government and progressive reform to the Filipino people. In some villages the inhabitants formed vigilante committees and drove the guerrillas from their towns. Indeed, when General Miguel Malvar surrendered, he claimed that the major factor in his decision was the realization that he was now being pursued by the "people."[74] Finally, the US Navy was able to effectively blockade the Philippines, stopping almost all imports of arms, ammunition, supplies, and food, which left the insurgents in dire material straits by early 1901.

It is also unclear whether Aguinaldo's capture and capitulation were even the *primary* factors leading to the increase in surrenders by revolutionary leaders and soldiers. Martin Delgado in Panay, Nicolas Capistrano in Mindanao, and Simon Tecson in northern Luzon all surrendered in the months *before* Aguinaldo's capture. Extensive negotiations in Cavite province between American officers and Lieutenant General Mariano Trias—the commander of southern Luzon and the man who the isolated Aguinaldo believed would assume leadership of the insurgency upon his capture—culminated on March 15, 1901. Trias turned in not only himself but most of his men and arms as well, and published an appeal to his compatriots to abandon resistance. MacArthur, unaware of the status of Funston's mission, called Trias's capitulation a "most auspicious event" that indicated the "final stage [of] armed insurrection." Civilian commissioners Bourns and Taft also saw Trias's surrender as an event of greater significance than Aguinaldo's capture.[75]

Anecdotal evidence suggesting MacArthur's new offensive of November 1900 was more important than Aguinaldo's capture is supported by quantifiable data. In November and December 1900, there were over 1,300 surrenders per month, compared with a total of less than 500 for the previous three months combined. After a slight drop to approximately 900 and 750 respectively, in January and February 1901, they increased again to almost 7,000 in March, the month *before* Aguinaldo's surrender proclamation. Statistics on the surrender of weapons show a similar pattern: from August to December 1900, a total of less than 200 firearms were surrendered. In January and February 1901, however, over 900 were turned in each month. Asked to explain the sudden wave of surrenders by the top guerrilla leadership in the first months of 1901, Lieutenant Colonel Bernardo Marques stated, "They surrendered for various things; some because they tired of staying in the field; some through fear and because they lost hope; because some of them had been injured or lost their health through life in the field and some because their families obliged them to surrender."[76]

Finally, Aguinaldo's capture failed to decisively stem the violence in the Philippines. On April 4, General Malvar, revolutionary commander of Batangas province, convened a meeting of all the remaining leaders and vowed to continue the fight until the Americans were worn down by "*esta guerra interminable.*" By the summer of 1901, five thousand guerrillas under Malvar had regained control over the population south of Manila and most local governments. The United States responded with its most brutal counterinsurgency campaign in the islands, and by the end of the year fifty-four thousand civilians had died in Batangas as collateral damage in the conflict. Sick, famished, and almost out of ammunition, Malvar and his forces finally surrendered on April 16, 1902. Although President Roosevelt declared the war over on July 4, 1902, the American conquest of the Philippines would not be complete for a decade.[77] The single worst defeat suffered by US forces in the Philippines occurred *after* Aguinaldo's capture, when on September 28, 1901, guerrillas attacked the seventy-four officers and soldiers of Company C, Ninth US Infantry at the town of Balangiga, Samar, killing forty-eight men and literally chasing the twenty-six survivors into the ocean. The press rated it as the worst disaster for the US Army since Custer's defeat at Little Big Horn, and the one hundred rifles, twenty-five thousand rounds of ammunition, and other provisions captured fueled the insurgency on Samar for another year.[78]

This is not to say that the pursuit of Aguinaldo had no effect on the outcome of the war. The very act of targeting Aguinaldo and making him evade capture rendered him ineffective as a commander. As Linn notes, Aguinaldo "may have envisioned retaining personal control over strategy and operations throughout the island, but such plans were vitiated by his flight from the Americans." General Isidoro Torres, commander in Central Luzon's letter book, showed only two incoming communications from Aguinaldo between November 9, 1899, and August 12, 1900. In February 1901 a guerrilla major told his captors that Trias had received no word from his president for six months. Thus, the Philippine insurgency degenerated into a number of regional conflicts that suffered from the lack of central strategic direction.[79]

✳

BY THE SPRING OF 1901, the American public was weary of the grinding counterinsurgency being fought half a world away with no tangible benefits and no end in sight. With the news of Aguinaldo's capture providing a respite from the unrelenting bad news from the Philippines, they instantly took the bantamweight general from Kansas to their hearts. Vice President Theodore Roosevelt, no doubt sensing a kindred spirit, wrote Funston: "This is no perfunctory or formal letter of congratulation. I take pride in this crowning exploit of a career filled with feats of cool courage, iron endurance and gallant daring because you have added

your name to the honor roll of American worthies."[80] Funston was rewarded for his success by promotion to brigadier general in the Regular
Army, and returned home to a hero's welcome.

Amid the cavalcade of praise for Funston, there were voices of dissent. Mark Twain composed a sarcastic diatribe, "In Defense of General Funston," in which he took issue with Funston's begging for food
and then capturing his benefactor. While on furlough from the army,
Funston went on a national speaking tour. At a banquet in Chicago he
announced he had personally strung up thirty-five Filipinos without
benefit of a trial, a number he increased to fifty in a later speech. Egged
on by applause, Funston then suggested that some impromptu domestic
hangings might also hasten the end of the war, starting with those who
had recently petitioned Congress to sue for peace in the Philippines. At
the same time, a former captain in the Kansas regiment appeared before
a Senate committee investigating American atrocities in the Philippines
to testify that Funston had personally administered the water cure to
numerous suspects and prisoners, and on several occasions had ordered
his men to "take no prisoners." When Funston mocked the "overheated
conscience" of the leading antiwar senator, George Hoar of Massachu-
setts, now-President Roosevelt ordered Root to silence the general and
terminate his furlough.[81]

Despite his penchant for controversy, Funston went on to further
distinguish himself in his military career. In the aftermath of the 1906
San Francisco earthquake, Funston saved the city from greater destruction by using artillery to create firebreaks and later directed an effective
relief effort. Eight years later, when American forces seized Vera Cruz
during the Mexican revolution, Funston acted as the city's military
governor, surprising many by his diplomacy under adverse conditions.
Funston was promoted to major general and placed in command of the
Army's Southern Department, a position he held in 1916 when a Mexican bandit launched a deadly raid into New Mexico.

CHAPTER THREE

PANCHO VILLA AND THE PUNITIVE EXPEDITION, 1916–1917

It was only through sheer luck that John J. Pershing missed out on the first two US strategic manhunts. An 1886 graduate of West Point, where he was Captain of the Corps of Cadets, he reported for duty with the Sixth Cavalry in September 1886, barely missing service in the Geronimo Campaign. In 1899, while his brother Ward chased Aguinaldo with Major General Lawton, Pershing was assigned to the archipelago's southern reaches to subdue the Islamic Moros.

Nevertheless, by 1915 Pershing was already renowned in the army. As a first lieutenant with the Tenth Cavalry in 1898, Pershing had stormed San Juan Hill in the same charge as Theodore Roosevelt, and his commanding officer declared that Pershing was "the coolest man I ever saw under fire in my life."[1] Pershing proved so successful at counterinsurgency in the Philippines that in 1906 President Roosevelt promoted him to general over the heads of 862 officers with more seniority. Pershing's promotion from major to brigadier general generated bitter resentment in some quarters of the army, and Pershing himself never inspired the warm, personal enthusiasm of a Crook or Lawton. One veteran referred to Pershing as an "S.O.B" and hated his guts, but added: "As

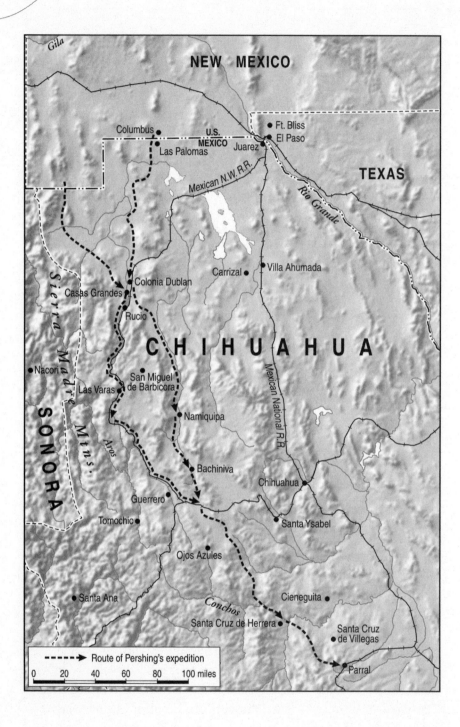

a soldier, the ones then and the ones now could not polish his boots."[2] In the 1913 attack on Mount Bagsak, Pershing's men—from privates to captains—were so impressed with his personal courage that they gathered testimonials and affidavits and sent them to the Adjutant General in Washington, seeking the Medal of Honor for their leader.

Although Pershing was "a no-nonsense disciplinarian whose glacial stare when he was angry could instill fear into even the most veteran trooper,"[3] he possessed one significant soft spot. A bachelor at forty-five years old, in 1904 he met and fell in love with Helen Frances Warren, the twenty-five-year-old daughter of Wyoming senator Francis E. Warren. Pershing called her "the dearest girl in all the world." They were married in Washington in January 1905 in a ceremony attended by more than five hundred guests, including President Roosevelt, who declared it "a bully match."[4] For the next decade, they were inseparable, traveling the world together to Pershing's various duty stations with their four small children beside them. In the fall of 1913, Pershing was assigned as commander of the Eighth Infantry Brigade at the Presidio of San Francisco, but when the Mexican Revolution threatened to spill over the border the following year, the brigade was transferred to Fort Bliss, Texas. Pershing thought the assignment would only be temporary, but as US–Mexican relations deteriorated he realized he would be in El Paso for some time and made arrangements for his wife and four children to join him in Texas.

Only a few days before they were to be reunited, tragedy struck. Before dawn on August 27, 1915, Pershing was awoken with the message that a fire had destroyed the house at the Presidio, killing his wife and three daughters, sparing only his six-year-old son. When informed of the tragedy, Pershing cried out in anguish: "My God! My God! Can this be true!"

Among the outpouring of condolences the devastated Pershing received was a note signed "Francisco Villa." It was an unusual act of compassion from the notorious Mexican revolutionary leader, who had met Pershing only briefly in August 1914, and whom the American found to be "coarse . . . suspicious and distasteful."[5]

This kind gesture would quickly be forgotten, however, as barely six months later Pershing would be ordered to hunt down the man known more commonly as Pancho Villa.

✳

IN 1916, COLUMBUS, NEW MEXICO, was little more than "a cluster of adobe houses, a hotel, a few stores and streets knee deep in sand" filled with cactus, mesquite, and rattlesnakes.[6] Only about 300 people lived in this desolate town three miles from the Mexican border, and if not for Camp Furlong, home to a 350-man detachment of the Thirteenth US Cavalry in Columbus's southeast quadrant, the town would have little more significance than the desert that surrounded it.

The night was still on March 9, and the moon had nearly disappeared over the horizon, when First Lieutenant John P. Lucas was awoken at 4:30 AM by the sound of hoofbeats outside his adobe hut. Columbus's streets were unlit, causing sentries to complain they could not see twenty feet in front of them. Yet through the darkness, Lucas discerned the shadowy figures of several mounted men wearing sombreros and instinctively knew Columbus was under attack. He retrieved his .45 pistol from its holster and, wearing only his underwear, quietly slipped into the center of the room facing the door, "determined to get a few of them before they got me" when they stormed the hut.[7]

The eerie silence was broken by a shout. Private Fred Griffin, on guard duty outside the regiment's headquarters a few hundred feet away, had spied the invaders outside Lucas's hut. Griffin issued a challenge, but was answered by a rifle shot that hit him in the stomach. Griffin fired as he reeled backward, killing his assailant and two other Mexicans before slumping to the ground and dying.

Lucas did not hesitate. Taking advantage of the sudden confusion, he put on his pants and raced barefoot out of his hut toward the barracks of the Machine Gun Troop he commanded. All hell was about to break loose in Columbus.

The legendary Mexican revolutionary and bandit Pancho Villa was leading five hundred men in a cross-border raid on Columbus. Villa had divided his men into two columns: one column struck Camp Furlong simultaneously from the east and west, while the other moved to attack Columbus's business district from the west. Panic erupted among the residents when the *Villistas* rode into Columbus shouting "Viva Villa! Viva Mexico!" and wildly shooting into houses and at any civilians in their path.

At Camp Furlong, Villa's men mistook the stables for the sleeping quarters of the garrison and directed most of their fire at horses rather than soldiers. Lieutenant Lucas was able to marshal his men and his machine guns. Deciding the first priority should be the defense of Camp Furlong, he set up the guns where they could cover the railroad crossing leading into camp. Yet because of the darkness, Lucas and his men could only aim bursts of fire in the direction of the Villistas' muzzle flashes.

Meanwhile, Lieutenant James P. Castleman, serving on staff duty, heard the gunfire and ran out of his hut. As he turned the corner of the building, he collided with a dismounted Mexican, whom he promptly shot and killed. By the time he reached his unit's barracks, his sergeant had already rallied F Troop. Castleman led his men toward the regiment's headquarters, advancing under heavy fire from nearby Villistas. As soon as the fire slackened, Castleman ordered the troop into Columbus, where the Mexicans had penetrated as far as the Commercial Hotel in the center of town. There the raiders dragged civilian men into the street, robbing and murdering them. Others were killed on the stairs and in the lobby. The Mexicans made a serious tactical error, however, by setting fire to the hotel. Lucas's and Castleman's troops had linked up and took up firing positions on Main Street. The conflagration from the hotel illuminated the streets and allowed the cavalrymen to distinguish Americans from the Villistas. The US forces trapped the enemy in cross fire, and within ninety minutes Lucas's four machine guns fired close to twenty thousand rounds.

Finally, at 7:30 AM a Villista bugler signaled retreat.

As soon as Columbus was clear of invaders, Major Frank Tompkins left his family's house in town and ran to the only high ground, Cootes Hill. The Thirteenth Cavalry's commander, Colonel Frank Slocum, was directing the efforts of a group of riflemen firing at the retreating Mexicans, now clearly visible in the breaking dawn. "Realizing that the Mexicans were whipped," Tompkins asked Slocum for permission to mount up a troop and pursue.[8] Slocum assented, and Tompkins—who sixteen years earlier had led then–Company H up the cliffs at Tirad Pass—organized H Troop for a counterattack. Within twenty minutes, thirty-two men were riding after Villa's force, soon to be joined by the twenty-seven men of Castleman's F Troop. Tompkins's detachment chased the Villistas fifteen miles into Mexico. Although he had not lost a single man, on the way back to Columbus he counted nearly one hundred dead Villistas.

Back in Columbus, the corpses of sixty-seven raiders had been dragged to the outskirts of town, doused in kerosene, and set ablaze, "adding to the stench of smoldering wood from the gutted area along Main Street." Seventeen Americans were killed during the fighting, including nine civilians. Four troopers, two officers, and one civilian were wounded as well.[9] Captured Mexicans and copies of correspondence from Villa to other revolutionary commanders found on the body of a Villa aide confirmed that Pancho Villa had led the attack.

In three brief hours, Columbus was transformed from a poor, desolate desert town into the sight of the deadliest attack on US soil by a foreign military force between the War of 1812 and Pearl Harbor.

＊

THE COLUMBUS RAID WAS NOT the first time the Mexican Revolution had spilled over the border. During the second half of 1915 and early 1916, the pace of violence along the Mexican–US border increased dramatically. A series of raids, marked by theft, robbery, kidnapping, and murder in the lower Rio Grande valley, began in the summer of 1915. In September alone, attacks occurred on Brownsville, Red House Ferry, Progresso Post Office, and Las Paladas. In October a passenger train was wrecked by bandits, killing several people, north of Brownsville. During the two-and-a-half-month siege of Naco, Sonora, at least fifty-four Americans in neighboring Naco, Arizona, were killed or wounded by stray fire from Mexican forces. As one army officer noted, the frontier was in "a state of constant apprehension and turmoil because of the frequent and sudden incursions into American territory and depredations and murders on American soil by Mexican bandits."[10]

The Columbus raid was particularly troubling because of the man who planned and executed it. "Stockily built and of medium height," Pancho Villa possessed "a mouth which is cruel even when smiling" and dark eyes "full of energy and brutality . . . intelligent as hell and merciless."[11] One contemporary remarked that Villa "had more of a jaguar about him than a man."[12] Villa was born in 1878, the illegitimate son of a wealthy *hacienda* who had an affair with his maid. At age seventeen he joined a bandit gang that roamed Durango and Chihuahua provinces, and for the next two decades he robbed, kidnapped, and committed arson and murder.[13] Yet Villa epitomized the Mexican ideal of *macho* and carefully cultivated a Robin Hood image by donating a portion of his booty to the poor of northern Mexico. Consequently, he became a popular folk hero, the subject of numerous ballads and poems.

When the revolution against dictator Porfirio Díaz erupted in 1910, Villa readily took to the battlefield as a guerrilla. On March 13, 1913, Villa and eight followers crossed into Mexico from a temporary exile in Arizona, riding stolen horses and possessing meager supplies. By September he had risen to head the Division of the North, placing him in command of some eight thousand followers. In late 1914 and early 1915, Villa and the Division of the North seemed invincible, winning an impressive string of military victories. The American journalist John Reed wrote that Villa's name "was a legend already with the enemy—whenever Pancho Villa appeared in battle, they had begun to believe it lost."[14]

During this period, however, Villa also left a trail of savagery notable even amid the vicious backdrop of the Mexican Revolution. After each victory, Villa ordered the mass executions of hundreds of prisoners. He oversaw the torture and slaughter of hundreds of ethnic Chinese in the towns he captured. And any individual who crossed him, including friends who fell out of favor such as the American writer Ambrose Bierce, were murdered without hesitation.[15]

Despite his depredations, Villa's flamboyance and reputation for helping the poor made him a popular figure with the American press and the public, and even the staid *New York Times* referred to Villa as "the Robin Hood of Mexico."[16] *The Life of General Villa,* filmed by the Mutual Film Corporation with Villa's permission, premiered at the Lyric Theater in New York City on May 9, 1914. Villa's popularity extended to US policymakers in the Wilson administration. General Hugh Scott, chief of staff of the US Army, had commanded the Southern Department for five years and was close friends with the revolutionary. Secretary of State William Jennings Bryan gave Villa credit for "valuable services" in "restoring order in Sonora," adding: "Your patient labors in this matter are greatly appreciated by the State Department and the President."[17] President Woodrow Wilson himself declared that Villa was "not so bad as he had been painted," and that amid the turmoil of the revolution, "Villa was perhaps the safest man to tie to."[18]

In mid-1914, however, Villa broke off relations with the political leader of the revolution, Venustiano Carranza, and soon the former allies were fighting against each other. In 1915 Carranza's military commander, General Álvaro Obregón, defeated Villa in four major battles. By the fall of 1915 the Wilson administration understood Villa's power was waning, and on October 19 officially recognized the Carranza government. Yet Villa continued fighting and on November 1 attacked *Carrancista* forces at the border town of Agua Prieta. The United States allowed the Carrancistas to rush reinforcements via rail through US territory and supplied the electricity that allowed searchlights to illuminate the Villistas during the battle. By the end of 1915, only a few hundred followers remained from Villa's army, which had once numbered between thirty and fifty thousand men.

Villa blamed the Wilson administration for his defeat at Agua Prieta, which, with American recognition of the Carranza government, led him to swear revenge on the United States. Villa and his remaining men, mostly his elite guard of Dorados, started a campaign of harassment of both Carrancistas and Americans. On January 10, 1916, Villa's forces stopped a train of the Mexican North Western Railway Company near Santa Ysabel, Chihuahua. They dragged seventeen American miners off the train, and amid cries of "Viva Villa," they stripped and shot the Americans in cold blood. News of the massacre "set off violent agitation in Congress," and a "wild anger and excitement greater than any since the sinking of the *Lusitania* surged through part of the American people."[19]

Because an Associated Press correspondent was staying in the Columbus Hotel during the March 9 attack, President Wilson learned of the raid only three hours after Villa had recrossed the border into Mexico. Wilson immediately summoned his private secretary and personal friend, Joseph P. Tumulty, and told him to convene a Cabinet meeting early the next morning.

Despite the calls for retaliation after Santa Ysabel, the Wilson administration insisted it was an internal matter for Carranza to deal with. Yet after the Columbus attack the clamor for intervention was irresistible, and even US officials who had been close to Villa recognized the threat he posed. Wilson now regarded Villa as little more than a bandit who threatened the security of the southwestern United States. Scott's successor as commander of the Southern Department, Major General Frederick Funston, delivered his assessment to the War Department the day after the Columbus raid: "Unless Villa is relentlessly pursued and his forces scattered he will continue raids. As troops of the Mexican Government are accomplishing nothing and as he can make his preparations undisturbed, he can strike at any point on the border."[20] The American consul in Torreon wrote to General Scott: "This is a different man than we knew. All the brutality of his nature has come to the front, and he should be killed like a dog."[21]

On March 10, Wilson's Cabinet unanimously agreed to use limited military force against Villa lest Congress adopt a resolution forcing the president into a full-scale war. Wilson adamantly told Tumulty: "There won't be any war with Mexico if I can prevent it."[22] To guard against this danger, the president announced: "An adequate force will be sent at once in pursuit of Villa *with the single object* of capturing him and putting a stop to his forays."[23]

✳

AS SOON AS CARRANZA RECEIVED NEWS of the Columbus raid, he ordered his commander in Chihuahua to apprehend Villa—a task at which he had thus far been unsuccessful—in an attempt to convince Wilson that intervention was unnecessary. Carranza also proposed reinstituting the agreement that was active during the Geronimo Campaign, which allowed the reciprocal pursuit of bandits across the border, in case of *future* raids. He had no intention, however, of accepting intervention by a large American force. The Wilson administration responded by accepting Carranza's proposal but considered the agreement to be in force presently rather than in the future. Consequently, US forces would enter Mexico without the official approval of the Mexican government.

As soon as the Cabinet meeting ended, Secretary of War Newton Baker proceeded to General Scott's office. "I want you to start an expedition into Mexico to catch Villa," Baker said.

"Mr. Secretary," Scott replied, "do you want to make war on one man? Suppose Villa should get on the train and go to Guatemala, Yucatan, or South America: are you going to go after him?"

Baker was new to his position, had practically no experience in military affairs, and thus deferred to Scott's judgment. The War Department subsequently sent orders to General Funston that did not even mention Villa by name:

> You will promptly organize an adequate military force of troops from your department under the command of Brigadier General John J. Pershing and will direct him to proceed promptly across the border in pursuit of the Mexican band which attacked the town of Columbus, New Mexico. These troops will be withdrawn to American territory as soon as the de facto government of Mexico is able to relieve them of this work. The work of these troops will be regarded as finished as soon as Villa's band or bands are known to be broken up.[24]

Whereas the White House had informed the press—and initially trans-mitted orders—that US troops would be sent in pursuit of Villa to cap-ture him, the final military orders were merely to pursue Villa's band until it was dispersed.

The wording of these orders was also unusual in that it specified the officer who was to command the expedition, a choice normally left to the department command. By 1916, Funston was "considered to be the army's foremost field commander."[25] He outranked Pershing, was five years younger and fit for duty, and had recent command experience in Mexico, having successfully led the Vera Cruz occupation. Moreover, Funston wanted to command the expedition himself, a fact General Scott was aware of when he made his decision. Yet given Funston's re-cord of outspokenness, Scott preferred Pershing for the campaign. Fun-ston accepted higher orders and pledged his full support to Pershing.

✳

PERSHING'S COMMAND, which would become known as the "Punitive Expedition," initially consisted of three brigades—two cavalry and one infantry, totaling 4,800 men and 4,175 animals—as well as a squadron of eight airplanes. Funston promised Pershing reinforcements as soon as they could be transported to the border. Pershing assumed Villa had taken refuge somewhere in Chihuahua, a territory roughly the size of Virginia and the Carolinas combined. Chihuahua is dominated by the barren and rugged Sierra Madres, whose peaks average ten to twelve thousand feet, rising abruptly from the five-thousand-foot plateau be-low, and are separated by deep canyons that offered Villa and his band endless hiding places, as they had for Geronimo thirty years earlier.

Somewhere in that desolate landscape, Pershing hoped to locate one solitary man.

As General Crook had done in 1885, the Punitive Expedition en-tered Mexico in two parallel columns. The first column, with Major Tompkins and the Thirteenth Cavalry granted the honor of riding point, left Columbus on March 15. Pershing crossed into Mexico on horseback with the other column fifty miles to the west just past mid-night on March 16. The two columns were to converge at the Mormon settlement, Colonia Dublan, about 125 miles into Mexico. Pershing hoped to move as quickly as possible, either to trap Villa or to make up for his week's head start.

Pershing's column marched twenty-five miles in the dark the first night, arriving at Geronimo's Rock at six AM. Pershing allowed the men and horses to rest until noon before resuming the march for another thirty miles, making a total of fifty-five miles in less than twenty-four hours. It had not rained in northern Chihuahua for nine months, and great choking clouds of white alkaline dust were whipped up by the passage of so many feet and hooves. One sergeant reported: "The alkali got in our eyes and down our throats, it sifted into our shoes and through our clothing."[26] The next day, March 17, Pershing's column covered sixty-eight miles, arriving at the Casas Grandes–Colonia Dublan complex at eight PM. The Second Brigade covered the longest distance ever recorded in the annals of the US Cavalry, and their march in the moonlight would prove to be the last hurrah for the American horse cavalry, soon to be replaced by the trucks, cars, and planes following behind them.[27]

The natives of Casas Grandes reported that Villa was somewhere near San Miguel de Babicora some sixty miles south on a high plateau deep in the Sierras, where William Randolph Hearst owned a vast ranch. Pershing deployed the Seventh and Tenth Cavalry southward down two approaching valleys to approach Babicora from the east and west simultaneously. The Seventh Cavalry would leave for Babicora via the Santa Maria Valley right away. The Tenth Cavalry would follow the western valley by rail in order to flank Babicora through the Sierra Madres.[28]

At three AM on March 18, Colonel James B. Erwin's Seventh Cavalry marched out of Casas Grandes. After a few miles the regiment picked up the Santa Maria River and turned south. The Seventh Cavalry marched under extreme conditions. The temperature in that rough hill country soared above ninety degrees in the daytime only to plummet below freezing at night. During the Seventh Cavalry's drive south, "The men were so weary that orders were issued that every one would remain standing during the short halts, otherwise men would immediately drop off to sleep, and there was so much difficulty and delay rousing them."[29]

As difficult as the Seventh's march was, the Tenth Cavalry's movement by rail may have been worse. The transport train they took was in a dangerous state of disrepair and ran out of either water or fuel five times over ten hours. As the train approached Rucio, the engine proved insufficiently powerful to pull the twenty-five boxcars up the grade. Colonel W. C. Brown detrained his squadron at the foot of the hill and left on horseback for Babicora, already seven hours behind schedule. The shortened train was able to reach Rucio, but shortly thereafter two cars loaded with horses jumped the track and plunged down the steep embankment at the Cumbre Pass, sending the black troopers riding on top of the cars crashing into the rocks and brush. Eleven men were injured, some seriously.[30]

These trials turned out to be unnecessary, for when Colonel Brown's squadron reached, Babicora he discovered not only that Villa was not there but that he had not been within miles of the town.

Shortly after learning his trap had come up empty, General Pershing gave a press conference for the correspondents traveling with his headquarters. "Our troops seem to be pressing him," Pershing said. "But I won't hazard any predictions. Villa is no fool. It may be that campaigning has just started."

Nearby, one of the Punitive Expedition's scouts listened, chewing a straw as he squatted on his haunches. In a drawl reminiscent of that of Will Rogers, he interrupted: "As I figure it, General, we've got Villa surrounded . . ." He paused for effect before adding, ". . . on one side."

The reporters collapsed in laughter, and the normally taciturn Pershing, still carrying a heavy heart, laughed with them.[31]

✳

WITH THE FAILURE OF THIS initial operation, Pershing put his longer-term plan into action. He ordered the Seventh Cavalry to continue south down the Santa Maria River Valley and the Tenth Cavalry to continue down the railway line on horseback. Both regiments were ordered to scout the plain between the two valleys in order to screen a large portion of the Chihuahua plain. Pershing appointed Colonel George A. Dodd to command the flying columns. A sixty-three-year-old "tough, rangy, cigar-chewing" old Indian-fighter, Dodd attached himself to the Seventh Cavalry and raced the regiment through the Santa Maria Valley after Villa's band.[32]

On March 25 Colonel Brown sent a message to Dodd from Namiquipa reporting: "Villa's whereabouts unknown, but it is thought possible he has gone through the mountains towards Bachiniva."[33] At Bachiniva, on March 28, Dodd learned that Villa had been involved in a battle with Carrancista forces at Guerrero thirty-six miles to the south. This intelligence supported other rumors Dodd had heard placing Villa in the Guerrero Valley, and for the first time he believed he was on the right trail.

As the Seventh Cavalry prepared to march south, Lieutenant Herbert A. Dargue of the First Aero Squadron descended and brought Dodd an order from Pershing to retire to Namiquipa. The Seventh Cavalry had marched fourteen of the past fifteen days, covering an incredible four hundred miles, and Pershing decided they needed a rest. Dodd considered the general's message but gave Dargue a reply informing Pershing: "I am now satisfied that Villa is not far distant. I shall proceed farther south, and shall continue in such touch as is possible to attain (and attack if possible) with Villa."[34]

Dodd allowed his men to rest and refit for a few hours at Bachiniva, and then at eleven PM, in gentle defiance of General Pershing's orders, took to the saddle to catch Pancho Villa.

Dodd hoped to surprise Villa and his band at dawn. However, none of his maps indicated a trail that would lead the Seventh Cavalry through the mountains between them and Guerrero. The civilian guide attached to the regiment had been reliable thus far, but now informed Dodd it had been several years since he had been to Guerrero, and even then he had approached the town from a completely different direction. They were unable to hire any native guides, and when they finally forcibly impressed two Mexicans they were taken on a circuitous route that nearly doubled the distance of their march. Through the dark and bitter cold, the regiment accordioned its way up rocky slopes, down gullies, and through arroyos. There were frequent halts while the point groped along the terrain ahead, seeking passable terrain. During these halts men in the column lay down on the frozen ground, reins in hand, and caught what fragments of sleep they could, waking to find their beards covered in hoar frost. By the time the 370 officers and men of the Seventh Cavalry reached Guerrero the next morning, they had covered fifty-five miles in the preceding seventeen hours.[35]

Guerrero lay in a horseshoe-shaped canyon, with the open end to the north. The Seventh Cavalry emerged on the bluff overlooking the town at 6:30 AM, but were still three miles south of the town, separated by deep arroyos that made a mounted charge impossible. It was eight AM by the time Dodd had deployed his squadrons to their assault or blocking positions. The element of surprise had been lost.

The combat suddenly opened everywhere at once. Mounted Villistas attempted to flee into the hills and were engaged by E and C troops, while the Machine Gun Troop opened fire on the town from a range of one thousand yards. Amid the chaos of battle, a squadron of Mexican cavalry calmly rode out of town and up a ravine, the lead rider carrying a large Mexican flag. The Americans thought they were witnessing the exit of Carrancista cavalry and allowed the procession to leave town unmolested, unaware that a large body of Villistas were escaping under their noses.[36]

Despite the exhausted condition of the horses, the Seventh Cavalry vigorously pursued the Villistas. The running fight continued until the Villistas reached the mountains, where they scattered and disappeared into the broken terrain. The engagement had begun shortly after eight AM, and it was 11:30 AM before the regiment reassembled. At least thirty Villistas were killed, and more were likely wounded but carried off. The Seventh Cavalry suffered only five wounded.[37]

Although Villa had been at Guerrero, an incredible twist of fate saved him from capture. In the previous day's battle against the Carrancistas, an impressed irregular attempted to assassinate Villa during the heat of the battle, shooting the bandit leader from behind as he led a charge. Villa's shin bone was shattered, and doctors had to pick out splinters of bone through the exit wound in front. His leg in a splint, and wild with pain, Villa was gingerly loaded into a wagon and, shortly after midnight, was carried out of Guerrero with 150 men as an escort. Thus, Villa departed Guerrero to the north on March 29 as Dodd and the Seventh Cavalry approached from the south. Had Dodd known the direct route from Bachiniva to Guerrero, he would have encountered Villa's wagon along the way. As it was, the Seventh Cavalry missed Villa by only a few miles on its night march to Guerrero.

Regardless, the exhausted condition of the American horses prevented Dodd from launching an immediate pursuit of the incapacitated revolutionary.

✳

ON MARCH 30 PERSHING'S HEADQUARTERS learned the details of Dodd's fight at Guerrero. Correspondents were optimistic about the campaign in the wake of the skirmish, but Pershing remained cautious. "You fellows mustn't be too sanguine," he said. "It may take weeks, perhaps months. It's like trying to catch a rat in a corn-field." As if to punctuate his point about the difficulty of the campaign ahead, a sandstorm mixed with snow hit Pershing's headquarters that day. The snow and sand "cut like a knife, filling the eyes and hair and mouth, filtering through the clothing and into boots and shoes."[38]

The next evening, April 1, Pershing went to Bachiniva, where Major Tompkins was camped with the Thirteenth Cavalry. "Tompkins," Pershing said as they sat before a fire, "where is Villa?"

"I don't know," Tompkins replied. "But I would like mighty well to go find out where he is."

"Where would you go?" Pershing asked.

"I would head for Parral and would expect to cut his trail before then," Tompkins said.

"Why?"

"The history of Villa's bandit days shows that when hard pressed he invariably holes up in the mountains in the vicinity of Parral," Tompkins explained. "He has friends in that region."

Pershing sat silently thinking. Tompkins suggested a small command could move faster, conceal itself better, and live off the land more easily than a regular squadron. It might even tempt Villa to give battle because of its size, he argued.

About noon the next day, Pershing sent for Tompkins. "Go find Villa wherever you think he is," the general said. He gave Tompkins twelve mules from the Eleventh Cavalry, five hundred Mexican silver pesos, five days' rations, and grain for two days. At 1:55 PM on April 2, Tompkins set off with K and M troops of the Thirteenth Cavalry to search for Pancho Villa.[39]

Tompkins's command covered more than eighty-five miles through rugged country in its first two days. On April 4 they found Colonel Brown and elements of the Tenth Cavalry at San Antonio, who relayed the news that Villa was badly wounded and moving from San Borja to Parral. Tompkins decided to go to San Borja, arriving the following afternoon. On the outskirts of town a party of Mexicans delivered a note from General Cavazos, the commander of the town's Carrancista garrison: "I would esteem it very much," Cavazos courteously wrote, "if you would suspend your advance."[40]

Tompkins entered the town for a parley, which was conducted with a strained civility. Cavazos insisted that Villa was dead and buried at

Santa Ana, and that he was taking his men there to search for the body. Then Cavazos warned Tompkins that he could not give the Americans permission to pass through San Borja. Although Tompkins believed he was following a hot trail, he chose discretion and headed to Cieneguita instead.

Three days later, on April 8, Major Howze's Eleventh Cavalry passed through San Borja without incident.

At three AM on April 11, Howze's command attacked the small town of Santa Cruz de Herrera. After a brief skirmish, the band of Villistas escaped into the darkness. Howze's column had been on the move almost constantly for seventy-two hours and was in no condition for a hot pursuit. Instead, like Crawford's Apache scouts at the Aros River thirty years before, the troopers flopped down beside the Balleza River, unrolled their blankets, and collapsed in exhaustion.[41]

At daylight Howze ordered a search of the town. The natives were nervous and uncommunicative, however, claiming they did not know any of the Villistas. Howze gave up on these interrogations and bivouacked the squadron south of town to let the horses graze. Lieutenant S. M. Williams recalled:

> While in the town I saw coming from a ranch house about a mile distant, 14 Yaqui Indians, in full war paint but unarmed. When they came into town the natives were tense with excitement.... Several of us urged [Major Howze] to send a troop to this ranch house and search it, but he ... prohibited any of us from going to this ranch house, and the following morning we marched south.

Williams claimed to have read an article later in which Villa said he was indeed hiding in the ranch house, which would have conformed to his practice of never staying overnight inside a pueblo.[42] Thus, Howze may have unknowingly come within a mile of Villa at Santa Cruz de Herrera.

Similarly, Modesto Nevares, the conscript who drove the wagon carrying Villa out of Guerrero, recalled that "We went to a place called Santa Ana, near San Borja," and that after Villa was transferred to a litter, Tompkins's column passed the now-empty wagon on April 5. In October Tompkins's former adjutant, Lieutenant James B. Ord, wrote to Tompkins: "Had a talk with a Villista who was with Villa when he went south. Villa was in the Santa Ana Mountains within sight of us while we were talking with old General Cavazos that day at San Borja, and Major Howze's outfit passed by him near San Borja."[43] Thus, the Punitive Expedition may have narrowly missed Villa twice in one week.

✳

WHILE HOWZE AND THE ELEVENTH CAVALRY were en route to Santa Cruz, a Carrancista Captain named Antonio Mesa arrived at Tompkins's camp. He was friendly, and told Tompkins he would call ahead to Parral and officially arrange for the troops to enter the town. "Captain Mesa had led us to believe that we would be received with friendship and hospitality," Tompkins wrote later. "We pictured the hot baths we should have, the long cool drinks, and the good food."[44]

Tompkins's squadron arrived at Parral just before noon on April 12. He proceeded to the garrison's headquarters, where he met the Carrancista commander, General Ismael Lozano. Lozano said he had never received any message from Captain Mesa, and that Villa was likely somewhere to the north near Saveto. He ominously suggested that Tompkins should never have entered Parral. Tompkins agreed to be escorted to a campsite outside town while Lozano arranged for the Americans to purchase supplies.

By the time they left Lozano's office, however, a mob had gathered in the town square to taunt the Americans with shouts of "Viva Villa!" and "Viva Mexico!" Tompkins calmly ordered his men to form into columns and march out of Parral. The crowd pressed menacingly behind the Americans, and in an attempt to break the tension Tompkins wheeled his horse around and shouted "Viva Villa!" The crowd paused, and then broke into laughter. But they kept coming.[45]

Lozano led the Americans a few hundred yards north of town into a "perfect cul-de-sac." The crack of rifle fire filled the air as armed civilians began shooting at the American rear guard, killing one trooper. Tompkins saw Carrancista troops forming on the crest of a hill a few hundred yards to his right and decided to forego securing the promised supplies and try to extract the squadron from the hole in which Lozano had placed them. Tompkins rode point to lead the column toward the road leading back to Santa Cruz de Villegas eighteen miles away, which would provide a better defensive position for his one hundred men. It was now 1:30 PM. Tompkins estimated that Santa Cruz was nearly three hours away.

One hundred Carrancistas left the group on the hill and rode forward, attempting to flank the Americans. First Lieutenant Clarence Lininger and eight handpicked rifleman opened fire, stopping the Mexican advance. Lininger's sharpshooters killed twenty-five Carrancistas and wounded as many, while the rest of the column reached the Santa Cruz road. Badly outnumbered, the column rode briskly north toward Santa Cruz. Although the civilian mob was left behind, the mounted Carrancistas shadowed the column, riding parallel to the US column through the fields alongside the road, shooting whenever possible, and wounding Tompkins in the shoulder.[46]

The running fight lasted through the afternoon. Finally, one mile south of Santa Cruz, the Carrancistas formed for a final charge. When Tompkins's squadron dipped temporarily out of sight over a ridge, he deployed twenty men under Captain Frederick Turner to ambush the Mexicans as they came over the ridge. "In a minute or two they came," Tompkins recalled, "hell-bent-for-election, firing in the air, yelling like fiends out of hell, and making a most beautiful target."[47] When the Mexicans came within two hundred yards, the Americans opened fire, the initial volley decimating the front ranks of the Carrancistas, sending men and horses rolling in the dust. Turner's men stood and began pouring rapid fire into the Mexicans, who quickly retreated, leaving forty-two dead comrades behind. The US column trotted into the sanctuary of Santa Cruz's adobe houses.

Two Americans were killed in the Parral fight, and six were wounded. But the strategic damage was far more significant. On April 14 Pershing cabled Funston: "It is very probable that the real object of our mission to Mexico can only be attained after an arduous campaign of considerable length."[48] Parral shocked the Wilson administration, making it even more cautious. Wilson met with his Cabinet on April 14. Although he decided Pershing should not be recalled until Carranza's government had demonstrated either the will or the capacity to hunt Pancho Villa itself, Parral signaled the effective end of Pershing's pursuit.

✳

RATHER THAN RISK AN IMMINENT WAR with Mexico, the Wilson administration decided on a partial retreat. US forces would be withdrawn from most of Chihuahua and concentrated near Colonia Dublan. On April 29 Pershing issued orders organizing the territory occupied by the

Punitive Expedition—a rough parallelogram one hundred miles long and thirty miles wide—into five districts, each patrolled by a cavalry regiment. If possible, each sector commander would continue to search for Villa while (in theory) the Carrancistas scoured southern Chihuahua and Durango province. The principal aim of US forces would not be to capture Villa themselves, however, but to remain as an incentive to Carranza's forces to kill or capture Villa.[49]

Despite these new constraints, the Punitive Expedition scored some significant victories over Villista forces. On April 22, after leading his men on another all-night ride at altitude and in cold that "left the men's legs numb from the knees down," Dodd attacked a force of two hundred Villistas under Colonel Candelario Cervantes at the hamlet of Tomochic. Dodd's men, despite being partially hypoxic and suffering nosebleeds and headaches, killed about thirty Villistas and wounded another twenty-five in close-quarters combat.[50] On May 5, after a forced march of more than thirty-six miles, six troops of cavalry, with Apache scouts in the lead "shrieking shrill, weird war whoops," attacked a force of 120 Villistas at Ojos Azules ranch.[51] Although the fight at Ojos Azules lasted only twenty minutes, Howze's command killed sixty-one Villistas. Amazingly, not a single American was wounded in the battle.

The Punitive Expedition also enjoyed some success in hunting Villa's subordinates. On May 14, Pershing placed an aide in command of an expedition to buy corn from nearby haciendas. Lieutenant George S. Patton, thirty years old, was a tall, thin, reedy-voiced officer already renowned as one of the army's best athletes and pistol shots. When he learned in March that his regiment would not go to Mexico, Patton literally begged Pershing to take him along, offering to perform any job, no matter how menial.[52]

While purchasing feed in Rubio, Patton noticed a group of fifty or sixty unarmed Mexicans. One of the guides, an ex-Villista named E. L. Holmdahl, recognized "a number of old friends" among them.[53] Although Villa was still in hiding somewhere south of Parral, the commander of his Dorados, General Julio Cardenas, was believed to be in hiding in the vicinity of Rubio. Patton and his party—a corporal, six privates, Holmdahl, and another civilian interpreter—drove to Las Ciengas, where Patton interrogated Cardenas's uncle. The uncle's nervousness aroused Patton's suspicions, and on a hunch, he ordered his convoy to drive six miles to San Miguelito Ranch, where Cardenas's family was rumored to be residing.

As Patton's car sped toward the house, he saw three old men and a boy skinning a cow in the front yard east of the house. One of the men ran into the house, but quickly returned and resumed his work. Patton's car halted at the house's northwest corner, and the other two cars took up positions at the southwest. Pershing jumped out and, carrying a rifle and pistol, raced along the ranch's northern edge. Two soldiers made a similar dash along the southern wall while the privates covered the windows in case any Mexicans jumped out. Patton reached the eastern side first and moved toward the gate. When he was fifteen yards from the large arched door, three armed men on horseback burst out from the house. Seeing Patton standing with his pistol drawn, they dashed toward the southeast corner until they saw the soldiers coming from the south. The Mexicans turned and rode straight at Patton. "All three shot at me," Patton recalled. "One bullet threw gravel at me. I fired back . . . five times" from a range of twenty yards. Two of Patton's shots hit their targets, one entering a horse's belly, the other breaking the rider's right arm.[54]

Patton's soldiers began firing from the southeast corner, putting him in the line of fire. Patton ducked behind the corner and reloaded as three bullets hit a foot above his head and covered him in adobe dust. Consequently, he did not see the man he had shot turn back into the house's courtyard.

When Patton came around the corner again, he was nearly stampeded by a horseman. Patton fired and broke the horse's hip, bringing it crashing down on the rider. When the Mexican disentangled himself and rose to fire, Patton and several other Americans cut him down at a range of about ten yards. The third rider had made it a hundred yards east of the hacienda before the soldiers fired at him. He pitched forward dead in the sand near a stone wall.

Two of the three Mexicans were now dead. The first man, who had reentered the inner patio and climbed out a window, was spotted running from a gate in the southwest corner toward the nearby fields when a fusillade brought him down. When Holmdahl approached him, the man "held up his left hand in surrender, but when H[olmdahl] was 20 feet from him he raised his pistol and shot at H[olmdahl] but fortunately missed him and H[olmdahl] blew out his brains."[55]

A search of the hacienda turned up no further Villistas, only Carde-nas's family. Nobody would identify the bodies, however, so the corpses were strapped across the hoods of the three automobiles like hunt-ing trophies. As they prepared to leave, Patton saw some forty men on horseback racing toward the hacienda, likely intending to rescue Carde-nas. Outnumbered, the Americans retreated toward Rubio, where the first man Patton had shot was identified as Cardenas.

Pershing allowed Patton to keep Cardenas's saddle and saber as trophies, began referring to him as "the Bandit," and promoted him to first lieutenant. The Rubio exploit quickly appeared in the US press, and newspaper readers were thrilled to have an attractive, young hero with whom they could associate the Punitive Expedition. Meanwhile, in Mexico, the Americans buried the rapidly decomposing Mexicans. Against the backdrop of a blood-red sunset, a veteran sergeant offered an impromptu eulogy: "Ashes to ashes, and dust to dust / If Villa won't bury you, Uncle Sam must."[56]

✳

SINCE THE FIGHT AT TOMOCHIC, Candelario Cervantes had been play-ing a game of cat-and-mouse with Dodd and the Seventh Cavalry. Cer-vantes, whom Pershing called "the most able and the most desperate of Villa's band," was bold enough to raid in the area around Namiquipa, right under the nose of Pershing's headquarters.[57] On May 25 a small detachment of mappers and riflemen from the Second Engineers and Seventeenth Infantry under Lance Corporal Davis Marksbury left Las Cruces, twelve miles south of Namiquipa, intending to study the Santa Maria Valley. While one group sketched the terrain, another began hunt-ing for pigs in the brush of Alamia Canyon.

A band of Mexicans suddenly appeared on the horizon, firing and riding furiously toward the Americans. Marksbury was killed and three others wounded as the US troops were quickly pinned down. Several sol-diers noticed the leader of the Mexican band, mounted on a large black horse. He wore an elegant sombrero turned up at the brim and a "fancy coat that looked like velvet or plush, with a white braid in front."[58] In-fantry Private George D. Hullett emptied his pistol at the Mexicans and then picked up Marksbury's rifle. He calmly aimed his weapon, drawing a bead on the flashily dressed Mexican. He fired once, knocking the tall man from his horse. The Mexicans withdrew and when inspecting the personal effects of the bandit, the Americans realized they had killed Cervantes, Villa's deputy at the Columbus raid.

Since Parral, the Mexicans in Chihuahua were becoming increasingly resentful of Pershing's penetration so deep into Mexico. Pershing attributed his lack of success to this hostility, writing to Funston on April 17: "[It is] inconceivable that [a] notorious character like Villa could remain in country with people ignorant of his general direction and approximate location. Since [the] Guerrero fight it is practically impossible [to] obtain guides."[59] Newspaper correspondents seconded Pershing's assessment, noting Villa "has disappeared in a way which, considering the relentlessness of the American pursuit, seems mysterious. The American troops have not encountered any natives who will even admit they have seen Villa."[60] Pershing also noted that Carrancista forces had usually acted to obstruct the Punitive Expedition, telling Funston: "Carranza officers have stated openly that they would not allow Americans to capture Villa."[61] To a friend, he summarized his dilemma: "I feel just a little bit like a man looking for a needle in a haystack with an armed guard standing over the stack forbidding you to look in the hay."[62]

✳

REPRESENTATIVES OF THE TWO GOVERNMENTS met in Juarez and El Paso at the end of April to resolve the increasing US–Mexican tensions. General Scott and now–Secretary of War Obregón eventually hammered out an agreement by which the Americans would gradually withdraw and the Mexicans would increase their efforts to capture Villa. Wilson quickly agreed, noting: "The Government of the United States has no pride involved in who makes the capture, and its only interest is that it should be done expeditiously so that American troops can be withdrawn and the peace of its borders secured."[63] Carranza, however, refused to sign the agreement since it did not set a date for US withdrawal.

Events on the ground quickly made the pact irrelevant. Funston received intelligence reports from one of his Arizona commanders who had intercepted orders from Carranza to General Arnulfo Gomez to cut off Pershing's forces unless the United States agreed to completely withdraw from Mexico.[64] Despite repeated protestations by Obregón that the border was secure, on May 6 a band of sixty Mexicans crossed the Rio Grande shouting both "Viva Villa!" and "Viva Carranza!" They attacked Glen Springs and Boquillas, Texas, killing three US soldiers and a nine-year-old boy. Elements of the Eighth and Fourteenth Cavalry pursued the raiders across the border, eventually penetrating 160 miles into Mexico. This raid exasperated Wilson, who called up 4,500 National Guardsmen from Arizona, New Mexico, and Texas.

On June 15, Carranza ordered his commander in Chihuahua, General Jacinto B. Trevino, to keep US troops from moving any direction except north, even if it led to another armed confrontation. The next day, Trevino warned Pershing: "I have orders from my Government to prevent, by the use of arms, new invasions of my country by American forces and also to prevent the American forces that are in this state from moving to the south, east or west of the places they now occupy."[65] Although Pershing was not intimidated, the increasing tensions and rumors of war dried up his human intelligence as potential sources feared retribution.

Shortly after Trevino's threatening telegram, Pershing received reports that a Carrancista army was assembling a force of ten thousand men at Villa Ahumada, about seventy miles east of Dublan. Fearing for his lines of communication, Pershing summoned Captain Charles T. Boyd, commander of Troop C, Tenth Cavalry. Boyd had served as the general's adjutant in the Philippines and was considered reliable. Pershing ordered Boyd: "Take your troops and reconnoiter in the direction of Ahumada and obtain as much information as you can regarding forces there." He further cautioned: "This is a reconnaissance only and you will not be expected to fight. In fact, I want you to avoid a fight if possible." Similar orders were given to Captain Lewis S. Morey of Troop K, Tenth Cavalry.[66]

The two troops, totaling seventy-six soldiers, converged at a ranch twelve miles west of Carrizal on the evening of June 20. The combined forces set out for Villa Ahumada early the next morning with Boyd in command. As they approached Carrizal, a Mexican messenger emerged to warn that the Americans would be attacked if they attempted to go through Carrizal. General Felix Gomez personally came out to offer to telegraph his superiors to request permission for the Americans to enter the town.

Boyd refused.

Boyd was determined to ride straight through Carrizal to Villa Ahamuda despite Pershing's orders, the Mexicans' warnings, and the advice of the other US officers to simply bypass the town. Perhaps he thought audacity would cow the Mexicans. Perhaps he thought any armed resistance would be easily overcome. Perhaps he thought a successful skirmish would bring a promotion and fame. Whatever Boyd's reasons, he ordered his men to charge the Mexicans who had entrenched themselves in an irrigation ditch to the west and south of Carrizal. Although the Buffalo Soldiers fought valiantly, killing forty and wounding thirty Carrancistas, their small force was easily outflanked and cut down by machine-gun fire. Fourteen Americans—including Boyd—were killed, twelve were wounded, and twenty-four were captured.[67]

✳

EIGHT HOURS AFTER THE FIGHT at Carrizal, President Wilson was sitting at his desk in the White House when he heard newsboys shouting on Pennsylvania Avenue. He sent an aide to buy a copy of the extra and thus learned of the American defeat. Incensed, Wilson demanded the immediate release of the American prisoners and the US Government property seized at Carrizal. Assuming the Carrancistas to be at fault, Wilson followed this ultimatum with preparations for war. He approved military contingency plans, asked for permission to address Congress, and began drafting a declaration of war.

Tensions between the United States and Mexico were at a breaking point. Anti-American demonstrations, largely staged by Carranza himself, erupted in all major Mexican cities. Carranza's attitude changed, however, when he learned of Wilson's anger. Although Carranza recognized the value of patriotic rhetoric, he knew Mexico could not win a war with the United States. The Mexican economy was in ruin, and his army suffered from acute shortages of food and munitions.[68] Precipitating a war he could not win would likely cost Carranza not only his position, but in the manner of revolutionary politics, his life as well.

Consequently, Carranza ordered the American prisoners freed on June 28. When they were released and the truth about Carrizal discovered, Wilson tried diplomacy once again and on June 30 publicly disavowed the possibility of war with Mexico. On July 4, Carranza reopened negotiations, and on July 28 the Wilson administration agreed to the creation of a joint commission to convene in September. Wilson later confessed that had Carranza not released the American prisoners and renewed diplomacy, he probably would have declared war on Mexico.[69]

✳

ALTHOUGH CARRIZAL WOULD BE the Punitive Expedition's last battle, Wilson could not withdraw US forces without giving the Republicans an issue in the upcoming elections.[70] Consequently, Funston instructed Pershing that his forces were to remain at Colonia Dublan, where the cavalry and infantry regiments dug in for the balance of the summer. There they lived "no better than the poorest Indian." Troopers sweltered in field khakis as the days grew longer and hotter, and desert winds made the camp seem like a blast furnace. Similar to expeditions during the Geronimo Campaign, swarming flies, crawling insects, and snakes tormented US forces. For a stretch of sixty-two days, the men of the Fourth Field Artillery were fed beans three times a day. One veteran recalled: "I have been in three wars, and for unmitigated hardship, the Punitive Expedition was the worst of all."[71]

With the campaign's original objective—the capture of Pancho Villa—now forgotten, Pershing set his troops to intensive drilling. Meanwhile, two US agents resorted to unconventional means of eliminating Villa. A Bureau of Investigations agent named Stone and a Captain Reed from Pershing's intelligence department arranged with some Japanese living in Mexico who knew Villa to poison the bandit. On September 23, two of the Japanese agents, Dyo and Sato, reported they had placed poison in Villa's coffee. However, "Villa having been suspicious that he might be poisoned through his food for a long time, poured half of this cup of coffee which contained the poison into another cup and handed it to the Mexican who sat on his right."[72] Pershing learned about this bizarre conspiracy only after the fact.

While American forces were confined to Colonia Dublan, Pancho Villa was able to recover his health and rebuild his army. In early September, just as the US and Mexican commissioners were convening in Connecticut, Villa led five hundred men in an attack on Saveto, killing two hundred Carrancistas. A week later he seized a military train at Santa Ysabel, and on September 16, leading eight hundred men, briefly occupied the provincial capital Chihuahua City. By the end of 1916, Villa controlled a significant part of the Chihuahuan countryside and headed an army of between six and ten thousand men. His prestige soared, "the defeats of 1915 were forgotten, and he was once again Villa the Invincible."[73]

As his revolutionary career was resurrected, Villa's rhetoric adopted an increasingly belligerent tone toward the United States. He released *General Villa's Manifesto to the Nation,* which expressed hostility to foreigners in general and toward "the abhorred Yankee" in particular.[74] A British vice-consul in Mexico was troubled by Villa's incendiary language. "The army that now follows him," Patrick O'Hea wrote, "Villa has called to his standard like a mad mullah, preaching a holy war, a crusade against the foreigner, and particularly against the 'gringo.'"[75] When his army retook Chihuahua City on November 27, Villa's wrath once again fell upon the city's Chinese residents, more than one hundred of whom were murdered in cold blood.

On November 2, Pershing warned Funston that "Villa's prestige continues to grow, and his numbers are increasing." He argued that it would be militarily sound to strike at Villa now and eliminate the threat before it grew worse. Although Funston agreed with Pershing's assessment, Wilson refused to authorize offensive operations. On December 9 Pershing wired Funston, again requesting permission to move his rested and well-drilled forces against Villa's army. Funston endorsed Pershing's request in writing to Secretary Baker, but Wilson hesitated, fearing even the slightest risk of an escalation of the US military involvement in Mexico while US relations with Germany continued to deteriorate. Consequently, Secretary Baker ordered Funston to take no action.[76]

Alarmed by Villa's conquests, Carranza deployed an elite force to Chihuahua under the command of General Francisco Murguia. Murguia drew Villa into battle at Jiménez on January 6, badly defeating Villa's forces. Now that Carranza had apparently demonstrated the ability to potentially defeat Villa, Wilson finally had the pretext he sought for withdrawing the Punitive Expedition. On January 12, Wilson told Baker he wanted US forces withdrawn, and a week later Pershing received orders to ready the command for return to the United States.

On January 27, Pershing's vanguard started north toward the border. Trailing behind the nearly 11,000 troopers were 2,030 Mexican, 533 Chinese, and 197 Mormon refugees. By February 4 the entire column was assembled at Palomas, and the next morning they crossed the border heading toward Columbus. Although the Punitive Expedition failed to capture Villa, Pershing's men were greeted with enthusiastic cheers as they returned home.

✳

DESPITE THE FAILURE TO KILL or capture Pancho Villa, he was never again a serious threat to the security of the US border states. Pershing succeeded in scattering Villa's forces, killing 203, wounding 108, and capturing 19 of the 485 Villistas who had attacked Columbus. By the beginning of April 1916, several members of Wilson's Cabinet were urging the withdrawal of the Punitive Expedition, as it appeared to have accomplished its objectives.[77] Had the US withdrawn from Mexico before the Carrizal incident, it is doubtful whether Villa could have recovered from the losses he had suffered. Even when he reappeared at the head of a reconstructed army in the fall of 1916, he never dared to approach US forces nor to attack Americans in Mexico in spite of his bellicose threats. And although Wilson's decision to maintain the inactive expedition in Mexico contributed to Villa's resurrection by aiding his recruitment, it also forced Villa to go to ground for several months and bought the Carrancista forces time to improve their ability to deal with Villa themselves.

Ironically, two years after the Punitive Expedition's withdrawal, US forces finally engaged and defeated a force personally led by Villa. Despite the defeat at Jiménez, Pershing's withdrawal left Villa free to raid anywhere he wished. He spent the first part of 1918 preying upon isolated villages, but increasingly he resorted to kidnappings to finance his operations. On June 14, 1919, Villa raided Juárez, and the stray bullets from the ensuing battle with Carrancista forces indiscriminately wounded civilians and soldiers in El Paso. General James B. Erwin, who had commanded the Seventh Cavalry during the Punitive Expedition, had his artillery shell Villa's positions as a cavalry force under Colonel S. R. H. "Tommy" Tompkins (Frank Tompkins's brother and a fellow veteran of the Punitive Expedition) crossed the border, flanked Villa's force, and routed them in a mounted pistol charge.[78]

Villa's strength ebbed and flowed between 1917 and 1920, but he was increasingly checked by competent Carrancista forces. Two months after Carranza died in 1920, Villa decided to lay down his arms, signing a pact with interim President Adolfo de la Huerta that gave him title to a twenty-five-thousand-acre hacienda at Canutillo, thirty-five miles south of Parral. Villa was allowed to keep fifty of his Dorados as a personal bodyguards, whose salaries were paid by the Ministry of War. Unlike Geronimo and Aguinaldo, however, Pancho Villa would not enjoy a long, peaceful retirement. Having made innumerable enemies during his days as a bandit and revolutionary, on July 20, 1923, the forty-six-year-old Villa was killed when eight gunmen ambushed his automobile in Parral as he returned from the christening of one of the children of his former Dorados.[79]

✳

AS PRESSURE INCREASED FOR AMERICA to enter World War I, Major General Frederick Funston emerged as the leading candidate to command the American Expeditionary Force. On February 19, 1917, Secretary of War Baker threw a dinner party at his home with President Wilson as guest of honor. Major Douglas MacArthur, the son of Funston's former commander in the Philippines, was on night-watch duty for the General Staff. Peyton March, now a lieutenant colonel, was also on staff duty that night. At about ten PM, March brought MacArthur a telegram that both officers agreed was important enough to be delivered to Baker at once. MacArthur writes:

> When I reached the Secretary's home, the butler refused to let me enter, saying that he had orders to admit no one. The dining room looked out on the entrance hall and I could see it plainly. It was a gay party, with lights and laughter, the tinkle of glasses, the soft music from an alcove, the merry quips and jokes of a cosmopolitan group. I finally pushed by the butler and tried to attract the attention of the Secretary so I could report to him privately what had occurred. But the President saw me and sang out in the most jovial manner, "Come in, Major, and tell all of us the news. There are no secrets here." There was a general clapping of hands at this, and I knew I was in for it. So I clicked my heels together, saluted him, and barked in a drill-sergeant tone, "Sir, I regret to report that General Funston has just died." Had the voice of doom spoken, the result could not have been different. The silence seemed like that of death itself. You could hear your own breathing. Then, I never saw such a scattering of guests in my life. It was a stampede.[80]

Frederick S. Funston had survived the extremities of deserts, tundra, and jungles, multiple tropical diseases, and five wounds from enemy fire. While sitting in the lobby of the Saint Anthony Hotel in San Antonio, he heard an orchestra playing and commented, "How beautiful it all is," when his own heart finally failed him at the age of fifty-one. His body was the first to ever lay in state at the Alamo, before eventually being buried at the Presidio.

With Funston's passing, "Black Jack" Pershing became the logical choice to command the American Expeditionary Force in France. He successfully led US forces to victory in World War I, and was rewarded in 1919 with promotion to the artificial rank of "General of the Armies," a grade occupied only by himself and the posthumously promoted George Washington. Pershing became Chief of Staff of the Army in 1921, and over the next quarter century was a key mentor to two of his former aides: General George C. Marshall, to whom he provided useful advice during World War II; and General George S. Patton, who before deploying to North Africa made the pilgrimage to Pershing's bedside at Walter Reed Army Hospital to seek the aging warrior's blessing. General John J. Pershing died at Walter Reed in 1948.

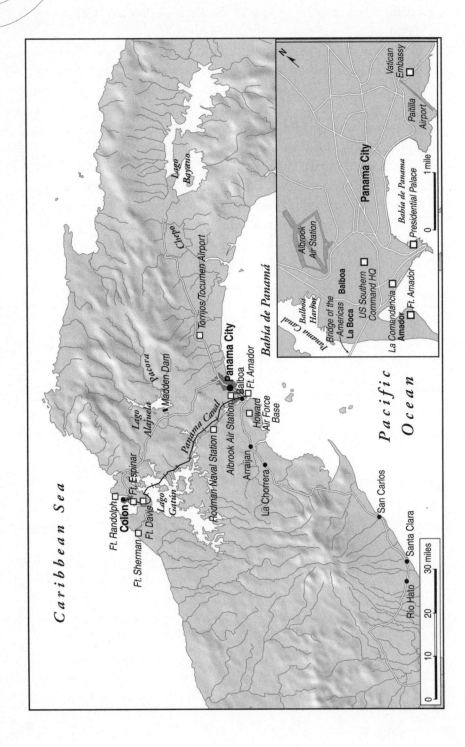

Caribbean Sea

Ft. Randolph
Colón
Ft. Espinar
Ft. Davis
Ft. Sherman

Lago
Gatún

Lago
Alajuela

Madden Dam

Pacora

Lago
Bayano

Chepo

Torrijos/Tocumen Airport

Panama City
Balboa
Ft. Amador

Howard
Air Force
Base

Albrook Air Station

Panama Canal

Rodman Naval Station

Arraiján

La Chorrera

San Carlos

Santa Clara

Río Hato

30 miles

0 10 20

Bahía de Panamá

Pacific
Ocean

Panama City

Vatican
Embassy

Paitilla
Airport

Bahía de Panamá

Presidential Palace

US Southern
Command HQ

Albrook
Air Station

Balboa
Bridge of the
Americas
La Boca
Balboa
Harbor

Ft. Amador

La Comandancia
Amador

Panama Canal

1 mile

N

CHAPTER FOUR

THE POPE, HEAVY METAL, AND THE VOODOO CHILD

THE HUNT FOR MANUEL NORIEGA

Sunday, December 17, 1989, was supposed to be a day of celebration at 1600 Pennsylvania Avenue. The halls of the White House were festively decked as President George H. W. Bush entertained old friends and family at one of the Bushes' numerous Christmas parties. The normally reserved president embodied the holiday spirit by accessorizing his blue blazer and gray slacks with gaudy, bright red socks, one emblazoned with the word "Merry," the other with "Christmas." At two PM, as carolers in eighteenth-century costume entertained the guests, Bush politely excused himself and headed upstairs to the second-floor residence.

Bush was met there in his office by his "War Council" and took a seat beneath the large oil painting "The Peacemakers," depicting Lincoln with his top military leaders near the end of the Civil War. Two days before, Panamanian dictator Manuel Noriega had declared his nation to be in a state of war with the United States. On Saturday night, Panamanian troops opened fire on four off-duty American officers—killing a Marine lieutenant—and detained and abused a Navy lieutenant and his wife.

President Bush now had to decide how America would respond.

Perhaps no man has entered the presidency as experienced in foreign affairs as George H. W. Bush. A decorated fighter pilot in World War II, he had served as director of the Central Intelligence Agency, US Ambassador to China, US Permanent Representative to the United Nations, and as Vice President for eight years. For nearly two hours he listened to his generals lay out plans for invading Panama. Bush asked hard and detailed questions on the myriad diplomatic and logistical details of the proposed military action. Finally, Chairman of the Joint Chiefs of Staff General Colin Powell concluded: "My recommendation is that we go with the full [invasion] plan. I can tell you that the chiefs agree with me to a man."

Secretary of Defense Dick Cheney concurred: "I support what the Chairman just recommended to you."

Secretary of State James Baker told Bush, "I think we ought to go," and National Security Advisor Brent Scowcroft agreed the time for diplomacy had passed.

The president sat pensively, his chin resting on his chest, chewing his lower lip. "Noriega," he said finally, "is not going to lay off. It will only get worse."

At 3:50 PM, he gripped the arms of his chair and rose to his feet. "Okay, let's do it," he quietly said. "The hell with it!"[1]

Within fifty-six hours, ten thousand airborne troops were en route to Panama to join the thirteen thousand soldiers and Marines already stationed there for what would become the largest US military operation since Vietnam. But what began as one of the largest strategic manhunts in US history ended in a bizarre standoff involving the Pope, black voodoo, heavy metal music, and the Delta Force.

✳

HISTORICAL REVISIONISM HAS BEEN KIND to many individuals targeted by US strategic manhunts. Geronimo and Pancho Villa have been romanticized by Hollywood. Augusto Sandino and Che Guevara are icons to anti-American leftists throughout the world. Even Osama bin Laden is revered by a significant portion of the Islamic world despite the large number of Muslims killed in al-Qaeda's attacks. Despite the appealing image of a third-world David battling the Goliath of the US military, it is highly unlikely that history will be so kind to General Manuel Antonio Noriega.

Whereas most of America's other antagonists had some admirable quality—whether it be sheer physical courage or commitment to some cause, however misguided—it is difficult to find any redeemable traits in Noriega. Short and coarse, an inveterate alcoholic with a reputation for sexual violence, Noriega was stuck with the sobriquet "*La Pina*" ("the pineapple") in reference to his acne-scarred face. He seemed to elicit hatred in almost everyone he encountered. Former Assistant Secretary of State Elliott Abrams recalled the dictator as "a remarkably ugly man whose true nature shown through—greasy and thoroughly off putting."[2] Colin Powell, not normally a man given to hyperbole, recalled meeting Noriega: "I found Noriega an unappealing man, with his pock-marked face, beady, darting eyes, and arrogant swagger. I immediately had the crawling sense that I was in the presence of evil."[3] Or, as James Baker put it more colloquially, Noriega "was a case of what we in Texas call 'bad chili.'"[4]

Noriega rose to power in 1983 after the death of Panamanian strongman Omar Torrijos, outmaneuvering his fellow officers to seize control of the Panama Defense Force (PDF). Noriega enjoyed a productive relationship with US intelligence agencies and served as an important conduit for US aid supporting the Nicaraguan contras. Although this effort was the backbone of the Reagan administration's anticommunist strategy in Central America, Secretary of State George Shultz observed that "You can't buy [Noriega], you can only rent him."[5] Even as Noriega helped the Contras, he was simultaneously shipping arms to the Marxist rebels in El Salvador who opposed the US-backed government. He was also known to be passing classified information to Cuba, Libya, and Warsaw Pact states. By 1987, Noriega was dealing with outright terrorist organizations, such as the more radical factions of the Palestine Liberation Organization and the Colombian M-19 group. Despite this pattern of double-dealing, the US intelligence agencies continued to believe that Noriega's benefits outweighed his costs.[6]

Yet not even the strongman's friends in the intelligence community could mitigate the damage done within US policymaking circles by Noriega's profitable side venture in international narcotics trafficking.

American law enforcement officials rated Noriega one of the world's most significant narco-traffickers as early as 1971, and in 1972 proposed Noriega's "total and complete immobilization," a euphemism for assassination. Noriega's ties to the Medellín cartel deepened over the next two decades, and on February 4, 1988, two separate grand juries indicted the dictator on drug trafficking and associated racketeering charges. The cumulative sentences for Noriega, if convicted, were 145 years of imprisonment. The indictments, which technically could not be enforced due to the lack of an extradition treaty with Panama, limited the options of first the Reagan and, later, the Bush administration with regard to policy toward Noriega, lest they appear to condone drug dealing.[7]

Noriega responded to the US indictments with a systematic campaign to harass US military personnel and dependents stationed in Panama. From February 1988 to May 1989, over six hundred incidents involving the harassment of US civilians and troops were reported.[8] The crisis deteriorated even further after Panama's May 1989 presidential elections. Fearful of defeat, Noriega ordered the PDF and his personal paramilitary organization, the "Dignity Battalions," to seize the ballot boxes, close select polling stations, and intimidate the opposition and its supporters. When exit polls conducted by the Catholic Church still showed the opposition candidate Guillermo Endara ahead, Noriega quickly canceled the elections and installed a crony as president.[9]

On May 10, the cheated opposition candidates organized a protest rally near Noriega's military headquarters, La Comandancia. Thousands of demonstrators honked car horns and chanted, "Down with the pineapple." As the march proceeded down the Via Espana in Panama City, men wearing red T-shirts inscribed "Dignity Battalions" descended upon the crowd, furiously swinging steel pipes, tire irons, and planks with jutting nails. Endara was quickly knocked unconscious, lying in the street bleeding from a gash in his head. The bodyguard of vice-presidential candidate Guillermo "Billy" Ford was shot dead. Ford himself staggered desperately along the sidewalk, his white shirt drenched in his bodyguard's blood, hounded by Noriega's goons at every step. Television cameras captured the horrifying, indelible images of the patrician, white-haired Ford being punched repeatedly, a look of sheer terror in his eyes.[10]

For many Americans, this would be the symbol that defined Manuel Noriega's Panama.

*

IN MAY 1988, Ronald Reagan declared that "Noriega must go." But the question of *how* to remove the dictator proved to be far more difficult to resolve.

State Department officials advocated military force be used to oust Noriega. Elliott Abrams suggested a surgical strike by special operations teams to capture Noriega, and the notion of a commando raid targeting Noriega persisted well into the Bush administration. In an internal State memorandum dated April 14, 1989, the department's point man on Panama, Michael Kozak, maintained that the preferred strategic option was to incite a PDF coup. However, "If the PDF has not [acted] by September 1 the President should order Noriega's removal by a snatch or US military operation."[11]

Although the State Department took a more aggressive view, Defense officials and military commanders argued against the use of force. United States Southern Command (SOUTHCOM) viewed the probability of successfully executing a snatch operation as remote. Noriega was difficult to track, and US intelligence only occasionally knew where he had been, rarely knew where he was, and never knew where he was going to be. One exception was Master Sergeant Santos Alfred Matos of the Seventh Special Forces Group (Seventh SFG) headquartered in Panama. Matos was a legend within the special operations community for his skydiving prowess, and informed his superiors that he had taken Noriega tandem jumping four times. If the commanders wanted Noriega snatched, Matos proposed, he could simply call the strongman up, propose they meet for a jump, and then instead of steering him to the drop zone he would guide their parachute to a van parked somewhere and abscond with Noriega. Matos was immediately told his comments were now classified and not to discuss them with anybody else.[12] Even if Noriega could be captured in a raid, SOUTHCOM sources within the PDF suggested he might have prearranged the abduction or killing of any number of US citizens residing in Panama. Military officials derided the proposed snatch operations as "Looney Tunes" or a "Rambo operation," and worked to delay initiatives proposed in the interagency. Admiral Jonathan Howe—Chairman of the Joint Chiefs Admiral William Crowe's representative at the National Security Council Deputies' Committee—argued that all US dependents would have to be moved before an operation could be launched against Noriega. When asked how long this would take, he eventually replied it would take roughly nine months, citing the availability of commercial moving companies, which were completely booked in the interim.[13]

Instead of military force, the Reagan administration attempted to apply a carrot-and-stick approach to persuade Noriega to relinquish power. In April 1988 the administration imposed economic sanctions against Panama, while simultaneously offering Noriega a deal by which the United States would agree not to extradite him for prosecution if he agreed to asylum in a third country. Although the sanctions created the intended economic crisis in Panama, they disproportionately harmed the country's poor and middle classes, as Noriega and his supporters were buoyed by limitless drug revenues. Similarly, although the negotiations appeared promising at times, in May Noriega abruptly rejected the US proposal.[14]

Although military force had been ruled out to remove Noriega, US forces could still be used to apply indirect pressure on the dictator. On July 22, 1989, the Bush administration issued National Security Directive–17, which invoked a provision of the canal treaty that allowed US troops unlimited training exercises. This allowed SOUTHCOM to increase its troop movements, patrols, and training flights in and around Panama. SOUTHCOM also inaugurated a series of small-scale exercises dubbed "Sand Fleas" that mimicked US contingency plans in the event of an invasion.

These operations were ultimately intended as a show of force to intimidate Noriega. As Secretary Baker recalled: "We wanted Noriega to believe we were coming if he didn't leave first."[15] Yet Noriega was not so easily cowed. The dictator had written a textbook on psychological warfare and envisioned himself portrayed in the movies by Clint Eastwood because "he is very macho. He doesn't take [xxxx] from anybody." During one American exercise involving a US military police quick reaction force, Noriega showed up with an entourage and directly approached the US forces. He shook hands with one MP and, in front of Panamanian cameramen, offered himself up for arrest.

"Here I am," he taunted.[16]

A second purpose of the exercises was to send the PDF a message: "Noriega is the problem; either you remove him or the US military will."[17] President Bush made the US desire for a PDF coup explicit in extemporaneous remarks on May 13, 1989. While aboard Air Force One, he summoned the reporters traveling with him to his cabin. He said he had no quarrel with the PDF, just with Noriega and his "thuggery."

"The will of the people should not be thwarted by this man," Bush said. When a reporter asked what Panamanians should do, the president replied, "They ought to just do everything they can to get Mr. Noriega out of there." The remarks were widely interpreted as official American encouragement of a coup.[18]

It took nearly four months before the president's wish came to fruition. On Sunday, October 1, SOUTHCOM learned of a planned coup against Noriega by Major Moises Giroldi. In the Panamanian tradition of bloodless coups, Giroldi proposed neither to arrest nor kill Noriega, but rather to detain him in the Comandancia and convince him to retire. The CIA agents in contact with Giroldi estimated the chances of success at less than 50 percent. SOUTHCOM commander General Max Thurman quickly concluded the coup was "ill-motivated, ill-conceived, ill-led, and fatally flawed."[19]

Despite American misgivings, the coup actually took place on October 3 as forces under Giroldi seized the Comandancia for several hours. Giroldi's aides met with SOUTHCOM representatives, but informed them they would not turn him over to the Americans. Unfortunately, Thurman's assessment of the plotters' competency proved accurate. They "detained" Noriega alone in a room with a telephone, which he used to call in loyal PDF units that subsequently overwhelmed the rebels and freed him. By the time President Bush and his advisors had thoroughly discussed their options, the coup was over, and Giroldi was dead soon thereafter.[20]

Despite the Keystone Cop nature of the Giroldi coup, both Republicans and Democrats in Congress excoriated the Bush administration for failing to exploit the opportunity. The Democratic chairman of the House Armed Services Committee, Les Aspin, admonished, "We ought to be ready at any opportunity . . . to do something about Mr. Noriega." Editorials compared the incident to the failed Desert One and Bay of Pigs missions. Bush's response that to unleash America's armed forces under such dubious circumstances was "not prudent" recalled the "wimp factor" charges that had plagued him during the 1988 campaign, and became a staple of satirical caricatures of the president.[21]

However vigorously administration officials defended their caution during the coup attempt, its collapse prompted considerable introspection. "It was apparent that a prime opportunity to remove Noriega had been squandered," Baker recalled. "All of us vowed never to let such an opportunity pass us by."[22] "Amateur hour is over," President Bush declared to his National Security Council. "I want some follow-through planning" for *when*, not if, Noriega would overstep his bounds.[23] Returning to Panama from Washington after the coup, General Thurman chided himself, "Get your shit straight because if this ever happens again or if an American is hurt, then there will be a takedown here. That will be the end of it." The Bush administration and SOUTHCOM began revising its existing war plan, BLUE SPOON, and in late October the administration launched another covert program to depose Noriega, which one official summarized: "What it boils down to is that we want him alive in the United States or dead."[24]

Once again, General Thurman turned out to be unfortunately prophetic.

✳

ON DECEMBER 15, NORIEGA initiated the penultimate crisis when he had his puppet National Assembly declare him "Maximum Leader of National Liberation" and head of government. The assembly proceeded to pass a resolution declaring Panama "to be in a state of war" with the United States. Noriega strode triumphantly to the podium, wielding a machete, and boasted, "We the Panamanian people will sit along the banks of the canal to watch the dead bodies of our enemies pass by."[25]

The next evening, four US officers took a wrong turn in Panama City and approached a checkpoint at the Comandancia. PDF guards brandishing AK-47s stopped the car and tried to drag the Americans from the vehicle. The driver hit the gas pedal, and as the car sped away, the PDF opened fire, killing twenty-four-year-old Marine Corps Lieutenant Roberto Paz. The shooting was witnessed by an American naval officer and his wife, who had been stopped at the same checkpoint about a half hour earlier. They were subsequently blindfolded and driven to an unknown location. For the next four hours the lieutenant was repeatedly kicked in the head and groin as his wife was forced to watch. The PDF soldiers threw her against a wall and threatened to rape her. Finally, at about one AM, December 17, the Panamanians gave up and released the couple three blocks from the Comandancia.

Although US commanders had previously not considered Noriega worth expending American lives to depose, these events erased any doubts about the advisability of using force.

✳

AT THE OUTSET OF THE December 17 war council, President Bush said, "Look, here are my objectives. I want to get Noriega."[26] He asked whether a commando raid to apprehend Noriega was feasible. Powell explained that Noriega was extraordinarily skilled at hiding. He rarely slept in the same location on consecutive nights and traveled in as many as seven identical limousines. Despite the efforts of an elite tracking team, SOUTHCOM knew his whereabouts only perhaps 80 percent of the time and could not reliably predict where he would appear next. Thus, Powell could offer no assurance that a covert operation to kidnap or arrest Noriega would be successful. Worse, if the US military went after Noriega and missed, the lives of every American in the Canal Zone would be in jeopardy.

Consequently, Powell presented General Thurman's preferred option: to use massive force to overwhelm and demolish the PDF. This would minimize the time available for the PDF to seize US citizens as hostages. Even if Noriega escaped at H-Hour, he would have no forces to command. "Wherever he is," Powell told the president, "he won't be El Jefe. He won't be able to show his face."[27]

Bush and his advisors concurred with Powell's recommendation. The execute order was given for an operation involving twenty-three thousand US forces—including the thirteen thousand already stationed in Panama—to invade and remove Noriega from power. The heart of the invasion force would be four thousand special operations forces— Green Berets, SEALs, Rangers, Air Force commandos, and the Delta Force—that would execute a series of raids all over Panama at H-hour.

General Thurman set H-hour for one AM, December 20, the timing of which proved to be the worst-kept secret in Panama as the massive movement of US aircraft to Panama compromised strategic surprise. At ten PM Dan Rather appeared on a CBS News special report to announce: "US military transport planes have left Fort Bragg. The Pentagon declines to say whether or not they're bound for Panama. It will only say that the Fort Bragg-based 18th Airborne Corps has been conducting what the Army calls an emergency readiness measure."[28] Similar stories and images compromising the secrecy of the invasion appeared on CNN and NBC. At midnight, the Comandancia sent out a message to PDF commanders: "They're coming. The ballgame is at 1AM. Report to your units . . . draw your weapons and prepare to fight."[29] Consequently, General Thurman ordered the special operations forces to launch their operations fifteen minutes ahead of schedule, at 12:45 AM.[30]

Because SOUTHCOM could not be sure of Noriega's location at H-hour, an emphasis was placed on cutting off his potential means of escape. If intelligence, radar, or AWACS planes discovered Noriega trying to escape by air, F-16 fighters or AC-130 gunships would intercept his aircraft and force it to land. If the dictator's pilot refused to obey, the US military aircraft, upon authorization of Secretary Cheney, were to shoot down the suspected aircraft.[31]

In order to cut off another potential escape route for Noriega, two combat rubber raider craft departed Rodman Naval Station at eleven PM. They silently crossed the canal in the darkness and tied up in a mangrove stand near the docks at Balboa Harbor. Two two-man SEAL teams slipped over the sides of the crafts, and using sophisticated scuba gear that left no trail of air bubbles, swam to their target—the Panamanian fast patrol boat *Presidente Poras,* which US commanders feared Noriega would use to flee Panama. The SEAL demolition teams placed haversacks filled with explosives in the propeller shaft, set the detonators for one AM, and quickly swam away to their extraction point. Above the water's surface they could already hear the roar of the initial firefights erupting between US and Panamanian forces. At one AM the explosion ripped a hole in the *Presidente Poras,* rocking downtown Panama City as the vessel slowly sank to the bottom of the harbor.[32]

As one team of SEALs was navigating the waters of Balboa Harbor, SEAL Team Four was coming ashore at Panama City's downtown Paitilla Airport, where Noriega based his personal Learjet. At 12:45 AM the sixty-two-man force—comprised of three sixteen-man SEAL platoons and a command element led by Lieutenant Commander Pat Toohey—came ashore. The SEALs hurried up the trail from the beach and snuck through a hole in the airport's security fence. Two platoons each started moving up one side of the runway, while a third platoon remained on the southern edge of the airfield to provide security. By 1:05 AM the

SEALs had reached their assault positions in front of the three northern-most hangars. One squad of nine commandos lay prone on the tarmac in front of the middle hangar, which housed Noriega's jet. Another platoon was positioned just to the north, providing cover and observing the northern side of the airfield.

A radio transmission reported that three PDF armored vehicles were racing down the road that circles the northern end of Paitilla airfield. Toohey quickly ordered the northernmost platoon to move to the road to either ensure the vehicles passed by the airport or, if necessary, ambush them. As the SEAL team rose from the tarmac, a Panamanian guard in the northernmost hangar saw them and raised his weapon. A SEAL fired first, but missed. A split second later the crack of AK-47 fire echoed through the humid night as the guard fired a burst on automatic. The bullets ripped through the line of exposed SEALs, two of whom were killed instantly. The remaining SEALs dove for cover in a drainage ditch, but were struck by shots ricocheting off the tarmac, wounding six others. The SEALs in front of Noriega's hangar unleashed a hail of covering fire at the northern hangar, which now appeared to hold at least two Panamanians, but their line of fire was obstructed by two small aircraft parked in front of the hanger. The third platoon to the south was ordered up to attack the hangar.

A minute of intense fire gave way to a heavy silence. The hangar was riddled with bullet holes, the Panamanians were dead, and anti-armor rockets had destroyed the cockpit of Noriega's plane. But although SEAL Team Four achieved its objective, the price paid was steep: four SEALs dead and eight more wounded. The unexpected casualties from such an elite force shocked the Special Operations community and would remain a source of controversy for years.[33]

In addition to cutting off Noriega's avenues of escape, another critical H-hour mission was to destroy the units that had come to his rescue during the October coup. The PDF numbered nearly 12,800 troops, but only one-third of these could be classified as combat troops. Although the infantry units were judged "a well-trained and disciplined force at the small unit, tactical level," they suffered from reliance on overly centralized command and control. The two exceptions were the Seventh Infantry Company and Battalion 2000.[34]

The black-uniformed, bearded "*Macho de Monte*" (literally, "Mountain Men") of the Seventh Infantry were a well-armed commando unit trained by Cuban military advisors for a single purpose: to protect and, if necessary, rescue Noriega. They were stationed at Rio Hato about sixty-five miles from Panama City on the Pacific Coast, but as demonstrated during the Giroldi coup, were able to rapidly deploy by air to the capital. The mission of attacking Rio Hato was given to the US Army's elite light infantry, the Seventy-Fifth Ranger Regiment under Colonel William F. "Buck" Kernan.

At precisely one AM, two F-117A "Stealth" bombers, in their first-ever combat mission, swooped in at four thousand feet to drop a pair of two-thousand-pound bombs next to the Seventh Infantry's barracks. The idea was to terrify and confuse the Panamanians into surrendering quickly. Yet instead of stunning the Macho de Monte, the massive bombs roused the Panamanians from their beds and out of their barracks, leaving them better prepared to resist the incoming Rangers.

The Mountain Men moved into position, while thirteen C-130 transports carried 1,300 Rangers from the Second and Third Ranger battalions into battle. As they prepared to jump into the warm, humid night, one Ranger recalled: "[We] just went around and started hitting one another on the head and got motivated, because if anybody deserved to be slammed, [Noriega] was the one. Because he was an evil man . . . There was no death wish, but we wanted to get him bad, and he deserved to be got." The lights of the airfield and barracks were visible as the planes approached, leading the Rangers to think they had achieved strategic surprise. But as soon as they began to exit the aircraft, the skies filled with tracer fire.[35]

The Rangers jumped from an altitude of only five hundred feet, three hundred feet below the standard training jump. This meant their main parachutes would open at just one hundred feet. While limiting their exposure to ground fire, it also meant their reserve parachutes were virtually useless in case of a malfunction, and with their hundred-pound packs, every Ranger was assured a brutal landing. Four soldiers were killed on the jump, and another eighty-six formed part of an "orthopedic nightmare" of broken legs and ankles.[36]

Although the runway was cleared within thirty minutes, the fighting in the barracks area was intense. The PDF withdrew through the rear of a building and took up firing positions in nearby gullies or trenches. When the Rangers worked through to the building's exit, the PDF ambushed them and withdrew to the next building to repeat the tactic. Finally, after five hours of room-to-room, building-to-building combat, the Macho de Monte had all either surrendered or melted into the surrounding jungle.

The other PDF unit that concerned US commanders was Battalion 2000, an elite fighting unit of two hundred mechanized infantry that had smashed the abortive October revolt. One of Noriega's most loyal units, they were stationed at Fort Cimarron, approximately sixteen miles from Panama City's Torrijos/Tocumen airport, which could serve as either an escape hatch for Noriega or an entry point for Cuban or Nicaraguan reinforcements. Thus, another critical H-hour mission was to seize the airport complex before Battalion 2000 could secure it.

While First Battalion, Seventy-Fifth Ranger Regiment captured the airfields, elements of Third Battalion, Seventh Special Forces Group were tasked with conducting surveillance missions at Fort Cimarron and the Pacora River Bridge to monitor Battalion 2000's movements. Major Kevin Higgins was preparing to take off in three helicopters with a twenty-four-man element of Company A, Third/Seventh SFG, when an intelligence officer came running onto the helipad. "We just got reports that . . . a ten-vehicle convoy is leaving Cimarron Cuartel for Panama City," he said.[37] Higgins's mission instantly shifted from reconnaissance to direct action, with the goal of seizing Pacora River Bridge and blocking Battalion 2000 from entering the capital.

As the helicopters approached the bridge at 12:45 AM, the lead pilot spotted six PDF vehicles on the road. It was now a race between the Green Berets and the Panamanians to see who could get to the bridge first. The helicopters dropped Higgins's element on the western shore of the river. His men quickly clambered up the steep slope to the road and found themselves directly in the headlights of the first PDF vehicle crossing the bridge from the east. The soldiers hit the lead vehicle with two light antitank weapons and poured machine-gun fire and M203-launched grenades into the column. The Air Force combat controller with Higgins's element directed AC-130 fire onto the stalled column, driving the Panamanians from their trucks. The battle continued for several hours, as the Panamanians attempted to outflank the small element, but Higgins's men repelled all PDF attempts to cross the bridge or the river.[38]

Meanwhile, eleven transport aircraft approached Tocumen airfield in a straight line over the runway. At 1:03 AM, the clear evening sky filled with the dark silhouettes of parachutes as the First Ranger Battalion jumped from the planes. The seizure of the airfield was flawless, and once again, more Rangers suffered torn knee ligaments, broken legs, and other injuries from the low jumping altitude and unforgiving concrete of the tarmac than from hostile fire. As the other Ranger companies assaulted objectives held by the PDF, Bravo First/Seventy-Fifth was tasked to secure the perimeter and establish roadblocks around the airfield. Bravo landed on target and received only sporadic enemy fire as it quickly moved to its blocking positions. The biggest obstacle these Rangers faced were Panamanian vehicles ignoring their warning sign and barricades. These vehicles typically turned and fled once the Rangers fired warning shots. But one convoy of two hatchbacks refused to heed the warnings and hurtled toward Bravo Company at full speed. The Rangers took aim and shot out the front tires of the lead vehicle. The second car came to a screeching halt and turned around, disappearing into the night.

It would not be discovered until later that General Noriega was in the car that got away.

✳

THE SIMULTANEOUS H-HOUR ASSAULT on dozens of targets with overwhelming force decimated the PDF, who proved to be no match for American firepower and training, and had little stomach for a genuine fight. "Essentially, the leaders didn't show," said Major General James Johnson, commander of the 82nd Airborne. "The troops were deserted."[39] The Panamanians would typically empty the magazines of their rifles and disappear. The exception to this pattern was at the Comandancia, where elements of the PDF's Sixth, Seventh, and Eighth Rifle Companies, reinforced by two public-order companies, vigorously defended PDF headquarters for a day. Resistance finally collapsed on the morning of December 21, thereby immobilizing resistance in outlying provinces as well.[40]

American forces were greeted by the long-suffering Panamanian people as liberators. In Colón, one officer recalled, "The streets came alive as people appeared from every door and window, cheering us."[41] In a scene eerily foreshadowing the liberation of Baghdad more than a decade later, "People were out there looting their asses off. They had armfuls of televisions, pillows, anything they could get. When they saw

us, they shouted, '*Viva Bush! Viva the United States!*'"[42] Another soldier
noted, "There was people out partying and waving US flags and cheering for us. And then we would turn a corner and start heading down
another way, and all of a sudden we'd start getting shot at."[43]

On the home front, however, the failure to capture Noriega dominated the perception of Operation Just Cause. At the first press conference on the morning of December 20, reporters wanted to know
about Noriega. "If we did not catch him, what was the point of invading
Panama?" they asked Powell. "Wouldn't it make life miserable for the
US forces down there," a reporter asked, "if Noriega was still running
around in the Panamanian wilds?"

Powell assured the press that "we'll chase him and we will find him.
I'm not quite sure he's up to being chased around the countryside by
Army Rangers, Special Forces, and light infantry units."

But the reporters persisted: "Could we really consider Just Cause
successful as long as we did not have Noriega in custody?"[44]

✳

PRIOR TO THE INVASION, Noriega had been constantly tracked by members of Delta Force, aided by experts from the National Security Agency
and Central Intelligence Agency. This surveillance and intelligence cell,
code-named CENTRA SPIKE, reported directly to General Thurman
and monitored radio and telephone communications and directed a
network of informants that traced the dictator's movements. Noriega's
last known location was in a house in Colón at six PM on December
19. Shortly thereafter, he left in a convoy of cars and buses south toward
Panama City. Part of the convoy turned off the road toward Tocumen
and Torrijos airfields, while the other half headed straight toward the
Comandancia. Although the Joint Special Operations Command was
confident that Noriega had not returned to his headquarters, they could
not definitely say where he actually was. At H-hour, US troops raided
Noriega's beach house at Farallon and his apartment near Colón, but
found both of them empty.[45]

In reality, Noriega had returned to Panama City around eight PM,
heading straight to a PDF club. Despite the mounting evidence of the
impending invasion, he dismissed the possibility of a US attack, insist-
ing reports of troop mobilizations were disinformation designed to
scare him into fleeing. He proceeded to get drunk, eventually deciding

another form of entertainment was needed. A sergeant on his staff was dispatched to pick up a prostitute, who met the intoxicated strongman at the Ceremi Recreation Center, a PDF rest area just east of Tocumen military airfield. His dalliance was interrupted at one AM, when the thumping sound of an AC-130 gunship's 105 mm and 40 mm cannon prepping the objective at Tocumen for the First Ranger Battalion's assault shook the room. Noriega's bodyguard, Captain Ivan Castillo, went outside and saw the sky filled with 750 parachutes descending upon the airfield. Castillo rushed back inside to collect his boss, and the dictator's entourage piled into the two Hyundai hatchbacks.[46]

The next day, elements of Bravo Company, First Ranger Battalion, secured the recreation center, discovering some of Noriega's personal belongings, including his uniform and shoes.

After narrowly avoiding capture at B-1/Seventy-Fifth's roadblock, Noriega took the main highway into Panama City, where he spent the night moving between the houses of various friends and associates. He had no plan, and his only goal was to evade capture. At 3:39 AM SOUTHCOM received a signals intelligence report that the dictator had fled and was still safe. Shortly after five AM, another intercept indicated that Noriega was hiding in a reinforced house somewhere in the capital city, a needle among a pile of needles.

Administration and military officials tried to downplay the significance of missing Noriega. On December 20, Powell declared: "The operation is a success already because we cut off the head of that government, and there is a new government that was elected by the Panamanian people."[47] Military briefers suggested his capture was imminent, but in reality had no clue where he was. Whatever their public nonchalance, in private there was genuine consternation regarding Noriega's disappearance. Intelligence analysts speculated that Noriega might execute a contingency plan for setting up a guerrilla base in the mountains or escape to a friendly country like Cuba. From there, he could mount a propaganda campaign and orchestrate terrorist attacks against US forces and the newly installed Endara government. US commanders feared Noriega had made his way out of the capital to rural Chiriquí, where, under the command of his friend Major Luis del Cid, the PDF command structure was still intact.[48]

This scenario was especially troubling given the activities of Noriega's "Dignity Battalions," fourteen paramilitary units containing two thousand members, comprised mainly of Noriega loyalists from within the PDF and common street thugs. Working in groups of a dozen or fewer men, the Dignity Battalions kept fighting in tactics that, although borderline suicidal, nevertheless posed considerable problems to US forces trying to restore law and order. These loyalists fought on in the hope that Noriega might reappear to lead them. The government radio station, Radio Nacional, stayed on the air throughout the twentieth, broadcasting news about American "atrocities" and giving assurances that Noriega was still in command of the resistance. From an undisclosed location, Noriega recorded a speech exhorting his supporters: "We're in trench warfare now and we will maintain the resistance. We must resist and advance. . . . Our slogan is to win or die, not one step back."[49]

General Thurman believed their predations to be "centrally controlled" and that the key to neutralizing the Dignity Battalions and isolated pockets of PDF resistance was the capture or death of Noriega. "This operation is . . . pretty well wrapped up," President Bush said on December 21, but "I won't be satisfied until we see him come to justice."[50] A $1 million bounty for information leading to Noriega's capture was announced, although one senior officer cautioned: "We don't want to make him a fugitive bandit being hunted by marines. He's not Pancho Villa, he's John Dillinger."[51]

The avenues of escape were slammed shut throughout Panama by various special operations forces. As SEALs watched Panama's ports and Seventh Group's Green Berets combed the streets of the capital, primary responsibility for hunting Noriega was given to Delta Force. Noriega sightings flooded into the SOUTHCOM intelligence network, and analysts tried to separate truth from falsehood. In Colón, an old woman appeared at the front gate of the hotel being used as headquarters for the 504th Parachute Infantry Regiment, "pointing a crooked finger and raving that Noriega had a secret tunnel under the hotel that he had used for an escape route upon the 7th Infantry's arrival." Other locals corroborated this claim, but a search of the hotel's basement quickly dismissed the notion of a secret tunnel.[52] For intelligence that was deemed credible, Delta Force could go "from tip to takeoff" in thirty minutes, and between December 21–24 launched forty-two raids on every known or suspected safe house where Noriega could hide.[53]

Yet for all Delta's considerable skill, they could apparently never catch up to the elusive dictator. Often they thought they were getting close: at one seaside villa on the Pacific Ocean US forces found lit cigarettes and warm coffee cups; at other locations they found PDF soldiers. But no matter how rapidly they kicked down doors and poured in through windows, the operators would be told Noriega had either just left or was at another location. As this cycle repeated itself in the days after the invasion, raiding troops made a series of bizarre discoveries. At Noriega's residence at Fort Amador, US troops found pictures of Hitler, an extensive pornography collection, a "witches diary" chronicling visits by two voodoo priestesses from Brazil, and fifty kilograms of white powder initially believed to be cocaine, but later identified as flour for making tamales. At Noriega's home at Altos del Golfo, Delta uncovered more stacks of hard-core pornography, $8 million in US currency, and two religious altars, one of which was decorated with jars containing human internal organs.[54]

But there still was no sign of Noriega.

∗

EARLY ON THE MORNING of December 24, Ivan Castillo left the Panama City apartment where he and Noriega had been hiding for the past three days. He told his boss he was searching for the next place to hide, and that if he did not return by seven AM Noriega was to move without him. Noriega trusted Castillo completely.[55] But Castillo was tired of running and ready to give up. He set out to look for an American to take him to the Spanish-speaking Major General Marc Cisneros, to whom he hoped to betray Noriega in exchange for his own safety. At 6:30 AM Castillo found a patrol from the Seventh Infantry, but none of the soldiers spoke Spanish. Castillo tried to explain who he was, but was taken into custody as a prisoner of war, and Cisneros did not find out about Castillo's surrender until 10:30 AM.

"General," Castillo told Cisneros, "if I could have gotten word to you when I wanted to, I could have found you Noriega."

"Well, where could he be?" Cisneros asked.

Castillo handed Cisneros a list of possible hiding spots. Although it was several hours past the time he told Noriega to leave from their last safe house, Castillo said Noriega probably left his baggage behind and might return to the location. But when the team arrived, they found nothing except the dictator's wallet and briefcase.

Castillo was not the only person trying to contact Cisneros on Christmas Eve. Monsignor José Sebastián Laboa, the papal nuncio to Panama, was desperately trying to reach Cisneros by telephone for hours to warn him that Noriega was seeking asylum. US commanders had stationed forces outside several foreign embassies to which Noriega might seek asylum, but they neglected to block the Vatican's embassy. Although Noriega kept pictures of two popes on his office desk, he claimed to be a Buddhist and was known to practice black voodoo.

Around 3:30 PM Laboa's call finally got through to the general. As Cisneros picked up the phone, he heard the priest whisper, "He just walked in."[56]

✳

WHILE DELTA FORCE WAS HUNTING for Noriega, elements of the Seventh SFG were conducting what came to be called the "Ma Bell" operations. In order to avoid direct attacks on the remaining PDF garrisons spread throughout the Panamanian countryside and the casualties such missions would entail, Captain Charles Cleveland suggested they telephone the Panamanian commander at each barracks and give him an ultimatum to surrender peacefully or be attacked. Between December 22–31, these missions produced the surrender of fourteen garrisons and two thousand PDF troops.[57]

Perhaps the most significant capitulation was the first, when Major del Cid in Chiriquí announced he would surrender on December 23. The news depressed Noriega, who subsequently told an intermediary to call Monsignor Laboa and request asylum. Noriega requested that the Vatican's emissary pick him up at the Panama City Dairy Queen. There, a visibly exhausted Noriega—wearing a T-shirt, Bermuda shorts, and an oversized baseball cap—jumped into the backseat of the nunciature's car, and sunk low in his seat to avoid being seen on the short drive to the nunciature, arriving at the Vatican's embassy at 3:30 PM.

Manuel Noriega had begun the invasion with a prostitute. He would end it surrounded by nuns.

✳

DELTA FORCE HAD RECEIVED A TIP that Noriega was en route to the nunciature, and was speeding through the air in six Black Hawks to intercept the blue all-terrain vehicle carrying Noriega when they were told they were too late. Instead of capturing the dictator, they landed two helicopters on Avenida Balboa, the main street in front of the nunciature. They were quickly joined by armored personnel carriers, who pointed their .50-caliber machine guns outward to deter a rescue attempt by Noriega loyalists. Military police arrived and cordoned off the area with concertina wire.[58]

In Washington, Secretary Cheney told Powell, "Don't let that guy out of the compound."[59] The State Department immediately informed the Vatican of the situation and requested it deny Noriega asylum. Since most of the Vatican hierarchy were about to celebrate Midnight Mass at Saint Peter's, State did not receive an immediate response. On Christmas Day, the papal secretary of state responded to Secretary Baker's request for Noriega's release with a polite but firm refusal. A Church spokesman explained that Noriega was being urged to leave of his own free will, but "at the same time, we cannot force Noriega to leave nor . . . can we consign him to US forces."[60]

On Christmas morning, General Thurman spoke personally with Monsignor Laboa at the gate of the nunciature. American officers noticed that the third-floor balcony of the Holiday Inn, less than one hundred yards away, was filled with reporters, many of whom held long boom mikes directed at the nunciature. Fearing they would use them to eavesdrop on either the negotiations or internal US military discussions, General Thurman ordered loudspeakers be directed to create a sound barrier around the nunciature.

In what would become one of the more comically surreal aspects of the Noriega manhunt, on December 27 the Fourth Psychological Operations Group went to work. As Delta commander Jerry Boykin recalled, "Being twenty-year-olds, the psy-ops guys started playing loud rock music. *Really* loud."[61] As the music blared around the clock, it became apparent it could also be used to agitate Noriega, a reported opera aficionado. Consequently, the Fourth Psy Ops used a playlist heavy on ironically titled songs, such as "Voodoo Child," "You're No Good," and "I Fought the Law." Thurman embraced the tactic, proudly telling reporters, "I am the music man."[62] The noise drove the nunciature staff crazy, however, keeping Laboa and others awake. (Noriega later claimed he could not hear the music.) On December 29 Laboa insisted the music stop, and the White House issued a directive not to "make things any more difficult or unpleasant for Monsignor Laboa than necessary." Powell ordered Thurman to turn off the music. The music was replaced by Spanish-language reports carrying stories of the surrender of the PDF in outlying areas in order to demoralize Noriega.[63]

Although the loudspeaker gambit failed to dislodge Noriega, Thurman had other levers by which to influence the dictator and the priest. US forces acted as if they were preparing to assault the nunciature, shooting out the street lights and cutting down the tall grass and brush surrounding the white stucco building. US patrols circled the embassy walls while other soldiers took up positions in a parking garage fifty feet away. US troops cleared a landing zone for a helicopter that made several landings in an attempt to intimidate Noriega. Thurman also arranged for Archbishop Marcos McGrath, the senior Catholic prelate in Panama, to tour Noriega's former residences and office to "gain insight into the man's soul." In addition to the Hitler and voodoo paraphernalia, the archbishop was shown a large poster of all the priests and other high Catholic officials in Central America, implying they were on a hit list. Archbishop McGrath subsequently convened a conference of Panamanian bishops, who then wrote Pope John Paul II a letter urging the pontiff to order Noriega's release to US custody.[64]

But the key to influencing Noriega proved not to be an American officer or policymaker, but rather Monsignor Laboa. A small man with white hair and spectacles, hailing from Spain's Basque region, Laboa was a seasoned Church diplomat and a former *advocatus diaboli*—only now he would be attempting to persuade the devil rather than advocating on his behalf. Laboa had shaped Vatican policy toward Panama for years and knew that Noriega was "a man, who without a pistol, is manageable by anyone."[65] He set about applying both subtle and direct pressure on the dictator in order to get him to surrender willingly.

Upon Noriega's arrival, Laboa had the dictator disarmed and confined to the same bare bedroom with no air-conditioning and a broken television set in which so many of the dictator's victims had sought refuge. Laboa denied the alcoholic Noriega any liquor, save for a single glass of beer. He also avoided repeating Giroldi's mistake and removed the telephone from Noriega's quarters. Laboa told Noriega he would never evict him, and he meant it. But he also informed Noriega that he had granted approval to US forces to raid the compound should Noriega and his men use their weapons to seize control of the nunciature. He then avoided contact with Noriega to isolate the deposed strongman and let him stew for a week.

As the days passed, increasing numbers of Panamanians began to gather at the barricades erected about two hundred yards from the embassy. They banged pots and waved white handkerchiefs, shouting, "Kill the Hitler!" and "Justice for the Tyrant!" Some skewered pineapples on long sticks and pumped them up and down in the air, taunting, "Pineapple face! Pineapple face!" The crowd handed flowers to the US forces surrounding the nunciature, and when Laboa asked what would happen if the demonstrators tried to storm the barricades, Joint Special Operations Task Force commander Major General Wayne Downing replied, "I'm not going to kill a single innocent person to protect that SOB."[66]

By January 2, Laboa was ready to apply pressure. In a brief fifteen-minute meeting, he urged Noriega to see that his best option was to surrender to US justice and defend himself in an American courtroom. The next day a crowd of more than ten thousand Panamanians descended upon Avenida Balboa to demonstrate. Against the backdrop of the angry crowd and a chorus of anti-Noriega slogans, Laboa again invited the dictator to talk. Once again he assured Noriega that he could stay. But Laboa suggested he consider the mob outside who wanted to kill him and might overrun the nunciature.

"But we have the US Army out there," Noriega protested.

"They will not fire on the Panamanian people," Laboa replied. He ominously suggested Noriega could end up like Mussolini, killed by his own people and strung up for the world to see. Besides, Laboa asked, even if he were to remain safely within the confines of the nunciature, "Do you really want to spend the rest of your life having nuns wash your underwear?"[67]

Noriega was out of options. It was clear from the US troops and mass of demonstrators outside that he had no hope of regaining power. Later in the afternoon, he told Laboa, "Your solution is best. I am going."

Just before nine PM, January 3, Noriega emerged from the nunciature wearing a wrinkled tan uniform with four stars on each shoulder board. Carrying a Bible and a toothbrush, he looked stunned and submissive in the glare of the television camera lights. He was met at the gate by Major General Cisneros.

"*Yo soy el General Noriega. Me rindo a las fuerza de los Estados Unidos.*" (I am General Noriega, and I am surrendering to US forces.)

"*Su rendición es aceptada.*" (Your surrender is accepted.)

The ex-dictator was quickly seized by Delta Force operators and hustled aboard a helicopter. Minutes later, at Howard Air Force Base, he was formally placed under arrest by DEA agents and read his Miranda rights in Spanish. The agents made him trade his uniform for a prisoner's flight suit and escorted him aboard a C-130. Within two hours the man who had controlled a tropical paradise as the "Maximum Leader" was on the ground in the United States, heading to a Miami jail cell as prisoner no. 41586.

✳

LATE ON THE EVENING of January 3, President Bush announced that with Noriega's surrender, all Operation Just Cause's strategic objectives had been achieved. SOUTHCOM's initial tally of casualties, released in mid-January, were 23 American KIA and 323 wounded, 314 Panamanian military fatalities, and 202 Panamanian civilians killed.[68]

In 1992 Noriega was convicted of drug-trafficking charges and sentenced to forty years in prison. His sentence officially ended in September 2007, but he remained in a US prison while fighting extradition requests by both France and Panama. He was extradited to France in 2010, where he is currently serving a seven-year sentence for murder and money laundering.

In the end, the Noriega manhunt is one of the few cases in which the capture or killing of the targeted individual correlates with accomplishing the desired strategic objective. Although Panama's democratic legitimacy was still very much in question in the aftermath of the invasion, the nation has witnessed four successful elections since Noriega's overthrow. The drug cartels suffered a brief setback as a result of Operation Just Cause, but the invasion failed to deliver a devastating blow to the international drug trade. Given Panama's proximity to the major cocaine-producing regions in South America, as well as its strategic central position as a transit route to North America, it is inevitable that some amount of narcotics and/or drug profits will pass through Panamanian ports and banks. The key difference from two decades ago is that this trafficking is no longer officially sanctioned as it was under Noriega's rule.[69]

In part, this success was due to the decision to demolish the entire PDF rather than *strictly* target Noriega. General Frederick Woerner—

Thurman's predecessor at SOUTHCOM—warned that even if Noriega were to be removed from power, it "merely created a promotion potential for the next thug. It didn't change institutional attitudes."[70] Powell similarly believed that the PDF was rife with Noriega clones who could replace him if he were captured or killed and the PDF were left intact. Consequently, when General Thurman revised US war plans in the fall of 1989, he made the destruction or radical reorientation of the entire PDF a US strategic objective.[71]

Although destroying the PDF was a primary *operational* objective, the key *strategic* objective was Noriega's removal. Both Secretary Shultz and Secretary Baker issued guidance to inform the PDF that the United States had no quarrel with the Panamanian military, only with Noriega.[72] In his initial remarks to the nation to announce the invasion on December 20, President Bush made this strategic objective clear:

> General Noriega's reckless threats and attacks upon American citizens created an imminent danger to the thirty-five thousand American citizens in Panama. As President I have no higher obligation than to safeguard the lives of American citizens. And that is why I directed our armed forces to protect the lives of American citizens in Panama and to bring General Noriega to justice in the United States."[73]

Moreover, even the operational objective of destroying the PDF was made easier by targeting Noriega individually. Although US forces failed to apprehend Noriega at H-hour, he was on the run and was too frightened for his own safety to exercise any control over the remnants of the PDF and Dignity Battalions. Although the numerous post-D-Day raids failed to nab the dictator, they resulted in the capture of numerous senior officers and Noriega loyalists on the "Black List" who could have led resistance in the strongman's absence. Thus, the destruction of the PDF was in some ways a by-product of, not a prerequisite for, achieving US strategic objectives in Panama.

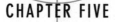

CHAPTER FIVE

THE WARLORD'S REVENGE

TASK FORCE RANGER AND THE SEARCH

FOR MOHAMMED FARAH AIDEED

Although August 23, 1993, was an overcast day when the chartered Boeing 737 touched down at Mogadishu Airport, the US Army officers who stepped off the plane were greeted by a blast of intense humidity. The air was filled with the suffocating stench of burning garbage, rotting ocean waste, and the sweat of the more than one million souls who dwelled in the Somali capital. Decrepit Soviet transport aircraft left from the 1960s sat rusting on the tarmac. Sloping upward beyond the airport's perimeter, the officers could see Mogadishu devastated "like Stalingrad after the battle." The city's streets were cratered and strewn with debris, its buildings bullet-ridden or collapsed.[1]

Among the officers disembarking was a tall, muscular lieutenant colonel with a gray crew cut wearing desert fatigues. To the casual observer, he was just another replacement officer for the US Forces Somalia staff. Yet in reality, Major General William F. Garrison was America's

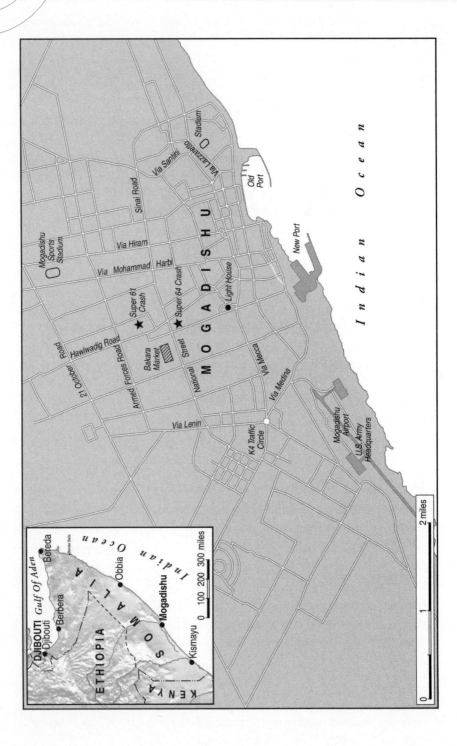

most accomplished commando. A veteran Green Beret with two tours in Vietnam—including participation in the Phoenix program—Garrison had run covert operations all over the world for twenty-five years, including a four-year stint as commander of the Delta Force. Now leading the Joint Special Operations Command (JSOC), Garrison was traveling incognito in hopes of surprising the man he had been sent halfway around the world to capture: the Somali warlord General Mohammed Farah Aideed.

✳

THOMAS HOBBES LIKELY KNEW NOTHING about Somalia when he wrote his treatise *Leviathan* in 1651. Yet in 1992, Mogadishu epitomized Hobbes's vision of man's existence in a state of nature as "nasty, brutish, and short." In January 1991 an alliance of Somali clans overthrew dictator Siad Barre after more than two decades of oppressive rule. The members of the temporary front that deposed Barre quickly turned on each other, however, and throughout 1991 the clans fought among themselves as government, civil society, and basic services collapsed. Anarchy reigned, and within Mogadishu one thousand people were killed each week from random artillery and rocket fire in densely populated neighborhoods. By the end of 1991 there were an estimated twenty thousand casualties of the civil war, more than six hundred thousand refugees, and several hundred thousand more internally displaced persons.[2] The most conspicuous symbols of this anarchy were the warlords' "technicals," land cruisers with the canopies shorn away and fitted with American 106 mm antitank cannons, Chinese recoilless rifles, or Soviet antiaircraft guns bolted to the chassis. The technicals, and the khat-addicted young men who operated these battle wagons, made the streets of Mogadishu appear to be a *Mad Max* movie come to life.[3]

Compounding Somalia's problems, Barre's forces had laid waste to Somalia's farming region in a scorched-earth campaign, which, combined with a widespread drought, triggered a famine. By late 1992, more than three hundred thousand Somalis had perished, and the United Nations (UN) estimated that as many as three thousand people per day were dying of starvation. Beginning in August 1992, the US-led Operation Provide Relief flew almost 2,500 flights into Somalia, delivering more than 28,000 metric tons of relief supplies to airfields in the famine belt. Although the volume of food arriving in Somalia increased significantly, the percentage actually reaching people in need fell by 40 percent, as relief supplies from nongovernmental organizations were looted or hijacked. By early November 1992, up to half a million Somalis had died during the two years of civil war, famine, and disease, all recorded by the dispassionate eye of the burgeoning international twenty-four-hour news media.[4]

On November 25, President George H. W. Bush met with his senior advisors to discuss Somalia. As General Colin Powell recalled, the "images of the fleshless limbs and bloated bellies of dying children continued to haunt us."[5] After broad discussion, President Bush decided to send US ground troops to lead an international force to stop the death and famine in Somalia. On December 4, Bush announced the American-led intervention. By December 8, Operation Restore Hope was under way as Navy SEALs went ashore at Mogadishu, and by the end of the month more than twenty-eight thousand Marines and soldiers from the First Marine Expeditionary Force and Tenth Mountain Division had arrived in Somalia.

Yet to a large degree, the success or failure of Operation Restore Hope did not rest on the diplomats in New York, the policymakers in Washington, or even the US generals in Somalia, but rather on the son of a Hawiye camel trader whose name literally meant "one who tolerates no insult."

∗

MOHAMMED FARAH AIDEED was a slender man with Semitic features, a bald head, small black eyes, and "the bearing of a hawk in constant pursuit of prey."[6] Sixty-two years old at the time of the US intervention, Aideed had been trained at military academies in Rome and Moscow. He was chief of staff of the Somali army in 1970 when Barre, fearing Aideed posed a threat to his regime, imprisoned him without trial for six years. Aideed was fluent in several languages, and in the 1980s served as Somalia's ambassador to India.[7]

Aideed returned to Somalia to command the United Somali Congress's armed component, and after overthrowing Barre, arguably had the best claim to power. His militia—the Somali National Alliance (SNA)—was the best armed and best organized, and his lead role in toppling the hated dictator gave him popular support outside his Hawiye clan and Habr Gidr subclan. Although Marine General Anthony Zinni found him to be "articulate and statesmanlike," he was also ruthless, in-stitutionalizing the looting of desperately needed relief supplies from the ports of Mogadishu and Kismayu. American officials noted the war-lord had almost a split personality, and Zinni admitted he "could never be sure which mood I would find when I arrived at his compound."[8]

On December 7 and 8, US envoy Robert Oakley met separately with Aideed and his main rival in Mogadishu, Ali Mahdi, to enlist their cooperation in ensuring the uncontested arrival of US forces. Each leader promised to keep his followers away from the proposed landing sites. Consequently, when the SEALs came ashore on December 8, they were greeted not by hostile fire from Somali gunmen, but instead by Dan Rather. Beneath a battery of bright lights that revealed the SEALs' position, washed out their night-vision goggles, and blinded them, Rather reported, "What you are seeing now, live through our night vi-sion cameras, is the arrival of the first Navy SEAL units on the beaches of Somalia."[9]

Ambassador Oakley and Unified Task Force (UNITAF) commander Marine Lieutenant General Robert Johnston worked to avoid direct confrontation with Aideed while consolidating UN relief operations. Aideed generally cooperated with US-sponsored initiatives to encourage local and regional reconciliation through a series of peace conferences. Oakley convinced Aideed and Ali Mahdi to place their heavier weap-ons and technicals at UN-controlled storage sites. Aideed even proposed that his SNA forces and UNITAF undertake joint military action against the National Islamic Front in Mogadishu and other regions.

Although he lacked the ability to challenge UNITAF militarily, his cooperation may also have been due to some genuine affection Aideed possessed for America, where many of his fourteen children resided. Consequently, US troops "were treated like apostles bringing salvation, and President Bush was the returning messiah when he ushered in 1993 with a visit on New Year's Day."[10] Conversely, when UN Secretary Gen-eral Boutros Boutros-Ghali arrived in Mogadishu on January 3, Aideed incited his followers to riot outside UN offices.[11]

Aideed's goodwill toward the Americans began to fray by late Feb-ruary, however, when his ally Omar Jess was ousted from Kismayu by a former Barre commander under the unsuspecting watch of Belgian and US-UNITAF troops. Aideed, who was already under pressure from his rural lieutenants threatened by UNITAF's empowerment of traditional local councils, blamed the foreign troops for Jess's ouster. Thus, shortly after dawn on February 24, Aideed's supporters staged protests at the US embassy compound. The crowds threw rocks and Molotov cocktails, burned tires, and established roadblocks at other locations within Aideed's sectors of southern Mogadishu. At the same time, many of Aideed's technicals disappeared from the UN storage sites, having been surreptitiously moved to undisclosed areas outside Mogadishu.[12]

While Aideed clearly still harbored deep reservations about the threat foreign intervention posed to his interests, he was not in a mood to challenge them. The February demonstrations were the last violent flare-up to occur during UNITAF's deployment, and Zinni confidently concluded that although Aideed "was a dangerous character who required constant attention ... I believed he could be handled and controlled."[13]

Operation Restore Hope was an indisputable success. The protection provided by UNITAF to humanitarian relief operations enabled Somalia to survive the worst of the famine. On March 26, 1993, the UN Security Council adopted Resolution 814, calling for the replacement of UNITAF with a UN peacekeeping force with two objectives: to provide for the "consolidation, expansion, and maintenance of a secure environment throughout Somalia" and for "the rehabilitation of the political institutions and economy of Somalia." This expanded mission, called UNOSOM II, began on May 4, and would be one of "peace enforcement," in which warlords could be compelled to disarm.

Although twenty-three nations contributed troops to UNOSOM II, its decision makers remained primarily American. The Clinton administration, which inherited the Somalia operation in January, insisted that retired Admiral Jonathan Howe be named to head UNOSOM II as the Secretary General's special representative. Howe had served as Deputy National Security Advisor at the end of President Bush's administration. He was a slender man who always wore a Columbia-blue UN baseball cap over his graying, close-cropped hair and a white short-sleeved shirt that revealed a pale complexion, which not even seven months in the Somali sun could color in the slightest. "Polite and articulate," Howe directed UNOSOM II to engage in aggressive action to force various Somali militias to disarm and seemed particularly focused on marginalizing Aideed.[14]

Aideed recognized that the UN's plan would weaken his military power and political base, and thus began a vicious, no-holds-barred propaganda campaign on Radio Mogadishu. "Radio Aideed," as it was known, accused the UN of "imperialist designs" and "colonization" and called upon Somalis to defend their sovereignty. Shootings and rock-throwing confrontations increased around Mogadishu, and UNOSOM II began taking casualties. A CIA assessment around this time deemed Aideed "a threat to peace," and UNOSOM II's commander, Turkish Lieutenant General Cervik Bir, had seen enough and decided to respond.[15]

On June 4, UNOSOM II notified Aideed's interior minister, Abdi Hassan Awale, that various SNA weapons sites were to be inspected the next morning. "This is unacceptable," Awale replied to the messenger. "This means war."[16]

The next day, after inspecting the arms cache co-located with Aideed's radio station, a company-sized Pakistani force was ambushed while returning to their battalion's camp at Mogadishu's sports stadium. Another Pakistani unit protecting a food-distribution center was slaughtered after one soldier, trying to calm a growing mob, was pulled into the crowd and dismembered. Twenty-four Pakistanis were killed in the attacks, and another fifty-six were wounded. Ten of the dead were castrated and their eyes gouged out, while others were disemboweled and skinned.[17]

When the Quick Reaction Force (QRF) from the Tenth Mountain Division advanced to cover the Pakistani retreat, they saw nearby ruins with fresh graffiti declaring: "WELCOME TO HELL."[18]

Although Aideed denied ordering the attack and asked for an inquiry, Radio Mogadishu declared the firefights a victory for the Somali people. "Brothers and sisters," Aideed proclaimed, "I congratulate you today on the way you have defended with your lives your homes, religion, and your country. . . . [T]hey [UNOSOM II] are directly responsible for the events that happened today."[19]

Within twenty-four hours the US Ambassador to the UN, Madeleine Albright, and the Pakistani envoy presented a draft resolution to the Security Council placing responsibility for the attacks on Aideed and demanding his arrest. The other council members balked at singling out Aideed, however, so the final version of Resolution 837 instead authorized UNOSOM II to take "all necessary measures against all those responsible for the armed attacks." Nevertheless, from June 6 on, the UN's mission in Somalia was dominated by the hunt for Aideed.[20]

Although the Clinton administration later attempted to distance it-self from this decision, there is little doubt the president and his advisors agreed with Howe that the June 5 ambush demanded a strong response lest UNOSOM II lose all credibility. Ambassador Albright called Aideed a "thug," and Howe declared the warlord "a menace to public safety" and a "killer." In fact, the US Special Envoy to Somalia, Robert Gosende, had first suggested arresting Aideed in May, *before* the Pakistani massacre.[21]

Yet as with the early debates on whether to snatch Noriega, the military and Defense Department were more cautious than their State Department counterparts. A US Central Command (CENTCOM) in-telligence assessment team traveled to Mogadishu in June 1993 and re-ported that the capture of Aideed was "viable and feasible." In private, however, team members described the task as "extremely ugly . . . with numerous potential points of failure."[22] CENTCOM commander Ma-rine General Joseph Hoar estimated the chances of catching Aideed to be one in four. Similarly, Powell noted that "finding [Aideed] in the war-rens of Mogadishu was a thousand-to-one shot. Worse, we were person-alizing the conflict and getting deeper and deeper into ancient Somali clan rivalries."[23]

Powell resisted Howe's request on June 9 for a team of fifty Delta Force operators to snatch Aideed, though Lieutenant General Bir and UNOSOM II's Deputy Commander, US Army Major General Thomas Montgomery, both supported the request. But now–Secretary of De-fense Les Aspin rejected the idea. Even if Aideed could be found, Aspin thought, an already skeptical public would consider Delta's deployment to be a dangerous escalation.

Howe therefore tried to catch Aideed with the forces already in place. At four AM on June 12, a "steady, ominous buzz" was audible in the sky over Mogadishu. A distant pop was quickly followed by a deep thud—*pa-Daa, pa-Daa, pa-Daa*—again and again. American AC-130 Spectre gunships fired ten rounds at Radio Mogadishu and some of the SNA's weapons cantonments. The attack ended almost as quickly as it began, an orange glow from fires illuminating the city as the buzz of the gunships faded away.

As dawn broke over Mogadishu, Somalis woke to find Radio Aideed destroyed.[24]

Over the next two nights, AC-130s attacked Aideed's headquarters and the workshop where the SNA's financier—Osman Ato—converted stolen cars into technicals. At Aideed's residence, American PSYOPS units used mobile speakers similar to those that taunted Noriega to blast Aideed's house with the sounds of helicopter rotors, tank engines, and machine-gun fire in an attempt to intimidate the warlord.[25]

At 1:30 AM on June 17, Spectre gunships began striking weapons storage sites and knocking out selected roadblocks in southern Mogadishu. The PSYOPS teams' speakers warned anyone around Aideed's compound to drop their weapons, raise their arms, and walk to the main road. "Evacuate immediately, these buildings will be destroyed in 10 minutes. . . . You have five minutes to evacuate immediately, *immediately. . . .*" This announcement was followed by warning shots from a 40 mm cannon. Approximately thirty to forty people left Aideed's compound before 105 mm guns fired at targets in the area of the warlord's house.

Aideed was finally being directly targeted.

At four AM, hundreds of Pakistani, Moroccan, Italian, and French troops lined up for the ground assault, supported by US liaison officers and American attack helicopters. A tight cordon was in place by 5:45 AM, and two Pakistani infantry battalions assaulted the housing complexes of Aideed, Ato, and Jess. The international forces conducted a house-to-house search of Aideed's compound. Although reporters later found the pink earplugs he used to block the PSYOPS broadcasts, the warlord had slipped away. Local legend held that Aideed escaped under the UN troops' noses on a donkey cart, wrapped up in a sheet like a corpse.[26] In the end, the operation managed only to damage Aideed's house at the cost of five UN troops killed and forty-six wounded.[27]

One senior Clinton administration official who participated in the president's decision to mount the attacks acknowledged that "we didn't plan to kill him, but the president knew that if something fell on Aideed and killed him, no tears would be shed."[28] The administration subsequently portrayed the operations as a success. "The military back of Aideed has been broken," President Clinton declared. Howe similarly proclaimed a "tremendous victory," and just hours after the raid issued a UN warrant for Aideed's arrest. Over General Montgomery's objections, Howe had UNOSOM II helicopters drop leaflets offering a $25,000 reward for the warlord's capture, the same amount offered for Geronimo 107 years earlier. About eighty thousand copies of the yellow poster were dumped on Mogadishu, "floating down like canary-yellow ticker tape," urging Somalis to bring Aideed "to the UN, Gate 8." Aideed's subclan, the Habr Gidr, were insulted not by the threat to their leader, but rather by the paltry sum being offered. Within hours they countered with a defiant $1 million reward for the capture of the man they derisively nicknamed "Animal" Howe.[29]

Over the next month, the First Battalion, Twenty-Second Infantry, conducted several raids aimed at capturing Aideed. Yet having been alerted that he was a wanted man, Aideed went underground. He reorganized his intelligence service, purging suspected double agents or using them to spread disinformation regarding his movements. He changed his location once or twice a night, masquerading as a sheikh, a woman, an old man, an Islamic mullah, or a hospital patient. He appeared on television, weary yet defiant, declaring: "I'm not concerned by the search being conducted now. They are trying to arrest me unjustly." As the tempo of the strategic manhunt intensified, Aideed and the SNA kept the military pressure up, increasing their sniping at UN forces. On July 2, Aideed's men attacked an Italian checkpoint, killing three and wounding twenty-four. Five days later, six Somali UN employees died in an ambush. And on July 9, the SNA lobbed the first mortar rounds into the US embassy compound that housed the American QRF.[30]

As a fugitive, Aideed was becoming everything the Bush administration feared from Noriega three and a half years earlier.

After several weeks of escalating tensions, UN forces were tipped off about a meeting on the morning of Monday, July 12. The Habr Gidr leadership—possibly including Aideed himself—had been meeting regularly at Abdi Hassan Awale's house, where they planned attacks on coalition troops. UNOSOM II planned to encircle the house with attack helicopters, fire TOW missiles and cannon rounds into it, and then raid the house to arrest survivors. Howe originally opposed the operation, questioning the need for the preparatory fire if the objective was surrounded. He was told that simply storming the house would subject UN forces to excessive risk, and that none of the units in Somalia was capable of policing a "sanitized" cordon. When Howe learned the operation had President Clinton's explicit approval, he put aside his doubts.[31]

At 10:15 AM, July 12, a Somali agent stepped outside the front door and walked across the compound toward the main gate as a prearranged signal to a communications helicopter circling above that everyone was present. Seconds later, an attack helicopter fired its first missile at the house. For six minutes, 16 TOWs and 2,020 rounds of 20 mm cannon struck the house at three points: the second-floor conference room, so that the roof would fall in on the militia leaders; the stairs leading from the conference hall to block any escape; and outside the main gate, so that the assault forces would have an unimpeded approach to the building. Immediately after the helicopter attack, air assault and ground forces from the First/Twenty-Second converged on "Abdi House." The fifty-three heliborne troops arrived in Black Hawks, landed on an adjoining street, and raided the compound while the ground element established blocking positions in the area. The targets were struck with such precision that only the slightest collateral damage showed on the walls of adjacent buildings, and from a tactical standpoint, the mission was a clear success.[32]

From a strategic standpoint, however, the operation backfired badly. Aideed later claimed he had been warned by his intelligence that a spy for the UN had infiltrated the group. Although Aideed had said he would be there, he postponed his arrival and thus was not present during the attack. Although Abdi and some of those present were close Aideed advisors with blood on their hands, that day the leadership had gathered to discuss how to respond to a peace initiative from Howe. Although the moderates' arguments were unlikely to prevail, there were many who disagreed with Aideed. Consequently, among the clan elders and intellectuals killed were the senior mullah of the Habr Gidr and his brother, who had met with Howe only three days before to explore paths for renewing dialogue.[33]

After the First/Twenty-Second withdrew, four Western journalists rushed to Abdi House to report on the attack, only to be beaten to death with blunt objects and stones, and then literally torn apart by an enraged mob. More damaging in the long term was the blowback created by the attack. The massacre badly undercut the UN forces' humanitarian image and bolstered Aideed's status. Any remaining moderates within the Habr Gidr and SNA now rallied behind him. The attack also caused many non–Habr Gidr to sympathize and even ally with the SNA. Any wavering Somali was now fully committed to opposing the UN.[34]

The SNA continued to escalate the violence. On August 8, four American MPs were killed when their Humvee was destroyed by a remotely detonated antitank mine similar to the improvised explosive devices (IEDs) that would become ubiquitous in Iraq and Afghanistan a decade later. Again, Howe asked for a strike team to snatch Aideed. Although Howe had stridently opposed a similar operation against Noriega during the Reagan administration, his obsession led one Aspin aide to observe that Howe had "adopted Aideed as his Great White Whale," and Howe's nickname in Washington became "Jonathan Ahab."[35] Again, General Hoar did not endorse Howe's request for Delta Force, and General Powell also expressed reservations about the aggressive pursuit of the SNA. Yet Howe's pleas finally won out when IED attacks on August 19 and 22 wounded ten more soldiers. Vacationing on Martha's Vineyard, President Clinton agreed to deploy what would become known as "Task Force Ranger."

*

ON AUGUST 27, SIX MASSIVE C-5B Galaxy jet transports arrived at Mogadishu airport. The men who stepped off these planes were the "best of the best, the very sharp tip of the spear" of American military might.[36] The Joint Special Operations Task Force (JSOTF) included 130 operators from Delta's Squadron C; Bravo Company, Third Battalion, Seventy-Fifth Ranger Regiment; and sixteen helicopters from First Battalion, 160th Special Operations Aviation Regiment (SOAR). These elite warriors would be led by the JSOC deployable headquarters element under General Garrison, "the picture of American military machismo" with a 9 mm Baretta strapped to his chest and a half-lit cigar perpetually jutting out of a corner of his mouth.[37]

With orders to capture Aideed, Garrison divided "Operation Gothic Serpent"—as the mission was designated—into three phases. The first phase was deploying the JSOTF and making it operational. Phase Two would concentrate exclusively on locating and capturing Aideed. If this objective appeared futile, then Garrison would initiate Phase Three, which would target the warlord's command structure and force Aideed into the open in order to control his forces.[38]

Garrison believed the key to capturing Aideed was "current actionable intelligence" provided by human intelligence (HUMINT). Yet when he checked the local intelligence trail upon arrival, there were no leads. The Intelligence Support Activity (Delta's special intelligence cell) and the CIA had lost track of the warlord, who had not been seen since July. Moreover, within days of Task Force Ranger's arrival, the top Somali CIA informant was mortally wounded in a game of Russian roulette. The original plan had called for the spy—a minor warlord loosely affiliated with Aideed—to present the SNA chief with an elegant hand-carved cane with a homing beacon embedded in the head. The plan seemed foolproof, until Lieutenant Colonel Danny McKnight—commander of the Third/Seventy-Fifth Ranger battalion and Task Force Ranger's intelligence chief—burst into Garrison's headquarters at the Mogadishu airport on their first day and exclaimed: "Main source shot in the head. He's not dead yet, but we're fucked!"

Garrison responded philosophically, quoting the opening lines of Ulysses S. Grant's memoir: "Man proposes and God disposes."[39]

✳

JUST AS PHASE TWO WAS SET to begin, at ten PM on August 29 the ground at the airport shook with a dull thud. A Somali mortar attack consisting of a half-dozen rounds wounded five Task Force soldiers. Garrison vowed "to kick somebody's ass" and, chewing his cigar, walked into the Joint Operations Center (JOC). "McKnight, tell me where the last place was we saw this sombitch."[40]

McKnight responded that it was at a house near the center of the city. "That's our target," Garrison said. "I don't care if Aideed's there or not.... [G]et the men ready."[41]

A little over an hour later, Garrison stood before the assembled task force in front of the JOC. Arms crossed, cigar jutting from his mouth, he spoke with a distinctive Texas twang: "Now, some of you have never been mortared before," he said casually. "I just wanted to tell you that if one of them piddly-ass mortars lands in your pocket, it's probably going to hurt. If it doesn't land in your pocket, you don't have to worry about piddly-ass mortars."

The tension broken, Garrison declared: "Now we're gonna go in there tonight and let 'em know we're here. And I have confidence in every one of you. So let's get it on and go do it."[42]

At three AM a dozen blacked-out helicopters rose from the tarmac, formed up, and then clattered over to the target, the nearby Lig Ligato house off Via Lenin. The birds pulled up one by one, hovering in loose formation above and around the sleeping compound before commandos swathed in black fast-roped down to the ground. While Ranger security teams sealed off the objective, Delta operators stormed the house and plasticuffed all eight occupants. They did not find Aideed, as hoped, but discovered cash, khat, and evidence of a black-market operation. It was a textbook lightning strike.

When the Task Force returned from the mission, before they had even finished shedding their gear, they were astonished to see themselves on CNN in footage shot from afar with an infrared camera. It turned out the house was a part of the UN Development Program, and their plasticuffed prisoners were members of the UN mission and their Somali assistants. Subsequent newspaper reports portrayed the Task Force as Keystone Cops. General Powell was so angry that "I had to screw myself off the ceiling," and Garrison reportedly received a brutal tongue-lashing from General Hoar.[43]

*

ON SEPTEMBER 14, GENERAL GARRISON sent his intelligence officer to the Italian embassy for consultations with his Italian counterpart. Five Rangers sent along as an escort swore they saw Aideed speeding away from the embassy in an SUV. A US reconnaissance helicopter followed the vehicle, and within twenty-two minutes Delta was launched. The suspect and thirty-eight others were arrested despite having gone to a house in Ali Mahdi–controlled territory in north Mogadishu. The assault force had stormed what turned out to be the residence of Somali General Ahmed Jilao, who despite possessing a balding, gray pate similar to Aideed's, was an ally of the UN and the man being groomed to lead the projected Somali police.

Given the paucity of intelligence on Aideed, Garrison initiated Phase Three and Task Force Ranger concentrated on dismantling Aideed's network by capturing his key lieutenants, who were designated "Tier One" personalities.

At 8:15 AM on September 18, Tier One personality Osman Ato was seen at a garage in Mogadishu. Yet by the time Task Force Ranger fast-roped onto the target at 8:46 AM, Ato was gone. Three days later, he was in a moving car being tracked by US sensors and pursued by a Black Hawk carrying a Delta team and an AH-6 "Little Bird" with a special operations sniper on board. The sniper leaned out of the Little Bird and disabled the car by firing three shots through the engine block. The Delta operators then landed and snatched Ato, the highest SNA target captured to date.[44]

Despite this success, Task Force Ranger's operations in September produced decidedly mixed results. Two other raids produced dry holes, and between thirty-five and forty other operations reached various degrees of planning before being aborted. For three nights between September 30 and October 2, the Task Force geared up to raid locations where Aideed was either present or expected. Every time, they failed to nail the intelligence down.[45]

Aideed acquired the code name Elvis for the frequency of his unsubstantiated sightings.

Aideed's forces remained active despite the Task Force raids. On September 5, SNA forces killed seven Nigerian soldiers and captured a prisoner in attacks on two separate locations. On September 26, a 101st Air Assault helicopter—"Cougar 53"—was shot down by a rocket-propelled grenade (RPG). Three Americans were killed, and the two injured pilots were rescued by a patrol of United Arab Emirates troops. The dead Americans were mutilated by a Somali mob, and the body of one decapitated corpse was stuffed in a food sack labeled "Gift from the USA." While on the run, Aideed managed to find the time to edit a biography of himself titled *The Lion of Somalia*. Ato, prior to his capture, warned that if the UN thought Aideed's clan support was splintering, "they are dreaming. He is far stronger now than when they started bombing the area."[46]

The only close call Aideed recalled came one night when a helicopter hovered above the house next to where he was staying for twenty minutes. It hovered so closely that Aideed's gunmen loaded an RPG and asked for permission to fire on it. "No, no, if we shoot they will have a clue where we are," Aideed replied.[47]

Aideed apparently felt enough pressure, however, to resort to the preferred tactic of many a besieged strongman in the last decade of the twentieth century: he contacted Jimmy Carter. On September 13, Carter informed President Clinton he had received a letter from Aideed in which the warlord portrayed himself and the SNA as under attack in an unjust war. Aideed appealed to Carter to "prevent an impending disaster" and restated his willingness to accept the findings of an independent commission regarding responsibility for the June 5 attack. Carter subsequently urged an end to the strategic manhunt and recommended renewed efforts to find a political solution.[48]

"After Carter's visit," a Clinton aide recalled, "the hard line began to weaken." Task Force Ranger's inability to immediately capture Aideed had led the Clinton administration to begin talking of a "two-track" solution. Under the new approach, the United States would launch an initiative aimed at a political settlement that could include Aideed. Yet as National Security Advisor Tony Lake noted: "The policy was never to stop trying to get Aideed" but rather "to move to more diplomatic efforts but snatch Aideed on the side." Consequently, there was no change in orders for General Garrison and Task Force Ranger in Mogadishu.[49]

Six days after the decision for a two-track policy, Aideed's top political advisor, Omar Salad, was the featured speaker at the weekly Habr Gidr rally on Via Lenin on October 3. When the rally broke up, his white Toyota Land Cruiser was tracked by Task Force air assets as it drove north toward the Bakara Market. Salad was observed entering a house one block north of the Olympic Hotel. Later, at 1:30 PM, the CIA station chief brought a Somali to the JOC. The Somali's name had appeared on a list of wanted men Task Force Ranger had published after capturing Ato. "My name shouldn't have been on that list," the Somali complained, and he offered to reveal the location of a secret meeting among Salad, Abdi Awale, and many of Aideed's lieutenants if his name was removed. Although nobody had actually seen him, the presence of so many SNA officials raised hopes that Aideed might attend as well.[50]

Bakara Market lay in the heart of an area Task Force Ranger called "the Black Sea," a labyrinth of narrow alleys and walkways that was an SNA stronghold. The Olympic Hotel served as a virtual headquarters for the Habr Gidr militia, and Garrison had once told his officers: "I will not send you in [the Bakara area] unless it is a lucrative target. I know if I send you guys in we'll get in a gunfight."[51] When informed of the Task Force's mission just minutes before it was launched, an astonished General Montgomery called Garrison. "Bill," Montgomery said, "that's really Indian country. That's a bad place."[52] Although US policy was to not even drive *through* Bakara Market, the chance of netting two Tier One targets was too good to resist.

Shortly after three PM the CIA's source marked the target for US overhead sensors by stopping his car outside and raising the hood. The squared-off, three-story building with whitewashed cinder-block walls and windows without glass that the source identified was the same house US surveillance had watched Omar Salad enter earlier in the day. With their tip confirmed, Task Force Ranger went from briefing to mission launch in less than an hour. At 3:32 PM, fourteen helicopters from the 160th SOAR took off from Mogadishu Airport. Three minutes later, a ground convoy of three five-ton trucks and nine Humvees moved out. In all, the mission on October 3 involved 160 men, 19 aircraft, and 12 vehicles.

At 3:40 PM, two Little Birds gave a final visual reconnaissance of the target building. They were immediately followed by four MH-6s, each carrying a four-man Delta team perched on the benches attached to each side of the helicopters. The Task Force swept in from the north, the beating blades of the rotors stirring up great clouds of orange dust. As the MH-6s settled on the street, the operators leapt from the skids and dashed into the building, while Rangers fast-roped from four Black Hawks to establish their security perimeter and blocking positions around the objective. The Delta operators, clad in black body armor, swept through the rooms, bellowing orders, and corralling the stunned Somalis together. Within twenty minutes they had secured twenty-four prisoners—including Salad and Awale—marching them out with their hands flex-cuffed behind their backs.

Other than a Ranger who had been critically injured from a fall while fast-roping, the mission was going like clockwork. The raiders radioed "Laurie," the brevity code for success, back to the JOC. At four PM the ground convoy commanded by Lieutenant Colonel McKnight—a veteran of the Ranger's jump into Rio Hato during the Noriega manhunt—headed toward the secured objective. As the vehicles arrived at the target building, both Delta and the Rangers pulling security on the perimeter were beginning to draw increasingly heavy fire. The passing bullets "made a loud snap, like cracking a stick of dry hickory." The volume of fire built steadily as thousands of people grabbed weapons and poured into the streets. Garrison and the officers watching the mission from the JOC could see them racing from all directions toward the Bakara Market, as if the raiders "had poked a stick into a hornet's nest."[53]

The Somalis began firing RPGs, and the Delta ground commander called the command-and-control helicopter overhead. "Hey, boss, I think we've got the guys you sent us in for," he told Lieutenant Colonel Gary Harrell, the C Squadron commander. "We're ready to get out of Dodge."[54]

But almost immediately, another radio call grabbed the attention of those listening.

*

CHIEF WARRANT OFFICER (CWO) CLIFF WOLCOTT had earned the nickname "Elvis" from his buddies in the 160th for both his unflappable cool and his uncanny impression of the singer. On January 3, 1990, when Manuel Noriega surrendered, it was Wolcott who piloted the Black Hawk carrying the deposed strongman from the papal nunciature to Howard Air Force Base.[55] On October 3, 1993, after disgorging his chalk of Rangers at 3:45 PM, his Black Hawk, Super Six One, provided fire support to the Rangers on the perimeter using its sniper team to disperse the growing crowd. At 4:15 PM, however, his voice broke through the radio clutter, calmly saying: "Six-One is going down." Wolcott's Black Hawk had been hit by an RPG-7 grenade, and dropped like a stone three hundred yards east of the target building. The two crew chiefs and three Delta snipers survived, albeit badly injured, but the two pilots were killed on impact.[56]

The Somalis had gotten Task Force Ranger's "Elvis" before the Americans could get theirs.

✳

GENERAL GARRISON HAD ANTICIPATED the loss of a helicopter, and with his planners had drafted three contingency plans:

- Insert fifteen soldiers from a combat-search-and-rescue (CSAR) Black Hawk circling nearby.
- Alert the Tenth Mountain's QRF.
- Move the main body of Task Force Ranger from the target building to the crash site to provide more firepower.

Garrison executed all three contingencies almost simultaneously.[57]

McKnight ordered the raiders to split up, and Delta operators and two chalks of Rangers dashed to the crash site through the narrow streets and alleyways against a growing barrage of gunfire emanating from seemingly every doorway, alley, and window. They reached Super Six One at 4:28 PM, just moments ahead of the onrushing mob of armed Somalis, and established a perimeter round the wreckage. At the same time, the lone CSAR helicopter—"Super 68"—moved over the downed Black Hawk to insert its medics and Ranger security team. As the last two men of the CSAR team fast-roped down, Super 68 was hit by an RPG. The helicopter was badly damaged, but managed to limp back to base.[58]

Garrison directed McKnight to move the convoy—with the prisoners and initial wave of wounded aboard the trucks—to reinforce the perimeter around Super Six One. As the trucks bounded east, every building spat tracers and RPGs. McKnight's lead Humvee—disoriented by dust, smoke, and roadblocks—quickly got lost in Mogadishu's maze of constricted, unfamiliar streets. As "scattered small arms fire . . . became a metal storm," the convoy went in circles, twice passing near the crash site but unable to link up with the detachment defending it. Of the sixty-five men who started from the original objective an hour earlier, nearly half—including McKnight—were wounded. There were now more casualties in the convoy than there were at the crash site. When the procession of shot-up vehicles passed the Olympic Hotel a second time at 5:15 PM, Garrison ordered McKnight to get his precious cargo of prisoners back to the headquarters at the airport. If the SNA leaders were not evacuated, the raid would certainly be a failure. Even then, the convoy had to fight its way back to the airport, suffering still more casualties before it made it back to base.[59]

✳

WHILE MCKNIGHT WAS ENDURING the abattoir, a second Black Hawk—Super 64—took an RPG through its tail and crashed about two miles south of the target building. As there was no preexisting plan to react to a second downed aircraft, Garrison and his staff tried several desperate courses of action, each unsuccessful. First, at about 5:03 PM, an improvised QRF of twenty-seven Rangers was dispatched from the airport to the second crash site. But this small force was quickly ambushed and pinned down at the K-4 traffic circle. A half hour later, Charlie Company from the Tenth Mountain's QRF left the airfield, but within ten minutes was ambushed. Fighting for their lives, one hundred US soldiers fired nearly *sixty thousand* rounds of ammunition and hundreds of grenades in thirty minutes before being forced to retreat.[60]

Another Black Hawk, Super 62, made a low pass over Super 64 and could see that pilot Chief Warrant Officer Mike Durant, his copilot, and two crew chiefs had survived the crash, but were badly injured. They also saw what seemed to be thousands of armed, angry Somalis massing and moving toward the crash site. Knowing the horrific fate of those who fell into the clutches of Somali mobs, two Delta snipers on board Super 62 volunteered to try to save Super 64's survivors. Lieutenant Colonel Harrell rejected Master Sergeant Gary Gordon and Sergeant First Class

Randall Shugart's request twice, but after learning of the QRF ambushes, approved their third request for insertion.[61]

Super 62 dropped the snipers off one hundred meters from the crash site in a deserted, garbage-strewn alley. When word was passed to the operators that it was time to jump, Gordon grinned and—despite the near hopelessness of their task—gave an excited thumbs-up. As they moved toward Super 64 and saw the hundreds of Somalis surging toward the wreckage, they must have known they would not survive. Super 62 hovered above the wreckage and pointed down—using its rotors to create a wind to blast back the mob—long enough for Gordon and Shugart to reach the downed bird. An RPG slammed through 62's cockpit, knocking the copilot unconscious and ripping the leg off the door gunner. Super 62's copilot, Chief Warrant Officer Michael Goffena, could not make it back to the airfield but managed a crash landing in the secure area near Mogadishu's port.[62]

At the crash site, the operators freed the crew from Super 64's wreckage. For a few minutes they held their own, methodically firing round after round in aimed fire at the onrushing crowd. But with the helicopters gone and their ammunition running low, the tide of Somalis pressed closer. Durant heard Gordon cry out as he was fatally wounded on the other side of the wreckage. Shugart brought the immobilized pilot's rifle and handed the weapon to Durant.

"Good luck," he said, and then returned to battle the Somalis who were now within thirty feet. Shugart defended the crash site with his pistol until he too went down and Super 64 was overrun. Gordon and Shugart's heroism bought enough time for SNA leaders to gain control of the mob before it could finish off Durant. Durant was taken prisoner, while laughing Somalis desecrated the bodies of the other Americans. For their sacrifice, Gordon and Shugart were awarded the first Medals of Honor since the Vietnam War.

✳

THE ROUGHLY NINETY SOLDIERS defending Super 61 took shelter in four houses near the downed helicopter. The troops termed the three city blocks around the wreckage "The Alamo," a fitting name given their dire situation. More armed Somalis were arriving and ammunition was running dangerously low. AK-47 bullets flew overhead with a loud pop, punctuated by the ominous *swoosh* of RPGs exploding every five or ten minutes. Even if they had been willing to abandon the bodies trapped in the helicopter, seven of every ten soldiers had been wounded—many unable to walk—thereby making it impossible for the raiders to fight their way out on foot. Consequently, the Rangers and Delta operators hunkered down for the night.

Even though it risked making a bad situation worse, at about seven PM General Garrison ordered a helicopter to resupply the besieged troops. As soon as the Black Hawk roared in and began hovering above the crash site, Somali gunfire and RPGs erupted from every direction. Two Delta operators kicked out water, ammunition, and IV bags, as the pilots held steady until the resupply was complete. Then, shot full of holes and leaking fluid, the helicopter returned to base, unable to fly again.[63] The Little Birds, which were capable of firing thousands of rounds per minute, made running and diving fire attacks against Somali groups throughout the night, probably saving the besieged Americans from being overrun.

✳

ANOTHER RELIEF FORCE WAS ORGANIZED, consisting of Pakistani tanks, Malaysian armored personnel carriers, and various US forces in a convoy of nearly one hundred vehicles that stretched almost two miles long. At 11:15 PM the convoy departed from the port into the pitch-black city and fought its way to the surrounded Rangers and Delta operators, who could hear the rumble of its engines and thunderclap of its guns from miles away, steadily edging closer. At 1:55 AM, October 4, the relief convoy finally reached Task Force Ranger's perimeter. The dash through the Somali gauntlet resulted in three Tenth Mountain soldiers killed and more than thirty wounded.[64]

The combined force waited almost three hours while Wolcott's body was extracted from Super 61. Seeing the preparations for withdrawal, the Somalis increased their fire and committed their last reserves. Finally, the combined force was able to depart the crash site at 5:37 AM. Some of the corpses were placed atop the Malaysian armored personnel carriers (APCs), a morbid spectacle given that "some bodies were missing pieces and others did not resemble a cadaver."[65] Because there were so many nonambulatory wounded, there was not enough room in the vehicles for all the soldiers. The nervous Malaysian drivers took off, leaving behind the Rangers and Delta operators who had been fighting for fourteen hours straight, and forcing them to run through the same streets they had already fought through in what became known in Ranger lore as "the Mogadishu Mile." Eventually they overtook and stopped a Pakistani M-113. By 6:20 AM all personnel were loaded, and movement continued until they reached the safety of the Pakistani perimeter at the stadium.

✳

OVERALL, IT WAS AN IMPRESSIVE FEAT. Task Force Ranger had raided into the heart of the adversary's stronghold in broad daylight and seized twenty-four prisoners, including the two Tier One leaders they were after. The cost had been steep: eighteen Americans dead, one missing, and eighty-four wounded. But the Somalis had clearly fared worse, suffering an estimated 500 to 1,000 fatalities. In the mind of at least one Delta operator, "they'd just fought one of the most one-sided battles in American history."[66]

Aideed later said he had been just to the east of the target house at the time of the raid. Within twenty minutes the SNA had sealed the roads and the warlord was moved to a safer location. Yet even if he personally escaped harm, the "Battle of Mogadishu" had cost the warlord dearly. Many families aligned with him had suffered casualties, and local spies reported some of Aideed's strongest clan allies had fled Mogadishu fearing the seemingly inevitable American retribution. Others were sending peace feelers, offering to dump Aideed to avoid further bloodshed. The SNA's arsenal of RPGs was depleted, and both General Garrison and Admiral Howe believed Aideed had been struck a mortal blow. Consequently, they pressed their US and UN superiors to take the initiative and finish the job.[67]

The perception in Washington, however, was shaped by the vivid television images of dead and naked bodies of US soldiers being dragged through the streets of Mogadishu. President Clinton was in a hotel room in San Francisco when he saw the horrifying pictures. Angered, he asked his staff, "How could this happen?" as if the raid were not the direct result of his policy decisions. Many in Congress demanded an immediate withdrawal from Somalia, and the outrage over US casualties caused the White House to throw in the towel. On October 6, Clinton convened an emergency policy review with his key national security advisors and senior military staff. The next day, he announced a new policy in which the United States would increase its military presence in Somalia by over five thousand troops until March 31, when all US troops would be withdrawn. Clinton personally ordered General Hoar to halt any further action by US forces against Aideed.

Aideed was still in hiding when Ambassador Oakley returned to Mogadishu on October 8 as President Clinton's new envoy. It took several days to arrange a meeting with the Habr Gidr leadership, but when they did, Aideed made sure the American delegation was greeted by cheering crowds. Aideed smiled broadly and hugged the Americans as they entered his compound. Recalling the dialogue that existed under UNITAF, Oakley assured the SNA of President Clinton's decision "to depersonalize Somalia policy." Although the Somalis were skeptical, Oakley informed the Habr Gidr leaders that US military operations against Aideed had ended and that Task Force Ranger was redeploying. Shortly thereafter Aideed emerged from hiding long enough to make a brief appearance on CNN and announce the release of Mike Durant.[68]

On November 16 the UN Security Council adopted Resolution 885, which suspended the call for Aideed's arrest and established an international commission to investigate the June 5 attacks. Aideed seemed content to wait for the Americans to leave, and he refrained from any large-scale violence. Simultaneously, the White House began referring to him as "a clan leader with a substantial constituency in Somalia."[69] The ultimate symbol of Aideed's rehabilitation was his flight to peace talks in Ethiopia in early December. He refused to travel on a UN plane, but accepted Oakley's offer to use an American transport. On December 2 Marines escorted the warlord to the plane in full view of US troops at the airport. The spectacle caused "anger and disappointment throughout the ranks," and the morale of US forces plummeted.[70] By March 25, 1994, all US forces had withdrawn from Somalia. In General Montgomery's opinion, "We wound up . . . giving a victory to Aideed that Aideed did not win on the third day of October."[71]

With the United States appearing to retreat under fire, most of the UNOSOM II contingents followed suit. When the last UN forces left Somalia in March 1995, the country quickly reverted to anarchy. The world soon forgot about Somalia except for the rare newspaper headline, such as the one that graced the front page of the New York Times in 2003, nearly a decade after the failed manhunt: "Somalia: Fights Break Out at Peace Talks."

✳

THE STRATEGIC MANHUNT for Mohammed Farah Aideed appears to be
a rare case where the US forces' failure to catch their quarry positively
correlates to a failure to achieve our broader strategic objectives. Yet it is
unclear whether killing or capturing Aideed would have made a difference. Although General Montgomery testified before the Senate Armed
Services Committee in May 1994 that Aideed was the "center of gravity"
for anti-UN attacks and that if Aideed were eliminated, "the consensus
opinion was that the SNA militia would have a hard time continuing
to conduct operations." Conversely, John Drysdale, the British Somalia
expert who advised Howe, warned: "Aideed can't stay in power for one
day without grass-roots support. Aideed is not one man, he is Aideed
because of his support, his following." Or as an SNA official noted at the
time of the manhunt: "What's the use of killing Aideed? Everybody is
Aideed. If he goes tomorrow you will have a million Aideeds around."[72]
Indeed, in the years after Aideed's death, little in the power dynamics in
Mogadishu or Somalia changed.

More significant than the failed manhunt's impact on Somalia,
perhaps, was the effect it had on US foreign policy for the remainder
of the Clinton administration. A week after "The Battle of Mogadishu,"
the USS *Harlan County* withdrew from the Haitian harbor of Port-
au-Prince due to an orchestrated riot by fewer than two hundred hostile, lightly armed demonstrators. Some protesting at the docks held
up signs proclaiming Haiti would be another Somalia for the United
States. The Clinton administration later declined to intervene to prevent repeated atrocities in Bosnia and genocide in Rwanda due to its
experience with the Aideed manhunt. As will be seen in the next chapter, the fear of another special operations failure would have far more
tragic repercussions.

Kofi Annan, then the UN undersecretary-general for peacekeeping,
noted the lesson of Somalia was that "one only has to kill a few Americans and the United States leaves."[73] Other observers, more sinister in
their intent, similarly noted:

> There is an important observation that we must not ignore, which is that
> the Americans were not defeated militarily in Somalia. Effective human and
> economic losses were not inflicted on them. All that happened was that the

Somali battle revealed many of their psychological, political, and perhaps military weakness.

The Somali experience confirmed the spurious nature of American power and that it has not recovered from the Vietnam complex. It fears getting bogged down in a real war that would reveal its psychological collapse at the level of personnel and leadership. Since Vietnam America has been seeking easy battles that are completely guaranteed.

This was the assessment of the lessons learned from Somalia by an al-Qaeda correspondent, discovered eight years later among documents captured in Afghanistan.

✳

IN JUNE 1995 AIDEED DECLARED himself president of Somalia. Like Pancho Villa and Augusto Sandino before him, however, Aideed's domestic rivals would eventually succeed where US forces failed. On July 24, 1996, he was fatally wounded in a shootout with a rival warlord. He died on August 1, which coincidentally was the same day William Garrison retired from active duty.

With Aideed's passing, leadership of the Habr Gidr and the SNA passed to his third son, thirty-three-year old Hussein Farah Aideed. Hussein returned to Somalia from his home in Orange County, California, where he had lived since 1980 and worked as a civil engineer. In addition to leaving behind Chinese food and his daily *Wall Street Journal,* Hussein Aideed was forced to say good-bye to another American institution with which he had forged strong ties: the United States Marines Corps. He had enlisted in the Marines in 1987, and actually served as an activated reservist in Somalia in January 1993. Although he never participated in the strategic manhunt against his father, he returned to reserve duty after his father was placed squarely in America's crosshairs.

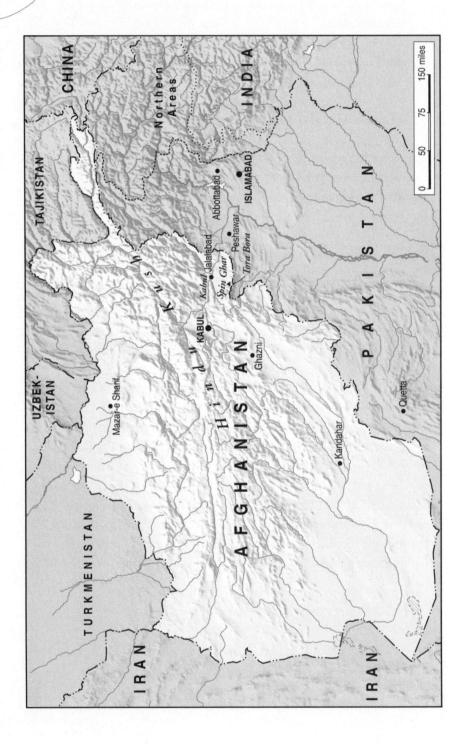

CHAPTER SIX

THE HUNT FOR OSAMA
BIN LADEN, PART I

On August 20, 1998, two old classmates from the Combined and General Staff College reunited for dinner in Islamabad, Pakistan. Both officers had come a long way since graduating from Fort Leavenworth: the guest, Air Force General Joseph Ralston, was now Vice-Chairman of the Joint Chiefs of Staff, the second-highest-ranking officer in the US military. His host, General Jehangir Karamat, had risen to become the Pakistani Army's Chief of Staff. They reminisced over a dinner of chicken tikka, and as the meal was winding down, General Ralston looked at his watch. At approximately 9:50 PM, as he prepared to leave, Ralston said, "By the way, General Karamat, at this moment missiles are coming over your airspace." He assured his host that they were US cruise missiles en route to targets in Afghanistan rather than an Indian attack against Pakistan's nuclear sites. Karamat was visibly unhappy, but understood Ralston's need for discretion.

The two classmates shook hands. Ralston thanked Karamat for his hospitality and departed for the Islamabad airport.[1]

Thus began the first strike in the longest strategic manhunt in US history—the hunt for Osama bin Laden.

*

PRIOR TO THE FIRST World Trade Center bombing in February 1993, Osama bin Laden was virtually unknown to US officials. It was not until the FBI found his telephone number amid the calls made by Ramzi Yousef and his cell from their New York safe houses that the Saudi appeared on America's radar screen. A CIA paper circulated on April 2, 1993, described bin Laden as an "independent actor [who] sometimes works with other individuals or governments" to promote "militant Islamic causes."[2] In the summer of 1993, the CIA began monitoring bin Laden and building a file on his activities. "Every time we turned over a rock, there would be some sort of connection to bin Laden," said one CIA official. "The conventional wisdom at the time was that he was some sort of financier and little else, a kind of Gucci terrorist. The more we dug, the more it became clear that there was more there."[3] Consequently, in January 1996, the CIA's Counterterrorist Center (CTC) formed a separate unit devoted to tracking him, the first of its kind devoted to a single individual. In a rare public statement, the CIA declared bin Laden to be "one of the most significant financial sponsors of Islamic extremist activities in the world."[4]

In May 1996, a few months after the formation of the task force dedicated to tracking the Saudi—"Alec Station"—bin Laden relocated to Afghanistan, where under the protection of the Taliban he launched his holy war against the United States. In a July 1996 interview with a British journalist, he said the world had reached "the beginning of war between Muslims and the United States."[5] He codified this belief on August 23 in a proclamation titled "The Declaration of Jihad on the Americans Occupying the Country of the Two Sacred Places," which stated: "Terrorizing you, while you are carrying arms in our land, is a legitimate right and a moral obligation." This declaration of war was followed by a series of increasingly bellicose interviews with CNN, ABC News, and Al Jazeera.

Despite these radical pronouncements, the Clinton administration was slow to appreciate the magnitude of the threat bin Laden posed. A 1997 National Intelligence Estimate on terrorism only briefly mentioned the Saudi. In the autumn of that same year, the State Department announced its first list of officially designated Foreign Terrorist Organizations, a list that did not include bin Laden and al-Qaeda despite knowledge of the organization's involvement in attacks against Americans in Yemen, Somalia, and Saudi Arabia. Two National Security Council (NSC) staffers later acknowledged there was little sense of urgency about bin Laden among counterterror planners in the White House until December 1997.[6]

Conversely, the analysts in Alec Station recognized that bin Laden was more than just a financier, and were actively planning for offensive operations against him. The CTC had on its payroll a group of well-organized Afghan tribal elements who could survey or harass bin Laden, and by the fall of 1997 had developed a plan for the tracking teams to capture bin Laden and hand him over for trial either in the United States or in an Arab country.[7] By early 1998 the snatch operation had been developed to the point where the tribal team was told they could launch an operation to kidnap bin Laden whenever the opportunity arose. The Afghans reported one unsuccessful ambush against bin Laden's convoy on a road near Kandahar, claiming that although the primary target escaped, several Arabs escorting him were killed. The CIA had no way to corroborate whether this assault had been a near miss or sheer fantasy.[8]

Recognizing the difficulty of capturing bin Laden while he was moving, the CTC began to focus on a raid on Tarnak Farms, bin Laden's compound on the outskirts of Kandahar comprising about eighty concrete or mud-brick buildings surrounded by a ten-foot wall. CIA officers were able to map the entire site from satellite photos, identifying the houses belonging to bin Laden's wives and the one where he was most likely to sleep. The plan was meticulously detailed. One team of Afghans would enter the compound through a drainage ditch that ran under the fence while another team would sneak through the front gate, using silenced pistols to eliminate the guards. When they found bin Laden, they would hold him in a provisioned cave thirty miles away until the Americans could take custody.[9] From May 20 to 24 the CIA ran a successful final rehearsal of the operation. The CTC planned to brief Cabinet-level principals and their deputies the following week. June 23 would be D-Day for the raid, with bin Laden in American custody by July 23.

Although a Principals Committee meeting to approve the operation was scheduled for May 30, it never took place. The White House Counterterrorism Strategy Group, led by Richard Clarke, perceived the Afghan tribals as a bunch of aging anti-Soviet mujahideen well past their prime and milking the CIA for easy money while avoiding any real operations on the ground. Moreover, the CIA's senior management did not believe the plan would succeed. Thus, on May 29, CTC Chief Jeff O'Connell informed the bin Laden unit that Cabinet-level officials thought the risk of civilian casualties was too high, and the decision had been made to abort the operation.[10]

The working-level CIA officers were disappointed, believing the raid to be the "best plan we are going to come up with to capture [bin Laden] while he is in Afghanistan and bring him to justice." The tribals' reported readiness to act was subsequently diminished. As the 9/11 Commission later noted, "No capture plan before 9/11 ever again attained the same level of detail and preparation."[11]

✳

WHILE THE CLINTON ADMINISTRATION debated a course of action, bin Laden escalated his holy war. On February 22, 1998, bin Laden announced the formation of the International Islamic Front for Jihad Against Jews and Crusaders. The new coalition's fatwa declared that "to kill the Americans and their allies—civilians and military—is the individual duty for every Muslim who can do it in any country in which it is possible."[12]

Six months later, on August 7, President Bill Clinton was awakened at 5:35 AM by a phone call from his National Security Advisor, Sandy Berger, who informed him of the near-simultaneous bombings of the American embassies in Nairobi, Kenya, and Dar es Salaam, Tanzania. The attack in Nairobi killed 12 Americans and 201 others, almost all Kenyan staff at the embassy. The death toll would have been even worse but for the courageous actions of the security guards who denied the terrorists access to the embassy's garage. As it was, nearly five thousand Kenyans were injured as the blast demolished the secretarial college next to the embassy. Four minutes later, a second bomb exploded outside the embassy in Dar es Salaam, killing eleven people and injuring eighty-five. The blast was so powerful that the body of the suicide bomber driving the van was split in half, his torso still clutching the steering wheel in both hands as it hit the embassy building.[13]

The determination was made quickly that al-Qaeda was behind the attacks. On Friday, August 14, a week after the bombings, CIA Director George Tenet delivered to the NSC the agency's formal judgment that bin Laden was responsible. Tenet began his presentation of the CIA and FBI's investigation by stating: "This one is a slam dunk, Mr. President," a phrase he would infamously repeat years later to a different president.[14] Although the embassy attacks, clearly constituted an act of war against sovereign US territory, there was no serious discussion of a US-led military campaign in Afghanistan.

Within days of the attacks the CIA received a report that senior leaders of terrorist groups linked to bin Laden had been summoned to a meeting on August 20 at the Zawhar Kili camp complex in eastern Afghanistan. The intelligence indicated that bin Laden himself would be present. Tenet called this information "a godsend. . . . We were accustomed to getting intelligence about where bin Laden *had been.* This was a rarity: intelligence predicting where he was *going to be.*"[15] The principals quickly reached a consensus on attacking the gathering, with the objective of killing bin Laden.

✳

ON THE NIGHT OF AUGUST 20, five Navy destroyers lined up in the Arabian Sea and began spinning Tomahawk cruise missiles in their launch tubes. At about ten PM local time, seventy-five missiles, each costing about $750,000, slammed into Zawhar Kili's rock gorges. The secret attack, code-named Operation Infinite Reach, killed at least twenty-one Pakistani jihadist volunteers and wounded dozens more.[16]

Half a world away, on Martha's Vineyard, a solemn Bill Clinton announced the military strikes to the media assembled there. Clinton quickly flew back to the White House, where he addressed the nation from the Oval Office. "Our target was terror," Clinton explained,

> our mission was clear—to strike at the network of radical groups affiliated with and funded by Osama bin Laden. . . . They have made the United States their adversary precisely because of what we stand for and what we stand against. . . . And so this morning, based on the unanimous recommendation of my national security team, I ordered our armed forces to take action to counter an imminent threat from the bin Laden network.

Ironically, many of these same themes—"war on a noun," the idea that al-Qaeda hated us for our values, and the doctrine of preemption—would be ridiculed when adopted by President Bush three years later.

The next day a radio broadcast emanated from somewhere in Afghanistan. "By the grace of Allah," bin Laden's voice announced, "I am alive!"[17] Although al-Qaeda's camps suffered extensive damage, bin Laden himself was unscathed. Worse, the attacks had the unintended consequence of transforming the Saudi from a marginal figure into a global celebrity. He had been targeted by history's most powerful military and survived. Two instant celebratory biographies appeared in Pakistani stores, his bearded face appeared on posters and T-shirts, and Osama became a common name for newborn boys in Pakistan. The head of Pakistan's largest religious academy explained that the strikes had made bin Laden "a symbol for the whole Islamic world. . . . He's a hero to us, but it is America that first made him a hero."[18]

✳

A FEW DAYS AFTER THE FAILED missile attack, President Clinton signed a Memorandum of Notification (MON) authorizing the CIA to let its tribal assets use force to capture bin Laden. CIA officers told the Afghans the plan was back on. Yet while the tribal agents' reporting about bin Laden's movements was "very good," this scenario was unrealistic given that the White House had warned the tribals that they would be paid only if they captured bin Laden, not if they killed him. In September and October 1998, the tribals claimed to have attempted at least four ambushes of bin Laden, but once again the CIA was unable to verify these claims. It was not until December 21 that the President approved a new MON allowing the tribals to be paid whether bin Laden was captured or killed.[19]

In February 1999 another draft MON went to President Clinton asking that the same guidance be given to Ahmad Shah Massoud's Northern Alliance. Yet for some reason Clinton crossed out key language he had approved in December and inserted more ambiguous wording. Consequently, one senior Massoud aide recalled, "We never heard the word 'kill' from any American we talked to."[20] When Massoud's forces moved to stage a rocket attack against bin Laden's Derunta training complex, the CIA's lawyers "convulsed in alarm," and the Agency pleaded with Massoud to call off the attack. When the CIA explained that the United States wanted bin Laden taken alive, an American official recalled, "The Northern Alliance thought: 'Oh, okay, you want to capture him. Right. You crazy white guys.'" Ultimately, neither the CIA's tribal assets nor the Northern Alliance were able to capture *or* kill bin Laden.[21]

✳

WITH THE POSSIBILITY OF INDIGENOUS forces nabbing bin Laden fading, US officials turned to foreign allies as a possible solution. Gary Schroen and other CIA officers hoped to enlist Pakistani intelligence officers whom bin Laden trusted to lure him into a trap near Kandahar. In July 1999, Pakistani Prime Minister Nawaz Sharif proposed to President Clinton that the CIA train a Pakistani commando team for the purpose of capturing bin Laden. Although US officials were skeptical— Pakistani intelligence could just as easily tell the CIA where bin Laden was so the United States could launch either a missile strike or a snatch operation—the White House approved the plan. The CIA began paying salaries and providing communications and other gear until Sharif was overthrown in a coup in October 1999 and the plan was terminated.[22]

In addition to Pakistan, other regional actors were considered in the bin Laden manhunt. Following an assassination attempt against dictator Islam Karimov by al-Qaeda-affiliated extremists, Uzbekistan agreed to accept CIA funding and training for a counterterrorism strike force. Although Langley hoped they would eventually carry out a covert snatch operation against bin Laden, bureaucratic inertia slowed the implementation of this program. Later, in July 2001, the CIA learned that Jordan's King Abdullah had determined that al-Qaeda posed a significant enough threat to the kingdom's security that he offered to send two battalions of Jordanian special forces to go door-to-door in Afghanistan, if necessary, to deal with al-Qaeda. But as with the Pakistani and Uzbek initiatives, this offer was never implemented.[23]

Part of the Clinton administration's eagerness to use foreign forces in the bin Laden manhunt stemmed from its reluctance to use US special operations forces. The White House first asked the Pentagon for detailed military plans to attack and arrest bin Laden in the fall of 1998. Officers within the Special Operations Command (SOCOM) were eager to go after bin Laden and al-Qaeda and hoped for action orders. One envisioned raid would involve some forty special operators inserted by air-refueled helicopters launched from US warships off Pakistan's Makran coast. Once the forces were in place, such a raid could launch with six to ten hours' advance notice of bin Laden's nighttime location. Some planners on the Joint Staff believed that with accurate intelligence, a small, stealthy raid would be able to successfully seize bin Laden. The CIA estimated a 95 percent chance of SOCOM forces capturing bin Laden if deployed.[24]

Yet the Chairman of the Joint Chiefs of Staff, General Hugh Shelton, and CENTCOM Commander General Anthony Zinni, disagreed. As Richard Shultz has observed, "The Mogadishu disaster spooked the Clinton administration as well as the brass." After Mogadishu, one Pentagon officer explained, there was "reluctance to even discuss pro-active measures associated with countering the terrorist threat through SOF [special operations forces] operations."[25] Shelton, a veteran of the special forces, was skeptical about the raids' feasibility, and insisted on including a force-protection package that significantly increased the number of troops required. Shelton repeatedly cited Desert One—the failed US special forces raid in 1980 to rescue American hostages in Tehran—as a cautionary tale for Clinton's aides. More important, perhaps, was Zinni's opposition. Zinni believed that a raid, even if successful, would hurt the United States diplomatically throughout the region, especially in Pakistan, whose airspace would need to be transited. Given his always tenuous relationship with the military, Clinton decided not to push the generals on their reluctance to consider a snatch operation in Afghanistan.[26]

By November 1998, the CIA's CTC admitted: "At this point we cannot predict when or if a capture operation will be executed by our assets."[27] Consequently, after Operation Infinite Reach, cruise-missile-bearing submarines remained on station off the coast of Pakistan beneath the Arabian sea, ready to fire if credible intelligence arrived concerning bin Laden's location. The coordinates of some of bin Laden's known camps and villas, such as the Tarnak Farm compound, were preloaded into the submarines' missile computers.

On December 20, 1998, intelligence indicated bin Laden would be spending the night at the governor's residence in Kandahar. From the field, Schroen advised: "Hit him tonight—we may not get another chance." The Principals Committee convened and considered a cruise-missile strike. However, General Zinni predicted that over two hundred civilians would be killed or wounded in the strike, and expressed concern about possible damage to a nearby mosque. Conversely, the senior intelligence officer on the Joint Staff estimated only half as many civilian casualties and no damage to the mosque. Yet knowing President Clinton's opposition "to any operation that might kill women and children," the principals decided against recommending a strike.[28]

Several weeks later, in February 1999, the CIA's tribal agents reported that bin Laden had traveled to an elaborate cluster of hunting camps—replete with elegant tents, a small fleet of Land Cruisers, and a plane parked nearby—in western Afghanistan. The CIA's confidence in the tribals' reporting had increased, and the collective feeling at the NSC was "*Bingo!* It had to be bin Laden."[29] Because of the remote location, a missile strike would have less risk of collateral damage, and on February 8 the military began to prepare for a possible strike.

Satellite reconnaissance confirmed the location and description of the largest camp, but it also revealed the plane was an official aircraft of the United Arab Emirates (UAE), and the falconers included several UAE princes. Although the satellite photos provided enough detail that analysts could make out the falcons roosting on their poles, the location of bin Laden's quarters could not be precisely determined. All the tribals could report was that bin Laden regularly visited the Emiratis from an adjacent camp, and that they expected him to be at the hunting camp for such a visit at least until midmorning on February 11.[30]

Without a picture of bin Laden standing outside his tent or the tracking team able to get close enough to the camp, neither the Islamabad station nor the CTC could provide a 100 percent guarantee of bin Laden's location. Policymakers were paralyzed by the fear that a strike on the main camp would kill an Emirati prince or senior official, and by February 12 bin Laden had moved on. On March 7, Richard Clarke—who had personal ties to the UAE royal family stemming from defense deals he had previously negotiated—called a UAE official to express his concerns about possible associations between Emirati officials and bin Laden. Satellite imagery soon confirmed that less than a week after Clarke's phone call, the camp was quickly disassembled and the site deserted. CIA officials were livid at having lost a possible site for targeting bin Laden.[31]

Finally, in May 1999, CIA assets in Afghanistan reported on bin Laden's location in and around Kandahar over the course of five days and nights. The reporting came from multiple sources and was very detailed. John Gordon, Tenet's deputy at the CIA, briefed that the intelligence "was about as good as it could get." Working-level officials at the Agency believed that if this intelligence was not considered actionable, then it was hard to imagine how any reporting from Afghanistan could ever meet the standard. By this point, however, the Clinton administration was reeling from the accidental bombing of the Chinese embassy in Belgrade during the NATO air war against Serbia, and required absolute certainty before ordering a strike. When the decision to stand down came back from the Principals Committee, "We all just slumped," said Major General John Maher, Deputy Director for Operations on the Joint Staff. Bin Laden "should have been a dead man" that night.[32]

From May 1999 to September 2001, US policymakers did not again seriously consider a missile strike against bin Laden.

The Clinton administration's pursuit of bin Laden was crippled by internecine bureaucratic squabbling that resembled the three-way gun fight at the end of *The Good, The Bad, and The Ugly.* Clinton's NSC aides believed they were the aggressive ones on the bin Laden manhunt, encumbered by resistance or incompetence within the CIA and Department of Defense. Clarke complained several years later of the "reluctance of the military to plan seriously for commando operations in Afghanistan and the fecklessness . . . of CIA's Afghan friends."[33] Yet the Agency's field operatives ("we who actually *did things*") felt they "certainly were not better by [Clarke and Berger's] intervention in ops matters in which they had no experience." Similarly, General Shelton and other generals felt Clarke and other Clinton advisors had "some dumb-ass ideas, not militarily feasible. They read something in a Tom Clancy novel and thought you can ignore distances, you can ignore the time-distance factors."[34]

Although President Clinton would later claim that "I tried to take bin Laden out . . . the last four years I was in office," he either failed to clearly convey his intent or its strategic importance to the entirety of the policymaking apparatus. As Steve Coll observes, "Clinton consistently goaded Clarke's efforts with 'need to do more'-style notations in the margins of the NSC memos, but he never insisted on final plans or attack decisions."[35] This indecision and refusal to consider military action in Afghanistan persisted despite the increasing volume of secret intelligence cables warning of active, yet unspecified al-Qaeda plans to attack US targets.

On October 12, 2000, a skiff piloted by two smiling Arabs approached a US Navy destroyer stopped for refueling in the Yemeni port of Aden. The bow of the skiff was laden with a shaped charge that, when it collided with the USS *Cole,* tore a forty-foot gash in the destroyer's steel siding. Seventeen American sailors were killed, and the *Cole* would have sunk if not for the heroic effort of its crew.

Al-Qaeda had further escalated its war against the United States. Bin Laden, anticipating American retaliation, dispersed his senior leadership throughout Afghanistan.

But no response ever came.

∗

DESPITE AL-QAEDA'S SECOND CLEAR act of war against the United States, terrorism was not an important topic in the 2000 presidential campaign. When President-elect George W. Bush and his senior aides were briefed on al-Qaeda before the inauguration, they were told that killing bin Laden would have an impact, but would not stop the threat the terrorist network posed to US security. Consequently, although the Bush administration began work on a more aggressive strategy against bin Laden, by August 2001 the only significant policy innovations were the determination that killing bin Laden constituted a legal act of self-defense rather than assassination and the arming of unmanned "Predator" drones with Hellfire missiles.[36]

The dual attacks on New York and Washington on September 11, 2001, and the scar they imprinted upon the national psyche, instilled a new sense of urgency to the bin Laden manhunt. On September 12, Secretary of Defense Donald Rumsfeld asked the principals, "Do we focus on bin Laden and al-Qaeda or terrorism more broadly?"

"Start with bin Laden, which Americans expect," President Bush told his war cabinet. "And then if we succeed we've struck a huge blow and can move forward."[37]

This sentiment was expressed more viscerally by Cofer Black, the head of the CTC. Before dispatching the first CIA paramilitary team to Afghanistan on September 19, he told the team leader:

> Your mission is to exert all efforts to find Usama bin Ladin and his senior lieutenants and to kill them. . . . I don't want bin Ladin and his thugs captured, I want them dead. . . . They must be killed. I want to see photos of their heads on pikes. I want bin Ladin's head shipped back in a box filled with dry ice. I want to be able to show bin Ladin's head to the president. . . . Have I made myself clear?[38]

It was decided that in order to get to bin Laden, the US and its allies would have to fight through the Taliban, who had rejected numerous entreaties to turn the Saudi over to US custody or to administer justice themselves. Schroen and a seven-man CIA team—code-named "Jaw-breaker"—were inserted into Afghanistan on September 26, where they linked up with the remnants of the Northern Alliance. On October 7, the US air campaign against al-Qaeda and the Taliban began as bombers, strike aircraft, and cruise missiles pounded targets. Measurable progress was initially difficult to discern, yet by November 10, the first major objective of the campaign—the northern city of Mazar-e-Sharif—was taken. Within the next few days, the Taliban's hold on the country began to rapidly disintegrate in the face of US precision-guided munitions (PGMs) and the Northern Alliance's ground assault.

Despite the quality and volume of intelligence the Northern Alliance procured for Team Jawbreaker, there was little reliable information on bin Laden. On November 10 the London *Sunday Times* reported the Saudi was seen entering Jalalabad in a convoy of white Toyota trucks surrounded by sixty commandos in green battle fatigues, armed with shiny new Kalashnikovs. He addressed a gathering of about one thousand Afghan and Pakistani tribal leaders at the Islamic Studies Institute, and the next day was spotted by Jalalabad residents standing outside a mosque, holding hands with the local Taliban governor. He barked orders to his bodyguards and left in a convoy of four-wheel-drive vehicles.[39]

At roughly the same time bin Laden fled Jalalabad, an American bomb destroyed an al-Qaeda safe house in Kabul. Buried in the rubble was Mohammed Atef, aka Abu Hafs, the former Egyptian policeman who was the head of bin Laden's security and number three in the terrorist organization. The United States appeared to be getting closer to its quarry.

Gary Berntsen, the new leader of Jawbreaker, received reports of bin Laden's exodus shortly after Northern Alliance forces entered Kabul on November 12. Berntsen, a bear-sized man with a Long Island accent, learned two days later of a convoy of two hundred Toyotas and Land Cruisers passing through the village of Agam two hours south of Kabul. A quick plotting of all the reports received from Afghan agents indicated a steady movement south and east toward the Pakistan border.

Bin Laden's flight toward Afghanistan's southeastern mountains made sense. His destination was Tora Bora (Pashto for "black dust"), a series of cave-filled valleys in the White Mountains where ridgelines rose from wooded foothills to jagged, snow-covered peaks separated by deep ravines. The Tora Bora complex covered an area roughly six miles wide and six miles long, and during the 1980s had been the object of multiple Soviet offensives. The Red Army had attacked with thousands of infantrymen supported by helicopter gunships and MiGs, yet the fortifications were so solid that the Soviets were held off by a force of 130 Afghans. Thus, Tora Bora appeared to offer as unassailable a redoubt as the natural fortress Geronimo occupied at Canon de los Embudos 115 years earlier.[40]

Moreover, bin Laden was intimately familiar with the terrain at Tora Bora. In 1987 he used bulldozers from his family's construction company to build a road through the mountains. Later, at the village of Jaji, bin Laden fought his first battle against the Soviets. During the years before September 11, bin Laden kept a house in a settlement near Tora Bora called Milawa. Tora Bora offered easy access to Parachinar, a region of Pakistan that juts into Afghanistan like a parrot's beak on the southern slope of Tora Bora. Bin Laden's son Omar recalled that his father would routinely hike from Tora Bora into Pakistan on excursions that could take from seven to fourteen hours. "My brothers and I all loathed those grueling treks," Omar said, but they "seemed the most pleasant outings to our father."[41]

Locals reported scores of vehicles loaded with al-Qaeda fighters and supplies moving toward Tora Bora. Estimates from Afghans who had traveled inside to meet with the Arabs put the number of fighters between 1,600 and 2,000. Villagers in the area said that bin Laden's core bodyguard was supported by a four-hundred-man force acting as pickets on the flanks as the terrorist leader moved back and forth between the Milewa Valley in the west and Tora Bora in the east. Another force of four hundred Chechens—highly regarded for their alpine fighting skills—guarded the perimeter of the Tora Bora complex.[42]

Thus, Tora Bora afforded bin Laden the option of fighting or fleeing.

In addition to the formidable terrain, Berntsen faced another problem. The Northern Alliance, which had served as the proxy ground force thus far in the campaign, had neither the capacity nor the desire to push as far south as Jalalabad. Consequently, Berntsen was forced to turn to the local warlords of the "Eastern Alliance," who had not been fully vetted. Hazaret Ali was a Pashai tribal leader who, despite being "physically small, quiet, and unassuming," had distinguished himself as a field commander in the war against the Soviets.[43] Although he seemed reliable, he led "a gang of skinny mountain boys in rags," and because his translator spoke only limited English, communicating the complexities of a rapidly evolving battlefield would be difficult. Conversely, Haji Zaman was well educated and spoke English. But he had only just returned from exile in France and commanded men who "could well have passed themselves off as a band of 18th-century cutthroats."[44]

Jawbreaker moved into a schoolhouse in the foothills near Tora Bora and established a command center. Because satellite imagery and photos from high-flying reconnaissance planes showed deep snow was stacking up in Tora Bora's valleys and passes, it was concluded that bin Laden would not be able to leave the mountains anytime soon. Radio intercepts further suggested al-Qaeda wanted a fight in the mountains, where their prepared positions would give them a tactical advantage. Finally, as the Delta Force commander noted, based on his constant praise over the years for the virtues of martyrdom, "We had no reason to doubt that bin Laden wouldn't fight to the death."[45]

Consequently, the plan for Tora Bora closely resembled the operations that had broken the Taliban lines north of Kabul. CIA paramilitary operatives and US special forces would infiltrate Tora Bora to identify targets for bombing, which would clear the way for the Afghan militias. Ali and Zaman, already fierce rivals, were given separate parallel axes of advance into the mountains: Ali's forces would take the center of the range, Zaman's men the western half of the base, with both attacking south. US forces would coordinate their movements and provide massive air support, while Pakistani forces would seal the border to the south and east.[46]

While Special Forces units worked with the Afghans to prepare for the assault on Tora Bora, on November 18 Berntsen sent an eight-man team to pursue bin Laden. By the end of November, this team divided itself into two groups of four, one of which included an Air Force combat controller. This team, using the call sign "VB02," would push forward into Tora Bora with ten Afghan fighters to serve as guides and provide additional firepower in case they were attacked by al-Qaeda.[47] The mission was delayed, however, when a poorly packed RPG carried on a donkey blew up, killing two of the guides and the unfortunate pack animal. Finally, on December 4, the team established their first observation post (OP) on a mountaintop from which they could see hundreds of bin Laden's men in the Milewa Valley below. Using a Special Operations Forces Laser Marker (SOFLAM), they began to designate targets for the US bombers and fighter jets circling high above Tora Bora.[48]

VB02 went without sleep for the next fifty-six hours while calling air strikes on the al-Qaeda positions, at one point requesting B-52s to drop bombs barely a kilometer from their OP. In all, about seven hundred thousand pounds of ordnance were dropped between December 4–7. The daring attacks, conducted without any possibility of rescue if their position was discovered, seemed to catch al-Qaeda by surprise, killing several hundred operatives. The fir and pine trees in the valley were stripped of all vegetation, and arms and legs amputated by the blasts hung from their branches instead.[49]

The devastating bombardment drove bin Laden and his forces from Milawa deeper into the White Mountains. Hazaret Ali deployed small scouting teams forward to locate al-Qaeda's new positions. They quickly discovered encampments in an area surrounded by caves. Berntsen hoped to deploy special forces to two new OPs south and west, while VB02's original OP was reestablished to the east. Ideally, bin Laden and his forces would be trapped in a kill box as the US forces called in fire from the surrounding promontories.[50]

Within a day, the teams established OPs and began calling in air strikes. B-52 and B-1 bombers from the United States and fighters stationed on aircraft carriers in the Persian Gulf responded to the calls for fire each day. At night, AC-130 Spectre gunships slowly circled above the valley, laying down a deadly blanket of machine-gun and cannon fire on the heat signatures below. Once again, al-Qaeda was driven into the valley's caves before abandoning their positions altogether and retreating further into the mountains.

On December 6, an Arab-American CIA operative named "Bilal" moved through Milawa with two Afghan guides to survey the destruction and look for clues as to bin Laden's location or plans. Clutching an AK-47, he made his way over the rolling hills and ravines until he found the first set of al-Qaeda caves. There he found sleeping mats, cases of Russian-made ammunition, and the mangled remains of al-Qaeda fighters stripped of their boots and uniforms. One corpse still clutched a Japanese-made handheld Yazoo radio, from which emanated a frantic voice speaking Arabic. Bilal listened to the transmissions and quickly realized the radio was tuned to al-Qaeda's frequency. He heard men talking excitedly, screaming: "Bring the food!" "We need water!" Al-Qaeda had apparently been surprised by the speed of the US assault and abandoned their supplies in the valley below.

After an AC-130 pass, Bilal heard a voice familiar from dozens of tape recordings. Osama bin Laden was exhorting his troops to keep fighting. The terrorist mastermind was alive and still hiding somewhere among the dusty, rocky peaks.[51]

✳

ON DECEMBER 7, one of Berntsen's team members reported that Hazaret Ali had allowed a source from Jalalabad to enter Tora Bora to deliver water and food to bin Laden's men. "He gave us an excellent description of three prominent Arabs," "George" said. "One was extremely tall, definitely bin Laden, another older man probably [bin Laden's top deputy] Ayman al-Zawahiri. The third man slightly resembled the tall one and was approximately 20 years old. I suspect he's bin Laden's son Saad."

"Did [Ali's] source give us a position?" Berntsen asked.

"We have coordinates near some large caves where they met," George replied. These coordinates appeared to corroborate the baseline location provided by a signal intercept of bin Laden communicating with his fighters.

Berntsen put in a request through the CTC to hit the location with a BLU-82 bomb. Word quickly came back that the BLU-82 would be dropped on the morning of December 9.[52]

✳

ON DECEMBER 9, a forty-man detachment from the Delta Force arrived at the base of Tora Bora. Under the command of a thirty-seven-year-old major who would later publish a memoir under the pseudonym "Dalton Fury," the Delta operators were supplemented by fourteen Green Berets, six CIA operatives, a few Air Force specialists, and a dozen British commandos from the elite Special Boat Service.[53] Originally, Delta had envisioned an operation in which they used bottled oxygen to climb the peaks of the Spin Ghar and surprise al-Qaeda from the rear. This unconventional thinking was rejected by higher commands, however, and on December 2 Delta was ordered to linkup with the Eastern Alliance strictly "to facilitate killing or capturing Osama bin Laden."[54]

On the ninth, US forces watched through binoculars as a car-sized bomb fell out the back of a C-130. Known as a "Daisy Cutter," the BLU-82 is a fifteen-thousand-pound bomb that was used in the Gulf War to clear minefields. An explosion rumbled through the mountains, followed by "a huge sucking, whooshing sound." Initially, it was assumed the bomb had failed to detonate properly because the expected mushroom cloud never materialized. But as US signal interceptors overheard al-Qaeda's anguished voices desperately crying for help, they realized the BLU-82 had been more effective than thought. Journalists who later toured the al-Qaeda positions at the point of detonation reported a path of complete devastation in a daisy pattern that was five football fields wide. One reporter found "nothing but scorched earth. Trees burned down to their roots, trucks, tanks, weapons—incinerated." The follow-on air strikes were equally destructive, and Berntsen recalled one abandoned al-Qaeda camp as being "pockmarked with bomb craters 50 feet wide and 20 feet deep." Consequently, most of bin Laden's troops moved to prepared fighting positions and caves in higher ground that were stockpiled with food and ammunition.[55]

The next day, a Delta OP received a report from an Afghan commander that bin Laden had been seen on a hilltop and was surrounded. He adamantly insisted that Delta immediately smash the hilltop, crying, "*Bouyahs! Bouyahs!*" ("Bombs! Bombs!")

"Where is bin Laden?" the commandos asked. "Show us!"

To overcome the language barrier, they resorted to drawing in the dirt and holding up fingers to represent the various crests and peaks. Finally, they deduced that the Afghan was saying bin Laden was on Hilltop 2685, a little more than seven kilometers away.[56]

About the same time, signals-intelligence operators picked up an intercept from Tora Bora: "Father [bin Laden] is trying to break through the siege line." It seemed possible that the combination of the bombing and an Afghan assault on the al-Qaeda stronghold could be flushing out the terrorists' command group.[57]

Later that evening, about thirty minutes before sunset, "George" received a new piece of signals intelligence. Bin Laden had apparently spent too long on his radio consulting with his subordinate commanders, and his general location had been determined. Combined with the earlier intercept, this report strongly suggested not only that bin Laden had been found, but that the Afghans actually had him surrounded.

George handed Fury a small piece of paper with an eight-digit grid location—accurate down to ten meters—scribbled upon it. About fifteen minutes later, another report from higher headquarters provided a less accurate six-digit grid placing bin Laden two kilometers from the original location. Although it was impossible to tell which report was more recent, bin Laden appeared to be in the open and on the move. It took about fifteen minutes for Fury and thirty-two other Delta operators to load into their vehicles and head out to meet Hazaret Ali.[58]

As Delta's main force moved out, "Team Jackal"—a three-man Delta outpost with Afghan guides—began taking machine-gun fire unexpectedly from its rear. With the mujahideen low on ammunition and increasingly skittish, the team's leader gave the order to initiate escape and evasion. The code word "Warpath! Warpath! Warpath!" went out over the radio network, followed by silence.[59]

Fury met Ali at "Mortar Hill" as dusk fell. But after only a few minutes of pleasantries, the Afghan commander returned to his SUV. Rather than joining the pursuit of bin Laden, Ali was returning home to break his Ramadan fast. Worse, all his men appeared to be leaving the battlefield with him. Not only did Fury no longer have bin Laden surrounded, he now had no Afghan allies to guide him in the darkness. Moreover, with Team Jackal on the run, Delta had no air support, because there was no combat controller to direct the planes. Al-Qaeda took advantage of the halt in the bombing to occupy the ridgelines directly to Delta's front and rear and opened fire. Fury and his men took cover as red and green tracer rounds zipped around them and rockets screamed overhead.

Delta was approximately 2,500 meters from bin Laden's last reported position, but that intelligence was more than an hour old. Fury had no Afghans to guide them through the unfamiliar, rocky terrain, nor to prevent a friendly-fire incident with any mujahideen who might still be out in the darkness. And they had not heard any report on Team Jackal's status. Fury quickly consulted with his NCOs. "Okay, we'll have another shot at bin Laden," he said. "We need to concentrate on recovering our boys first. If things change between now and then, we'll go for bin Laden too."

Reluctantly, Fury led his men back down the mountain, while bin Laden seemed to fade like a ghost into Tora Bora's moonscape.[60]

✳

ON DECEMBER 12. Haji Zaman informed the Americans he had opened negotiations with al-Qaeda for a surrender agreement. This was unwelcome news to Delta, which had pushed its operatives deeper into Tora Bora to bin Laden's two-room house in Milewa. A twenty-man Delta team was blocked at gunpoint by eighty of Zaman's men under orders to enforce the cease-fire. Fury was convinced the whole surrender gesture was a hoax, and that even if Zaman was not dirty, he was enabling al-Qaeda's stalling tactics.

Even as al-Qaeda dragged out discussions, Zaman told Fury, "This is the greatest day in the history of Afghanistan."

"Why is that?" Fury asked skeptically.

"Because al Qaeda is no more," Zaman boasted. "Bin Laden is finished."[61]

Although suspect, Zaman was close to the truth. Bin Laden was in significant jeopardy, a fact the Saudi himself seemed to acknowledge. On the afternoon of December 13, the sham cease-fire ended, and US signals operators picked up a transmission that "Father" was "moving to a new tunnel with two Yemeni brothers." Then bin Laden himself came on the air. "The time is now," he said. "Arm your women and children against the infidel!"[62]

After several hours of intense bombing, bin Laden was on the radio again. "Our prayers have not been answered. Times are dire," he said in despair. "We didn't receive support from the apostate nations who call themselves our Muslim brothers. Things might have been different." With the fatigue palpable in his voice, he concluded, "I'm sorry for getting you involved in this battle, if you can no longer resist, you may surrender with my blessing."

The Americans heard bin Laden gather his followers together in prayer. The sound of mules and a large group of people moving about was audible. And then the radio went dead.[63]

The next day, December 14, bin Laden's voice was picked up again. But according to Bilal and another Arab-American CIA operative, it sounded more like a prerecorded sermon than a live transmission. It was deduced that bin Laden had left the battlefield and the transmission was merely a decoy to make it seem as if he were still involved in the fighting.

The next day, however, Afghan fighters reported seeing bin Laden moving among a group of several dozen enemy fighters before he disappeared into a cave. Three Delta snipers heard the Afghans' frantic radio transmissions and relayed word back to the command center at the schoolhouse. An air controller stacked up all available aircraft while the cave's location was plotted. The snipers took cover behind a small rock formation as the bombs from the first warplane descended onto the cave. Inside, something flammable ignited, and flashes and secondary explosions lit up the valley. For the next two hours, impact after impact from the GBU-31 bombs shook the ground and triggered secondary blasts and massive fireballs. Shrapnel and debris smashed into the rocks in front of the American snipers and raced over their heads.

Sundown brought with it the usual Afghan retreat. The Delta snipers, however, did not want to ease up and decided to stay the night behind enemy lines. They were exposed, however, on a six-foot-wide path along the spine of a ridgeline that was the only trail in the area. The terrain on both sides of the path dropped off severely, with occasional trees or stumps sprouting from the cliff walls. Knowing they could not remain on the path, the commandos sat down and eased themselves over the edge of the cliff. In the darkness, they slid about ten feet before finding a ledge to cling to for the night. After about an hour, they heard the sound of weapons rattling and hurried footsteps approaching. Like Funston and his men on the path to Palanan one hundred years earlier, they froze in place and held their breaths, their thumbs on the selector switches of their rifles and clutching grenades. Throughout the night they could hear groups of fighters running along the trail in both directions, unaware of the Americans in the darkness just feet away.

The three snipers remained on the ridgeline calling for fire for the next two days.[64]

On December 16, tactical radio intercepts picked up desperate calls by al-Qaeda begging for medicine, bandages, food, and water. The terrorists also requested guidance as to whether they should retreat into the villages or fade deeper into the mountains. But their calls went unanswered. Al-Qaeda's chain of command was destroyed, and throughout the day numerous reports of surrenders came into the schoolhouse. By the next day, the battle of Tora Bora was over. Estimates of al-Qaeda fighters killed ranged from 220 to 500, although the real number was likely higher as the bombing literally obliterated or buried the bodies of large groups of fighters. Fifty-two fighters, mostly Arabs, were captured by the Afghans, and another hundred were captured crossing the border into Pakistan. One group of twenty prisoners was paraded before the international media assembled near the schoolhouse. Sleep deprivation, shell shock, and battle fatigue had reduced the fearsome warriors into "a bedraggled, scrawny lot."[65]

Yet there was no sign of the target of the campaign, Osama bin Laden.

As with the Noriega manhunt, one of the first US officials to appear on television was now–Secretary of State Colin Powell. "There's some information that suggests he might still be there, and he might have got across the border. We don't know," Powell told NBC. "But you can be sure he is under hot pursuit. We'll get bin Laden. Whether it's today, to-morrow, a year from now, two years from now, we will not rest until he is brought to justice or justice is brought to him."[66]

The Saudi's fate remained unknown until December 27, when a vis-ibly aged bin Laden appeared on a videotape. Despite being left-handed and typically gesturing with both hands while speaking, bin Laden did not move his entire left side in the thirty-four-minute video, suggesting he had sustained a serious injury during the battle. "I am a poor slave of God," he said resignedly. "If I live or die the war will continue."[67]

The hunt for Osama bin Laden would continue for almost another decade until it reached its climax on a cloudless night in a quiet neigh-borhood in Abbottabad, Pakistan.

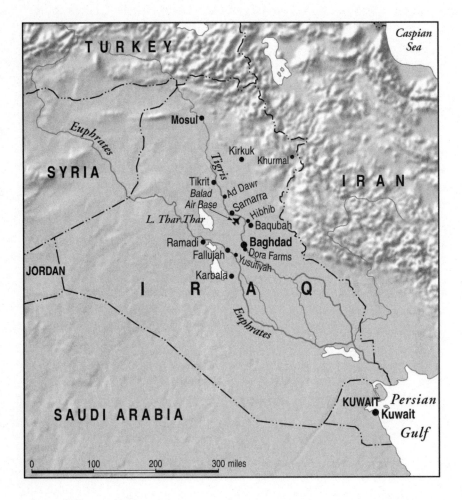

CHAPTER SEVEN

STRATEGIC MANHUNTS IN MESOPOTAMIA

SADDAM HUSSEIN AND

ABU MUSAB AL-ZARQAWI

The Coalition Provisional Authority's (CPA) conference center was packed tightly on Sunday, December 14, 2003, as the three men walked to the podium. Adnan Pachachi, the silver-haired patrician serving as President of the Iraqi Governing Council, led the way. He was followed by Ambassador L. Paul Bremer, the handsome statesman in charge of America's struggling effort to reconstruct Iraq. Following the two diplomats was Lieutenant General Ricardo Sanchez, the dour commander of Coalition forces in Iraq. When they reached the massive podium emblazoned with the CPA seal, they turned to face the crowd of Western, Iraqi, and regional Arab reporters who filled every seat. An electricity was in the air as Bremer approached the microphone at 3:15 PM Baghdad time.

"Ladies and gentlemen," he said, pausing briefly, "we got him!"

Bremer did not have to even say the name. Instantly, Iraqi reporters sprang to their feet and began cheering wildly, forcing Bremer to wait half a minute for the outburst to subside before resuming his remarks. Later, when Lieutenant General Sanchez showed video of the haggard-looking fugitive undergoing a medical exam, there were again shouts, cries, and weeping from the Iraqis in the audience. Several Iraqi reporters cast aside any semblance of objectivity and vented the emotions suppressed during thirty-five years of tyranny, shouting, "Death to Saddam! Down with Saddam!"[1]

Outside the heavily fortified International Zone, Baghdad erupted in euphoria. People took to the streets, many in tears and holding tattered pictures of family members killed during Iraq's reign of terror. The normally reserved judges and lawyers studying the Iraqi High Tribunal statute—under which the dictator would eventually be tried—"dissolved in a frenzy of joy and palpable relief as Iraqis literally jumped and hugged and cried on each other's shoulders. It was a scene of joyful pandemonium."[2] Celebratory gunfire was audible throughout the Iraqi capital and continued to crackle through the night.

Saddam Hussein, one of the twentieth century's deadliest tyrants, had been captured.

✳

ALTHOUGH THE DEBATES SURROUNDING the planning and execution of Operation Iraqi Freedom will persist long after the last US soldier leaves Iraq, the war was *initiated* with the strategic objective of removing Saddam from power. Deposing Saddam had been official US policy well before the Bush administration took office in 2001. Both political parties and both houses of Congress overwhelmingly passed—and the Clinton administration signed—H.R. 4655, the Iraqi Liberation Act of 1998, which declared: "It should be the policy of the United States to seek to remove the Saddam Hussein regime from power in Iraq."[3] No more than token resources were devoted to this objective, however, and Iraq played only a minor role in the 2000 presidential campaign. Iraq continued to be a back-burner issue during the first eight months of the Bush administration until the 9/11 attacks changed the strategic calculation regarding Saddam's assumed possession of weapons of mass destruction and suspected ties to extremist terrorist organizations. Although President Bush chose to address the problem of demolishing al-Qaeda's sanctuary in Afghanistan before dealing with Saddam, Richard Haass notes that by July 2002 President Bush "had reached the conclusion that it was both necessary and desirable that Saddam should be ousted, and that he was prepared to do what was necessary to bring it about."[4] Eventually, as Douglas Feith observes, by December "President Bush concluded that he had to remove Saddam's regime from power by war."[5] Thus, although the war in Iraq evolved numerous times over the years, it began as the largest strategic manhunt in US military history.

After months of steady military buildup in the Persian Gulf region and Sisyphean diplomacy at the United Nations, on March 17, 2003, President Bush announced that Saddam could avoid war under one condition: if he and his sons left Iraq within forty-eight hours. Speaking from the White House following a meeting abroad with allied leaders, Bush declared: "The decades of deceit and cruelty have now reached an end," and that if Saddam and his sons did not accept this final offer, their refusal "will result in military conflict."[6] The intricately planned military timetable for "D-Day"—which involved commando raids, the beginning of the "Shock and Awe" air strikes, and the ground invasion led by the First Marine Expeditionary Force and the Army's V Corps—was synchronized with the expiration of President Bush's deadline.[7]

On March 19, however, a CIA source learned of a possible meeting that night at Dora Farms, an estate owned by Saddam's wife southeast of Baghdad on the bank of the Tigris River. Although it was unclear who would be present, indications were that Saddam's sons, Uday and Qusay, and perhaps the entire family, might be planning a meeting there to discuss what to do if the coalition invaded. "At that point," CIA Director George Tenet recalled, "we ordered U.S. overhead reconnaissance to examine the site closely. What we saw was a large contingent of security vehicles, precisely the kinds that would typically precede and accompany Saddam's movements, hidden under trees at the farm." Sometime after 12:30 PM (8:30 PM Baghdad time) the CIA's source on the scene reported Uday and Qusay were definitely at the farm, that he had actually seen Saddam, and that the dictator would be returning to spend the night with his sons sometime between 3:00 and 3:30 AM Baghdad time. Tenet told the President's war cabinet: "I can't give you 100 percent assurance, but this is as good as it gets."[8]

Given CENTCOM's elaborate plan of attack, attempting to strike Dora Farms posed a significant risk. If Saddam was not present, the United States would be telegraphing that a major air and ground attack was forthcoming, thereby forfeiting strategic surprise. Yet when President

Bush met with his war cabinet that afternoon, all Bush's advisors recommended the strike, with Secretary of State Colin Powell saying, "If we've got a chance to decapitate them, it's worth it."[9]

The latest information indicated that while at Dora Farms, Saddam would be staying in a *manzul,* an Arabic word that could be translated either as "place of refuge" or "basement/bunker."[10] If there were a bunker at Dora Farms, cruise missiles would not be able to take it out. Chairman of the Joint Chiefs of Staff General Richard Meyers called CENTCOM commander General Tommy Franks on a secure phone. Could a stealth fighter be loaded with EGBU-27 bunker-busting bombs in time for the attack? The Air Force been following the intelligence and had prepared the planes at the Al Udeid air base in Qatar. Franks sent word to the White House that an attack would indeed be possible.[11]

There was one important tactical problem, however. To execute the mission the F-117s would have to fly into the heart of Iraq's air defenses, which surrounded the capital with surface-to-air missile sites and antiaircraft artillery. Although F-117s are virtually invisible to radar and ground observers while flying at night at high altitude, in daylight they become relatively slow, defenseless targets. According to the weather and light data, first twilight—when aircraft become visible from the ground—would be at 5:39 AM.

General Meyers called again, asking how long the President had to make a final decision on the attack. "Tom, I need your drop-dead, no-shit decision time."

In order to get the planes in and out of Iraqi airspace before dawn, Franks said, "Time on target must be no later than 0530 Iraq time, Dick, with takeoff from Al Udeid no later than 0330. . . . I need the President's decision by 0315, so the jets can start engines and taxi."

It was already 2:27 AM.

Time passed slowly in CENTCOM's headquarters. At 2:59 AM Franks received word that the aircraft were armed, and the pilots were briefed and sitting on the runway in their planes.

Finally, at 3:12 AM, the phone rang. "The mission is a go, Tom," General Meyers said. "Please execute."[12]

At 3:38 Qatari time, Lieutenant Colonel Dave Toomey and Major Mark Hoehn were airborne, flying north toward Baghdad in a race with the dawn. An hour later, forty-five Tomahawk land attack missiles (TLAMs) were fired from surface vessels and submarines in the North

Arabian Gulf. Each TLAM carried a thousand-pound warhead, and once launched was impossible to recall.

The campaign to kill Saddam Hussein was under way.

As Toomey and Hoehn neared Baghdad, the GPS on one of Toomey's bombs went dead. The EGBU-27s had never been used in combat and had arrived in Qatar only the day before the mission. So Toomey, a combat veteran and the squadron's director of operations, literally pulled out the instruction manual, rebooted the computerized guidance system, and hoped for the best. As Toomey and Hoehn approached Dora Farms along oval flight paths from the east and west, the sun was almost above the horizon. Clouds shielded them from ground observation, but also hid the target complex. At the last moment, however, the pilots found a break in the clouds that gave them six seconds to visually identify the targets and drop the bombs at 5:36 AM Baghdad time.[13]

Reconnaissance photos showed all four bombs hit their target squarely. When the first intelligence reports from the scene started coming in, the CIA's source reported that someone who appeared to be Saddam was pulled from the rubble, looking blue and receiving oxygen. He had been put on a stretcher and loaded into the back of an ambulance, which did not move for half an hour before leaving the complex. Around 4:30 AM, Tenet called the White House Situation Room and told the duty officer, "Tell the President we got the son of a bitch!"[14]

Several hours later, however, Saddam appeared on Iraqi television. He was wearing an army uniform, a beret, and glasses. For seven minutes he read from a notepad, denouncing the American attack. It was not clear to US analysts whether the address was live or taped, or whether it was Saddam or a body double.[15] Consequently, US forces launched two more missions during the invasion of Iraq targeting Saddam. Early on April 3, Navy SEALs conducted a nighttime heliborne raid against the dictator's palace in the middle of Lake Thar Thar near Tikrit. Although the SEALs encountered "fierce" antiaircraft fire, resistance on the objective itself was light, and the raiders found only intelligence documents rather than Saddam or any other high-value targets (HVTs). Four days later, as US ground forces began probing the capital's defenses, an intelligence source reported seeing Saddam in the affluent Baghdad neighborhood of Mansour, where he allegedly visited a popular restaurant. The source claimed to have seen Saddam entering a nearby building for a meeting with his intelligence service. Two B-1B bombers already airborne were diverted to Baghdad, where they dropped four tons of bombs on the supposed meeting place. Communications chatter picked up by the National Security Agency (NSA) suggested Saddam had been killed, and Pentagon officials telephoned CIA headquarters and heard analysts proclaim: "We got 'em."[16]

Whereas Saddam's fate remained uncertain, his army melted away under the irresistible force of the First Marine Expeditionary Force (MEF) and V Corps's offensive. By April 9, US troops had seized Baghdad, and the enormous statue of Saddam looming over Firdos Square was pulled down in a tangible symbol of the fall of Saddam's dictatorship. The US intelligence community was split over whether Saddam was killed in the Mansour bombing. On April 18 an Abu Dhabi television network broadcast a videotape—allegedly made on April 9—showing Saddam surrounded by supporters in the Adhamiya district of Baghdad. Once again, US intelligence officials could not determine the film's date or authenticity.

US forces began to concentrate on rounding up the high-ranking officials from the deposed regime's leadership before they could flee the country. A deck of playing cards bearing the pictures of the top fifty-five "most wanted" members of the "Black List" was distributed to American soldiers, with Saddam depicted as the ace of spades. The search was led by Task Force 20, a secret joint special operations unit that included members of Delta Force, Navy SEALs, and the British Special Air and Boat Services. By May 1, when President Bush proclaimed "Mission Accomplished" aboard the USS *Abraham Lincoln,* fifteen of the men on the cards had surrendered or been captured. Seizure missions continued through the spring, and coalition troops netted another twelve top fugitives in May, including one of Saddam's sons-in-law.[17]

Despite the euphoria of liberation and the tentative signs of progress following the initial looting of Baghdad, ordinary Iraqis were plagued by a sense of growing unease and disbelief. As the nascent insurgency began to coalesce in increasing attacks against coalition forces and Iraqi civilians, graffiti praising Saddam began to emerge in Iraq's Sunni Triangle, bearing messages such as "Saddam is still our leader" and "Saddam the hero will be back."[18] By late June, US intelligence officials had intercepted communications among Saddam loyalists indicating they believed he was alive. General John Abizaid—Franks's replacement as CENTCOM commander—acknowledged: "It's important even to know if he's alive or dead; and if he's alive, it's important either to capture or kill him." Ambassador Bremer agreed: "It is important to kill Saddam or capture him because his continued uncertain state has allowed people to play on that uncertainty and make the argument that, in some fashion, the Ba'athists would come back." This sentiment was perhaps best expressed by an old Bedouin near Tikrit, who warned soldiers of the Fourth Infantry Division that "unless you catch Saddam and show his head to the people, they won't believe he is gone. This will not end."[19]

Military engineers began excavating the site of the Mansour bombing on June 3 to try to find traces of Saddam's DNA, but the search came up empty. An apparent breakthrough in the hunt for Saddam occurred on June 16, when US forces captured Abid Hamid Mahmud al-Tikriti. Al-Tikriti, sometimes called "Saddam's Shadow," was the dictator's personal secretary and, as the ace of diamonds on the deck of cards, the fourth-most-wanted man in Iraq behind Saddam and his sons. Although the Associated Press declared in a headline, "Captured Iraqi May Know Fate of Saddam," al-Tikriti told interrogators he and Saddam's sons had separated from the dictator in April after Saddam became convinced they could survive longer apart.[20] In July, the CIA confirmed that the scratchy voice heard on an audio recording played on Al Jazeera, exhorting Iraqis to resist the "infidel invaders," belonged to Saddam. Consequently, in order to erase Saddam's value as a symbol to hard-core resisters, US officials announced a $25 million reward for information either proving his demise or leading to his capture, as well as a $15 million reward for each of his sons.

※

AT TEN AM ON JULY 22, the doorbell to Nawaf al-Zaydan Mohammed's house in the northern city of Mosul rang. Outside, among the tall, Greek-style columns, were twenty Delta operators and SEALs from Task Force 20. Reinforcing them were some two hundred soldiers from the 326th Engineer Battalion and the 3/502 Infantry of the 101st Air Assault Division under Brigadier General Frank Helmick. The 101st had established support-by-fire positions on the south and northeast sides of the huge stone and concrete house, with additional troops in blocking positions on the road parallel to the house. Three days earlier, Mohammed had approached US forces and told them Uday and Qusay Hussein were staying at his house in Mosul's Falah district. Mohammed answered the door and then, as arranged, fled with his son. An interpreter with a bullhorn called out for Uday and Qusay to surrender, and at 10:10 Task Force 20 stormed the house.[21]

As the commandos climbed the stairs, they received intense small-arms fire from behind a barricade on the house's second floor. Three Task Force operators were wounded, as well as one soldier in the street. The commandos withdrew, and the 101st opened up with vehicle-mounted .50-caliber machine guns. But when the operators attempted to storm the house again, they were repelled by AK-47 fire. At 10:45 AM the 101st fired AT-4s and Mark 19 automatic grenade launchers, but the house had two-foot-thick concrete walls and bulletproof windows—reinforced with mattresses used as sandbags—and the light antitank rockets and 40 mm high-explosive grenades failed to penetrate the structure or stop the return fire coming from the house.[22]

Although only four men defended the house—Uday, Qusay, a body-guard, and Qusay's son Mustafa—the commanders on the ground decided against simply laying siege to the house as US forces had done with the papal nunciature in Panama City back in 1990. Because of the house's prepared fortifications, commanders feared there might also be an escape tunnel to nearby buildings, and that Uday and Qusay would escape. Moreover, the brothers had spent much of the firefight frantically calling for reinforcements. Consequently, a prolonged siege might have given insurgents time to assemble and surround the two hundred troops encircling the house, thereby trapping US forces in an ambush similar to Mogadishu in 1993. As it became increasingly clear that Uday and Qusay were not going to let themselves be taken alive, US forces evacuated the residents from nearby houses and escalated their attack.[23]

At eleven AM a team of two Kiowa Warrior helicopters flew southeast to northwest, firing their .50-caliber machine guns and 2.75-inch rockets at the target. Around noon, Task Force 20 tried to move in and seize the objective, but once again were forced back. The 101st fired more .50-caliber and Mark 19s, and fifteen minutes later launched a barrage of eighteen Humvee-mounted TOW wire-guided antitank missiles, enough to knock out a company of tanks. Brigadier General Helmick had communicated by radio with the 101st's commander, Major General David Petraeus, and they decided to "put TOW missiles right into the window" of the house in order to shock the inhabitants and to damage the building structurally so that it was unfeasible to fight in. Fired from two hundred meters away, they were guided through the windows from which the blocking force had drawn fire and knocked holes through the mansion's walls.[24]

At about 1:20 PM, Task Force 20 made a final assault on the house. Blasted furniture lay everywhere, and the walls were pockmarked and gouged by the intense American barrage. Although two of the defenders had survived the volley of TOW missiles, there was no movement upstairs. Uday had barricaded himself in a bathroom, clinging to a briefcase full of condoms, Viagra, and cologne. The operators forced entry with an explosive charge and killed the notorious psychopath with aimed shots to the head. Mustafa, firing from under a bed, was killed the same way.[25]

✳

ALTHOUGH THE JULY 22 KILLING of Uday and Qusay was celebrated throughout Iraq, it did not bring US forces any closer to capturing their father, as Saddam appeared to have completely separated himself from the Ba'ath Party leaders who made up the deck of cards. Consequently, US forces began to shift the focus of their seizure operations from concentrating on HVTs to Saddam's "enablers." In Tikrit, the First Brigade Combat Team (BCT) of the Fourth Infantry Division (ID) began to focus on the middle tier of bodyguards in and around Saddam's hometown who were easier to locate than the Ba'ath functionaries. Eventually, the raids designed to net these operators also uncovered photographs of Saddam posing with associates previously unknown or overlooked by US forces. Eventually, the Fourth ID's intelligence officers were able to create a Link Analysis Diagram—nicknamed the "Mongo Link"—detailing more than 250 top- and mid-level Ba'athist activists' functional and tribal ties to the fugitive tyrant.[26]

The increase in intelligence produced by the Fourth ID's social network analysis led to an intensified series of raids that produced new intelligence about Saddam and the insurgency. This additional information generated new missions and, even when unsuccessful, bit by bit aided the planners' understanding of the rising Sunni insurgency. By the end of October, of the fifty-five Iraqis most wanted by the Coalition in the wake of the invasion, only Saddam and eleven others remained at large.

While this intelligence allowed the analysts to fill their link diagrams with more tidbits of information, it did not appear to be getting US forces any closer to their original target. In September and October alone, US forces launched eleven seizure raids against Saddam.

Although several times the raiders were told they had missed their target by hours, each mission was still a "dry hole." Tips about Saddam became so frequent and unreliable that they became known as "Elvis sightings." As Lieutenant Colonel Steve Russell, commander of the First Battalion, Twenty-Second Infantry, noted: "Rarely would we get an Elvis sighting that was timely. Usually it would be third- or fifth-hand information and almost always, 'He was here four days ago.'" Saddam was reported posing as a cab driver, a janitor, and in countless other disguises.[27] One Iraqi said he saw Saddam selling ice cream on a street corner. Despite the absurdity of some sightings, Saddam's image and reputation still haunted Iraq and its people. Such was the tyrant's effect that allegedly an Iraqi policeman looked into the backseat of a taxi as it tried to enter a police compound near Tikrit and saw Saddam hiding beneath a blanket. The man's bladder emptied on the spot "in a spontaneous reaction of fear and surprise."[28]

More significant, the specter of Saddam continued to have a damaging effect on Iraqi morale and reconstruction. From hiding, Saddam had issued at least five audio recordings calling upon Iraqis to attack Coalition forces. At the same time, the level of violence in Iraq rose dramatically in the late summer and fall of 2003. Nearly one soldier per day was being killed by hostile action, and in August alone, car bombs had destroyed the Jordanian embassy and UN Headquarters in Baghdad, and killed more than two hundred Shi'a worshippers at the sacred Imam Ali mosque in Najaf. On October 26, insurgents launched a brazen rocket attack on the International Zone's Al Rashid Hotel while Deputy Secretary of Defense Paul Wolfowitz was staying there. General Sanchez deemed killing the fugitive Iraqi leader to be critical, as it would "relieve the people of Iraq of the fear of his return."[29]

Meanwhile, in one of Saddam's ornate palaces along the Tigris in Tikrit, Task Force 20's intelligence analysts were independently coming to a similar conclusion as the Fourth ID. When interrogation specialist Staff Sergeant Eric Maddox joined the secretive unit in July, an interpreter showed him a list of all the former bodyguards who lived in the area, as well as their kin. On September 6 the Iraqi police arrested a former bodyguard named Nasir Yasim Omar al-Muslit, one of forty al-Muslits on Maddox's list. Under questioning, Nasir eventually provided Maddox with the blueprint to the operation of Saddam's bodyguards. Whereas the Task Force analysts had been working off a list of two hundred bodyguards of uncertain importance, Nasir gave them the key to the inner circle of thirty-two *Hamaya*, the individuals most trusted by Saddam.[30]

Through countless hours of interrogation, the Task Force analysts were further able to refine this list to key in on four specific al-Muslits: the brothers Radman Ibrahim, Muhammad Ibrahim, and Khalil Ibrahim, along with their cousin Farris Yasin. Task Force 20 (now redesignated as Task Force 121) captured Radman Ibrahim on November 8 and sought to question him immediately to exploit any intelligence for follow-on raids. Yet against the Tikrit team's wishes, Radman was flown to Baghdad, where less than twenty-four hours after being detained he dropped dead of a coronary.[31]

Shortly after this setback, in mid-November one of Farris Yasin's closest associates turned himself in to the local police. During his interview with Maddox, "Shakir" explained that "aside from Abid Mahmood, his personal secretary, there was no one Saddam trusted more than Muhammad Ibrahim."[32] With this revelation, US forces shifted their focus to Muhammad Ibrahim al-Muslit, a balding, paunchy middle-aged man who—although a veteran of Saddam's feared Special Security Organization—was on neither the coalition's Top 55 or Top 200 fugitives list. Nicknamed "the Fat Man," Muhammad Ibrahim had been seen by Iraqis driving Saddam's white Mercedes out of Adhamiyah when the dictator made his final public appearance there on April 9. US forces had raided his farms twice in July, but he eluded capture and at the time was not considered important enough to pursue further. Now US forces were convinced that if they found him, Saddam would not be far behind.[33]

On December 4, US forces conducted five simultaneous raids on suspected Muhammad Ibrahim hideouts in Tikrit, but each was a dry hole. The next night, Task Force 121 raided a rental house in nearby Samarra, where they seized $1.9 million in US currency and Muhammad's eighteen-year-old son, Musslit. Musslit, as Maddox recalled, "was a pretty pathetic specimen" who quickly broke down under questioning.

"When was the last time you saw your father?" Maddox asked.

"He was at the house two hours before your soldiers came," Musslit replied, and directed the Task Force to a hatchery where his father and a friend often went fishing.[34] For two nights, Task Force 121 staked out the fish farm in Samarra. At two AM on December 8, the team descended upon the farm and captured two Iraqi men, neither of whom was Muhammad Ibrahim. One of the men, however, was a cousin of Muhammad Ibrahim's business partner and fishing buddy, Mohammed Khudayr. The fisherman said he and his cousin owned a house in Baghdad that he thought Muhammad Ibrahim might use as a safe house.[35]

Unfortunately, just as the Task Force was closing in on its best lead to date, Maddox's deployment was ending. He returned to Baghdad to outprocess and brief Task Force 121's commanders. On his last night in Iraq, he was hanging around the Task Force's interrogation cell headquarters at Baghdad International Airport when an officer came by and casually mentioned a raid on a Baghdad house. A few hours later, at two AM, December 13, the commandos returned with four hooded and handcuffed prisoners. The team commander told Maddox that although they all carried a fuzzy black-and-white photograph of Muhammad Ibrahim and knew who they were looking for, they had not found him at the safe house.[36]

They detained Muhammad Khudayr, however, whom Maddox began questioning even though he was due to board a plane to Qatar in six hours. After several hours of back and forth, Khudayr admitted that Muhammad Ibrahim *had* been at his house that evening. Maddox initially misunderstood Khudayr's meaning, until his interpreter said, "Eric, he is saying that Muhammad Ibrahim was at the house *during* the raid."

Maddox sprinted back to the prison where the other detainees were being held and started pulling the hoods off the other three men who had been picked up at the safe house. The first two bore no resemblance to Muhammad Ibrahim, but the last prisoner had a belly that lapped over his belt buckle. "When I lifted the hood," Maddox recalled, "I didn't need to raise it any further than his chin. He had a distinctive dimple. I would have known it anywhere."

✳

AT 10:50 AM, DECEMBER 13, Colonel James Hickey—commander of First Brigade Combat Team, Fourth ID—received a call notifying him that Task Force 121 had Muhammad Ibrahim in custody and requesting he prepare a covering force for a seizure mission that night. After four hours of grueling interrogation, Muhammad Ibrahim had finally revealed two possible locations for Saddam: a house and a farm in the town of Ad Dawr, a Ba'athist stronghold about fifteen kilometers

southeast of Tikrit. Hickey, confident that this time they would capture Saddam, assembled a six-hundred-plus-strong force mounted in
twenty-five M2/M3 Bradley fighting vehicles and thirty HMMWVs to
support the two dozen special operators of Task Force 121. The mission was code-named "Operation Red Dawn," and the two objectives
were labeled "Wolverine One" and "Wolverine Two." These names
were appropriate, if somewhat coincidental. The operations staff for
the "Raider" Brigade habitually named each day's operations after the
movies they had watched the night before. Had they viewed *When
Harry Met Sally* or *The Wedding Planner* the previous night, it is possible the names for the operation would have evoked less martial images than those inspired by the 1980s movie about teenage guerrillas
resisting a Soviet invasion of the United States.[37]

At six PM, Hickey's force moved out of the brigade base at Camp
Raider, a former palace built on a bluff overlooking the Tigris south of
Tikrit. The night was cold and crisp as the covering force moved out to
an assembly area at an old granary north of Ad Dawr, while engineers secured the west bank of the Tigris several hundred meters away. The force
then moved quietly into position to block any escape and reinforcement
routes and stand ready to reinforce Task Force 121 in case of heavy resistance. At eight PM, the special operators—identifiable by their black
uniforms and night-vision goggles (NVGs)—fast-roped onto the objectives from hovering helicopters.[38]

The beam of red-lensed Maglite flashlights and laser sights on rifles
sweeping across the ground contrasted with the clear night sky over Ad
Dawr. Task Force 121 searched the two objectives, but they appeared
to be empty of any targets. The team leaders conferred and talked with
Muhammad Ibrahim, who had been flown from Baghdad to Tikrit and
then brought to the farm by the special operations team. Al-Muslit suggested another nearby location, northwest of Wolverine Two, where a
ramshackle shack stood. There was an animal stench in the air, mingled
with the scent of nearby fruit trees. The operators burst into the structure, which had been an orange-picker's hut, and seized two men. One
was Saddam's cook, the other was the cook's brother and owner of the
farm, Qies Niemic Jasim, a former bodyguard. The operators found two
AK-47s and $750,000, but Saddam was not there.[39]

US forces appeared to have struck another "dry hole" in the search
for Saddam.

✳

TO THE SUPPORT AND COMMAND ELEMENTS following the operation's progress via radio, the code words transmitted suggested the operators were fruitlessly going back over the same ground, desperately searching for any signs of their quarry.

Then a call went over the command net: "We have Jackpot."

The Joint Operations Center operations officer coordinating the mission asked for clarification, and an excited operator replied, "We've got Jackpot."

A voice that had never been heard before on the Task Force's countless missions came on the radio. Admiral William McRaven, Task Force 121's commander and a living legend within the special operations community, asked: "Do you mean *Big Jackpot?*"

"Yes, we have Big Jackpot."[40]

✳

MINUTES EARLIER, MUHAMMAD IBRAHIM had yelled at Qies Niemic Jasim in Arabic to show the operators where Saddam was hiding. The Fat Man apparently knew the exact spot, but wanted to be able to say that it was Jasim who had betrayed Saddam. Finally, he realized it was going to be up to him, and moved to an area a few meters away from where the US soldiers were concentrated. He began kicking the ground until he had uncovered a length of rope. The operators noticed Muhammad Ibrahim's activities and dug up the rope to reveal a trapdoor. The door was opened to reveal the entrance shaft to a "spider hole," about six feet deep.[41]

A sergeant shone a flashlight down the shaft. "I think there's something down there," an operator said, as another took the pin out of his grenade.

Then someone shouted, "Movement! We have something coming up!"[42]

The operators held their fire when they saw the upraised hands of a dirty, bearded man with unkempt gray hair appear. Although armed with a 9 mm Markarov pistol, the man, who looked like a vagrant, put up no resistance as the soldiers grabbed him and yanked him out of the hole. As he was roughly deposited on the ground, he said in halting English: "I am Saddam Hussein, the president of Iraq. I am willing to negotiate."

The operators replied, "President Bush sends his regards."[43]

✳

AT 8:26 PM, DECEMBER 13, the hunt for Saddam Hussein came to a successful conclusion. Saddam was captured on the same farm where he had taken refuge in 1959, when, as a young hit man for the Ba'ath party, he had been part of a failed assassination attempt on Iraqi President Abdul Kareem Qassem, an episode that served as the founding myth to the dictator's legend. Yet the tyrant who had terrified millions and buried hundreds of thousands of his own citizens in mass graves, who had urged his countrymen to violently resist US forces and bragged about going down in a blaze of glory and defiance, was captured without a shot being fired. As the Arab scholar Fouad Ajami observed:

> Great evil never quite lives up to our expectations. The image of Saddam Hussein in captivity was true to Arendt's theme. The haggard, disoriented man at the bottom of the "spider hole" was the very same man who had inflicted unspeakable sorrow on his people, and on the peoples of two neighboring lands. The discovery of the smallness of the men behind the most terrible of deeds is always an affront: if Eichmann was only a clerk, Saddam was only a thug.[44]

In the end, more US soldiers were wounded by celebratory gunfire in Baghdad returning to earth than in Operation Red Dawn itself.

For a brief period of time, US forces and the Iraqi people once again were united in joy and a sense of deliverance. For the first time since the early days of the occupation of Iraq, American flags appeared on the streets of Baghdad. In the weeks following Saddam's capture, US forces obtained the best intelligence they had seen in months. Along with the money and guns, Task Force 121 found a briefcase with Saddam that contained a letter from a Baghdad insurgent leader. The message included the minutes from a meeting of a number of resistance leaders who came together in the capital. These documents provided targets for further raids in the ensuing days, and within a week these raids had netted over two hundred wanted personnel. Knowing Saddam was in US custody, some detainees who had previously withheld information about insurgent networks began talking. At one point, some five hundred insurgents petitioned for amnesty, and cell leaders put out feelers for surrender.[45]

Consequently, in the four weeks after Saddam's capture, attacks against coalition forces in Iraq dropped 22 percent. After suffering eighty-three deaths in November 2003, US forces reported fewer than half that number—thirty-eight—in December. Major General Ray Odierno, who saw attacks against his Fourth ID soldiers drop from twenty-two to six a day, told the media in January 2004 that loyalists of the former regime "have been brought to their knees."[46] General Sanchez was even more optimistic, saying, "I expect that the detention of Saddam Hussein will be regarded as the beginning of reconciliation for the people of Iraq and as a sign of Iraq's rebirth."[47]

＊

OTHER US OFFICIALS were more restrained in their assessments. In his address marking Saddam's capture, President Bush congratulated US forces, but warned: "The capture of Saddam Hussein does not mean the end of violence in Iraq. We still face terrorists who would rather go on killing the innocent than accept the rise of liberty in Iraq."[48] On December 17 the Defense Intelligence Agency (DIA) concluded: "Saddam's capture will have little impact on foreign terrorist operational planning in Iraq. Sunni extremist groups are fighting against the U.S.-led occupation, not to restore the Hussein regime to power. Saddam's capture will have little impact on their motivation and operational capacity."[49]

Events would quickly prove President Bush and the DIA to be more prescient than Sanchez.

In January 2004, Kurdish forces captured an al-Qaeda courier named Hassan Ghul near the Iranian border. Ghul was carrying a compact disc containing a 6,700-word letter from Jordanian-born terrorist Abu Musab al-Zarqawi addressed to "the men on the mountaintops," a reference to Osama bin Laden and Ayman al-Zawahiri. In the letter, Zarqawi updated al-Qaeda's leaders on the situation in Iraq and proposed his strategy for conducting jihad there, the centerpiece of which was to foment a civil war between Iraq's Sunni and Shi'a communities.

Zarqawi had met bin Laden in Kandahar in December 1999, seeking support to open a training camp for his *al-Tawhid wal-Jihad* (Monotheism and Holy War) network. Although many al-Qaeda leaders distrusted Zarqawi, he was given roughly $5,000 in "seed money" to set up his own facility outside the western Afghan city of Herat. When US forces invaded Afghanistan in the wake of the 9/11 attacks, Zarqawi was wounded in an American air strike when the ceiling of the building he was operating from collapsed on him. After the Taliban fell in December 2001, he fled to Iran with about three hundred of his followers. In May 2002 he crossed into northern Iraq and made contact with the Islamist terror group Ansar al-Islam, but also spent time in Baghdad and the Sunni triangle to establish support networks for operations following the impending US invasion of Iraq.[50]

Although Zarqawi planned and facilitated the October 2002 assassination of US diplomat Lawrence Foley in Amman, he was largely unknown to Americans until February 5, 2003, when Secretary Powell made the Bush administration's case for going to war in Iraq at the United Nations. Powell charged that Saddam "harbors" a "deadly terrorist network" headed by Zarqawi, whom he described as a "collaborator of Osama bin Laden and his al Qaeda lieutenants" and the crucial link between al-Qaeda and Saddam's regime. Subsequently, on the second day of the war in Iraq, more than forty US cruise missiles were fired at a terrorist facility near the northern town of Khurmal in hopes of killing Zarqawi. Yet by the time the Coalition invaded Iraq, the Jordanian had already fled back across the Iranian border.[51]

Zarqawi fell off the radar screen after Baghdad fell in April 2003. As US forces focused on hunting Saddam, Zarqawi was lumped together with other foreign Arab terrorists. In the summer of 2003, Zarqawi returned to the Sunni Triangle and, beginning with the bombing of the UN headquarters, masterminded an eight-month wave of suicide attacks across Iraq. Whereas other insurgents targeted Americans or other coalition military personnel, Zarqawi's network terrorized Shi'a civilians with attacks in marketplaces, cafes, or other crowded, everyday locations. This spree of suicide bombings culminated with the murder of an estimated 185 Shi'a worshippers celebrating the religious festival of Ashura in twin bombings in Karbala and Baghdad.

Zarqawi's reputation for barbarism was sealed on May 11, 2004, when a video titled "Sheikh Abu Musab Zarqawi Slaughters an American Infidel" appeared on an Islamist website. The video showed a thin, bearded man—who identified himself as Nicholas Berg of West Chester, Pennsylvania—wearing an orange jumpsuit bound and seated before a row of five men dressed in black, their faces obscured by scarves and ski masks. One of the masked men, later identified as Zarqawi, read a proclamation in Arabic. "For the mothers and wives of American soldiers," the short, stocky man said, "you will receive nothing from us but coffin after coffin slaughtered in this way." The men then pushed Berg to the floor as Zarqawi pulled a long knife from his shirt. He stepped forward and put the blade to Berg's neck. As the men yelled *"Allahu Akbar!"* (God is great!), Berg's bloodcurdling screams filled the air. Zarqawi began to cut until Berg fell silent, and finally held the American's severed head to the camera.[52]

*

US COMMANDERS BEGAN to focus intently on hunting Zarqawi after the March massacre of the Shi'a pilgrims. During the abortive offensive on Fallujah the next month, Task Force 121 operators approached Marine commanders for help to insert "certain devices" in a house near city hall that would aid the search for the Jordanian. The mission was scrubbed, however, for fear that inserting such a small force into the middle of hostile territory in an urban battlefield would lead to a reprise of Mogadishu. Consequently, early attempts to apprehend Zarqawi were dependent upon a decidedly unsupportive local population. When the CIA determined the torture studio in which Zarqawi murdered Berg was located in Fallujah's Jolan district, Major General James Mattis proposed joint US-Iraqi patrols to pursue Zarqawi. But the ineffectual commander of the "Fallujah Brigade" declined. In June, US aircraft began dropping pamphlets over Fallujah urging residents to turn in Zarqawi, who had a $10 million bounty on his head. But this effort also produced no tangible results.[53]

US forces began kinetic action against Zarqawi's network in Fallujah through the only means available to them—killing eighteen Iraqis in an air strike against a suspected safe house on June 19. On July 1 the reward for Zarqawi's capture was raised to $25 million, the same amount as bin Laden. In August, US forces began conducting almost nightly air strikes against targets in Fallujah believed to be affiliated with the terrorist. Although Zarqawi himself was never touched, his organization suffered significant losses, including the deaths of his spiritual advisor and a Palestinian advisor described as his right-hand man.

On October 14 the Iraqi Interim Government raised the stakes when Interim Prime Minister Ayad Allawi warned insurgents: "If Zarqawi and his group are not handed over to us, we are ready for major operations in Fallujah."[54] When the leaders of Fallujah's insurgents refused, US forces launched a massive offensive to retake the city. For over a week, US forces engaged in intense house-to-house fighting against heavily fortified positions defended by approximately three thousand insurgents, destroying much of the city in the process. Major combat in Fallujah effectively ended with the destruction of Zarqawi's command center on November 16. Although US commanders determined that Zarqawi had fled the city before the offensive, Zarqawi later released an audiotape condemning Sunni clerics for abandoning him in Fallujah.[55]

Although the offensive deprived Zarqawi of a key base of operations, his influence and prominence, as well as the levels of violence in Iraq, only increased. With Saddam in captivity, Zarqawi successfully tapped into the anger and frustration of Iraq's leaderless Sunni minority. On October 17, Zarqawi issued an online statement in the name of his Tawhid group pledging allegiance to bin Laden and adopting the name "Al Qaeda in Iraq" (AQI) for his group. Bin Laden reciprocated in December by recognizing Zarqawi as the amir of the *Tanzim al-Qa'ida fi Bilad al-Rafidayn* (Al-Qaeda Organization in the Land of the Two Rivers) in an audiotape that aired on Al Jazeera on December 27, 2004. Despite their previous doctrinal and strategic disagreements, al-Qaeda recognized that Zarqawi had developed an effective network and a fierce reputation, and thus presented an opportunity for the immobilized organization to gain prestige from the fight in Iraq.[56]

Buoyed by bin Laden's endorsement, Zarqawi tried to undermine the event the Bush administration hoped would mark a turning point in the Coalition's flailing counterinsurgency effort. In an Internet audiotape posted a week before Iraq's first free election in a half century, Zarqawi warned: "We have declared an all-out war on this evil principle of democracy and those who follow this wrong ideology." Given his demonstrated ability to slaughter large numbers of Iraqis gathered in public places, his threat to fill the streets with blood was taken seriously. Despite AQI's threats and more than one hundred armed attacks on polling stations on January 30, 2005, more than 8.4 million Iraqis voted to select a 275-member assembly and transitional government, with only forty-four deaths on election day.

Shortly thereafter, Task Force 121 learned Zarqawi would be traveling on a particular stretch of road alongside the Tigris between Fallujah and Ramadi on February 20. Delta operators and Rangers set up an ambush and waited, but Zarqawi was late. Believing they had received another false lead, the operators began packing up when a vehicle blew through Delta's roadblock and came bearing down on the checkpoint manned by the Rangers. The Ranger M240B machine-gunner had the SUV in his sights and requested permission to fire. But the lieutenant in charge hesitated, refusing clearance because he lacked positive identification of the vehicle's occupants. The vehicle roared past the checkpoint with Zarqawi staring wildly out the window, clutching an American assault rifle.[57]

The Delta operators quickly took off in hot pursuit while a Shadow unmanned aerial vehicle tracked the high-speed chase from above. Zarqawi was "shitting his pants," one operator later recalled. "He was screaming at the driver. He knew he was caught."[58] With the Task Force operators about thirty seconds behind, Zarqawi's driver pulled off the main highway and onto a secondary road. The Shadow's camera showed the vehicle slowing down. An occupant jumped out and disappeared into a nearby field as the SUV sped off.

Inside the command center, a split-second decision had to be made: should the Shadow follow the vehicle or the runner? The officer in charge, likely reasoning that the truck could move faster than the man on foot, kept the unmanned aerial vehicle (UAV) on the moving vehicle.

Unfortunately, Zarqawi was the runner. When the Delta operators caught the truck, they captured his driver, another terrorist, $100,000 in euros, and his laptop. The hard drive contained everything from tactical information to Zarqawi's photographs of himself, which he stored in the banally titled file "My Pictures." But Zarqawi disappeared into the shadows once again.[59]

On May 24, a militant Islamic website announced Zarqawi had been wounded during a battle with US forces near Ramadi. Subsequent insurgent statements claimed he had either been shot between his shoulder and chest, or through his lung. Initially, US military officials said there was no record of any ambush such as that described by the militant websites and speculated the announcement could be a ruse to throw off the coalition manhunt. Yet in late May, US and Iraqi forces surrounded Karkh Hospital in central Baghdad after receiving a tip that Zarqawi had gone there for treatment. Subsequently, on June 1, General Myers said US analysts believed Zarqawi *had* been injured, not near Ramadi, but during anti-insurgent sweeps in western Iraq near the Syrian border. By this time, however, Zarqawi himself released an audiotape claiming he had suffered a "light wound" after combat with US troops and was now healthy again.[60]

As the violence in Iraq continued to escalate, in November US forces received a tip that Zarqawi was meeting with lieutenants at a safe house in Mosul. On November 19, a Special Forces "A-Team," supported by Iraqi forces, surrounded the house. An intense three-hour firefight erupted, killing an American soldier and four Iraqi policemen. The A-Team's team sergeant, Master Sergeant Tony Yost, somehow managed to work his way into the house despite the fierce resistance by the AQI fighters. Six foot four, thirty-nine years old, and nicknamed "Chief" because of his Apache heritage, Yost killed the three lieutenants with whom Zarqawi was meeting, but was killed himself when an explosion collapsed the building. Zarqawi's blood was later found in a tunnel through which he escaped and had detonated the charge that blew up the house.[61]

Although the Task Force had once again missed Zarqawi, its continuous operations appeared to be taking a toll on Zarqawi's network. A slide published by the Department of Defense in May 2005 showed twenty-one senior Zarqawi lieutenants: seven were listed as killed, thirteen as captured, and only one as "wanted." By August, JSOC forces had captured or killed "upwards of 200" Zarqawi associates senior enough to have had contact with the Jordanian himself.

Moreover, Zarqawi's brutal tactics appeared to be undermining his strategic leadership within the insurgency and creating unnecessary enemies. In July 2005, Zawahiri wrote a six-thousand-word letter urging Zarqawi to prepare for the inevitable US withdrawal by carrying out political as well as military actions, and strongly criticized the targeting of Iraqi civilians. Zawahiri warned Zarqawi that the "majority of Muslims don't comprehend this" and wondered whether such targeting is a "wise decision." He said fellow Muslims "will never find palatable" the televised scenes of hostage beheadings that threatened to undermine al-Qaeda's media battle "for the hearts and minds" of the Islamic world. This point was reinforced in December when Abu Muhammad al-Maqdisi, Zarqawi's spiritual mentor when both were imprisoned in Jordan in the 1990s, published a long treatise of "support and advice" to Zarqawi arguing that killing ordinary Shi'a citizens was not permitted in Islam, and warned against "acts that have no purpose other than revenge or outrages that terrify people . . . and tarnish the mujahideen."[62]

On April 2, 2006, a leading Islamist announced that the "Iraqi resistance's high command" had stripped Zarqawi of his political role and relegated him to military operations. Huthaifa Azzam, son of bin Laden's mentor Abdullah Azzam, cited the Jordanian's "many political mistakes" as the reason for his demotion within the Mujahideen Shura Council. At the same time, skirmishes began to erupt between Sunni tribal leaders and Zarqawi's group in the Sunni Triangle and along the Syrian border.[63]

In order to demonstrate his continued relevance, Zarqawi stepped out of the shadows in an Internet video released on April 24, 2006. After years of anonymity, Zarqawi was shown wearing black commando gear, a black do-rag, and shiny white New Balance sneakers ("looking vaguely like a wannabe hip-hop artist" according to one Task Force interrogator), strolling among dozens of masked followers. The chipmunk-cheeked terrorist mastermind could be seen pouring over maps and tactics with his associates, and later, in the desert, emptying round after round from a large-caliber machine gun held on his hip. Even if the video aided recruitment, by voluntarily revealing his face for the first time, Zarqawi was taking a significant risk with his security.[64]

Yet even this gambit backfired on Zarqawi, as in May the Pentagon released unedited clips of the video captured in a raid on an AQI safe house. In the version released by the Pentagon, Zarqawi is seen with his men spouting bilious rhetoric one moment, but then he is seen outside, fumbling badly with the machine gun. He fires a few rounds before it jams and appears befuddled about how to clear the chamber. A hooded terrorist steps from off camera left and charges the weapon by pulling back its bolt. Whereas the AQI-released video attempted to make Zarqawi appear Rambo-esque, the unedited version revealed him to be a buffoon who knew nothing about guns.[65]

Despite these embarrassments, Zarqawi's strategic plan was unfolding with tragic consequences in the spring of 2006. On February 22, at 6:55 AM, an explosion destroyed the golden dome of the Askariyya Mosque in Samarra. Containing the remains of the tenth and eleventh Imams, it is one of the holiest shrines in Shi'a Islam. Although AQI denied involvement, the Iraqi government blamed the attack on Zarqawi. Regardless of who conducted the attack, it triggered a nightmarish campaign of ethnic cleansing against Sunnis by Shi'a militias. In the first six months of 2006, the number of Iraqi civilians violently killed rose by nearly 80 percent (from 1,778 in January to 3,149 in June) as each day dozens of slain Sunnis appeared in vacant lots, often bearing signs of horrific torture. Sunnis were forced to turn to AQI for protection, and between January and June multiple fatality bombings increased nearly 300 percent, from twenty-one to fifty-seven per month. As Iraq slowly entered a downward spiral of sectarian slaughter, Task Force 145 (Task Force 121's new designation) refocused its hunt for Zarqawi. In March, the Colonel commanding the Task Force—a Delta Force veteran of the Aideed manhunt and the Battle of Mogadishu—told his intelligence cell: "From now on, you have only one objective: find Zarqawi and kill him" before he can spark a civil war between Sunnis and Shi'a.[66]

Unbeknownst to anyone in the Task Force at the time, detainee interrogations were already producing the intelligence that would eventually lead to "the sheikh of slaughterers." In February a detainee who admitted his association with the "Anger Brigades" (a Sunni group affiliated with AQI) revealed several residences in Yusufiyah—a town twenty miles southwest of Baghdad in the heart of the Sunni Triangle—that the insurgent leadership sometimes used as safe houses. They were placed under heavy surveillance, which did not turn up anything until around two AM, April 16, when a blue truck and white sedan were spotted parked in front of one of the houses. Within minutes, SEAL Team Six operators and Rangers were en route to conduct a raid.[67]

As US troops arrived, the enemy opened fire with small arms. The Americans killed five terrorists, three of whom wore suicide belts. Two of the suicide bombers were killed with headshots before they could detonate their vests, while the third detonated while falling to the ground, tearing his body in half but injuring no one else. As the SEALs cleared the house room by room, they realized the fighters were protecting five well-dressed Iraqi men inside the house, each of whom claimed "they'd gone to the house to attend a wedding." Intelligence later suggested Zarqawi "was probably 1,000 meters away" at the time of the raid.[68]

One of the men detained in the Yusufiyah raid was "Abu Haydr," a genial forty-three-year old with a penchant for Harry Potter books, whose girth nearly buckled the white plastic chairs in the interrogation rooms. For three weeks he was questioned twice daily but gave up nothing. Finally, an interrogation ruse tricked the Iraqi into revealing the existence of Abd al-Rahman, a Sunni cleric from a mosque in Baghdad's Mansour district. "He is Abu Musab al Zarqawi's personal spiritual advisor," Abu Haydr said. "If you want Zarqawi, watch al Rahman." He said that whenever they met, Rahman would change cars a number of times in the middle of his trip. Only when he got into a blue sedan would he be taken directly to Zarqawi.[69]

The task force began watching Rahman on May 20. US agents and informants tracked his every move on the ground while Predator drones watched from overhead. On May 31 a Predator observed Rahman switching cars to a blue sedan. The sedan weaved through Baghdad traffic, making numerous turns to shake any possible tail. After one sudden turn it disappeared behind a tall building. The Predator's camera panned up and down the street, but could find no sign of the car. The Predator flew around the building, continuing to pan its camera in all directions, but the blue sedan had simply vanished, and with it possibly the best chance of catching Zarqawi to date.[70]

A week later, however, a Predator picked up Rahman at his mosque late in the afternoon of June 7, getting into the blue sedan. The drone followed him as he made his way northeast out of Baghdad, staying on the highway for about forty minutes into Diyala province. Near Baqubah, the car turned onto a minor road and pulled up to a white, two-story farmhouse at the edge of a date palm forest in the village of Hibhib. No other buildings were nearby. Rahman opened the passenger door, exited the sedan, and walked inside the house, trailed by his driver. As the Task Force officers watched through the Predator camera, a man wearing a black *dishsasha* (long robe) walked from the house to the edge of the paved road. The man looked to his right, then to his left, before walking back inside.

Everybody was certain it was Abu Musab al-Zarqawi.[71]

As the Predator tracked Rahman, a Task Force assault team sat in a helicopter on the tarmac at Balad. The moment Zarqawi's location was revealed, they were airborne, en route to Hibhib. Yet the Task Force commander decided not to wait for the shooters to get into position. With no heavy concentration of coalition troops in the area, it would take time to muster a ground assault comparable to those that snagged Saddam and his sons. Moreover, a large ground force would likely be seen by Zarqawi's lookouts, who would subsequently warn the Jordanian. Even if a force could cordon off the farmhouse, storming the structure would likely result in a firefight, and the resulting confusion might allow Zarqawi yet another opportunity to slip away. Consequently, the commander decided to call in an air strike.

Two Air Force F-16Cs that had spent the day conducting aerial reconnaissance for roadside bombs were quickly located. The pilots were told only that the target was "high value." Although one of the planes was hooked up to a refueling plane, the second jet was ordered to peel off and fly solo for the mission, something "that is not done in the Air Force," underlining the urgency of the mission.[72]

In Balad, Task Force members waited, watching the farmhouse on a grainy black-and-white video. Suddenly, the screen grew dark, and billows of gray smoke emerged in four directions around the house, "in the shape of a cross." At 6:12 PM the jet dropped the first laser-guided five-hundred-pound bomb, creating a blast so large villagers said the earth shook. About two minutes later, before the smoke had cleared, a second blast produced a smaller, more contained plume of white smoke. Both bombs hit the target, leaving nothing but a pile of rubble and twisted metal in a grove of splintered palm trees. Other than a pair of thin foam mattresses and a small carton of pineapple juice, little else inside the house was intact.[73]

Several local Iraqi men raced to the sound of the explosions and pulled Zarqawi from the rubble, unaware the man they were trying to rescue was the most wanted man in Iraq. As they dragged him from the ruins, an ambulance and Iraqi forces arrived. The Task Force operators arrived at about 6:40 PM, fast-roping from Black Hawk helicopters. They took the stretcher that Zarqawi lay upon and placed it on the ground. Because of numerous reports that Zarqawi slept in a suicide belt, they tore off his dishsasha. But despite his declaration that he "would rather blow [him]self up and die as a martyr—and kill a few Americans along the way" than be captured, it turned out the vicious killer was wearing nothing but boxer shorts under his robes.[74]

Zarqawi spat blood and drifted in and out consciousness. When he realized American soldiers were standing over him, he attempted to roll off the stretcher and escape. The operators resecured him and tried to save his life. Although he had no external injuries except for a few cuts, his breathing was labored and shallow, his lungs collapsed from the concussive blast waves of the air strike. Finally, at 7:04 PM, his breath faded and his pulse gave out, his last sight an American soldier.[75]

*

ASIDE FROM SOME DANCING in Shi'a neighborhoods, the Iraqi celebration of Zarqawi's death was more subdued than that which marked Saddam's capture. The images of Iraqi men and women dancing in groups that filled the screen on Al Iraqiya, interspersed with shots of

Iraqi landmarks, were simply stock footage of Shi'a tribesmen celebrating. "Zarqawi is dead," President Bush said at an early morning announcement in Washington, "but the difficult and necessary mission
in Iraq continues. We can expect the terrorists and insurgents to carry
on without him."

Again, the President was sadly prescient. Seventeen raids were
launched in and around Baghdad in the twenty-four hours after Zarqawi's death, generating more intelligence and more raids, and putting
AQI on the defensive, so that suicide bombings temporarily declined.
But just as Saddam's capture had little long-term impact on the insurgency's strength, so too did Zarqawi's death fail to quell the rising cycle
of violence. Zarqawi held sway over just a fraction of the fighters in Iraq,
and the sectarian bloodletting continued to escalate to the point that by
November the American media was describing Iraq as a "civil war." As
one Task Force member said: "Zarqawi's death was an achievement, but
it was only symbolic. Zarqawi had hoped to incite a sectarian war, according to his letters, and he accomplished that."[76]

CHAPTER EIGHT

THE HUNT FOR OSAMA BIN LADEN, PART II

TORA BORA RECONSIDERED, ABBOTTABAD, AND MANHUNTING LESSONS LEARNED

In the wake of Tora Bora, the Bush administration downplayed the importance of capturing or killing Osama bin Laden. In February 2002, General Myers said, "I wouldn't call [getting bin Laden] a prime mission."[1] At a March press conference, President Bush dismissed bin Laden as "a person who's now been marginalized."[2] In the summer of 2002, when asked about the hunt for bin Laden, the commander of US forces in Afghanistan, Lieutenant General Dan McNeill, replied, "I'm not solely fixated on Osama bin Laden. If [his capture] is incidental in our operations and we get to him, that's fine."[3] Later, during the 2004 presidential election, the administration latched on to General Franks's dubious assertion that "we don't know to this day whether Mr. bin Laden was at Tora Bora in December 2001."[4] Even Bush's successor, Barack Obama, began to downplay the importance of apprehending bin Laden once he saw how few leads actually existed. Although he had promised during the 2008 presidential campaign that "We will kill bin Laden" and after being elected stated that killing or capturing al-Qaeda's mastermind was "critical" for the United States, on the eve of his inauguration Obama declared: "My preference obviously would be to capture or kill [Osama bin Laden]. But if we have so tightened the noose that he's in a cave somewhere and can't even communicate with his operatives, then we will meet our goal of protecting America."[5]

Indeed, in the decade following Tora Bora, the hunt for bin Laden was marked by occasional audio and videotapes starring the terrorist mastermind that alternately fueled speculation as to their authenticity and bin Laden's possible mortality, or when demonstrated to be genuine, where in the Afghanistan-Pakistan border region he was hiding. Yet truly significant events in the campaign, such as the March 2003 arrest of Khalid Sheikh Mohammed, the May 2005 arrest of al-Qaeda's most recent number-three leader, Abu Farraj al-Libbi, or the July 2009 killing of bin Laden's son Sa'ad, were few and far between, and the trail of al-Qaeda's mastermind himself appeared to have gone stone-cold.

Then on May 1, 2011, five helicopters took off from a Coalition airfield in Jalalabad, Afghanistan, on a cloudless night. The two modified Black Hawks and three Chinooks were piloted by aviators from the 160th SOAR, the same unit that had flown Task Force Ranger into the Bakara Market in Mogadishu two decades earlier and flown every special operations raid during the hunts for Saddam and Zarqawi. Their destination was a small city named Abbottabad 125 miles across the Pakistani border. An affluent suburb thirty-five miles north of Pakistan's capital, Islamabad, Abbottabad hosted a Pakistani army division headquarters, a prestigious military academy, and one hundred thousand residents. But the two dozen members of SEAL Team Six were only concerned with one of Abbottabad's residents that night.

The Chinooks hung back as the Black Hawks raced toward a compound at the end of a dirt road barely a kilometer from the military academy. The compound was roughly eight times larger than the other houses in the area and was surrounded by security walls twelve to eighteen feet high. At approximately 12:30 AM local time, the Black Hawks hovered over the compound. The first helicopter was supposed to hover above the main three-story house and disgorge its commandos via fast-rope onto the roof, but it unexpectedly got caught in an "air vortex" that robbed its lift capability. The Black Hawk fell quickly, clipping the compound wall on its way down. Despite the hard landing, the SEALs were unhurt and quickly dashed into the courtyard to assault the compound. Consequently, the other helicopter—from which SEALs were supposed to fast-rope into the courtyard—did not even attempt hovering and landed its SEALs outside the compound.[6]

The commandos started blowing their way in with explosives. They came under fire from the compound's guesthouse and killed a man and a woman in the ensuing firefight. The SEALs swiftly cleared the compound room by room, pausing only to blow through locked doors, walls, and barriers at each stair landing, the explosions rattling windows throughout the sleepy neighborhood. The SEALs killed two more men before reaching the main house's third floor. There, through the darkness, they saw the tall figure for whom they were searching.

Half a world away, President Obama and his advisors were huddled in the White House Situation Room watching video of the raid. As soon as the helicopters landed, however, they were unable to see what was transpiring inside the compound main house. For twenty-five minutes, the room was filled with an agonizing silence as the SEALs conducted their assault. Then, at approximately 1:10 AM Pakistan time, 4:10 PM in Washington, CIA Director Leon Panetta heard a familiar voice on the command net.

"Geronimo!" announced JSOC Commander Admiral William McRaven, the square-jawed Texan who eight years earlier had commanded the Task Force that captured Saddam Hussein.

A few moments later, McRaven declared, "Geronimo, EKIA [enemy killed in action]!"

With an ironic sense of history, the name of the first target of a US strategic manhunt was used as the brevity code for the successful conclusion of America's most recent manhunt.

After thirteen years, US forces had finally killed Osama bin Laden.

As the excitement over the killing of the man responsible for the nearly three thousand deaths in the September 11 attacks wanes, the question remains: why did it take the United States thirteen years to kill Osama bin Laden, a span of time longer than all seven previous successful strategic manhunts combined?

Unfortunately, much of the debate on this topic has been dominated by pundits and politicians more interested in gaining partisan advantage or settling scores. Rather than reasoned analysis based upon the broader history of strategic manhunts, these armchair strategists have generated more heat than light and done future US policymakers and commanders a disservice. Ultimately, the lessons drawn from the strategic manhunts discussed in preceding chapters explain why bin Laden remained at large for so long, how he was caught and killed in Abbottabad on May 2, and suggest available courses of action for the future.

In particular, it is worth examining six variables that may influence the outcome of a strategic manhunt: the level of technology employed (both relative and absolute); troop strength; terrain; human intelligence (HUMINT); indigenous forces; and bilateral cooperation. In the end, the bin Laden manhunt conforms to the lessons of more than a century's worth of American experience in conducting manhunts. Specifically:

- Although the United States almost always enjoys an edge in technology over its quarry, this advantage is never decisive;
- US troop strength is less important than the presence of reliable indigenous forces;
- Although terrain can influence individual campaigns, it does not predict success or failure across the spectrum of cases;
- More important than physical terrain is *human* terrain, which refers specifically to the ability to obtain HUMINT from local populations or support from neighboring states to assist in the US strategic manhunt.

Taken together, these lessons explain both why the United States has been successful in some of its strategic manhunts, and why Osama bin Laden eluded US forces for so long.

TECHNOLOGY

Ever since General Miles erected heliograph stations throughout the area of operations in the Geronimo Campaign, US forces have attempted to exploit their relative advantage in technology while engaged in strategic manhunts. Yet there is little to no correlation between advances in technology levels and operational success. Funston was able to capture Aguinaldo even though US forces in the Philippines enjoyed no significant technological advantage over the Filipino insurgents, whereas Pershing failed to catch Pancho Villa despite being equipped with planes, trucks, and radios. The United States enjoyed perhaps its greatest relative ad-

vantage in technology during the four-month pursuit of Aideed in Somalia. Task Force Ranger had access to the full range of US intelligence
capabilities and assets, including sensors that previous generations of
raiders "could only dream about." The Centra Spike signals-intelligence
team was pulled off the hunt for Colombian drug lord Pablo Escobar
in order to assist the search for Aideed.[7] Theater and joint task force
imagery assets included the navy's tactical airborne reconnaissance pod
system (TARPS) slung under low-flying jet aircraft; a specially modified
Navy P3 Orion patrol plane; a single-engine, super-quiet airplane with
a real-time downlink to JTF HQ; the Pioneer unmanned aerial vehicle
with a downlink to the JOC, and the Night Hawk ground FLIR (For-
ward-Looking InfraRed sensor) system. All the observation birds were
equipped with video cameras and radio equipment that would relay the
action live to the JOC, meaning Garrison and his staff had more instant
information about unfolding operations than any other commander in
history.[8]

Yet the highly sophisticated technological assets utilized by Task
Force Ranger were ultimately ineffective because they could not pick
up the low technology used by Somalis. Aideed communicated with his
militia by using either couriers or dated walkie-talkies too low-powered
to be detected by the sophisticated American electronic eavesdropping
equipment. In other words, Somalia's complete and utter technological
backwardness actually was an asset to Aideed.

Even in cases such as the Saddam and Zarqawi manhunts where
high degrees of absolute technology positively correlate to operational
success, these technologies played only a peripheral role. US forces hunting Saddam and Zarqawi possessed satellites that recorded suspicious
changes in the Iraqi terrain, spy aircraft scoured hiding spots with ther-
mal scans, and UAVs fed live video to military headquarters in Iraq. The
radar in Apache helicopters, originally designed to target moving tanks,
was reprogrammed to track cars and detect unusual traffic patterns,
such as fast-moving convoys. And the RC-135 River Joint aircraft—a
converted Boeing 707 loaded with antennae for picking up electronic
communications—flew over Iraq for up to ten hours at a time, detecting
signals up to 230 miles away and pinpointing the source of the conversation to within 1 to 3 miles.[9] But this advanced technology contributed
little to the successful conclusion of the Iraqi manhunts. Saddam and his
sons were extremely careful not to use phones or other communications
equipment that might give their positions away. Other than the single

phone call intercepted during the raid that killed his sons, there were reportedly few, if any, direct intercepts of Saddam available. Similarly, Zarqawi "knew well how much the Americans relied on high technology to track down suspects: he and his men refrained from using cell phones, knowing how easily they could be tracked."[10]

The unprecedented level of technology devoted to locating and killing bin Laden similarly failed to translate into operational success until May 2011. Beginning in 1997, the NSA and CIA monitored bin Laden's personal phone calls despite his use of an Inmarsat satellite phone and two electronic "scramblers" designed to protect the security of conversations. Bin Laden's "voice-print" was on file in the NSA's massive computers, and satellites scanned cellular and satellite phone calls originating from Afghanistan for a match. Yet these technologies were rendered useless when bin Laden stopped using these devices in 1998, relying exclusively on face-to-face meetings and couriers to transmit orders to his minions. Despite the ability of satellites and U-2 reconnaissance photography to identify fixed targets such as buildings, these systems could not single out individual faces or mobile targets.[11]

In addition to unsurpassed surveillance technology, US forces have also unleashed an arsenal against bin Laden that was unprecedented in both its technological sophistication and sheer destructive potential. By the end of November 2001, F-14s, F-16s, F/A-18s, B-52s, and B-1Bs had dropped approximately ten thousand bombs in Afghanistan, 60 percent of which were precision-guided munitions (PGMs).[12] Major Fury estimates that an additional 1,100 PGMs were dropped during the siege of Tora Bora, including an AGM-142 Have Nap missile equipped with a rock-penetrating warhead delivered by a B-52. These totals do not include the less sophisticated—but equally lethal—40 mm and 105 mm ordnance fired from AC-130s in the thousands. Yet while this massive release of ordnance gave US forces a lopsided technological advantage against al-Qaeda and literally changed the topography of Tora Bora, it did not kill Osama bin Laden.[13]

TROOP STRENGTH

The prevailing conventional wisdom regarding the bin Laden manhunt as executed at Tora Bora is that the Bush administration failed to deploy enough US troops to Tora Bora and thereby let bin Laden escape certain capture or death. On December 3, 2001, Gary Berntsen sent a request to CIA headquarters asking for eight hundred Rangers to assault the cave complexes at Tora Bora and to block their escape routes. He also appealed directly to the head of CENTCOM's special operations forces during a meeting in Kabul on December 15. Similarly, Brigadier General James Mattis, the commander of the Marines in Afghanistan, reportedly asked to send the 1,200 Marines stationed near Kandahar into Tora Bora. But CENTCOM denied all requests for more US troops. Consequently, as Peter Bergen concluded, "there were more American journalists at the battle of Tora Bora than there were US soldiers."[14] The Democratic staff of the Senate Foreign Relations Committee subsequently argued in 2009 that "the vast array of American military power, from sniper teams to the most mobile divisions of the Marine Corps and the Army, was kept on the sidelines" while "bin Laden, and an entourage of bodyguards walked unmolested out of Tora Bora and disappeared into Pakistan's unregulated tribal area."[15] Even former Bush administration defense official Joseph Collins noted, "It was the lack of expert infantry that allowed Osama bin Laden to escape at Tora Bora."[16]

Yet the history of US strategic manhunts suggests additional troops are not a guarantor of success. Indeed, the Punitive Expedition deployed twice as many troops as the Geronimo Campaign operating over the same terrain, yet it was the latter campaign that was successful. Similarly, both Operation Just Cause and Operation Gothic Serpent both involved approximately twenty thousand troops pursuing an individual in urban terrain, yet the former succeeded in capturing Noriega while the latter failed to capture Aideed.

Returning to the case of Osama bin Laden, CENTCOM commanders cited three broad arguments for why troop levels were kept so low during the Tora Bora operation. First, former Deputy Commander of CENTCOM Lieutenant General Mike DeLong argued, "The simple fact is, we couldn't put a large number of our troops on the ground [at Tora Bora]."[17] The roads from Jalalabad to Tora Bora were horrible and ran through villages loyal to the Taliban and al-Qaeda, making the stealthy or efficient deployment of large numbers of US forces improbable. Moreover, the weather conditions at Tora Bora's high altitudes and the lack of potential landing or drop zones for air insertion and resupply would have made such a mission dangerously unpredictable and logistically unprecedented.[18]

Second, General Franks later told a Senate committee, "I was very mindful of the Soviet experience of more than ten years, having introduced 620,000 troops into Afghanistan."[19] CENTCOM believed that the deployment of large-scale US forces would inevitably lead to conflict with Afghan villagers and alienate our Afghan allies. Both Ali and Zaman had made it clear that eastern Afghans would not fight alongside the American infidels, and Fury was "convinced that many of Ali's fighters, as well as those of his subordinate commanders such as Zaman and Haji Zahir, would have resisted the marines' presence and possibly even have turned their weapons on the larger American force."[20]

Finally, Franks firmly believed that the light-footprint approach—US airpower supporting indigenous ground forces—had already succeeded in overthrowing the Taliban, and would succeed in Tora Bora too. Franks was concerned that taking the time to introduce significant numbers of US ground forces would disrupt the momentum of the Coalition-Afghan offensive, thereby giving bin Laden a chance to slip away.[21]

Even where CENTCOM's logic is questionable, it is doubtful that a larger US ground force would have significantly increased the chances of capturing bin Laden. In an early December 2001 meeting at the White House, President Bush asked Hank Crumpton—the CIA official heading the Agency's Afghan campaign—whether the Pakistanis could seal their side of the border during the Tora Bora operations. "No sir," Crumpton said. "*No one has enough troops to prevent any possibility of escape in a region like that.*"[22] Indeed, if we apply the planners of March 2002's Operation Anaconda assumption that between 90–100 troops were required to block each pass out of comparable terrain in the Shah-i-Kot Valley, then it would have taken between 9,000–15,000 US troops to completely cordon off the 100–150 potential escape routes out of Tora Bora, a number that was logistically impossible to deploy to Tora Bora in December 2001.[23] Moreover, Fury noted, "We had to operate in virtual invisibility to keep Ali on top of the Afghan forces," and, "It would have been a major slap in Ali's face had" thousands of Rangers and Marines shown up. If the Afghan militias "didn't turn on [US forces] then they definitely would have gone home."[24] With regard to operations after Tora Bora, Rohan Gunaratna, author of *Inside al Qaeda*, says, "Even if Pakistan and Afghanistan were to put their complete armies there, they couldn't seal the border."[25]

Two historical operations conducted over the same terrain reinforce this point. In March 2002, three months after bin Laden escaped from

Tora Bora, roughly two thousand US troops from the Tenth Mountain and 101st Infantry Divisions, in addition to Special Operations Forces and Afghan allies, were deployed to the Shah-i-Kot Valley in eastern Afghanistan to trap several hundred al-Qaeda fighters and a suspected al-Qaeda senior leader. But as Sean Naylor notes, "at least as many al-Qaeda fighters escaped the Shahikot as died there," despite the reliance upon thousands of US conventional forces.[26] And whereas the Bush administration has been faulted for not deploying an additional eight hundred to three thousand forces, in the 1930s and 1940s the British hunted the Faqir of Ipi with forty thousand troops over similar terrain in Waziristan, but never caught their prey.[27]

In reality, because of the need for operational surprise, smaller is often better in strategic manhunts. When General Miles ordered Gatewood not to go near the hostile Chiricahua Apaches with fewer than twenty-five soldiers, Gatewood disobeyed, later recalling, "Hell, I couldn't get anywhere near Geronimo with twenty-five soldiers."[28] One Marine officer involved in the hunt for Nicaraguan insurgent leader Augusto Sandino from 1927 to 1932 noted, "Large bodies of troops had not the mobility necessary to overtake bandit groups and force them to decisive action."[29] Delta's initial plan in June 1993, code-named "Caustic Brimstone," called for a small force of fifty operators to be deployed to Mogadishu to capture Aideed.[30] And a raiding force was eschewed altogether on June 7, 2006, for fear it would tip off Zarqawi's lookouts. As with the cases previously examined, it appears troop strength was not the determining variable of success in the bin Laden manhunt that some commentators assert.

TERRAIN

A better argument for the failure to capture or kill bin Laden at Tora Bora lies in the forbidding terrain over which the operation was waged. Describing the difficult terrain there, Major Fury told *60 Minutes* that on a scale of one to ten, attacking bin Laden's position "in my experience, it's a ten."[31] Colonel John Mulholland, the commander of Fifth Special Forces Group in Afghanistan during Operation Enduring Freedom, noted "there was no shortage of ways for [al-Qaeda], especially for people who knew that area like the back of their hands, to continue to infiltrate or exfiltrate."[32] After Tora Bora, US forces had to monitor an Afghanistan-Pakistan (Af-Pak) border that stretches 1,500 miles—roughly the distance from Washington, DC, to Denver. Consequently, in 2008, CIA Director General Michael Hayden ascribed the failure to capture or kill bin Laden to the "rugged and inaccessible" terrain of the border area.[33]

Physical terrain is obviously a factor in every military operation, whether a tank battle or a special operations raid. Hence, it is true that terrain can play a role in any individual strategic manhunt. Marine officers in Nicaragua, for example, attributed Sandino's ability to elude his pursuers to the unique difficulties of fighting in the inhospitable terrain of Nicaragua's jungles. Similarly, General Hoar believed the odds were against capturing Aideed due to the warlord's ability to simply disappear into the narrow alleyways of Mogadishu. Yet despite these examples, US forces have demonstrated their ability to successfully corner their quarry in mountains (Geronimo, Che Guevara), in jungles (Aguinaldo, Charlemagne Péralte[34]), and in urban environments (Noriega, Pablo Escobar). Thus, it would be incorrect to say that any single type of terrain determines success or failure in a strategic manhunt.

Although the terrain of Tora Bora and the Af-Pak border was undeniably a hindrance in the pursuit of bin Laden, it was not the decisive variable. For during the first three years of the bin Laden manhunt, the Saudi terrorist was not hidden among mountains and caves, but rather lived openly in the plains around Kandahar. Five hundred al-Qaeda fighters were killed by US forces at Tora Bora, and the terrain apparently did not save bin Laden from being wounded. Moreover, since the 2007 advent of the "Drone War" against al-Qaeda in Pakistan's tribal areas, nine of al-Qaeda's top twenty senior leaders have been killed despite the forbidding terrain. Since bin Laden is reported to have been stationary at his Abbottabad compound from 2006 to 2011, the problem was not one of terrain masking his movements but rather of pinpointing his fixed location.[35] Thus, intelligence is as significant a factor as terrain.

HUMAN INTELLIGENCE

Perhaps the clearest dividing line between successful strategic manhunts and failed campaigns is the ability to obtain actionable intelligence on the target. The Geronimo Campaign was at a standstill in 1886 until the chance encounter with some Mexican acorn packers revealed the Apaches were near Fronteras. Funston's interception of Aguinaldo's courier breathed new life into a manhunt that had been moribund for over a year. Summarizing the Saddam manhunt, author David Isby notes, "The critical element had been . . . the all-important HUMINT." The successful targeting of Zarqawi, Amatzia Baram noted, was "a feather in the cap of American intelligence. It has very little to do with drones. This is HUMINT."[36]

Conversely, in every failed strategic manhunt there has been a distinct inability to obtain intelligence on the targeted individual's movements or location from the local population. Obtaining timely human intelligence on Pancho Villa, for example, proved to be an insurmountable challenge. Early in the campaign, Pershing lamented, "If this campaign should eventually prove successful it will be without the real assistance of any natives this side of [the] line."[37] Frank Tompkins recalled: "There was among the people a resentment toward us that was clearly shown in the brazenly false news they disseminated. Practically all information from native sources was either entirely misleading, or if based on fact, located Villa's band at places several days later than the actual date."[38] As historian Herbert Mason summarized Pershing's dilemma: "Going into Chihuahua to lay hands on Villa was like the Sheriff of Nottingham entering Sherwood Forest expecting the peasants to help him land Robin Hood. Pershing could not count on idolaters to help him catch the idol."[39]

From the outset of the Aideed manhunt, Somalia's social fabric of interwoven clans, tribes, and warlords posed a formidable intelligence challenge. Somalia's racial heterogeneity meant it was impossible for Task Force Ranger elements to move freely through Mogadishu collecting HUMINT. Using an agent outside his own clan territory rendered him suspect, and using an agent from within his own clan risked disinformation. Thus, General Hoar identified a "real problem with HUMINT. The people who provided information lacked credibility. . . . The possibility of getting predictive intelligence on Aideed was poor."[40]

The hunt for Osama bin Laden reinforces these lessons. Since the Clinton administration, the inability to obtain solid intelligence on bin Laden's movements was a constant source of frustration. Although the CIA was working eight separate Afghan tribal networks, and by the September 11 attacks had more than one hundred recruited sources inside

Afghanistan, these assets could rarely predict where bin Laden would be on a given day. Similarly, the CIA's liaisons with Pakistan, Uzbekistan, and the Northern Alliance generated volumes of hearsay, but nothing actionable enough to warrant a snatch operation or a missile strike. As General Ralston recalled, "There was always too much collateral damage relative to the confidence in the intelligence."[41]

Despite several years of effort, the CIA was unable to recruit a single asset with access to bin Laden's inner circle. Bin Laden's followers are defined by their strong religious orientation, and as a former senior US counterterrorist official told Peter Bergen, an al-Qaeda operative betraying bin Laden would have been like "a Catholic giving up the Pope."[42] A prominent Arab journalist reflected: "I don't believe they will surrender him. He's adored by the people around him. For them, he is not a leader. He is everything. He's the father; he's the brother; he is a leader; he is the imam."[43] Indeed, even the intelligence breakthroughs that led to the Abbottabad raid were based upon the revelation of a courier's existence, not on information directly relating to bin Laden's location.

In other words, of equal if not greater importance than the physical terrain of Afghanistan or Pakistan was the human terrain that provided bin Laden safe haven. The territory around Tora Bora was controlled by tribes hostile to the United States and sympathetic to al-Qaeda. Villagers turned the places where al-Qaeda fighters were buried into shrines honoring holy warriors fighting against the infidels. In the wake of the Taliban's collapse, the "Eastern Shura" became the principal political structure in the region, and its most influential leader was an aging warlord who had been there to welcome bin Laden at the airport in 1996 upon his return to Jalalabad from Sudan. Bin Laden had been providing jobs and funding for residents since 1985 through the construction of the trenches, bunkers, and caves in the area. Since moving back to the region, bin Laden had distributed money to practically every family in Nangarhar province. As Milton Bearden, former CIA station chief in Islamabad noted, bin Laden "put a lot of money in a lot of the right places in Afghanistan."[44]

This practice continued after US forces arrived on the ground in Afghanistan. At the November 10, 2001, banquet at the Islamic Studies Institute in Jalalabad, nearly one thousand Afghan and Pakistani tribal leaders rose and shouted, *"Zindibad, Osama!"* (Long live Osama!) without prompting. The tribal elders each received a white envelope full of

Pakistani rupees, its thickness proportionate to the chief's importance, with leaders of larger clans receiving up to $10,000. In exchange, the tribesmen promised to help smuggle Afghan and Arab leaders to freedom in Pakistan if escape became necessary. One leader later claimed his village escorted six hundred people out of Tora Bora and into Pakistan, receiving between five hundred and five thousand rupees per fighter and family for the use of mules and Afghan guides.[45]

INDIGENOUS FORCES

One way in which US forces are able to develop HUMINT or improve their understanding of terrain is through the use of indigenous forces. Two cases not discussed above are particularly illustrative of this phenomenon. In 1967, US Special Forces under Major "Pappy" Shelton were deployed to Bolivia to create and train the Second Ranger Battalion of the Bolivian Army, which would hunt the Cuban revolutionary Che Guevara. Two months later, CIA agent Felix Rodriguez and a team of covert operatives were deployed to assist the Bolivians in tracking Guevara and his band. In August and September, operating on tips from the local populace, the Bolivian army chased the previously untouchable guerrillas through the southeastern jungles of Bolivia, slowly attriting the group and killing Che's comrades. Rodriguez convinced the Bolivians to deploy the Second Ranger battalion to Vallegrande, where they trapped Guevara's band in a jungle canyon in Valle Serrano. On October 8, Guevara was shot multiple times in the leg and forearm during a three-and-a-half-hour battle, and was eventually captured and executed.[46]

Twenty years later, at the request of the Colombian government, the Bush administration deployed the top-secret army intelligence unit, Centra Spike, which specialized in locating individuals. Their target was the man listed by *Forbes* magazine as the seventh-richest man in the world—Pablo Escobar, the vicious kingpin of the Medellín Cartel. From January 1990 to July 1991, the intelligence produced by Centra Spike led to significant blows to Escobar's cocaine empire, but always barely missed out on capturing him due to the corruption or incompetence of the pursuing Colombian forces. In July 1992, following Escobar's escape from *La Catederal* prison, elements of the Delta Force under Colonel Jerry Boykin were deployed to assist the Colombian police's "Search Bloc." US and Colombian forces unsuccessfully pursued Escobar for the next sixteen months despite access to an array of technical assets that dwarfed anything used in previous strategic manhunts. Escobar was finally killed on December 2, 1993, in a middle-class neighborhood in Medellín. In the end, it was not the arsenal of sophisticated technology that revealed Escobar's location. Rather, it was the cooperation between US and Colombian forces that led to success, as the son of the Search Bloc's commander spied Escobar through the window of a row house after a failed raid in a nearby location.[47]

Similarly, Crook and Miles's forces would never have been able to pressure Geronimo's band if not for the familiarity with the terrain provided by their own Apache scouts. Funston would not have been able to get within miles of Palanan and Aguinaldo if not for the Macabebe scouts at his disposal. Conversely, because of the UN's mandate, UNOSOM II could not appear to take sides in Somalia's internal conflicts, and therefore could not use rival militias as scouts or a proxy force.

After 9/11, it appeared the United States would be able to draw upon indigenous forces in its pursuit of Osama bin Laden. Multiple sources suggested the majority of the Taliban opposed bin Laden and could possibly be recruited as allies in the subsequent manhunt. A Taliban official told a US diplomat in Pakistan that "Taliban leader Mullah Omar is the key supporter of his continued presence in the country, while 80 percent of Taliban officials oppose it." Hamid Mir agreed, claiming: "Mullah Omar was ready to sacrifice everything for Osama bin Laden. But the rest of the Taliban, they were saying that bin Laden is the biggest threat for the first ever Islamic government in modern times and if he is not forced to leave Afghanistan, then we will not be able to spread the word of God through our government." Immediately after September 11, an *ulema* of one thousand Taliban mullahs formally petitioned Mullah Omar to have bin Laden expelled from Afghanistan to a Muslim country.[48] As one analyst suggested prior to the start of Operation Enduring Freedom, "Informants might materialize in faction-ridden Afghanistan, where the extremist Taliban and its outside Arab allies such as bin Laden are much hated in some quarters."[49]

Thus, the United States was not obviously foolish in its choice of allies in the "Eastern Alliance": Ali had been fighting with the Northern Alliance against the Taliban for several years, and Tora Bora had been Zaman's own base of operations for several years during the Soviet War before the Taliban forced him into exile. Moreover, simply from a tactical standpoint, it was necessary to work with Afghan allies. As Fury observes: "To push forward unilaterally meant that we would be going it alone, without any muhj[ahideen] guides or security. Without a local guide's help in identifying friend from foe, we would have to treat anyone with a weapon as hostile."[50] And after two decades of persistent war, almost everybody in Afghanistan carried a weapon.

Although the decision to rely on Ali and Zaman was defensible at the time, they turned out to be, at best, unreliable allies. Ali insisted that the Eastern Shura—despite its obvious sympathies for bin Laden—had the final word on what should be done about the Arabs holed up in Tora Bora. Ali assigned a commander named Ilyas Khel to guard the Pakistani border, but instead Khel acted as an escort for al-Qaeda. "Our problem was that the Arabs had paid him more," one of Ali's top commanders later said. "So Ilyas Khel just showed the Arabs the way out of the country into Pakistan."[51] Zaman's men were from the local Khungani tribe, and many had been on bin Laden's payroll in recent months, hired to dig caves. "We might as well have been asking them to fight the Almighty Prophet Mohammed himself," Fury later concluded. "I am convinced that not a single one of our muhj fighters wanted to be recognized in their mosque as the man who killed Sheikh bin Laden."[52]

BILATERAL ASSISTANCE

There are two exceptions to the correlation between the use of indigenous forces and success in strategic manhunts. During the five-year hunt for Sandino in Nicaragua, US Marines used indigenous forces that spoke the language and understood Nicaragua's culture. First Lieutenant Mike Edson, for example, relied on native boats and crews during his legendary Coco River patrols because of the Indians' familiarity with the geography. Similarly, Lewis "Chesty" Puller's Company M became the "terror of guerrilla bands throughout Central Nicaragua" partly due to its reliance on Indians, who volunteered in large numbers to join his highly regarded unit. In the wake of the 1928 election, the thousand-man Guardia Nacional inherited the lead in operations against Sandino. Guardia contacts with the enemy rose from 26 in 1929 to 141 in 1931. Although Guardia performance was inconsistent, it continually improved. Puller's Company M, in particular, increased the pressure on Sandino through its persistent patrolling. By 1932 the Guardia whittled away at Sandino's men and supplies, and seemed to be an organization capable of dealing with the insurgent threat.[53]

Yet unlike other manhunts, indigenous forces did not prove sufficient to capture Sandino.[54]

One reason the Guardia was not enough to capture Sandino was that he could slip across the border into Honduras whenever conditions grew too tenuous in Nicaragua's northern departments. No amount of troops would have been sufficient to continuously occupy the whole five-hundred-mile border. Although Washington pressured Honduras to tighten the security along the border, Dana Munro, first secretary of the American legation in Managua, claimed the diplomats in Honduras never seemed to understand "that this was our war in Nicaragua and that getting Sandino was a matter of vital importance to the United States."[55] On April 2, 1929, Honduran public opinion forced the Honduran president to ask US forces to "retire from our territory." Four days later Marine officers met with a Honduran general on the border and established plans for joint operations against the Sandinistas, but when the Honduran president declared martial law along the Nicaraguan border his congress retaliated by reducing the size of the Honduran army.[56] Thus, despite the presence of a significant indigenous force aiding in the US strategic manhunt, Sandino could not be cornered due to the existence of a sanctuary contiguous to the Marines' area of operations.

Similarly, it was not just the Mexican peasants who worked against Pershing. The Carrancista government, although perceiving Villa as a mortal enemy, refused to provide anything resembling the assistance offered during the Geronimo Campaign. Pershing observed that Carranza's commanders "furnished us less cooperation and more deliberately false information than came from any other source."[57] In Somalia, other national contingents within UNOSOM II showed little stomach for pursuing Aideed, and some negotiated private agreements after the Pakistani massacre. Major General David Mead, commander of the Tenth Mountain Division, wrote to the Army Chief of Staff from Somalia: "This war is the United States versus Aideed. We are getting no significant support from any UN country."[58]

Conversely, the United States did not have a comparable Panamanian force to rely upon during Operation Just Cause, but were able to corner Noriega nevertheless. One of the explicit objectives of the Noriega hunt was to cut off possible avenues of escape, whether his yachts and planes or the potential sanctuaries to be found in sympathetic embassies in Panama City. The constraint imposed by a lack of foreign sanctuary is further illustrated by the two strategic manhunts this decade in Iraq. Saddam had attacked most of Iraq's neighbors, thereby eliminating them as possible sanctuaries. One of the few bordering countries he had not used force against, Syria, denied his sons asylum when they arrived there in 2003.[59] Although Zarqawi is rumored to have slipped into Syria for medical treatment, US officials explicitly warned Iraq's neighbors in June 2005 against providing refuge to the AQI leader. Such a warning was unnecessary in the case of Iran and Jordan due to Zarqawi's vicious attacks against Tehran's Shi'a brethren and in Amman itself.

Again, this corollary explains the failure to capture bin Laden at Tora Bora. Given bin Laden's ability to slip across the border between Afghanistan and Pakistan, a reliable partnership with Pakistan was critical for operational success. As with Mexico during the Punitive Expedition or Honduras during the Sandino Affair, however, Pakistan proved to be an imperfect ally at best. By the fall of 1998 the CIA and other US intelligence agencies had documented extensive links among Pakistan's Inter-Services Intelligence (ISI) directorate, the Taliban, and bin Laden. Although the ISI paid lip service to US counterterrorism goals, it simultaneously used bin Laden's training camps in Afghanistan to prepare its own allied extremist groups for attacks in Kashmir. Consequently, when Sandy Berger proposed a U-2 flight to recon bin Laden–related targets in 1999, Richard Clarke opposed him. Clarke noted such a mission would require Pakistani approval, and "Pak's intel is in bed with" bin Laden and would warn him that the United States was getting ready for a bombing attack. "Armed with that knowledge," Clarke wrote, Osama "will likely boogie to Baghdad."[60] Tenet concluded years later that "the Pakistanis always knew more than they were telling us, and they had been singularly uncooperative in helping us run these guys down. . . . That meant not cooperating with us in hunting down bin Laden and his organization."[61]

In the wake of the September 11 attacks, the Bush administration delivered a set of ultimatums warning Pakistan it was either an ally or an enemy in the coming fight. Despite internal opposition, Pakistani President General Pervez Musharraf agreed to the US demands and, on his own initiative, even replaced the religiously conservative head of the ISI and his cronies on October 8. The new, more moderate leadership of Pakistan's spy agency was ordered to fully cooperate with the CIA.

Part of Pakistan's designated responsibilities was to intercept al-Qaeda or Taliban fighters fleeing into Pakistan. This request from Washington came with little advanced warning, and Pakistan's tribal areas on the Afghan border had been off-limits to the Pakistani army since independence. Consequently, the best Musharraf could manage was to deploy four thousand "Frontier Forces" to the border, although due to poor logistics these troops did not arrive until mid-December, and even then many were likely influenced by local tribal and religious leaders sympathetic to al-Qaeda. At the same time, Musharraf rejected allowing US forces into Pakistan in a combat role. Thus, although approximately one hundred al-Qaeda fighters were captured fleeing Tora Bora into Pakistan, this avenue of escape was far from sealed.[62]

Since Tora Bora—and particularly since the assassination attempts against Musharraf in December 2003—Pakistan has actively assisted the United States in combating al-Qaeda and hunting bin Laden's lieutenants. As the 9/11 Commission noted in 2004: "[Pakistan's] authorities arrested more than 500 al Qaeda operatives and Taliban members, and Pakistani forces played a leading part in tracking down Khalid Sheikh Muhammed, Abu Zubaydah, and other key al Qaeda figures."[63] Consequently, al-Zawahiri wrote to Zarqawi in July 2005, "The real danger comes from the agent Pakistani army that is carrying out operations in the tribal areas looking for mujahideen."[64]

Yet even before the discovery of Osama bin Laden's compound just thirty-five miles north of Pakistan's capital, Islamabad, there was still reason to question Pakistan's reliability. According to Gary Schroen, the former Islamabad station chief who praised the ISI's cooperation in his book, First In, the Pakistanis delayed the arrest of al-Libbi for five months until May 2005 so they could determine that the intelligence provided by the United States did not lead to bin Laden himself. Although the CIA has been operating small, covert bases in northwestern Pakistan since late 2003, the American officers stationed there are strictly monitored by Pakistani officials and unable to effectively gather intelligence without the ISI knowing. Prior to July 2008, the United States shared all intelligence on proposed drone strikes against al-Qaeda or Taliban leadership in Pakistan with the Pakistani government, resulting in only seven successful attacks from June 2004 to June 2008 as the targets slipped away before they could be struck. When the Bush administration stopped sharing its targeting data with the Pakistanis (a policy that has been continued by the Obama administration), the number of senior leaders killed between July 2008 and December 2010 jumped to fifty-one.[65] Since 2008, Pakistan has committed 140,000 troops to offensives into its tribal areas, suffering thousands of casualties, including more KIA than the United States and NATO in ten years of war in Afghanistan. Yet Pakistani operations have been directed against groups that threaten Pakistani stability—such as the Tehrik-i-Taliban (TTP) and the Tehreek-e-Nafaz-e-Shariat-e-Mohammadi (TNSM)—rather than al Qaeda and affiliated groups. US military forces in Afghanistan lack the right of "hot pursuit" into Pakistan that allowed Generals Crook and Miles's forces to successfully pursue Geronimo into Mexico. And in the Spring of 2011, just weeks before the raid that killed bin Laden, Pakistan demanded that the CIA suspend drone strikes against militants in the tribal areas and requested that the United States reduce the number of US intelligence and Special Operations personnel in the country.[66]

As of this writing in early May 2011, however, there is no evidence to suggest that the Pakistani government was complicit in hiding bin Laden.

ABBOTTABAD

Although many details of the operation that killed bin Laden are shrouded in secrecy or likely to be revised as the fog of war lifts, as of this writing in May 2011, the initial accounts of the Abbottabad operation largely confirm the lessons of 125 years of US strategic manhunts outlined above. First, the Abbottabad raid clearly supports the contention of manhunters from Gatewood to Delta Force that bigger is seldom better when it comes to troop strength. The small force package comprised of two dozen SEALs and five helicopters from the 160th SOAR allowed a measure of operational surprise that was critical to the raid's success and that would not have been possible with a larger troop formation.

Although US intelligence agencies used the most advanced technology available in America's arsenal, once again this did not play the decisive role in tracking bin Laden. The Abbottabad compound had no phone lines or Internet service and was impenetrable to the National Security Agency's eavesdropping technology. Satellite imagery and "stealth drones" never provided a clear view of bin Laden's face, so no US spy agency was ever able to capture a recording of the voice of the mysterious male figure known as "The Pacer" suspected to be the al-Qaeda leader. Analysts at the National Geospatial-Intelligence Agency could only estimate the man thought to be bin Laden's height as somewhere between five foot eight and six foot eight.

Once again, al Qaeda proved itself to be savvy regarding countermeasures to US technology. When bin Laden's courier and host left the compound to make a call, he drove at least ninety minutes away from Abbottabad before even placing a battery in his cell phone. The house, built in 2005, appeared to have been specifically constructed to thwart a strike from a Predator drone. Because of its proximity to Islamabad and Pakistani military installations, any drone would have alerted and likely been shot down by Pakistani air defenses. Even had a Predator reached Abbottabad, the compound's multiple interior blast walls would likely have protected its inhabitants from the ordnance typically carried by US drones.

As with previous manhunts, technology made its greatest contribution to the Abbottabad raid when air- and space-based sensors corroborated HUMINT and assisted in the development of a mock-up of the compound on which the SEAL rehearsed. The intelligence path to Abbottabad began with detainee interrogations at Guantanamo and CIA "black" site prisons—including the questioning of Hassan Gul, the link between bin Laden and Abu Musab al-Zarqawi—during which multiple al-Qaeda operatives identified a man known by the nom de guerre "Abu Ahmed al-Kuwaiti" as one of the few couriers trusted by bin Laden. Painstaking detective work produced al-Kuwaiti's family name in 2007, which enabled an intercepted call with another al-Qaeda operative in 2009 to finally lead US intelligence to the region of Pakistan where al-Kuwaiti operated.

Although US forces did not have significant support from Pakistani forces—CIA Director Panetta said, "It was decided that any effort to work with the Pakistanis could jeopardize the mission. They might alert the targets."[67] US intelligence relied heavily on indigenous Pakistani assets. In July 2010 Pakistanis working for the CIA spotted al-Kuwaiti driving near Peshawar in his white Suzuki, which was subsequently tracked back to the Abbottabad compound. In Abbottabad, a CIA safe house relied on Pakistani informants to help develop the "pattern of life" portrait that led analysts to surmise that bin Laden was inside. Moreover, even if the residents of Abbottabad knew bin Laden was living among them, it is not clear they would have sheltered him as the Afghan Pashtuns did between 1998 and his escape from Tora Bora in December 2001. Although in 2003, 46 percent of Pakistanis had confidence in bin Laden according to a Pew Research survey, by 2010 this number had dropped to 18 percent. Given that Abbottabad was not considered a hotbed of extremist activity, the number of residents willing to shelter him was likely even smaller.

Thus, although the information available at this point is still rudimentary and may be subject to revision as more facts emerge, the Abbottabad raid appears to confirm the key lessons learned from 125 years of strategic manhunts.

*

AFTER THIRTEEN YEARS on the run, it can reasonably be asked whether killing bin Laden even matters anymore. To some observers, bin Laden's charisma and organizational skills still make him the indispensable figure for Islamic terrorism. As Lawrence Wright observes: "The international Salafist uprising might have occurred without the writings of Sayyid Qutb or Abdullah Azzam's call to jihad, but al Qaeda would not have existed" without bin Laden.[68] United Nations terrorism expert Richard Barrett argues, "Bin Laden represented a movement, he was almost mythic in his appearances and what he said—Zawahiri cannot equal that."[69] Other analysts stress that bin Laden continued to supply broad strategic guidance for al-Qaeda and its affiliates, and that his statements were always the most reliable guide to the future actions of jihadist movements around the world.[70] This contention appears to be supported by early reports that the trove of documents and computer hard drives recovered from the Abbottabad compound show that bin Laden played a direct role in plotting attacks from his hiding place.[71]

Yet it would be a mistake to overstate the significance of bin Laden's role based upon these reports. To date, no evidence has been revealed suggesting that bin Laden played any role in recent attacks on the US homeland, such as the December 2009 "underwear bomber," the failed May 2010 car bombing in Times Square, and the October 2010 plot to use printer toner cartridges packed with explosives to blow up airplanes over the eastern seaboard. Aguinaldo, Saddam, and Zarqawi were each in contact with their fellow insurgents when caught or killed by US forces, but their apprehensions failed to stem the violence perpetrated by the organizations they led. It is unclear at this time whether Osama bin Laden and al-Qaeda will break this precedent.

Moreover, bin Laden's importance to al-Qaeda today may not be what it was a decade ago. Even before being forced underground, bin Laden typically left much of the operational planning to trusted lieutenants such as Abu Hafs or Khalid Sheikh Muhammad. Judging by the failure of the 1989 siege of Jalalabad and of the 9/11 attacks to instigate a global war between Muslims and the United States, bin Laden's strategic judgment was of questionable value even if he remained actively involved in al-Qaeda's operational planning. While bin Laden's charisma may have been decisive in the formation and early years of al-Qaeda, throughout his decade in hiding his popularity plummeted throughout the Arab world.[72] This suggests that killing bin Laden in 1998, even if it would not have prevented 9/11, would have done more to stifle the al-Qaeda threat than his apprehension or death at Tora Bora. Although it certainly would have been preferable to kill him in 2001, by now al-Qaeda has evolved into an ideology of "bin Ladenism," and now even with bin Laden dead, dissatisfied Islamic extremists will not be deterred from their self-appointed mission to conduct holy war against America. Since 2001, al-Qaeda has evolved as the original group splintered, and regional affiliates planned high-profile attacks and encouraged radicalized followers to initiate their own strikes. Consequently, in February 2011, the head of the National Counterterrorism Center, Michael Leiter, told the House Homeland Security Committee that "Al Qaeda on the Arabian Peninsula" and its charismatic spiritual leader Anwar al-Awlaki are "probably the most significant risk to the U.S. homeland."[73]

In the end, bin Laden's death at the hands of US Navy SEALs was an important moment for American morale in the broader struggle against al-Qaeda and its affiliates. It represents a triumph of justice over evil. But the lessons drawn from previous manhunts suggest that it will not be decisive unless the United States continues to prosecute the war against the broader network that supported and was inspired by bin Laden to target Americans.

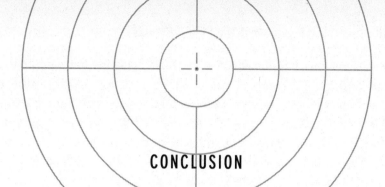

BEYOND BIN LADEN

THE FUTURE OF STRATEGIC MANHUNTS

The campaigns presented in this book suggest two almost paradoxical conclusions. First, the United States has historically been more successful than not at capturing or killing targeted individuals. With the killing of Osama bin Laden and including the Guevara and Escobar campaigns, US forces have apprehended their target in eight of eleven strategic manhunts. This positive record holds even if the universe of cases is expanded to include marginal cases that stretch the definition offered in the introduction, such as the pursuit of Charlemagne Péralte and the pursuit of Bosnian-Serb war criminals in the 1990s.

Yet the outcomes of strategic manhunts rarely correlate with the achievement of America's broader strategic objectives. Despite the capture of Emilio Aguinaldo, fighting continued in the Philippines for nearly a decade, and the most brutal phase of the counterinsurgency campaign occurred after Aguinaldo swore a loyalty oath to the United States; Pablo Escobar's death failed to stem the flow of cocaine from Colombia. And neither the capture of Saddam Hussein nor the killing of Abu Musab al-Zarqawi marked the turning point in defeating the Iraqi insurgency that was hoped for at the time. Even when operational success coincides with strategic success, it is often because of broader policies (for example, the exile of the Chiricahua and Warm Springs Apaches, Bolivia's broader counterinsurgency campaign, or the neutralization of the entire PDF in Operation Just Cause) beyond the manhunt itself. Conversely, US forces can also miss their target but still achieve their broader strategic objectives, as was the case with Pancho Villa and Sandino. Arguably, even before bin Laden's death the constant pressure exerted on al-Qaeda in Afghanistan and Pakistan by the Bush and Obama administrations similarly degraded al-Qaeda senior leadership's strategic effectiveness, given that they have not conducted a successful attack on the US homeland since the 9/11 attacks.[1]

Although strategic manhunts are at best imperfect policy instruments, future policymakers will continue to deploy US forces abroad in order to capture or kill individuals. One does not need to subscribe to Thomas Carlyle's "Great Man Theory" of history to recognize this. Reflecting upon the Noriega manhunt, Colin Powell lamented: "A President has to rally the country behind his policies. And when that policy is war, it is tough to arouse public opinion against political abstractions. A flesh-and-blood villain serves better."[2] Similarly, David Isby observes: "Americans love to personalize conflicts, even when they represent forces and movements much too complex and impossible to embody in a single individual."[3]

Beyond the inherent tendency of political leaders to bound complex problems by personalizing conflicts, operations aimed at capturing or killing individuals are likely to increasingly tempt future US policymakers for several reasons. First, Americans are sensitive to causing unnecessary suffering to civilian populations, and to some degree always have been. In 1863, amidst our clearest war of annihilation, American leaders were so horrified by the violations of customary noncombatant immunity that the Union government developed the first comprehensive set of regulations covering the conduct of land warfare. The "Lieber Code" specifically recognized the importance of distinguishing "unarmed" or "inoffensive" civilians, as well as the need to spare them from harm where possible during combat operations. The United States later signed and ratified the key international agreements—the Hague Conventions of 1907 and the Geneva Conventions of 1949—that enshrined the norm of noncombatant immunity as part of the Law of War.[4]

The immensely destructive nature of modern warfare has increased the aversion to causing collateral damage. Americans "have
grown ever more sensitive about casualties—our own military casualties, opponent and neutral civilian casualties, and even enemy military
casualties—and we seek to avoid them."[5] The death of three hundred
civilians in the bombing of the Al Firdos bunker, for example, almost
ended the air war over Iraq in 1991. It was several days before US commanders were permitted to bomb Baghdad again, and then only for a
few high-priority targets.[6] As previously discussed, this fear of causing
civilian casualties was a driving factor behind the Clinton administration's decision not to launch further missile attacks against Osama bin
Laden when he was thought to have been located in December 1998
and May 1999.

Because US policymakers risk losing public support for any military campaign if US forces are perceived to be acting immorally, they
will seek to win a conflict by focusing on as narrow a target set as possible. Beyond these moral considerations, US military leaders have come
to appreciate that in low-intensity conflicts, the people are the strategic
center of gravity. Population-centric strategies are critically undermined
if conducted through operations that either kill civilians indiscriminately or cause unnecessary suffering.

Second, since the end of the Cold War, *individuals* have increasingly
been perceived as posing a threat to US strategic interests. Traditionally,
the dominant paradigms of international relations theory dismissed the
importance of individual leaders in world politics. Structural realists, for
example, argue that all states are functionally equivalent, and that their
behavior is driven by their relative position—in terms of both geography and power—in the anarchic international system. Other schools of
thought cite domestic politics or institutional dynamics as the root of
state behavior, but seldom individual leaders.[7] Thus, during the Cold
War, it was not Khrushchev or Brezhnev who posed a threat to US security, but the entire Soviet Union.

Yet by the 1990s it appeared that American interests were being
threatened "not so much by countries, ideologies, nationalisms, or so-
cially mobilized populations as they are by a handful of leaders who put
their own interests ahead of the states they purport to represent." Although al-Qaeda's rise has subsequently demonstrated the danger posed
by a specific radical religious ideology, in autocratic countries foreign

policy does stem from the decision of a single leader rather than from popular demand or the international distribution of power. In such cases US policy should focus on this individual rather than trying to compel an entire population or reconfigure a regional balance of power.[8]

Taken together, therefore, US aversion to collateral damage and the importance of individual leaders to US interests imply a strategic impetus to kill or capture individuals who threaten our national security. Targeting leadership is arguably more defensible morally than is causing the widespread death of innocent civilians and soldiers and the destruction that inevitably accompany modern armed conflict. Or as Ralph Peters asks: "Why is it acceptable to slaughter—and I use that word advisedly—the commanded masses but not to mortally punish the guiltiest individual, the commander, a man stained with the blood of his own people as well as that of his neighbors?"[9] As the *Washington Post* recently editorialized regarding the NATO intervention in Libya, "Thousands of civilians have been killed, and more are dying every day. . . . Targeting Mr. Gaddafi may be the quickest way—and maybe the only way—to stop this carnage."[10]

Moreover, the evolution of modern technology increases the attractiveness of strategic manhunts for three reasons: the rise of the international media increases awareness of civilian suffering; the diffusion of potentially destructive technology empowers individuals, including the leaders of smaller states and transnational terrorists; and the seemingly increasing ability of US forces to lethally target individuals.

First, it is argued that the American public will tolerate significant killing in wartime "so long as the enemy dead do not have names, faces, and families."[11] Yet with the pervasive reach of twenty-four-hour international news networks such as CNN, the BBC, and Al Jazeera, governments are less able to control the dissemination of information emanating from war zones. As General Rupert Smith observes: "Television and the Internet . . . have brought conflict into the homes of the world."[12] In the hours before the end of Desert Storm, Bush administration leaders were on the phone to Riyadh complaining to General Schwarzkopf's headquarters about the images on CNN from the "Highway of Death." The pictures showed the smoldering wreckage of fleeing Iraqi convoys trapped by US aircraft, which as Colin Powell recalled, were "starting to make it look as if we were engaged in slaughter for slaughter's sake."[13] The global media are particularly eager to act as watchdogs for violations of noncombatant immunity, and are often manipulated by weaker forces in order to gain a strategic advantage by generating international sympathy. This creates a potentially serious tactical dilemma for democracies like the United States, whose military operations are conducted under the intense scrutiny of lawyers, judges, opposition politicians, and human rights activists. Consequently, US forces do not enjoy the latitude that European democracies possessed in suppressing colonial insurgencies in the 1950s and 1960s, or that an illiberal state such as Russia had in brutally crushing Chechen rebels in the 1990s.[14]

Even before the strategic lessons of counterinsurgency emerged, US operations in Operation Iraqi Freedom were dramatically shaped by the need to minimize civilian casualties. The US military ensured compliance with the principles of distinction and proportionality through the "Collateral Damage Estimation Methodology" and "weaponeering"—the process of selecting the type and quantity of weapon necessary to produce a desired effect. As the officer in charge of compiling the daily taskings for air strikes observed, "You couldn't swing a dead cat in the [Combined Air Operations Center] without hitting a JAG" lawyer. According to one study, the average monthly deaths of Iraqi civilians due to direct US action and cross fire are more than ten times lower than in Vietnam.[15]

At the same time that operations targeting civilian populations are becoming unthinkable, the diffusion of destructive technology is making individuals as great a threat to US national security as states were in a previous era. In 1987, a group of nuclear weapons designers concluded that building a crude nuclear device was "within reach of terrorists having sufficient resources to recruit a team of three or four technically qualified specialists" with expertise in "several quite distinct areas [including] the physical, chemical and metallurgical properties of the various materials to be used . . . technology concerning high explosives . . . electric circuitry, and others."[16] Another expert estimated that such a project would cost approximately $200 million. Considering that at the time of the 1995 Tokyo subway attack the apocalyptic cult Aum Shinrikiyo had assets worth $1.4 billion, this suggests the threshold for a terrorist group to be able to match the destructive power of all but a handful of nation-states is far from insurmountable.[17] In 2005, scientists in a lab in Atlanta resurrected the extinct 1918 Spanish flu and published its genome, meaning that people with resources well below those of nation-states will be able to re-create one of the most lethal disease agents in history. Far more dangerous biological weapons are on the horizon, and the technologies to develop them (i.e., advanced fermenting equipment and nanotechnology for coating microorganisms) are steadily becoming cheaper and more prevalent. Because of the dread such an attack would inspire, even a limited attack with a contagious agent would result in a shutdown of major segments of air travel, shipping, and trade.[18]

The diffusion of lethal technology, and particularly the increased lethality of dual-use technology, will allow increasingly smaller organizations, and possibly super-empowered individuals, to threaten US interests. Terrorists do not have to obtain weapons of mass destruction in order to attack America, but rather can utilize a wide array of dual-use or commercial technologies to conduct attacks. The explosive device used in the 1993 World Trade Center attack was made out of ordinary, commercially available materials, including lawn fertilizer and diesel fuel, and cost less than $400 to construct.[19] And the 9/11 attacks were carried out by turning commercial airplanes into guided missiles. As Chinese military theorists Qiao Liang and Wang Xiangsui predicted more than a decade ago, "[S]ome morning people will awake to discover with surprise that quite a few gentle and kind things have begun to have offensive lethal characteristics."[20] Worse, the Government Accountability Office recently concluded that "sensitive dual-use and military technology can be easily and legally purchased from manufacturers and distributors within the United States" and illegally exported without detection to rogue states and terrorist suppliers.[21]

The diffusion of destructive power downward to individuals is further accelerated through the rapid spread of the information revolution. As T. X. Hammes notes, "Systems that used to be highly classified are now commercially available to anyone with a computer, a modem, and a credit card." Thanks to the Internet and widely available encryption technology, anyone with a few thousand dollars can create a secure, worldwide communications system accessible from any Internet café or public library around the world.[22] The information revolution not only allows terrorists or other nonstate actors unprecedented communications capability but also gives them the ability to collect and disseminate intelligence on targets and on their enemies, including US forces. Iraqi insurgents used Google Maps to plot ambushes and IED emplacements. In November 2008, ten terrorists from Lashkar-e-Taiba were armed only with easily obtainable small arms, but used cell phones, BlackBerrys, and GPS locators to coordinate their three-day rampage that killed 173 and wounded 308 in Mumbai, India. Thus, the same information technologies empowering bloggers are allowing individuals and small groups to wage war on a more equal footing with states than ever before. As Bruce Hoffman notes, "Today, it is clear that the means and methods of terrorism are readily available to anyone with a grievance, agenda, or purpose."[23] As individuals increasingly are able to threaten US interests, the temptation for US policymakers to initiate military campaigns against the leaders of terrorist groups or of the rogue states that support them will increase as well.

The US military's increasing ability to target individuals with greater accuracy will also increase the appeal of targeting individuals rather than states in future military campaigns. Whereas in Operation Desert Storm only 7–8 percent of bombs dropped were precision-guided munitions (PGMs), this number rose to 35 percent in Kosovo, 60 percent in Afghanistan, and 68 percent during the major combat phase of Operation Iraqi Freedom. Once the war metastasized into a counterinsurgency, nearly all bombs or missiles were precision-guided as is currently the case in Afghanistan. With PGMs, any locatable object can be precisely targeted and probably destroyed. Moreover, with new assets in space and the increasing sophistication of airborne sensors, the number of objects that can be targeted has increased as well. As Martin Libicki notes: "Every trend in information technology favors the ability to collect more and more data about a battlefield, knitting a finer and finer mesh which can catch smaller and stealthier objects."[24] PGMs also significantly reduce the incidence of collateral damage to noncombatants, particularly when used in conjunction with penetrator munitions, delayed fuses, and smaller payloads that ensure the minimum necessary force required to destroy a target and that most blast and fragmentation damage is kept to a confined area. Thus, Ralph Peters concludes, "Current and impending technologies could permit us to reinvent warfare, once again to attack the instigators of violence and atrocity, not the representational populations who themselves have often been victimized by their leadership."[25]

✳

GIVEN THE PROBABILITY of future strategic manhunts, US policymakers should consider four broad policy recommendations:

1. Be careful about publicizing a strategic manhunt.

This sounds simple, but as seen with President Wilson's announcement the day after the Columbus raid and President Bush's statement a week after 9/11, senior policymakers often face political pressure to appear tough and to assuage the public's concern. Yet issuing statements before operations actually commence gives the targeted individual the chance to go to ground. A better course is to wait to declare any strategic objectives until after the campaign has started, such as Bush 41's patience in waiting to respond to Noriega's provocations until US forces had initiated Operation Just Cause or the Obama administration's secrecy regarding the Abbottabad campaign. Beyond tactical considerations, message discipline or cautious rhetoric minimizes the targeted individual's opportunity to turn an unsuccessful strike or raid into a significant propaganda victory akin to Aideed's after the Abdi House raid, or bin Laden's after the August 1998 missile strike. In both cases, global awareness that America had targeted a local warlord or terrorist and missed increased their standing with key demographics (non–Habr Gidr Somali and international Muslims, respectively) that rendered them exponentially more problematic from a strategic standpoint.

2. Do not allow gadgets to give you a false sense of security about the manhunt's outcome.

Despite the technological advances noted above that will make targeting individuals *appear* easier, the reality is that for every technology there is a countermeasure. Using the example of airpower during the Sandino campaign, when the Marines attacked Sandino with the most advanced Scout bombers, the Sandinistas adjusted their tactics to mitigate the United States' technological edge. "They move almost entirely at hours when the planes cannot reach them," Major Ross Rowell noted. "They camouflage their camps and stables and confine their operations to terrain offering the best cover from aerial observation and never fire on the planes unless they find themselves discovered and attacked."[26] The insurgents seldom moved in large groups, and if at all possible, marched only at night. Similarly, a guerrilla deserter informed Marine intelligence that Sandino had ordered his forces not to use horses, because aircraft could "spot them easily and horses could not be gotten through the brush quickly."[27]

When the United States developed technologies to intercept communications, bin Laden, Saddam, and Zarqawi simply stopped using their phones. Lieutenant General Lance Smith, former Deputy Commander of CENTCOM, once noted: "One of the reasons we're having difficulty getting Osama bin Laden and the other leadership of al Qaeda is because they recognize that technology is not their friend."[28] Indeed, as noted above, the compound in which bin Laden was hiding had neither a phone nor an Internet connection, and Abu Ahmed al-Kuwaiti waited until he was at least ninety minutes away from Abbottabad before placing a battery in his cell phone. Al-Qaeda and their Taliban allies have learned to surround themselves with human shields as a low-technology countermeasure to American drones thus embodying Rupert Smith's dictum: "Do not suppose the ingenuity that led to the technology is not matched by an equal ability to find the tactical solution."[29] Or, as former Delta Force commander Pete Blaber argues: "The reality and complexity of life virtually guarantee there will never be" an all-purpose technological panacea for finding people. "Instead, these types of capabilities should be looked at as part of an overall system. A buffet of capabilities that could be used in combination with our guys working the situation on the ground to assist in the vexing challenge of locating a wanted man."[30]

As the first "truth" of US Special Operations Forces posits: "Humans are more important than hardware."

3. *Human terrain is more important that physical terrain.*
In case after case, the attitudes of the local population—and by extension the availability and reliability of intelligence and indigenous forces— and neighboring countries are a more important variable in strategic manhunts than the terrain over which the campaign is conducted. If a targeted individual has committed acts that make him detested in his area of operations (as with Geronimo, Noriega, Escobar, Hussein, or Zarqawi), the lack of sanctuaries and available HUMINT will be proven as important to the manhunt as a mountain redoubt or an urban labyrinth. If, however, the target is perceived as a hero or a "Robin Hood" (Villa, Sandino, Aideed, or bin Laden in Afghanistan), the protection offered by the local population will thwart almost any number of satellites and elite troops. This is a deeply unsatisfying conclusion for US policymakers, as it suggests that some variables critical to operational success are not malleable by the decisions of US commanders. Instead, factors inherent to the individual and the cultural milieu in which he

operates—variables beyond our control at the outset of a strategic manhunt—may be more important.

4. Perseverance pays.

George Orwell observed that the quickest way of ending a war is to lose
it. When it comes to strategic manhunts, policymakers must be patient.
Excluding the bin Laden hunt as an obvious outlier, in the successful
campaigns cited above, US forces took an average of eighteen months to
capture or kill their quarry. Presidents Wilson and Clinton each gave up
on the respective manhunts for Pancho Villa and Aideed in less than four
months, refusing to press their advantage even when conditions seemed
propitious. In the end, if an individual is worth risking the lives of US
servicemen to capture or kill, then these forces should not be risked if
the policymakers are unwilling to ride out potential setbacks. This does
not mean that every strategic manhunt will end successfully, but rather
that you cannot eliminate the individual you stop pursuing.

If the initial raid or strike to capture or kill the targeted individual
fails, policymakers must have the patience to allow US commanders to
conduct social network analysis of the targeted individual or to reshape
the human terrain. In the months following Saddam Hussein's escape
from coalition forces seizing Baghdad, Task Force 20/121 and various
intelligence analysts pieced together the dictator's support infrastruc-
ture and were finally able to successfully target him at Ad Dawr nine
months later. Similarly, *seven years* passed between the discovery of
al-Kuwaiti's role as bin Laden's courier and the successful operation at
the Abbottabad compound. Conversely, Friedrich Katz notes that during the Punitive Expedition's period of inactivity from June 1916 to
January 1917, Pershing "succeeded in winning what later US strategists
would call 'hearts and minds' of the people in the regions he occupied."
Specifically, Pershing established an embryonic Mexican constabulary,
protected the region's inhabitants from the depredations of Carrancista
troops, and paid for supplies in hard currency, which neither the Villistas nor Carrancistas did. Consequently, Herbert Mason argues, Pershing's force—experienced in guerrilla warfare, familiar with the terrain,
and mounted on fresh horses—"could indeed have stood a better than
even chance of finding Villa and destroying him for good."[31]

In other words, the same strategies that make for an effective counterinsurgency strategy also help to improve the odds of success in a stra-

tegic manhunt, or increase the probability of a strategically satisfactory outcome even if the quarry is never apprehended. But as with counterinsurgencies, patience is a virtue for strategic manhunts.

Finally, another way in which policymakers planning for the long term matters for strategic manhunts is by working to prepare the human terrain well in advance of the decision to target an individual. Long-term investments in indigenous forces—especially partner-nation special operations forces—and the development of human intelligence networks in strategically vital regions can pay large dividends when emergencies occur that require intervention. Had the United States maintained significant intelligence ties with Pashtun sources in eastern and southern Afghanistan rather than washing its hands of the war-torn nation, and worked to develop Pakistani special forces capable of rapid deployment rather than sanctioning these forces throughout the decade because of Pakistan's nuclear proliferation, it is possible that Osama bin Laden would have been captured or killed well before that quiet night in May 2011.

✳

DESPITE THE CURRENT FASCINATION with tales of satellite surveillance, stealth helicopters, and signal intercepts that surround news accounts of the Abbottabad raid, strategic manhunts are not simply a modern phenomenon, nor are they strictly the provenance of the United States. Following the Battle of Gaugamela in 331 BC, Alexander the Great set his army in pursuit of Darius III all the way from Mosul to eastern Iran in order to cement his conquest of Persia. For nearly twenty years (202–183 BC) after the Second Punic War, the Romans attempted to kill Hannibal as he fled eastward in exile in order to remove the threat posed by the Carthaginian military genius. Even America's pre-colonial military history witnessed strategic manhunts, as in 1644 Virginia governor William Berkeley dispatched a militia to apprehend Powhatan chief Opchanacanough, eventually capturing the elderly chief after two years of pursuit.

Long after the operation that killed Osama bin Laden has faded into history, strategic manhunts will remain an important problem for US policymakers and military officials alike. Policymakers will have to determine whether a single individual poses a significant enough threat to warrant military intervention given the costs and the possibility that operational success will not necessarily translate into strategic success.

Similarly, military leaders will have to continually reevaluate how to capture or kill targeted individuals in a rapidly changing tactical environment, often while operating on unfriendly human terrain. By looking backward at such campaigns in US military history, this book has hopefully offered some lessons learned to guide policymakers and officers toward more effective strategies that will help secure the American people in an era when individuals may pose the greatest threats of all to US security and interests.

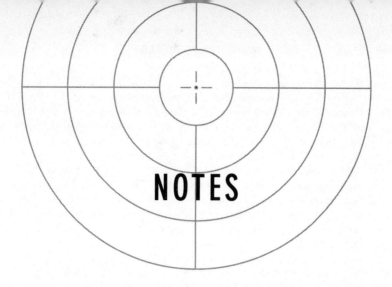

NOTES

INTRODUCTION: WHEN THE MAN IS THE MISSION

1. See Dan Balz, "Bush Warns of Casualties of War; President Says Bin Laden Is Wanted 'Dead or Alive,'" *Washington Post,* September 18, 2001; David Sanger, "Bin Laden Is Wanted in Attacks, 'Dead or Alive,' President Says," *New York Times,* September 18, 2001.

2. See, for example, CNN, "Interview with President George W. Bush," November 11, 2008.

3. On the Clinton administration's authorizations to capture or kill Osama bin Laden, see Steve Coll, *Ghost Wars: The Secret History of the CIA, Afghanistan, and Bin Laden, from the Soviet Invasion to September 10, 2001* (New York: Penguin, 2004), 410–11, 423–28.

4. House of Representatives Joint Resolution, May 3, 1886, National Archives, Record Group 94, M689, as quoted in Charles B. Gatewood, *Lt. Charles Gatewood and His Apache Wars Memoir,* Louis Kraft, ed. (Lincoln, NE: University of Nebraska Press, 2005), 119.

5. *New York Times,* March 11, 1916, as quoted in James A. Sandos, "Pancho Villa and American Security: Woodrow Wilson's Mexican Diplomacy Reconsidered," *Journal of Latin American Studies* 13, no. 2 (November 1981): 293.

6. Marlin Fitzwater, as quoted in Bob Woodward, *The Commanders* (New York: Simon & Schuster, 1991), 161.

7. For the most comprehensive explanation and critique of the theory of decapitation, see Robert Pape, *Bombing to Win: Air Power and Coercion in War* (Ithaca, NY: Cornell University Press, 1996), 79–86.

8. See Mark Moyar, *Phoenix and the Birds of Prey: The CIA's Secret War to Destroy the Viet Cong* (Annapolis, MD: Naval Institute Press, 1997); Daniel Byman, "Do Targeted Killings Work?" *Foreign Affairs,* March/April 2006; and Peter Bergen and Katherine Tiedemann, "The Drone War: Are Predators Our Best Weapon or Our Worst Enemy?" *The New Republic,* June 3, 2009.

9. See Hiroyuki Agawa, *The Reluctant Admiral: Yamamoto and the Imperial Navy,* trans. John Bester (Tokyo: Kodansha International, 1979), 344–53.

CHAPTER ONE: THE GERONIMO CAMPAIGN

1. John G. Bourke, *On the Border with Crook* (1891; repr., Lincoln, NE: University of Nebraska Press, 1971), 1.

2. Britton Davis, *The Truth about Geronimo* (Lincoln, NE: University of Nebraska Press, 1976), 142, 144; on Geronimo's appearance, see Henry W. Daly, "The Capture of Geronimo," *Winners of the West* 11, no. 1 (December 1933), in Peter Cozzens, ed., *Eyewitnesses to the Indian Wars, 1865–1890: The Struggle for Apacheria* (Mechanicsburg, PA: Stackpole Books, 2001), 448.

3. Davis, *The Truth about Geronimo*, 145.

4. Davis recalled: "Rain was so infrequent that it took on the semblance of a phenomenon when it came at all. Almost continuously dry, hot, dust- and gravel-laden winds swept the plain, denuding it of every vestige of vegetation. In summer a temperature of 100 degrees was cool weather." See ibid., 31. An Apache who lived there and fought by Geronimo's side recalled: "Dust storms were common the year round and in all seasons except the summer the locality swarmed with flies, mosquitoes, gnats, and other pesky insects. The place was almost uninhabitable, but we had to stay there." See Jason Betzinez, with Wilbur Sturtevant Nye, *I Fought with Geronimo* (1959; repr., Lincoln, NE: University of Nebraska Press, 1987), 54.

5. An article in the October 24, 1882, *Arizona Star* noted:

   > Fraud, peculation, conspiracy, larceny, plots, and counterplots seem to be the rule of action on [San Carlos] reservation. . . . With the immense power wielded by the Indian agent, almost any crime is possible. There seems to be no check upon his conduct. . . . Government contractors, in collusion with Agent Tiffany, get receipts for large amounts of supplies never furnished, and the profit is divided mutually and a general spoliation of the United States Treasury is thus effected.

   See James H. Toole, "Agent Tiffany Torn to Tatters," *Arizona Star* (Tucson), October 24, 1882, in Cozzens, *Eyewitnesses to the Indian Wars, 1865–1890: The Struggle for Apacheria*, 319–20. On the encroachment of the Apaches' land, see Robert M. Utley, *Frontier Regulars: The United States Army and the Indian, 1866–1891* (New York: Macmillan, 1973), 380.

6. Davis, *The Truth about Geronimo*, 141. Also see Odie Faulk, *The Geronimo Campaign* (repr., Oxford: Oxford University Press, 1993), 50.

7. Britton Davis, "A Short Account of the Chiricahua Tribe of Apache Indians and the Causes Leading to the Outbreak of May, 1885," Arizona Historical Society, Tucson, Gatewood Collection, p. 6, quoted in Louis Kraft, *Gatewood and Geronimo* (Albuquerque: University of New Mexico Press, 2000), 85.

8. Kraft, *Gatewood and Geronimo*, 86, citing an undated manuscript by Britton Davis (who was present at the time of the conversation).

9. Davis, *The Truth about Geronimo*, 148.

10. See C. L. Sonnichsen, "From Savage to Saint: A New Image for Geronimo," in C. L. Sonnichsen, ed., *Geronimo and the End of the Apache Wars* (Lincoln, NE: University of Nebraska Press, 1990), 9; Charles Gatewood, "Gatewood on Experiences among the Apaches," Gatewood Collection, Box 3, Folder 48, pp. 3–4, as quoted in Kraft, 3.

11. See Sherman to William K. Belknap, January 7, 1870, quoted in John Upton Terrell, *Apache Chronicle* (New York: World Publishing, 1972), 265; Bourke, *On the Border with Crook*, 444. David Roberts says that the estimated death toll of Victorio's campaign "is probably exaggerated, but not wildly so." See David Roberts, *Once They Moved Like the Wind : Cochise, Geronimo, and the Apache Wars* (New York: Simon and Schuster, 1994), 185.

12. One warrior recalled that Geronimo "seemed to be the most intelligent and resourceful as well as the most vigorous and farsighted. In times of danger he was a man to be relied on." Betzinez, *I Fought with Geronimo*, 58.

13. See Angie Debo, *Geronimo: The Man, His Time, His Place* (Norman, OK: University of Oklahoma Press, 1976), 132; Roberts, *Once They Moved Like the Wind*, 210; John G. Bourke, *An Apache Campaign in the Sierra Madre* (New York: Charles Scribner's Sons, 1958), 108.

14. Roberts says this attack was more likely perpetrated by Chihuahua than Geronimo. See Roberts, 258.

15. Commander of the Army William Tecumseh Sherman defended General Crook from his critics in the media, writing, "The Apaches know Genl. [*sic*] Crook, and fear him." Sherman to Secretary of War, August 2, 1882, as cited in Charles Collins, *An Apache Nightmare: The Battle at Cibecue Creek* (Norman, OK: University of Oklahoma Press, 1999), 210–11. On Crook's physical description, see Bourke, *On the Border with Crook*, 110, 268.

16. Utley, *Frontier Regulars*, 185.

17. Bourke, *On the Border with Crook*, 181.

18. Utley, *Frontier Regulars*, 390. On the Tonto Basin Campaign, see ibid., 203–04. More than 120 years before the US Army revamped its counterinsurgency manual, George Crook championed innovations that brought him unique success in irregular warfare against the Apaches. First, rather than using horses and wagons for transportation and logistics, Crook relied on pack mules that increased his forces' mobility in mountainous terrain and lasted longer than horses in the harsh desert climate of the American Southwest and northern Mexico. Second, Crook made extensive use of Indians to fight Indians. Finally, perhaps even more radical given the context of his times, Crook realized that a successful Indian strategy involved more than simply fighting Indians. Crook framed four precepts to guide his officers in dealing with the Apaches under their jurisdiction: first, to make no promises that could not be kept; second, to tell the truth always; third, to provide remunerated labor; and fourth, "to be patient, to be just, and to fear not." Crook's insistence on honest treatment of the Indian amounted almost to an obsession, and in time the Indians grew to trust him.

19. George Crook, *Resume of Operations against Apache Indians* (London: Johnson-Tawnton Military Press, 1971), 573.

20. On the ambush at Devil's River, see Kraft, 90–92; Charles B. Gatewood, *Lt. Charles Gatewood and His Apache Wars Memoir*, Louis Kraft, ed. (Lincoln, NE: University of Nebraska Press, 2005), 64–65; and Leighton Finley to James Parker, September 7, 1885, as quoted in James Parker, *The Old Army: Memories, 1872–1918* (Philadelphia, PA: Dorrance & Company, 1929), 157–59.

21. W. B. Jett, "Engagement in Guadalupe Canyon," *Winners of the West* 14, no. 9 (August 1937), in Cozzens, 495. A soldier who came upon the scene later described what he found: "Poor old Sergeant Neihaus was propped up against a tree, the scalp ripped off his head, and two or three chunks of bacon gripped tight between his teeth—a gory, grinning satyr of what had been a kindly, lovable man. Moriarty, a recruit, lay on his back with his abdomen slashed open and bunches of hay stuck in the cuts." See Harry R. Wright, "In the Days of Geronimo," *Pearson's Magazine* 26 (February 1950), in Cozzens, 500. Also see Michael M. Rice, "Across Apache Land," *The Great Divide* 12 (July 1895), 158–60; and Faulk, *The Geronimo Campaign*, 64–65.

22. Charles P. Elliott, "The Geronimo Campaign of 1885–1886," *Journal of the United States Cavalry Association* 21, no. 80 (September 1910), in Cozzens, 434.

23. Ibid., 436–37; Britton Davis, "The Difficulties of Indian Warfare," *Army and Navy Journal* 33, no. 13 (October 24, 1885), in Cozzens, 491.

24. On the engagement at Opunto, see Elliott, "The Geronimo Campaign of 1885–1886," in Cozzens, 433.

25. On Davis's scouts' engagements, see Bourke, *On the Border with Crook,* 467; Henry W. Daly, "The Geronimo Campaign," *Journal of the United States Cavalry Association* 19, no. 69 (July 1908), in Cozzens, 452; and Kraft, 103.

26. Gatewood to his wife, July 11, 1885, Fort Bayard, New Mexico, Letter no. 7, Gatewood Collection, as quoted in Faulk, 64.

27. "The information given to the troops by citizens is often untrustworthy and misleading," wrote Lieutenant James S. Petit, recalling a June 1885 incident in which several companies of the Tenth Cavalry were deployed to a town due to a report of recent Apache attacks, only to discover the telegraph operator had been in league with a professional gambler hoping to win money off the troops. Lieutenant Charles Elliott similarly noted that "Lack of veracity on the part of the civilians in reporting movements of Indians was frequently the cause of unnecessary loss of life among themselves.... In a sparsely settled country with few railroads, few roads, high and very rough mountains, with water long distance apart, information was hard to obtain, and when wrongly given, many weary miles were necessary to discover the error." Similarly, Gatewood recalled:

> [I]n following the trail of a hostile party, the officer would be informed by a "reliable citizen" that depredations were being committed at such & such a ranch perhaps fifteen or twenty miles off at a right angle to the direction the enemy had evidently gone. Making a forced march & arriving there, it would be found that the Indians had not been near the place but had kept on their straight course.

See James S. Petit, "Apache Campaign Notes—1886," *Journal of the Military Service Institution of the United States* 7 (September 1886), in Cozzens, 533; Elliott, 431; and Gatewood, *Lt. Charles Gatewood and His Apache Wars Memoir,* 74.

28. Davis, *The Truth about Geronimo,* 178, 179.

29. Kraft, 107; Faulk, 68.

30. Utley, *Frontier Regulars,* 393.

31. On Josannie's raid, see Faulk, 70–73; Kraft, 111–12; and Roberts, 263.

32. Davis, *The Truth about Geronimo,* 31; Faulk, 75.

33. William E. Shipp, "Captain Crawford's Last Expedition," *Journal of the United States Cavalry Association* 5, no. 19 (December 1892), in Cozzens, 524.

34. On the Aros River engagement, see ibid., 524–25; and Faulk, 78.

35. Daly, "The Geronimo Campaign," 464; Shipp, "Captain Crawford's Last Expedition," 529; and Roberts, 265.

36. Daly, "The Geronimo Campaign," 464; Faulk, 80.

37. Faulk, 83; Roberts, 265.

38. Sam Haozous, quoted in Debo, *Geronimo,* 250.

39. See Bourke, *On the Border with Crook,* 473, 476–77; Crook, *Resume of Operations against Apache Indians,* 579.

40. Crook, *1886 Annual Report,* 9–10, quoted in Kraft, 119.

41. For a transcript of the Crook–Geronimo negotiations at Canon de los Embudos, see Bourke, *On the Border with Crook,* 474–76.

42. Bourke, *On the Border with Crook,* 475–76.

43. Roberts, 270.

44. Kraft, 123.

45. Quoted in Davis, *The Truth about Geronimo,* 209.

46. Quoted in Faulk, 91.

47. George Crook, *General George Crook: His Autobiography*, ed. Martin F. Schmitt (Norman, OK: University of Oklahoma Press, 1946), 261.

48. Roberts, 273.

49. In his characteristically understated way, Geronimo simply recalled that "We started with all our tribe to go with General Crook back to the United States, but I feared treachery and decided to remain in Mexico." See Geronimo, *Geronimo: His Own Story*, as told to S. M. Barrett (New York: Meridian, 1996 [1906]), 132.

50. Charles Fletcher Lummis, *Dateline Fort Bowie*, ed. Dan L. Thrapp (Norman, OK: University of Oklahoma Press, 1979 [1886]), 34; Roberts, 273, 274.

51. P. H. Sheridan to General George Crook, March 31, 1886, quoted in Crook, *Resume of Operations against Apache Indians*, 578.

52. P. H. Sheridan to General George Crook, April 1, 1886, quoted in Davis, *The Truth about Geronimo*, 216.

53. Crook wrote to Sheridan:

> That the operations of the scouts in Mexico have not proved as successful as was hoped is due to the enormous difficulties they have been compelled to encounter from the nature of the Indians they have been hunting and the character of the country in which they have operated, and of which persons not thoroughly conversant with both can have no conception. I believe that the plan upon which I have conducted operations is the one most likely to prove successful in the end. It may be, however, that I am too much wedded to my own views in this matter, and as I have spent nearly eight years of the hardest work of my life in this department, I respectfully request that I may now be relieved from its command.

George Crook to Lieutenant General P. H. Sheridan, April 1, 1886, as quoted in Crook, *Resume of Operations against Apache Indians*, 581.

54. Lummis, *Dateline Fort Bowie*, 70.

55. Roberts, 278.

56. Later, he cautioned his former deputy that "Genl [*sic*] Miles is too apt to mistake the dictates of his personal ambition for wisdom." See Sherman to Sheridan, March 9, 1879, Sherman–Sheridan Letters, Sheridan Papers, Library of Congress, and Sherman to Sheridan, July 19, 1879, Sherman–Sheridan Letters, Sheridan Letters, Volume 2, Sheridan Papers, Library of Congress, as quoted in Utley, *Frontier Regulars*, 294, 295.

57. See William A. Thompson report (Apr. 20, 1886), Sen. Exec. Doc. 117, 49th Cong., 2nd sess., p. 2, as quoted in Geronimo, *Geronimo*, 172; Nelson A. Miles, *Serving the Republic: Memoirs of the Civil War and Military Life of Nelson A. Miles* (New York: Harper & Brothers Publishers, 1911), 225.

58. Faulk, 102.

59. House of Representatives Joint Resolution, May 3, 1886, National Archives, Record Group 94, M689, as quoted in Gatewood, *Lt. Charles Gatewood and His Apache Wars Memoir*, 119.

60. Miles, *Serving the Republic*, 224. See also Faulk, 106. Miles's biographer, Peter DeMontravel, argues that this flying column was formed from just two companies, and that therefore the selection of enlisted personnel "was not as selective as Miles wished his readers to believe." See Peter R. DeMontravel, *A Hero to His Fighting Men: Nelson A. Miles, 1839–1925* (Kent, OH: The Kent State University Press, 1998), 164.

61. Nelson A. Miles, "On the Trail of Geronimo," *Cosmopolitan* 51 (June 1911), in Cozzens, 537; and Miles, *Serving the Republic*, 224.

62. Hermann Hagedorn, *Leonard Wood: A Biography,* Vol. I, (New York: Harper & Brothers, 1931), 54; and Henry W. Daly, "The Geronimo Campaign [Concluded]," *Journal of the United States Cavalry Association* 19, no. 70 (October 1908), in Cozzens, 479.

63. Charles F. Lummis, *General Crook and the Apache Wars,* ed. Turbese Lummis Fiske, (Flagstaff, AZ: Northland Press, 1966), 142. On the strategic failure of Lawton's command, see Kraft, 120; and Roberts, 284–85.

64. See Faulk, 109; Gatewood, *Lt. Charles Gatewood and His Apache Wars Memoir,* 128; and Leonard Wood, *Report of Assistant Surgeon Leonard Wood, US Army, Fort Bowie, A.T., September 8, 1886, to Brigadier General N.A. Miles, USA., Albuquerque, New Mexico,* in Cozzens, 549, 550.

65. Faulk, 109, 110; Wood, *Report of Assistant Surgeon Leonard Wood,* 551. As if the terrain and weather were not difficult enough, "In our bivouacs we suffered much from ants and various insects that crawled under our bedclothes. Scorpions, tarantulas, and centipedes abounded." See Parker, *The Old Army,* 20.

66. Lawton to Adjutant General, September 9, 1886, *SW Annual Report,* as quoted in Davis, *The Truth about Geronimo,* 220, 221.

67. In the end, one survivor simply concluded, "It was only pure American grit that kept us going." See Clarence Chrisman, "The Apache Campaign of 1885–1886," *Winners of the West,* nos. 4–8 (March–July 1927), in Cozzens, 543; Faulk, 111.

68. Miles to Mary Sherman Miles, July 5, 1886, Ft. Apache, Arizona, in Virginia W. Johnson, *The Unregimented General: A Biography of Nelson A. Miles* (Boston: Houghton Mifflin, 1962), 240.

69. Miles to Howard, July 7, 1886, Ft. Apache, as quoted in Faulk, 154–55. Miles was not the first to propose the removal of all Chiricahua and Warm Springs Apaches, however. On November 29, 1885, at Secretary of War William C. Endicott's request, Sheridan informed Crook of the growing conviction in Washington that satisfactory resolution of the Apache problem depended upon relocating them to a location far away from the Southwest. Crook, supported by Crawford, strongly opposed the measure, arguing that such a scheme would decimate and demoralize the scout companies upon which their campaign depended. See Utley, *Frontier Regulars,* 394.

70. Davis, *The Truth about Geronimo,* 223; and Faulk, 38.

71. Anton Mazzanovich, *Trailing Geronimo,* edited and arranged by E. A. Brininstool (Los Angeles: Gem Publishing Company, 1926), 246.

72. Gatewood to Miles, October 15, 1886, Gatewood Collection, as quoted in Kraft, 134.

73. James B. Parker, "Service with Lieutenant Charles B. Gatewood, 6th US Cavalry," Gatewood Collection, as quoted in Faulk, 114.

74. Lawton to Adjutant General, District of Huachuca, August 8, 1886, Gatewood Collection, as quoted in Kraft, 145; Brigadier General James Parker, "The Geronimo Campaign," in John M. Carroll, introduction, and preface by Colonel George S. Pappas, *The Papers of the Order of Indian Wars* (Fort Collins, CO: The Old Army Press, 1975), 98. Hermann Hagedorn, based upon an August 4, 1886, letter from Lawton to his wife, argues that Lawton was just letting off steam and in fact was glad that Gatewood was there. See Hagedorn, *Leonard Wood,* 1:85.

75. Leonard Wood, *Chasing Geronimo: The Journal of Leonard Wood: May–September 1886,* edited, with introduction and epilogue by Jack C. Lane (Albuquerque, NM: University of New Mexico Press, 1970), August 19, 1886, 98. Earlier, upon meeting Gatewood on August 3, Wood noted, "He is not in especially good

health. Is suffering from an old inflammation of the bladder which renders riding difficult." See ibid., August 3, 1886, 88.

76. Lieutenant Charles B. Gatewood, "The Surrender of Geronimo," in Sonnichsen, *Geronimo and the End of the Apache Wars*, 58.

77. Ibid., 60. Wratten quoted in Albert E. Wratten, "George Wratten: Friend of the Apaches," in Sonnichsen, *Geronimo and the End of the Apache Wars*, 97.

78. Martine and Kayitah, "The Story of the Final Surrender of Geronimo," as told to O. M. Boggess, Superintendent of the Mescalero Indian Reservation, September 25, 1925, Gatewood Collection, p. 4, as quoted in Kraft, 162; Wratten, "George Wratten," 97.

79. Gatewood, "The Surrender of Geronimo," 61.

80. See ibid., 61; and Kraft, 163.

81. Gatewood, "The Surrender of Geronimo," 61; Kraft, 164.

82. Gatewood, "The Surrender of Geronimo," 63.

83. Ibid., 63.

84. Gatewood to Miles, October 15, 1886, Gatewood Collection, quoted in Kraft, 171.

85. Miles, *Serving the Republic*, 226.

86. Lawton to Mame Lawton, August 27, 1886, as quoted in Wood, *Chasing Geronimo*, 103.

87. Gatewood, "The Surrender of Geronimo," 68.

88. On September 1 he wrote Lawton seeking reassurance: "If you feel sure the Indians will surrender to me I will start tonight." See Roberts, 295; Faulk, 141.

89. As quoted in Faulk, 142.

90. The canyon was given its name from the still-visible remains of nineteen Mexicans ambushed and killed there by the Tombstone outlaw Curly Bill and his gang, who more than a century later would be immortalized as the Earp brothers' antagonists in the film *Tombstone*.

91. Thompson to Miles, September 3, 1886, Gatewood Collection, as quoted in Kraft, 190.

92. Miles later wrote that the old warrior "was one of the brightest, most resolute, determined looking men that I have ever encountered. He had the clearest, sharpest, dark eye I think I have ever seen.... Every movement indicated power, energy and determination. In everything he did he has a purpose." See Nelson A. Miles, *Personal Recollections and Observations of General Nelson A. Miles* (Chicago: The Werner Company, 1896), 520–22.

93. Roberts, 295.

94. Ibid., 296; and Faulk, 145.

95. Miles, Geronimo quoted in Faulk, 146.

96. Robert M. Utley, *A Clash of Cultures: Fort Bowie and the Chiricahua Apaches* (Washington, DC: National Park Service, 1977), 79.

97. Miles, *Personal Recollections*, 527–28.

98. Crook quoted in Bourke, *On the Border with Crook*, 483; Utley, *Frontier Regulars*, 400.

99. In his official reports and subsequent memoirs, Miles described success in terms of Lawton's tenacious pursuit and his own persuasiveness at Skeleton Canyon, as if the entire victory had been manipulated by puppet strings from his desk at Fort Bowie. In his list of tributes to officers who had served gallantly in the Geronimo campaign, Gatewood's name is conspicuously absent.

On November 8, 1886, the citizens of Tucson held a banquet to honor General Miles and the officers of the Geronimo campaign. Miles had relocated

Department headquarters to Los Angeles, where Gatewood now served as his aide. Just before they were to leave for Arizona to attend the ceremony, Miles informed Gatewood that he would remain behind to perform clerical work. Thus, while the citizens of Arizona hailed the conquering heroes—Miles received an ornamental Tiffany sword described in 1887 as "the most artistic weapon ever made in the United States"; Lawton was presented with a gold watch and chain—Gatewood remained in California performing tasks an ordinary clerk could have completed. When Miles was asked at the celebration about Gatewood's role in the surrender, the general stated that he was "sick of this adulation of Lieutenant Gatewood, who only did his duty." See Georgia to Gatewood Jr., Date Unknown/Letter Incomplete, quoting a San Francisco newspaper, Gatewood Collection, Letter 58, quoted in Kraft, 211–12. On Miles's sword, see DeMontravel, *A Hero to His Fighting Men*, 190.

100. See Frederick Turner, "Introduction," in Geronimo, 33. Despite the trivializing effect of such spectacles, Geronimo's name could still inspire fear on occasion. One day during their stay at the Omaha Exhibition in 1898, Geronimo, Naiche, and a few other Apaches hired a wagon to take a ride in the countryside. As darkness fell, they got lost among the endless cornfields. When word of their disappearance spread across eastern Nebraska, farmers bolted their doors and sat with rifles ready. By the time they found their way back to Omaha, the headline of the daily extra read: "GERONIMO AND NACHEE ESCAPE. APACHE MURDERERS THOUGHT TO BE ON THEIR WAY BACK TO ARIZONA."

Geronimo's legacy among the Chiricahua Apaches was decidedly mixed. One Apache who did not go on the warpath but was removed to Florida with the other reservation Chiricahuas later wrote: "I know plenty about [Geronimo]. I know that he and a few others like him were the cause of the death of my mother and many of my relatives who have been pushed around the country as prisoners of war. I know we would not be in our present trouble if it was not for men like him, and you honor him for that. . . . These people, these Chiricahua Apache, who lived at Fort Apache peacefully, and the scouts who had helped the army run down Geronimo's band, were taken to prison for what Geronimo had done." See Ross Santee, *Apache Land* (Lincoln, NE: University of Nebraska Press, 1971), 174–76; and Samuel E. Kenoi, recorded by Morris E. Opler, "A Chiricahua Apache's Account of the Geronimo Campaign of 1886," in Sonnichsen, 72, 84.

101. M. Salzman Jr., "Geronimo: The Napoleon of Indians," *The Border*, March 1909, and reprinted in *The Journal of Arizona History* 8 (Winter 1967), 215–47, as quoted in Faulk, 218.

CHAPTER TWO: THE CAPTURE OF EMILIO AGUINALDO

1. John R. M. Taylor, *The Philippine Insurrection Against the United States* (Washington, DC, 1906; 5 vols. of galley proof never published), galley 18AJ and 19AJ.

2. George Dewey, *Autobiography* (New York: C. Scribner's Sons, 1916), 245, 246–47; Henry F. Graff, ed., *American Imperialism and the Philippine Insurrection: Testimony Taken from Hearings on Affairs in the Philippine Islands Before the Senate Committee on the Philippines—1902* (Boston: Little, Brown, 1969), 3.

3. H. W. Brands, *Bound to Empire: The United States and the Philippines* (New York: Oxford University Press, 1992), 46; Leon Wolff, *Little Brown Brother: How the United States Purchased and Pacified the Philippine Islands at the Century's Turn* (New York: Doubleday, 1960), 77; and David F. Trask, *The War with Spain in 1898* (Lincoln, NE: University of Nebraska Press, 1981), 405.

4. Dewey to Long, July 26, 1898, in *Annual Reports of the Navy Department for the Year 1898*. Volume 2: *Appendix to the Report of the Chief of the Bureau of Navigation* (Washington, DC, 1898), 118.

5. Quoted in Wolff, 107.

6. Young, *The General's General*, 200–2.

7. Aguinaldo, *A Second Look at America*, 87. On Otis's advice to the president, see Olcott, *Life of William McKinley*, 2:110–11.

8. Specifically, Aguinaldo warned: "My government is ready to open hostilities if the Americans troops attempt to take forcible possession of such portion of the territory as comes under its jurisdiction. I denounce these acts before the world, in order that the conscience of mankind may pronounce its infallible verdict as to who are the true oppressors of nations and the tormentors of human kind. Upon their heads be all the blood which may be shed." See Aguinaldo Proclamation, January 16, 1899, Emilio Aguinaldo papers, Library of Congress, Washington, DC.

9. For example, in November, General Mascardo in San Fernando wrote Aguinaldo: "Most urgent. Have received telegraphic order from War Department which says: 'Prevent American troops from disembarking.' In case they insist what am I to do? May I begin firing?" Aguinaldo telegraphed: "Answered affirmatively." In January, Aguinaldo telegraphed the commander at Caloocan: "Tell the Filipino soldiers that they must keep on good terms with the Americans, in order to deceive them . . . since the hoped for moment has not yet arrived." See Wolff, 145, 202, 203–04, 206; and Stanley Karnow, *In Our Image: America's Empire in the Philippines* (New York: Random House, 1989), 135.

10. Brian MacAllister Linn notes, however, that the official US Army estimate was in reality little more than guesswork and that the battle was one-sided only in retrospect: almost all officers and many of the soldiers in the Army of Liberation were veterans of months, if not years, of fighting against the Spanish; the Filipinos were actually strengthened by a number of former Spanish soldiers; Filipino troop morale was very high; the Filipinos even had a slight weapons superiority, as their captured Mausers outranged the Volunteers' Springfields; and the insurgents could easily infiltrate troops to reinforce their sizable contingent of supporters in Manila and strike the Americans from the front and rear. Linn concludes that "With almost half a year to prepare for a showdown with the 8th Corps, to develop defensive positions, to train troops, to devise a coherent defense, to implement effective tactics, the Army of Liberation should have performed much better than it did." See Brian McAllister Linn, *The Philippine War, 1899–1902* (Lexington, KY: University Press of Kentucky, 2000), 52, 61.

11. Quotes taken from Bain, 12.

12. Brands, 50. See also Young, 231–34.

13. Linn, *The U.S. Army and Counterinsurgency in the Philippine War*, 12.

14. Kitchener comparison, *New York Times* quote in Miller, 70, 97. Also see Young, 240; and Dean C. Worcester, *The Philippines: Past and Present*, vol. 1 (New York: Macmillan, 1914), 320.

15. Russell Roth, *Muddy Glory: America's 'Indian Wars' in the Philippines, 1899–1935* (W. Hanover, MA: The Christopher Publishing House, 1981), 17; Young, 240; Worcester, *The Philippines*, 320; and Linn, *The Philippine War*, 115.

16. Worcester, 323.

17. See Wolff, 259, 260; Linn, *The Philippine War*, 139.

18. Gates, *Schoolbooks and Krags*, 158; Wolff, 260, 278, 279.

19. Linn, *The Philippine War*, 144–45; Wolff, 280.

20. See Linn, *The Philippine War*, 147. See also Young, 246, 247.

21. "The only reason the guide who led us to Manaoag instead of Pozorrubio was not shot," Young commented later, "was because he could not be found." Quoted in Wolff, 283. See also Linn, *The Philippine War*, 147, 148; and Miller, 96.

22. Young to Otis, November 17, 1899, in *Report of the War Department, 1898*, I:4:264, quoted in Linn, *The Philippine War*, 148. Linn notes that Young's best unit, Major John G. Ballance's Twenty-Second Infantry, was unfit for service at this point, and that three-fourths of its soldiers would soon be placed on sick report.

23. Wolff, 283, 284. There are two likely reasons for Wheaton's hesitance. First, despite the ease of his landing at San Fabian, high surf hampered the landing of supplies for a week, and on the twelfth a typhoon struck, flooding the countryside and rendering the march inland virtually impossible. Consequently, Wheaton did not push out patrols as far as Pozorubbio until November 16, a day after Aguinaldo had crossed the mountains into La Union province. More important, Otis had given Wheaton oral orders to place troops "on the roads leading north and near the coast, to prevent the retreat of the insurgent army to [the] north along the roads or trails leading in that direction." When MacArthur intercepted Aguinaldo's proclamation that he was relocating his capital to Bayombong, Otis, who suffered from a crippling lack of imagination, interpreted this to mean the president still planned to withdraw with the army and his cabinet. This would have limited his route to a few major trails. In reality, Aguinaldo had detached himself and his entourage from the bulk of his forces and could now travel rapidly over a more diverse option of routes. *Report of the War Department, 1900*, I:6:529, quoted in Linn, *The Philippine War*, 150.

24. Wolff, 284.

25. John T. McCutcheon, "Aguinaldo's Rear Guard," in Marrion Wilcox, *Harper's History of the War in the Philippines* (New York: Harper's, 1900), 317–20.

26. Bain, 195; Linn, *The Philippine War*, 155; and William Thaddeus Sexton, *Soldiers in the Sun: An Adventure in Imperialism* (Freeport, NY: Books for Libraries Press, 1939), 207.

27. Little wrote:

> We had seen him cheering his men in the fight. One of our companies crouched up close under the side of the cliff where he had built his first intrenchment [sic], heard his voice continually during the fight, scolding them, praising them, cursing, appealing one moment to their love of their native land and the next instant threatening to kill them if they did not stand firm. Driven from the first intrenchment [sic] he fell slowly back to the second in full sight of our sharpshooters and under a heavy fire. Not until every man around him in the second intrenchment [sic] was down did he turn his white horse and ride slowly up the winding trail. Then we who were below saw an American squirm his way out to the top of a high flat rock, and take deliberate aim at the figure on the white horse. We held our breath, not knowing whether to pray that the sharpshooter would shoot straight or miss. Then came the spiteful crack of the Krag rifle and the man on horseback rolled to the ground, and when the troops charging up the mountain side reached him, the boy general of the Filipinos was dead.

Little quoted in Wolff, 286. For accounts disputing Little's version of the Battle of Tirad Pass, see Linn, *The Philippine War*, 156.

28. Linn, *The Philippine War*, 156; Miller, 97.

29. *War Department, 1900* I:4:448, as quoted in Linn, *The U.S. Army and Counterinsurgency in the Philippine War*, 21.

30. Quoted in Wolff, 252. Typical was the August 1900 appeal of General Tomas Mascardo: "Let us for a little while longer put forth heroic deeds of arms," because "McKinley falls by the way side, the people abandon him, and incline to the political party of Mr. Bryan whose fundamental teaching is the recognition of our independence." See Linn, *The Philippine War*, 187.

31. See Linn, *The Philippine War*, 210, 211, 264, 267, 272, 281–82; and Linn, *The U.S. Army and Counterinsurgency in the Philippine War*, 23.

32. Linn, *The U.S. Army and Counterinsurgency in the Philippine War*, 22–23; see also Gates, 204, 209.

33. Wolff, 301, 302. See also Bain, 13; Villa and Barcelona, 45; and Miller, 167.

34. For accounts of Aguinaldo's harrowing journey through the mountains of Luzon after Tirad Pass, see Villa diary entries in Villa and Barcelona, 8, 14, 39, 72, 119. On Aguinaldo's flight to Palanan, see Bain, 275–94.

35. Linn, *The Philippine War*, 185; Taft quoted in Karnow, 173.

36. Frederick Funston, *Memories of Two Wars: Cuban and Philippine Experiences* (1911; repr., Lincoln, NE: University of Nebraska Press, 2009), 386.

37. Frederick Funston, *Memories of Two Wars*, 6.

38. Sexton, *Soldiers in the Sun*, 95–96.

39. Funston, *Memories of Two Wars*, 282, 285–86.

40. Linn, *The U.S. Army and Counterinsurgency in the Philippine War*, 70, 76, 81.

41. Bain, 95.

42. Bain, 97.

43. Specifically, Aguinaldo wrote:

> My dear cousin:
>
> After many and risky adventures we were able to reach Cagayan valley, where we are at present. I have not sufficient people of my confidence to garrison this province. I want, in the first place, that you take charge of the command of Central Luzon, residing wherever you deem it best; send me about 400 men at the first opportunity with a good commander; if you can not send them all at once, send them in parties, the bearer can serve as guide to them until their arrival here, he is a person to be trusted.
>
> We are preparing a large arsenal in this camp, which can furnish Central and even Southern Luzon with ammunition, some of the commercial houses of Cagayan and Isabela have promised us machinery and tools. I forwarded another copy of this letter by sea in case this one should be lost.
> (Signed) Colon de Magdolo

Letter quoted in Lazaro Segovia, *The Full Story of Aguinaldo's Capture*, trans. Frank de Thoma (Manila: Amigos del Pais, 1902: 1969 reprint by MCS Enterprises), 21. There is some controversy regarding how the precise location of Aguinaldo was extracted from Palanan. Segovia claims that Segismundo recognized him from their insurgent days and talked willingly. Aguinaldo claims that Segismundo was given the water cure without specifying how he came by this information. See ibid., 8–15; Aguinaldo, *A Second Look at America*, 126.

44. Funston, *Memories of Two Wars*, 395, 396.

45. Young, 286. Indeed, a Japanese editor warned: "It will amount to this, that when Aguinaldo is taken—if he ever is—and when the Philippine army is smashed,

people will not believe it. Most people will wink the other eye and say the Americans must be getting badly cornered again." Quoted in Miller, 168.

46. Funston, *Memories of Two Wars*, 398.

47. Funston, *Memories of Two Wars*, 399. Segovia claims to have met with Talplacido the night before, during which time he expressed doubts whether: a) they could surprise Aguinaldo, as it was widely known that Talplacido had defected; and b) whether he could accurately play the role of a colonel and leader of such a column. See Segovia, *The Full Story of Aguinaldo's Capture*, 46–50, 66.

48. See Segovia, 78–81; Funston, *Memories of Two Wars*, 402–03; and Bain, 213–14.

49. On the landing, see Funston, *Memories of Two Wars*, 404; Segovia, 82–87; and Bain, 219–20.

50. Segismundo had apparently kept busy after delivering his message to the village headman, for he greeted his colleagues with his arm wrapped around the shoulders of a village girl he had befriended during an earlier stay in the area. See Funston, *Memories of Two Wars*, 407; Segovia, 95.

51. Segovia, 89.

52. Ibid., 102; Bain, 255.

53. "Capt. Newton Tells of Aguinaldo's Capture," *Superior Evening Telegram*, May 23, 1901, as quoted in Bain, 321. See also Funston, "The Capture of Emilio Aguinaldo," *Everybody's Magazine*, October 1901, 472.

54. Funston, *Memories of Two Wars*, 412.

55. Segovia, 105–07.

56. Ibid., 109.

57. Ibid., 109; Bain, 324.

58. Funston, *Memories of Two Wars*, 414.

59. Funston, "The Capture of Emilio Aguinaldo," 472; Segovia, 121.

60. Segovia, 124–25.

61. Bain, 364.

62. Segovia, 140.

63. Segovia, 142.

64. Segovia, 142.

65. Funston, "The Capture of Emilio Aguinaldo," 474; Segovia, 143.

66. Funston spent part of the twenty-fourth with Aguinaldo, finding him to be "always courteous and self-possessed," and answering his questions about how he had been tricked. "Is there no limit to what you Americans can do!" Aguinaldo exclaimed upon learning the details of the plan. "It was a bold plan, executed with skill and cleverness in the face of difficulties which to most men, would have seemed insurmountable." Segovia also visited Aguinaldo several times. "I should never have believed it, that I could be deceived in this manner. . . . The whole thing seems yet to me a nightmare. I can hardly believe myself a prisoner," the Filipino confided. Ibid., 476; Brown to Roosevelt, Camp Wallace, Manila, April 27, 1901, in Theodore Roosevelt Papers, Serial 1, Reel 13, quoted in Bain, 370; Emilio Aguinaldo, "The Story of My Capture," *Everybody's Magazine* 5, no. 24 (August 1901), 140; Segovia, 147.

67. Young, 207, 286.

68. Funston, "The Capture of Emilio Aguinaldo," 478; Young, 286.

69. Funston, *Memories of Two Wars*, 425ff.; Sexton, 264–65.

70. Aguinaldo proclamation, April 19, 1901, Bureau of Insular Affairs records, National Archives, Washington, DC.

71. *New York Times*, MacArthur quoted in Miller, 171, 175.

72. Aguinaldo, *A Second Look at America*, 48, 66. In 1930, Aguinaldo appeared in a film for the Military Order of the Carabao (the fraternal organization for veterans of the Philippines War)'s "Main Corral Wallow" in Washington, DC, saying: "I greet you today with all the warmth of which my heart is capable. The Filipino associated veterans, seventy thousand strong, join me in this greeting. Some of them who were with me in many a campaign are present as I read this message to you, all reminiscent of how brave adversaries you all were in war and how good and sincere as friends in peace." Aguinaldo was less generous toward Funston. Despite expressing admiration immediately after his capture, with time he came to characterize the deception that led to his capture as "a clever but certainly unsporting ruse" and that "I would say that what Funston did was not exactly cricket." Given that his entire system of warfare was based upon similar deceptions and attacking American forces while in civilian attire, this is a fairly hypocritical critique. See ibid., 19, 124; and Roth, 205.

73. *Report of the War Department, 1901*, I: I:32, quoted in Linn, *The Philippine War*, 275; Bryan quoted in Bain, 384.

74. Major General Miguel Malvar, "The Reasons for My Change of Attitude," April 16, 1902, Taylor, *The Philippine Insurrection*, Exhibit 1172, p. 89 GV, quoted in Linn, *The U.S. Army and Counterinsurgency in the Philippines*, 158.

75. MacArthur to AG, March 16 and 19, 1901, *Correspondence Relating to the War with Spain . . .* , 2:1259–60, quoted in Gates, 230. See also 235.

76. See Gates, 229; "Testimony of Lt. Col. Bernardo Marques," *Gardener Board*, 153, as quoted in Linn, *The U.S. Army and Counterinsurgency in the Philippines*, 150.

77. The Dios-Dios sect on Samar went on harassing isolated US garrisons. On Luzon, aboriginal tribes defied submission, periodically staging head-hunting campaigns against Americans and their Filipino auxiliaries. And even as Luzon became pacified, the rebellion's center of gravity moved southward, especially toward the Moro islands. See Major General Miguel Malvar to Brigadier General Juan Cailles, April 4, 1901, PIR SD 692.3, as quoted in ibid., 148–49. See also Wolff, 358, 359; and Karnow, 194.

78. When a party was sent to bury the American dead, they "were stopped in their tracks by the sight of the mutilated bodies of their dead comrades." The company commander's head had been chopped off and set on fire; his finger and West Point ring were missing. Other bodies were slit open and stuffed with flour, jam, coffee, and molasses from the company's mess hall in order to attract fire ants. Even the dog that served as the company's mascot had not been spared—his eyes had been gouged out and replaced with rocks. See Miller, 204; and Linn, *The Philippine War*, 219, 311.

79. See Linn, *The Philippine War*, 16, 34; and Gates, 158.

80. Theodore Roosevelt to Frederick S. Funston, March 30, 1901.

81. Miller, 234–35.

CHAPTER THREE: PANCHO VILLA AND
THE PUNITIVE EXPEDITION. (1916–1917)

1. Quoted in Herbert Malloy Mason Jr., *The Great Pursuit: Pershing's Expedition to Destroy Pancho Villa* (New York: Konecky & Konecky, 1970), 77.

2. Quoted in Donald Smythe, *Guerrilla Warrior: The Early Life of John J. Pershing* (New York: Charles Scribner's Sons: 1973), 262.

3. Carlos D'Este, *Patton: A Genius for War* (New York: HarperCollins, 1995), 158.

4. Pershing, Roosevelt quoted in Mason, *The Great Pursuit,* 78.

5. D'Este, *Patton,* 158; John J. Pershing to General W. W. Wotherspoon, August 10, 1914, PP 214, quoted in Frank E. Vandiver, *Black Jack: The Life and Times of John J. Pershing* (College Station: Texas A&M University Press, 1977), 590.

6. Frank Tompkins, *Chasing Villa: The Last Campaign of the US Cavalry* (1934; repr., Silver City, NM: High-Lonesome Books, 1996), 50.

7. Lucas quoted in Tompkins, *Chasing Villa,* 51.

8. Tompkins, 55.

9. Mason, *The Great Pursuit,* 20, 24.

10. Tompkins, 38.

11. E. Alexander Powell, quoted in Joseph A. Stout Jr., *Border Conflict: Villistas, Carrancistas and the Punitive Expedition, 1915–1920* (Fort Worth, TX: Texas Christian University Press, 1999), 4.

12. Martin Luis Guzman, *The Eagle and the Serpent* (New York, 1930), 44.

13. Robert L. Scheina, *Villa: Soldier of the Mexican Revolution* (Washington, DC: Brassey's, Inc., 2004), 4.

14. John Reed, *Insurgent Mexico* (New York: International, 1964), 234.

15. One of Pancho Villa's biographers, Elias L. Torres, claimed to have been a witness to Ambrose Bierce's death, claiming that after Bierce insulted Villa and left the room, Villa turned to a subordinate and said, "Let's see if that damned gringo tells his last joke to the vulture of the sierra." See Elias L. Torres, *Twenty Episodes in the Life of Pancho Villa* (Austin: Encino Press, 1973), 36–37.

16. Mason, 60.

17. *New York Times,* September 2, 1914, as quoted in John S. D. Eisenhower, *Intervention! The United States and the Mexican Revolution, 1913–1917* (New York: W. W. Norton & Co., 1993), 155.

18. Wilson quoted in Vandiver, 579; Mason, 60.

19. Arthur S. Link, *Wilson: Confusions and Crises, 1915–1916* (Princeton, NJ: Princeton University Press, 1964), 201, 202. James Sandos suggests Villa also had "a deep financial motive for revenge against the railroad," as in December the Railway Company had refused to give Villa the $1.5 million he had demanded. See James A. Sandos, "Pancho Villa and American Security: Woodrow Wilson's Mexican Diplomacy Reconsidered," *Journal of Latin American Studies* 13, no. 2 (November 1981), 300.

20. Funston quoted in Mason, 66.

21. George Carothers, quoted in Larry D. Hill, *Emissaries to a Revolution: Woodrow Wilson's Executive Agents in Mexico* (Baton Rouge, LA: Louisiana State University Press, 1973), 370.

22. Joseph P. Tumulty, *Woodrow Wilson As I Know Him* (Garden City, NJ: Doubleday Page, 1921), 157.

23. Edward Haley, *Revolution and Intervention: The Diplomacy of Taft and Wilson with Mexico* (Cambridge, MA: MIT Press, 1970), 189. Emphasis added.

24. Hugh Lenox Scott, *Some Memories of a Soldier* (New York: Century Co., 1928), 520–21.

25. Ibid., 125.

26. *New York Times,* March 23, 1916, as quoted in Stout, *Border Conflict,* 47.

27. Eisenhower, 242.

28. On the Babicora plan, see Eisenhower, 245–46.

29. Samuel F. Dallam, "The Punitive Expedition of 1916," *Cavalry Journal* 36, no. 148 (July 1927), 386.

30. See Eisenhower, 246; Mason, 93.

31. Frank B. Elser, "General Pershing's Mexican Campaign," *The Century* 99, no. 4 (February 1920), 438.
32. Eisenhower, 246; Mason, 95.
33. Tompkins, 82.
34. Tompkins, 83. See also Eisenhower, 248.
35. Mason, 97–98; Stout, 52.
36. Mason, 98–99.
37. Tompkins, 87. Whereas Colonel Dodd reported the KIA figure of thirty, Herbert Mason says that fifty-six Mexicans were killed and thirty-five wounded. Another factor complicating the casualty estimates for the Guerrero battle is the fact that a significant portion of Villa's men were Yaqui Indians, who customarily took all their wounded with them to mask their casualties. See Mason, 99.
38. Elser, "General Pershing's Mexican Campaign," 440, 441.
39. Tompkins, 117–18, 128.
40. Quoted in Eisenhower, 268.
41. Mason, 160.
42. Quoted in Tompkins, 160–61.
43. Quoted in Tompkins, 163, 165.
44. Tompkins, 137.
45. Tompkins, 138; Mason, 133.
46. Mason, 134.
47. Tompkins, 141–42.
48. General Pershing to the Commanding General, Southern Department, "Report on the General Situation," April 14, 1916, State Department Papers, as quoted in Link, *Wilson: Confusions and Crises,* 280–81.
49. Haley, *Revolution and Intervention,* 200.
50. Cervantes managed to take some of his wounded with him as he withdrew under the cover of darkness, but others had crawled into the bush or ditches and were left behind. The Tamahuras, typhoid-ridden themselves, had no way to care for the wounded Villistas. So they simply dragged the dead and dying together, poured fuel over them, and set them on fire. See Mason, 148–51; and Stout, 58.
51. *New York Times,* May 9, 1916, as quoted in Stout, 76.
52. As Patton recalled the encounter, Pershing replied, "Everyone wants to go. Why should I favor you?"

    "Because I want to go more than anyone else," Patton said.

    "That will do," Pershing said, dismissing the supplicant.

    Undeterred, Patton went home and packed his gear. At five AM the next morning his phone rang, and when he answered it he heard Pershing's voice was on the other end. "Lieutenant Patton," the general asked, "how long will it take you to get ready?"

    Patton replied that he was already packed, to which Pershing exclaimed, "I'll be G-d damned. You are appointed aide."

    Patton's biographer Martin Blumenson notes, however, that in later years as Patton elaborated dramatically on how Pershing came to select him, he neglected to mention his sister Nita's presence at Fort Bliss. Although twenty-five years younger than Pershing, Nita had been keeping proper company with the general in El Paso, helping him cope with the grief of losing his family. Undoubtedly, Pershing's friendship with his sister helped Patton's chances to some degree. See Martin Blumenson, *Patton: The Man Behind the Legend, 1885–1945* (New York: William Morrow and Company, 1985), 82; and Martin

Blumenson, ed., *The Patton Papers: 1885-1940, Vol. I* (Boston: Houghton Mifflin, 1972), 347–48.

53. Patton, quoted in Blumenson, ed., *The Patton Papers*, 360–61.
54. Blumenson, *The Patton Papers*, 363.
55. Blumenson, *The Patton Papers*, 365.
56. Fred Ayer, *Before the Colors Fade* (London: Cassell, 1964), 73.
57. Eisenhower, 289.
58. Mason, 189.
59. Pershing to Funston, Namiquipa, April 17, 1916, in 3849 ACP 1886, as quoted in Vandiver, 634.
60. *New York Times*, April 2, 1916, quoted in Stout, 53.
61. Pershing to Funston (telegram), May 1, 1916, quoted in Vandiver, 639.
62. Quoted in Mason, 145.
63. Quoted in Link, *Wilson: Confusions and Crises*, 287.
64. See Mason, *Great Pursuit*, 152–53.
65. Quoted in Vandiver, 647.
66. Mason, 206, 208.
67. See Link, *Wilson: Confusions and Crises*, 304–05.
68. See Mason, 216.
69. Ray Stannard Baker, *Woodrow Wilson Life and Letters: Facing War 1915–1917* (New York: Greenwood Press, 1968), 80.
70. Michael Tate argues the Punitive Expedition was not withdrawn from Mexico lest it project US weakness that other Latin American governments might try to exploit through confiscation and nationalization. See Michael L. Tate, "Pershing's Punitive Expedition: Pursuer of Bandits or Presidential Panacea?" *The Americas* 32, no. 1 (July 1975), 67.
71. Captain Thomas L. Sherburne, Fifth Cavalry, quoted in Clarence C. Clendenen, *The United States and Pancho Villa* (Ithaca, NY: Cornell University Press, 1961), 264. See also Mason, 218.
72. National Archives, Records of the Punitive Expedition, Record Group 395, Dyo and Fusita report, September 23, 1916, as quoted in Charles H. Harris III and Louis R. Sadler, *The Border and the Revolution: Clandestine Activities of the Mexican Revolution, 1910–1920* (Silver City, NM: High-Lonesome Books, 1988), 16.
73. Friederich Katz, *The Life and Times of Pancho Villa* (Stanford, CA: Stanford University Press, 1998), 589. On the eventual failure of the Joint High Commission, see Mason, 223, 229–30.
74. Mason, 227.
75. Quoted in Katz, *The Life and Times of Pancho Villa*, 587. The description of Villa as a "Mad Mullah" is ironic, as it is an oblique reference to Sheik Mohammed Abdullah Hassan. At the same time the Punitive Expedition was pursuing Villa, British forces were pursuing Hassan in Somalia, who had raided and fought with the British and their tribal allies since 1898. After several unsuccessful campaigns, they finally succeeded in suppressing his rebellion after World War I, although they never actually captured Hassan, who died of old age in the Somalia bush, defiant to the end. See I. M. Lewis, *A Modern History of Somalia: Nation and State in the Horn of Africa* (Boulder, CO: Westview Press, 1988), 68–79.
76. Herbert Mason argues that Pershing's force—experienced in guerrilla warfare, familiar with the terrain, and mounted on healthy horses—"could indeed have stood a better than even chance of finding Villa and destroying him for good." See Mason, 228.

77. Secretary of War Baker told Wilson's confidant Colonel Edward House that he was in favor of "giving up the Villa chase and bringing the troops back from Mexico. He thought the purpose had been accomplished, that is the Villistas had already been dispersed and it was foolish to chase a single bandit all over Mexico." Chief of Staff Scott was even more explicit in this respect. "I do not know," he wrote two days later to a friend, "how long this thing is going to continue. It seems to me that Pershing has accomplished about all that he was sent for. . . . It does not seem dignified for all the United States to be hunting for one man in a foreign country." See Katz, 577.

78. Mason, 236.

79. On Villa's pact with Huerta and his assassination, see Scheina, *Villa*, 89–91.

80. Douglas MacArthur, *Reminiscences* (New York: McGraw-Hill, 1964), 46.

CHAPTER FOUR: THE POPE, HEAVY METAL, AND THE VOODOO CHILD: THE HUNT FOR MANUEL NORIEGA

1. On the December 17, 1989, White House meeting, see Thomas Donnelly, Margaret Roth, and Caleb Baker, *Operation JUST CAUSE: The Invasion of Panama* (New York: Lexington Books, 1991), 98–99; Colin Powell, *My American Journey* (New York: Ballantine Books, 1995), 410–12; and Bob Woodward, *The Commanders* (New York: Simon and Schuster, 1991), 143–47.

2. Major General Marc Cisneros, quoted in Lawrence Yates, *The U.S. Military Intervention in Panama: Origins, Planning, and Crisis Management, June 1987–December 1989* (Washington, DC: Center of Military History, 2008), 224; Elliott Abrams, interview with author, October 15, 2009.

3. Powell, *My American Journey*, 401.

4. James A. Baker III, *The Politics of Diplomacy: Revolution, War, and Peace, 1989–92* (New York: Putnam, 1995), 177.

5. George Shultz, *Turmoil and Triumph: My Years as Secretary of State* (New York: Scribner, 1993), 1052. On Noriega's relationship with US intelligence, see Ivan Musicant, *The Banana Wars: A History of United States Military Intervention in Latin America from the Spanish-American War to the Invasion of Panama* (New York: Macmillan, 1990), 392. See also ibid., 39; and Frederick Kempe, *Divorcing the Dictator: America's Bungled Affair with Noriega* (New York: G. P. Putnam's Sons, 1990), 58. On Noriega's rise to power, see Rebecca L. Grant, *Operation Just Cause and the U.S. Policy Process* (Santa Monica, CA: RAND, 1991), 7, and Yates, *The U.S. Military Intervention in Panama*, 10–11.

6. "The station chiefs loved him," a former US ambassador to Panama recalled. "As far as they were concerned, the stuff that they were getting was more interesting than what the Cubans were getting from Noriega on us." Quoted in Seymour M. Hersh, "Panama Strongman Said to Trade in Drugs, Arms, and Illicit Money," *New York Times*, June 12, 1986. See also Musicant, *The Banana Wars*, 391–92.

7. Russell Crandall, *Gunboat Democracy: U.S. Intervention in the Dominican Republic, Grenada, and Panama* (New York: Rowan and Littlefield, 2006), 191. On Noriega's relationships with the DEA and the Medellin cartel, see Seymour M. Hersh, "U.S. Aides in '72 Weighed Killing Officer Who Now Leads Panama," *New York Times*, June 13, 1986; Grant, 9, 31; Kevin Buckley, *Panama: The Whole Story* (New York: Simon and Schuster, 1991), 41; and Crandall, *Gunboat Democracy*, 188.

8. Crandall, *Gunboat Democracy*, 195. Thomas Donnelly, Margaret Baker, and Caleb Roth report that by February 1989 the number of incidents logged by

SOUTHCOM was "more than 1,000 since early 1988." The SOUTHCOM list of incidents catalogued broken fingers; loosened teeth; abrasions from billy clubs, rubber hoses, and pistols; strip searches; prolonged detention; and robberies and "fondling" of female military personnel. The worst incident came on March 3, 1989, when armed PDF "Transito" troops pulled over twenty-one US school buses transporting hundreds of American schoolchildren, many under twelve, and held them at gunpoint for several hours. See Donnelly, Roth, and Baker, *Operation JUST CAUSE*, 43; Buckley, *Panama*, 161, 172; and Yates, 145–46.

9. Crandall, 195–96; Yates, 167.

10. Buckley, 81; Woodward, *The Commanders*, 53.

11. Kozak quoted in Baker, *The Politics of Diplomacy*, 181. See also Donnelly, Roth, and Baker, *Operation JUST CAUSE*, 14, 65.

12. Major General (Ret.) Geoffrey Lambert, interview with author, September 30, 2009.

13. SOUTHCOM commander General Frederick Woerner noted: "Even if I succeeded, much less if I failed to get Noriega—I had a population of 50,000 Americans scattered throughout the country and I could not guarantee their protection against a PDF that might be a little upset with us, seeing that we would have just kidnapped their commanding officer. I could not resolve the problem of security with a strike-type operation, successful or not." Woerner quoted in Donnelly, Roth, and Baker, 17. See also Woodward, *The Commanders*, 58, 59; Abrams interview, October 15, 2009; Donnelly, Roth, and Baker, 140.

14. There are two possible explanations for Noriega's refusal to peacefully depart Panama. George Shultz argues that PDF officers insisted that Noriega remain in power for fear of their own safety should he leave the country. Conversely, journalist Kevin Buckley claims that "Noriega could not have retired because he would have been murdered by the Medellin Cartel. In power, Noriega was useful to them. Out of power, he was dangerous; he knew too much. Staying in power and staying alive were the same for Noriega." See Shultz, *Turmoil and Triumph*, 1077–78; and Buckley, 97.

15. Baker, 183.

16. Yates, 209. On Noriega's self-comparison to Clint Eastwood, see Buckley, 145.

17. Baker, 183.

18. See Woodward, 61; Buckley, 183; and Grant, 30.

19. The dictator was godfather to Giroldi's son and had been best man when the major and his wife renewed their wedding vows. Giroldi was one of a handful of men Noriega trusted enough to carry an automatic weapon in his presence, and had a history of being involved in entrapment operations. Consequently, Thurman had reason to suspect the reports were a ruse to get him to commit US troops to a nonexistent plot, thereby ruining his credibility as SOUTHCOM commander. See Woodward, 93; Yates, 250, 253.

20. See Powell, 466; Yates, 256–58.

21. Woodward, 99–100.

22. Baker, 186, 187.

23. Woodward, 100.

24. Quoted in Robin Wright, "U.S. in New Bid to Oust Noriega," *Los Angeles Times*, November 16, 1989; Thurman quoted in Yates, 262.

25. See Musicant, 396; Crandall, 200.

26. Buckley, 230.

27. Powell, 414.

28. Rather quoted in Ronald H. Cole, *Operation Just Cause: The Planning and Execution of Joint Operations in Panama, February 1988–January 1990* (Washington, DC: Joint History Office, Office of the Chairman of the Joint Chiefs of Staff, 1995), 34. Setting H-Hour for one AM allowed US commanders to minimize the risk of a civilian presence at key objectives such as Torrijos Airport; operate at high tide—which in Panama varies by as much fourteen feet—to allow the SEALs to avoid mudflats up to a mile long; and fight under the cover of darkness for at least four hours, during which time the better-equipped, better-trained US forces would have an added advantage. See Donnelly, Roth, and Baker, 101.

29. Cole, 34.

30. Despite the blatant endangerment of US forces due to the media's reporting, it was likely not the only source of the leaked H-hour. Intelligence sources in SOUTHCOM began picking up evidence that personnel at the Comandancia were aware of the movement of C-130s and C-141s into Howard Air Force Base as early as five PM. By six PM, December 19, congressional offices in Washington were receiving calls from Panama asking what time the Americans would begin their attack. And, of course, on Tuesday evening the impending invasion was the talk of Panama City, especially among the girlfriends of US servicemen. See Cole, 34; Musicant, 401; and Buckley, 233.

31. Cole, 35.

32. See Donnelly, Roth, and Baker, 120–21.

33. On the Paitilla Airfield mission, see Donnelly, Roth, and Baker, 114–17. Some Special Forces leaders reportedly questioned the use of SEALs for the Paitilla mission during the early stages of Just Cause planning, with some attributing the assignment to SEAL Team Four to bureaucratic politics within the military community. Although Lieutenant General Carl Stiner, Commander of the Eighteenth Airborne Corps, and US Special Operations Command (USASOC) Commander General James Lindsay claim the Paitilla mission was a suitable one for SEALs, in his memoirs, Colin Powell reflected: "We made the mistake of assigning the SEALs, however tough and brave, to a mission more appropriate to the infantry." In the end, exhaustive after-action reviews by the Joint Chiefs of Staff and USASOC determined that the SEALs had simply made a critical tactical error by standing up on the open tarmac. See Donnelly, Roth, and Baker, 119–20; Powell, 415–16.

34. Cole, 37; Yates, 38.

35. Quoted in Donnelly, Roth, and Baker, 334.

36. Cole, 39; Crandall, 203. Lieutenant General (Ret.) David Barno, who was the Operations Officer for Second Battalion, attributes most of these injuries to the intensity of the ground fire causing most Rangers to forget to perform a proper "PLF" (Parachute Landing Fall). Barno interview, February 23, 2010.

37. Linda Robinson, *Masters of Chaos: The Secret History of the Special Forces* (New York: Public Affairs, 2004), 44.

38. On the battle for the Pacora River Bridge, see Robinson, *Masters of Chaos*, 44–48.

39. Quoted in Donnelly, Roth, and Baker, 220.

40. See Musicant, 404.

41. Clarence Briggs, *Operation Just Cause: Panama, December 1989, A Soldier's Eyewitness Account* (New York: Stackpole Books, 1990), 94.

42. Russell Watson, "Invasion," *Newsweek*, January 1, 1990.

43. Sergeant Joseph Ruzic, quoted in Donnelly, Roth, and Baker, 313.

44. Powell, 417. See also Michael R. Gordon, "Fighting in Panama: The Chief of Staff; Vital for the Invasion: Politically Attuned General," *New York Times*, December 25, 1989.

45. See Donnelly, Roth, and Baker, 104, 107.

46. See ibid., 107; Buckley, 234–37.

47. Powell, 417.

48. See Buckley, 241.

49. Noriega quoted in Musicant, 408.

50. Bush quoted in Buckley, 241.

51. Musicant, 414.

52. Briggs, *Operation Just Cause*, 101.

53. Lieutenant General (Ret.) William G. Boykin, *Never Surrender: A Soldier's Journey to the Crossroads of Faith and Freedom* (New York: Faith Words, 2008), 211.

54. See Donnelly, Roth, and Baker, 105; Cole, 56; and Boykin, *Never Surrender*, 212.

55. It was the captain who had told him to put on civilian clothes rather than his uniform at the Ceremi Recreation Center, a decision that enabled him to evade US forces. Later that night, as Noriega and some bodyguards were leaving an associate's house and saw three US Black Hawk helicopters descending nearby, it was Castillo who warned them to stop running lest they draw the attention of another gunship hovering above. Consequently, when Castillo talked, Noriega listened. See Buckley, 236, 237.

56. Donnelly, Baker, and Roth, 112.

57. On the "Ma Bell" operations, see Robinson, 50–51.

58. Boykin, 213–14; Musicant, 414.

59. Cole, 57.

60. Quoted in Musicant, 415. See also Cole, 57, 62.

61. Boykin, 214.

62. Quoted Buckley, 248.

63. Buckley, 248; Cole, 60; Boykin, 218.

64. Woodward, 168–69; Cole, 62.

65. Quoted in Buckley, 246.

66. Downing quoted in Baker, 192. On the demonstrations, see also Buckley, 250; Donnelly, Roth, and Baker, 364; and Boykin, 218.

67. See Buckley, 251; Musicant, 416.

68. Although some left-wing groups claimed as many as four thousand Panamanian civilians died in the conflict, a charge that was unquestioningly trumpeted by CBS News's *60 Minutes*, investigations by other organizations in Panama and the United States indicated that SOUTHCOM's numbers were generally accurate. See Woodward, 172.

69. On the struggles to establish a functioning democracy in the immediate aftermath of the invasion, see John T. Fishel, *The Fog of Peace: Planning and Executing the Restoration of Panama* (Carlisle Barracks, PA: Strategic Studies Institute, 1992). On the continuation of drug trafficking, see Crandall, 208.

70. Quoted in Donnelly, Baker, and Roth, 33.

71. See Yates, 264–65; Cole, 29.

72. According to John Dinges, Shultz "secretly ordered US embassies in several Latin American countries to 'inform Panamanian military attaches of US desire to work with PDF, but inability to do so while Noriega remains.'" Similarly, Baker recalls: "All American officials in Panama were directed to deliver a similar message to their contacts in the PDF. The message reiterated that the United States had no quarrel with the military." See John Dinges, *Our Man*

in Panama: How General Noriega Used the United States—And Made Millions in Drugs and Arms (New York: Random House, 1990), 298–99; and Baker, 184–85.

73. Presidential Address, December 20, 1989, *Weekly Compilation of Presidential Documents,* 25: 1974–75.

CHAPTER FIVE: THE WARLORD'S REVENGE: TASK FORCE RANGER AND THE SEARCH FOR MOHAMMED FARAH AIDEED

1. William Boykin, *Never Surrender: A Soldier's Journey to the Crossroads of Faith and Freedom* (New York: Hachette Book Group USA, 2008), 251; and Anthony Zinni in Tom Clancy, with Anthony Zinni and Tony Koltz, *Battle Ready* (New York: Putnam, 2004), 239, 242.

2. John L. Hirsch and Robert B. Oakley, *Somalia and Operation Restore Hope: Reflections on Peacemaking and Peacekeeping* (Washington, DC: United States Institute for Peace, 1995), 15, 18; and William Shawcross, *Deliver Us from Evil: Peacekeepers, Warlords, and a World of Endless Conflict* (New York: Simon & Schuster, 2000), 85.

3. These battle wagons were called "technicals" because, in order to survive, relief agencies operating in Somalia were forced to hire gunmen for protection. They subsequently listed these expenditures on their budgets as "technical assistants," and hence the name "technical" was applied to any armed security vehicle. See Scott Peterson, *Me Against My Brother* (New York: Routledge, 2000), 24, 31.

4. Hirsch and Oakley, *Somalia and Operation Restore Hope,* 23, 25, 31.

5. Colin Powell, *My American Journey* (New York: Ballantine Books, 1995), 550.

6. Peterson, *Me Against My Brother,* 22; Mark Bowden, *Black Hawk Down: A Story of Modern War* (New York: Atlantic Monthly Press, 1999), 93.

7. On Aideed's background, see John Drysdale, *Whatever Happened in Somalia?* (London: HAAN Associates, 1994), 22.

8. Zinni quoted in Clancy et al., *Battle Ready,* 245, 260; also see Peterson, 22, 46.

9. Peterson, 52.

10. Peterson, 65.

11. Aideed distrusted the UN in general and harbored a specific, personal resentment toward Boutros-Ghali, who during Somalia's recent civil war had been Egypt's deputy foreign minister at a time when that country was supporting Siad Barre.

12. Peterson, 65–66; Robert F. Baumann, Lawrence A. Yates, and Versalle F. Washington, *"My Clan Against the World": U.S. and Coalition Forces in Somalia, 1992–1994* (Ft. Leavenworth, KS: CSI Press, 2004), 64, 82–83.

13. Zinni quoted in Clancy, et al., 260. Walter Clarke, the deputy chief of the mission, US Embassy, from March through July 1993, believed Aideed was being strategic in his cooperation with UNITAF: "I think he tended to look at the UNITAF period as a period for putting his force together, restoring some of his units, but certainly in preparation for other events after UNITAF had gone." See Walter Clarke, interview with *PBS Frontline: Ambush in Mogadishu,* available at http://www.pbs.org/wgbh/pages/frontline/shows/ambush/interviews/clarke.html.

14. Peterson, 75; R. D. Hooker Jr., "Hard Day's Night: A Retrospective on the American Intervention in Somalia," *Joint Forces Quarterly* 54, no. 3 (2009), 130.

15. Peterson, 72; Michael R. Gordon with John Cushman Jr., "Mission in Somalia: After Supporting Hunt for Aidid, U.S. Is Blaming U.N. for Losses," *New York Times*, October 18, 1993.

16. Quoted in Drysdale, *Whatever Happened in Somalia?* 181.

17. Peterson, 73; Bowden, *Black Hawk Down*, 93.

18. David C. Isby, *Leave No Man Behind: Liberation and Capture Missions* (London: Weidenfeld and Nicholson, 2004), 261.

19. Aideed quoted in Drysdale, 183.

20. Peterson, 76.

21. Albright and Howe quoted in Daniel Bolger, *Savage Peace: Americans at War in the 1990s* (Novato, CA: Presidio Press, 1995), 303.

22. Quoted in Hooker, "Hard Day's Night," 132.

23. Powell, *My American Journey*, 568.

24. On the June 12 AC-130 attack, see Peterson, 81.

25. Peterson, 83, 86.

26. Peterson, 88–90; Bowden, *Black Hawk Down*, 94.

27. Bolger, *Savage Peace*, 302–03.

28. Patrick J. Sloyan, "Mission to Somalia: "Somalia Mission Control; Clinton called the shots in failed policy targeting Aidid," *Newsday*, December 5, 1993.

29. Peterson, 90, 93.

30. Aideed quoted in Peterson, 95. See also Isby, *Leave No Man Behind*, 262.

31. Bowden, *Black Hawk Down*, 94.

32. There was significant controversy about how many Somalis were killed in the attack, however. UNOSOM II stated that seventeen Somalis were killed and ten wounded in the attack. The SNA claimed seventy-three people were killed, and the International Red Cross said fifty-four were killed. See Peterson, 119; Drysdale, 203; and Baumann, Yates, and Washington, *"My Clan Against the World,"* 118.

33. See Peterson, 118–19; Bowden, *Black Hawk Down*, 72.

34. See Bowden, *Black Hawk Down*, 95; Hirsch and Oakley, 121–22.

35. Quoted in Gordon, "Mission in Somalia."

36. Bolger, 307.

37. Bowden, *Black Hawk Down*, 23.

38. See Bowden, *Black Hawk Down*, 95.

39. See Rick Atkinson, "The Raid That Went Wrong: How an Elite U.S. Force Failed in Somalia," *Washington Post*, January 30, 1994; and Bowden, *Black Hawk Down*, 23.

40. Atkinson, "The Raid That Went Wrong"; Boykin, *Never Surrender*, 257.

41. Boykin, 257. There are three different accounts of how the target was selected. Rick Atkinson reported in the *Washington Post* that the intelligence cell at UN headquarters provided the target, Michael Smith says the information came from a tip and was subsequently confirmed by the CIA's station chief in Mogadishu, and Jerry Boykin says it was provided by a Task Force Ranger intelligence analyst. See Boykin, 257; Atkinson, "The Raid That Went Wrong"; and Michael Smith, *Killer Elite: The Inside Story of America's Most Secret Special Operations Team* (New York: St. Martin's Griffin, 2006), 183.

42. Quoted in Boykin, 257–58.

43. Bowden, *Black Hawk Down*, 26, 154; Atkinson, "The Raid That Went Wrong."

44. Accounts vary as to who fired the shot that disabled Ato's vehicle. Martin Smith claims it was a SEAL Team Six sniper, while David Isby says it was an all-Delta operation. See Smith, *Killer Elite*, 184–85; and Isby, 269.

45. Bowden, *Black Hawk Down,* 25–26.
46. Keith B. Richburg, "Under U.N.'s Nose, Somali Defiant," *Washington Post,* September 5, 1993. See also Isby, 270; and Peterson, 109, 140.
47. Peterson, 109.
48. Hirsch and Oakley, 126–27.
49. See Patrick Sloyan, "Hunting Down Aidid; Why Clinton Changed Mind," *Newsday,* December 6, 1993. Lake quoted in Isby, 271.
50. Bowden, *Black Hawk Down,* 28; Boykin, 260.
51. Quoted in Baumann, Yates, and Washington, 142.
52. Quoted in Atkinson, "The Raid That Went Wrong."
53. Bowden, *Black Hawk Down,* 17–18.
54. Atkinson, "The Raid That Went Wrong."
55. Chief Warrant Officer Michael Durant noted that the pilots of the 160th SOAR had nicknamed the Noriega dragnet "the Hunt for Elvis," and that therefore "Elvis captured Elvis." See Michael J. Durant, *In the Company of Heroes* (New York: Signet, 2003), 258.
56. Atkinson, "The Raid That Went Wrong"; Isby, 277.
57. Just ten days earlier, Task Force Ranger had simulated a helicopter crash to rehearse this scenario. By eerie coincidence, the Black Hawk used in the simulation was Super 61. See Rick Atkinson, "Night of a Thousand Casualties; Battle Triggered U.S. Decision to Withdraw from Somalia," *Washington Post,* January 31, 1994.
58. See Isby, 277–79.
59. See Bolger, 319; Bowden, 130–31; and Isby, 281.
60. See Isby, 279, 284; and Atkinson, "Night of a Thousand Casualties."
61. Isby, 282; Bolger, 323.
62. Peterson, 142; Bolger, 323.
63. Boykin, 270.
64. See Bowden, *Black Hawk Down,* 258, 263–64, 269.
65. Lawrence E. Casper, *Falcon Brigade: Combat and Command in Somalia and Haiti* (Boulder: Lynne Rienner, 2001), 83.
66. Master Sergeant Paul Howe quoted in Bowden, *Black Hawk Down,* 299.
67. Bowden, *Black Hawk Down,* 311.
68. Clancy, et al., 282; Baumann, Yates, and Washington, 171.
69. Quoted in "Letting Bygones be Bygones," *Time* (international edition), November 1, 1993.
70. Casper, *Falcon Brigade,* 125.
71. Quoted in Baumann, Yates, and Washington, 169.
72. Quoted in Peterson, 93, 95, 159–60.
73. Quoted in Refugee Policy Group, *Hope Restored? Humanitarian Aid in Somalia 1990–1994* (Washington, DC: Center for Policy Analysis and Research on Refugee Issues, 1994), 43.

CHAPTER SIX: THE HUNT FOR OSAMA BIN LADEN, PART I

1. The intent behind Ralston's meeting was not primarily to inform Karamat of the US attack, but to be on hand to personally assure him that they were not the first wave of an Indian preemptive strike in the aftermath of Pakistan's May 1998 nuclear tests. For accounts of the Ralston–Karamat meeting, see Mary Anne Weaver, "The Real Bin Laden," *The New Yorker,* January 24, 2000; Sandy Berger, testimony before the 9/11 Commission, March 24, 2004; and Steve Coll,

Ghost Wars: The Secret History of the CIA, Afghanistan, and Bin Laden, from the Soviet Invasion to September 10, 2001 (New York: Penguin, 2004), 411.

2. Quoted in Coll, *Ghost Wars,* 255.

3. Vernon Loeb, "The Federal Page: Where the CIA Wages Its New World War," *Washington Post,* September 9, 1998.

4. "Usama bin Laden: Islamic Extremist Financier," CIA assessment released publicly in 1996, quoted in Coll, *Ghost Wars,* 320. On Osama bin Laden's early years and rise as a terrorist leader, see Stephen Coll, *The Bin Ladens: An Arabian Family in the American Century* (New York: Penguin, 2008); Lawrence Wright, *The Looming Tower: Al-Qaeda and the Road to 9/11* (New York: Knopf, 2006); and Peter L. Bergen, *The Osama I Know: An Oral History of al-Qaeda's Leader* (New York: Free Press, 2006).

5. Robert Fisk, "Why We Reject the West—By the Saudis' Fiercest Arab Critic," *The Independent,* July 10, 1996.

6. See National Commission on Terrorist Attacks Upon the United States, *Final Report of the National Commission on Terrorist Attacks Upon the United States* (New York: W. W. Norton, 2004) [hereafter cited as *The 9/11 Commission Report*], 109, 188; Coll, *Ghost Wars,* 351, 620, footnote 15.

7. On the original snatch plan, see Coll, *Ghost Wars,* 375–77; *The 9/11 Commission,* 109–10.

8. See Coll, *Ghost Wars,* 379.

9. In a May 6 cable to CIA headquarters, the Islamabad station chief, Gary Schroen, declared the Afghans' planning "almost as professional and detailed . . . as would be done by any US military special operations element." He and the other officers who had worked through the plan with the Afghans judged it "about as good as can be." By that, Schroen told the 9/11 Commission, he meant that the chance of capturing or killing bin Laden was about 40 percent. See *The 9/11 Commission Report,* 111–12; Lawrence Wright, *The Looming Tower,* 265.

10. O'Connell, his deputy Paul Pillar, Jack Downing (chief of the Directorate of Operations), and his deputy Jim Pavitt all told CIA director George Tenet the Tarnak Farms raid was a bad idea. See *The 9/11 Commission Report,* 114; Coll, *Ghost Wars,* 396.

11. *The 9/11 Commission Report,* 114.

12. "Text of World Islamic Front's Statement Urging Jihad Against Jews and Crusaders," *Al-Quds al-Arabi,* February 23, 1998 (trans. Foreign Broadcast Information Service).

13. Simon Reeve, *The New Jackals: Osama bin Laden and the Future of Terrorism* (Boston: Northeastern University Press, 1999), 200.

14. Tenet quoted in Richard Clarke, *Against All Enemies: Inside America's War on Terror* (New York: Free Press, 2004), 184.

15. George Tenet, *At the Center of the Storm: My Years at the CIA* (New York: HarperCollins, 2007), 115. See also Coll, *Ghost Wars,* 409.

16. Coll, *Ghost Wars,* 411.

17. The CIA later reported to Clinton that it had received information that bin Laden had been at Zawhar Kili, but had left several hours before the strikes. Yet according to al-Qaeda sources, bin Laden was hundreds of miles away when the US cruise missiles struck his camps. According to his bodyguard Abu Jandal, bin Laden and his bodyguards were driving through Vardak province en route to Zawhar Kili when they stopped at a crossroads. "Where do you think, my friends, we should go?" bin Laden asked. "Khost or Kabul?" Abu Jandal and the

others said they would rather go to Kabul, where they could visit friends. "With G-d's help, let us go to Kabul," bin Laden decreed.

In reality, Abu Jandal's account is likely a cover story to protect al-Qaeda's allies in Pakistan's intelligence service, who other al-Qaeda sources say warned bin Laden about the imminent attack. There are at least three ways the Pakistanis could have known an attack was coming. One hundred eighty American diplomats were withdrawn from Islamabad, and all foreigners were evacuated from Kabul in the days before the attack. Additionally, the Pakistani navy in the northern Arabian Sea likely noticed the US naval activity prior to the attack and reported it back to the ISI.

See Khalid al-Hammadi, "The Inside Story of al-Qa'ida, as Told by Abu-Jandal (Nasir al-Behri), bin Ladin's Personal Guard," *Al-Quds al-Arabi,* translated by FBIS; Peter L. Bergen, *Holy War, Inc.: Inside the Secret World of Osama Bin Laden* (New York: Free Press, 2001), 124, 124; Reeve, *The New Jackals,* 202; and Clarke, *Against All Enemies,* 188.

18. Maulana Sami al-Haq quoted in Bergen, *Holy War, Inc.,* 129. See also Coll, *Ghost Wars,* 412; and Dexter Filkins, "World Perspective, Asia: Osama bin Laden is Wanted Here, Too: Babies and Businesses Are Named After the Suspected Terrorist, Who Is a Hero on Pakistan's Frontier for His Battle Against the West," *Los Angeles Times,* July 24, 1999.

19. See *The 9/11 Commission Report,* 126–27, 131–32.

20. Coll, *Ghost Wars,* 490. See also *The 9/11 Commission Report,* 133.

21. It is unlikely the restrictive guidance was the determining factor for the Northern Alliance's efforts to kill bin Laden. A senior Massoud aide noted that if Massoud's men found themselves "in a position to kill Osama bin Laden, we wouldn't have waited for approval from the United States." Moreover, bin Laden's base of activity near Kandahar was far from the Northern Alliance's front line of operations against the Taliban. See Coll, *Ghost Wars,* 469, 488–89.

22. See Coll, *Ghost Wars,* 439–44.

23. Coll, *Ghost Wars,* 454–56; Tenet, *At the Center of the Storm,* 156.

24. David C. Isby, *Leave No Man Behind: Liberation and Capture Missions* (London: Weidenfeld & Nicolson, 2004), 307, 310; *The 9/11 Commission Report,* 143.

25. See Richard Shultz, "Nine Reasons Why We Never Sent Our Special Operations Forces after al Qaeda before 9/11," *The Weekly Standard,* January 26, 2004.

26. Shelton also assumed that if Pakistan detected a US raiding mission, it would alert the Taliban, who would then alert bin Laden, allowing him to escape or prepare an ambush for American forces. See Coll, *Ghost Wars,* 499; Daniel Benjamin and Steven Simon, *The Age of Sacred Terror* (New York: Random House, 2002), 296, 318; Isby, *Leave No Man Behind,* 308, 309.

27. Quoted in *The 9/11 Commission Report,* 127.

28. See *The 9/11 Commission Report,* 130–31. On Clinton's aversion to collateral damage, see Bob Woodward, *Bush at War* (New York: Simon & Schuster, 2002), 6.

29. Benjamin and Simon, *The Age of Sacred Terror,* 281.

30. *The 9/11 Commission Report,* 137. Lawrence Wright asserts that the intelligence tip actually came from one of the princes' bodyguards, which would explain the ignorance of bin Laden's whereabouts when not physically present in the Emirati encampment. See Wright, *The Looming Tower,* 290.

31. Clarke later wrote in a memo of this conversation that the call had been approved at an interagency meeting and cleared with the CIA. When the former bin Laden unit chief found out about Clarke's call, he questioned CIA officials, who denied having given such a clearance. See *The 9/11 Commission*

Report, 138. For other accounts noting Clarke's ties to the UAE as a factor in the decision not to strike the hunting camp, see Coll, *Ghost Wars,* 449; and Wright, 291.

32. See *The 9/11 Commission Report,* 140–41.
33. Clarke, *Against All Enemies,* 199.
34. Quoted in Coll, *Ghost Wars,* 489, 498.
35. Coll, *Ghost Wars,* 500. President Clinton quoted in Susan Page, "Why Clinton Failed to Stop bin Laden," *USA Today,* November 12, 2001.
36. *The 9/11 Commission Report,* 211, 212, 398.
37. Woodward, *Bush at War,* 43.
38. Gary Schroen, *First In: An Insider's Account of How the CIA Spearheaded the War on Terror in Afghanistan* (New York: Presidio Press, 2005), 38.
39. Gary Bernsten, *Jawbreaker: The Attack on Bin Laden and Al-Qaeda: A Personal Account by the CIA's Key Field Commander* (New York: Crown, 2005), 108, 239.
40. See Peter Bergen, "The Long Hunt for Osama," *Atlantic Monthly,* October 2004, 92.
41. Omar bin Laden quoted in Peter Bergen, "The Battle for Tora Bora," *The New Republic,* December 30, 2009, 17.
42. Philip Smucker, *Al Qaeda's Great Escape: The Military and the Media on Terror's Trail* (Washington, DC: Potomac Books, 2004), 72–73.
43. Dalton Fury, *Kill Bin Laden: A Delta Force Commander's Account of the Hunt for the World's Most Wanted Man* (New York: St. Martin's Press, 2008), 84, 124.
44. Smucker, *Al Qaeda's Great Escape,* 10, 44.
45. See Fury, *Kill bin Laden,* 78, 125.
46. Smucker, *Al Qaeda's Great Escape,* 77, 89.
47. "VB02" was the personal call sign of the Delta operator, code-named "Warf," who accompanied this team, which also included an air force controller and two CIA paramilitary operatives.
48. Bergen, "The Battle for Tora Bora," 18.
49. Tenet, 226; Smucker, *Al Qaeda's Great Escape,* 75.
50. Berntsen, *Jawbreaker,* 274.
51. Berntsen, 283–84.
52. Berntsen, 291.
53. Dalton Fury and three other Delta operators arrived at the schoolhouse on December 7 and assumed control of the battle from Jawbreaker. The Green Berets and CIA operatives were already present in the vicinity of Tora Bora when Delta arrived.
54. Bergen, "The Battle for Tora Bora," 19; Fury, 76, 78, 82.
55. NBC reporter Kevin Sites quoted in Berntsen, 296. See also ibid., 292, 295; and Fury, 159.
56. Fury, 170–71.
57. Bergen, "The Battle for Tora Bora," 20; Fury, 173, 174.
58. Fury, 174–75.
59. Fury, 176, 178.
60. Fury, 180–85.
61. Bergen, "The Battle of Tora Bora," 20; Fury, 211, 217.
62. Fury, 233.
63. Bin Laden quote in Fury, 233–34. See also Berntsen, 307.
64. Fury, 254–56.
65. Bergen, "The Battle for Tora Bora," 21; Fury, 264, 266.

66. Powell quoted in Philip Smucker, "Bin Laden Flees as Tora Bora Fighters Are Routed," *The Telegraph,* December 17, 2001.

67. Peter L. Bergen, *The Osama I Know,* 335.

CHAPTER SEVEN: STRATEGIC MANHUNTS IN MESOPOTAMIA: SADDAM HUSSEIN AND ABU MUSAB AL-ZARQAWI

1. On the December 14 press conference in Baghdad, see L. Paul Bremer, *My Year in Iraq* (New York: Simon & Schuster, 2006), 253.

2. Michael A. Newton and Michael P. Scharf, *Enemy of the State: The Trial and Execution of Saddam Hussein* (New York: St. Martin's Press, 2008), 21.

3. H. R. 4655, The Iraqi Liberation Act of 1998, Public Law 105-338, available at http://thomas.loc.gov/cgi-bin/query/z?c105:H.R.4655.ENR:.

4. Richard N. Haass, *War of Necessity, War of Choice: A Memoir of Two Iraq Wars* (New York: Simon & Schuster, 2009), 216.

5. Douglas J. Feith, *War and Decision: Inside the Pentagon at the Dawn of the War on Terrorism* (New York: Harper, 2008), 223.

6. George W. Bush, "President Says Saddam Hussein Must Leave Iraq Within 48 Hours," March 17, 2003, as quoted in Feith, *War and Decision,* 393.

7. On the D-Day plan, see Michael R. Gordon and Bernard E. Trainor, *Cobra II: The Inside Story of the Invasion and Occupation of Iraq* (New York: Pantheon Books, 2006), 164–65.

8. Tenet quoted in Bob Woodward, *Plan of Attack* (New York: Simon & Schuster, 2004), 387. On the Dora Farms intelligence, see ibid., 374, 382, 385; and George Tenet, *At the Center of the Storm: My Years at the CIA* (New York: HarperCollins, 2007), 391–93.

9. Tenet and Powell quoted in Woodward, *Plan of Attack,* 386–87.

10. Woodward, 385. Tenet uses the word *malja* in his recounting of the Dora Farms intelligence and planning. See Tenet, *At the Center of the Storm,* 393.

11. Woodward, 388, 389.

12. Tommy Franks, *American Soldier* (New York: Regan Books, 2004), 453, 456–57.

13. On the Dora Farms strike, see Gordon and Trainor, *Cobra II,* 174–75; Franks, *American Soldier,* 459–60; and Eric Schmitt, "Back From Iraq, High-Tech Fighter Pilots Recount Exploits," *The New York Times,* April 25, 2003.

14. Woodward, 399.

15. For an explanation of why Saddam was wearing glasses in the March 20 video, see Gordon and Trainor, 177.

16. On the Thar Thar raid, see Mark Green, *A Night With Saddam* (Lexington, KY: lulu.com, 2009), 86–87; and David C. Isby, *Leave No Man Behind: Liberation and Capture Missions* (London: Weidenfeld & Nicolson, 2004), 342. On the Mansour air strike, see Rowan Scarborough, "Diligent Hunters Track Down Prey," *Washington Times,* December 15, 2003. Once again, however, the CIA's enthusiasm was premature. According to Abu Tiba, a bodyguard for Uday Hussein, the incident was a sting by Saddam Hussein against one of his own officers. Suspecting a captain on his staff of informing the Americans, Saddam gave him word that the top brass would be meeting at a house in Mansour on April 7. "We went inside and then out the back door," Abu Tiba said. "Ten minutes later it was bombed. So they killed the captain. One of Saddam's bodyguards did it." See Matthew McAllester, "Ex-Bodyguard for Uday Tells of Near Misses, Defiance, Defeat," *Long Island Newsday,* July 25, 2003.

17. Chris Wilson, "Searching for Saddam: The Social Network That Caught a Dictator," *Slate.com*, February 22–26, 2010, available at http://www.slate.com/id/2245228/.

18. Rajiv Chandrasekaran, "Many Iraqis Fear Hussein Is Plotting Return to Power," *Washington Post*, July 7, 2003.

19. See John Hendren, "Defense Officials Profiling the New Enemy," *Los Angeles Times*, July 21, 2003; Dana Priest, "Reported Sightings of Hussein Increase," *Washington Post*, July 24, 2003; and Brian Bennett, "Inside the Hunt for Saddam," *Time*, July 28, 2003.

20. Wilson, "Searching for Saddam."

21. Before Mohammed's walk-in tip, US forces had received a tip that the brothers were hiding in Mosul. The informant failed a polygraph test, however, causing US military officials to dismiss the tipster. But intelligence units soon picked up signal intercepts suggesting the possible presence of HVTs in the same location in Mosul that the source had identified. Just as they began investigating this lead, Mohammed arrived with his information. See Romesh Ratnesar, "Hot on Saddam's Trail," *Time*, August 11, 2003; Isby, *Leave No Man Behind*, 344–46; Robin Moore, *Hunting Down Saddam: The Inside Story of the Search and Capture* (New York: St. Martin's Press, 2004), 86–87.

22. Moore, *Hunting Down Saddam*, 88–89.

23. Isby, 346–47. See also Eric Schmitt and David E. Sanger, "U.S. Defends Move to Storm House Where Hussein Brothers Were Hiding," *New York Times*, July 24, 2003.

24. Anderson quoted in Moore, 90; See also Donald P. Wright and Timothy R. Reese, *On Point II Transition to the New Campaign: The United States Army in Operation IRAQI FREEDOM, May 2003–January 2005* (Washington, DC: Department of the Army, 2008), 226-227; and Isby, 347.

25. Isby, 347.

26. Wilson, "Searching for Saddam."

27. Lieutenant Colonel Steve Russell, "Letters from Tikrit," in Moore, 209, 222.

28. Newton and Scharf, *Enemy of the State*, 14.

29. Lieutenant General Sanchez quoted in John F. Burns, "General Vows To Intensify U.S. Response To Attackers," *New York Times*, November 12, 2003.

30. Eric Maddox, *Mission: Black List #1: The Inside Story of the Search for Saddam Hussein—As Told by the Soldier Who Masterminded His Capture* (New York: HarperCollins, 2008), 84, 86.

31. Wilson, "Searching for Saddam"; Maddox, *Mission: Black List #1*, 95.

32. Maddox, 129.

33. Eric Schmitt, "How Army Sleuths Stalked the Adviser Who Led to Hussein," *New York Times*, December 20, 2003.

34. Maddox, 177, 179.

35. Wilson, "Searching for Saddam."

36. Maddox, 221–22.

37. Author interview with brigade staff officer, March 30, 2010, Carlisle Barracks, PA; see also Isby, pp. 350–51.

38. Isby, 351.

39. Isby, 351–52; Moore, 252–53.

40. Green, *A Night with Saddam*, 11–12.

41. Maddox, 252–53.

42. Newton and Scharf, 17.

43. Newton and Scharf, 17; Isby, 352.

44. See Federal Bureau of Investigation interview with Saddam Hussein, February 8, 2004, available at http://www.gwu.edu/~nsarchiv/NSAEBB/NSAEBB279/03 .pdf; Fouad Ajami, *The Foreigner's Gift: The Americans, the Arabs, and the Iraqis in Iraq* (New York: Free Press, 2006), 192.

45. See Isby, 353; and Thomas E. Ricks, *Fiasco: The American Military Adventure in Iraq* (New York: Penguin, 2006), 263.

46. Odierno quoted in Patrick J. McDonnell, "Iraqi Insurgency Is As Lethal As Ever Since Hussein's Capture," *Los Angeles Times,* February 4, 2004. See also Ajami, *The Foreigner's Gift,* 190.

47. Sanchez quoted in Anthony Shadid, *Night Draws Near: Iraq's People in the Shadow of America's War* (New York: Henry Holt, 2005), 309.

48. George W. Bush, "Speech on the Capture of Saddam Hussein," December 14, 2003, available at http://www.cnn.com/2003/US/12/14/sprj.irq.bush.transcript/ index.html.

49. DIA report quoted in Ajami, 194.

50. See Mary Anne Weaver, "Inventing al-Zarqawi," *Atlantic Monthly,* July/August 2006, 96.

51. See Colin Powell, "Speech to the United Nations on Iraq," February 5, 2003, available at http://www.washingtonpost.com/wp-srv/nation/transcripts/powell text_020503.html; and David S. Cloud, "Elusive Enemy: Long in U.S. Sights, A Young Terrorist Builds Grim Resume," *Wall Street Journal,* February 10, 2004.

52. Dexter Filkins, "Zarqawi Is Named as Killer," *New York Times,* May 13, 2004.

53. See Bing West, *No True Glory: A Frontline Account of the Battle for Fallujah* (New York: Bantam Books, 2005), 154–55, 225–26.

54. Allawi quoted in Edward Wong, "Iraq Demands Falluja Give Up Its Militants from Abroad," *New York Times,* October 14, 2004.

55. See Robert F. Worth and Edward Wong, "House in Falluja Seems to Have Been Base for Top Jordanian Terrorist," *New York Times,* November 19, 2004; and West, *No True Glory,* 315.

56. See Dexter Filkins, "Wanted Rebel Vows Loyalty to bin Laden, Web Sites Say," *New York Times* October 18, 2004; Walter Pincus, "Zarqawi Is Said to Swear Allegiance to Bin Laden," *Washington Post,* October 19, 2004; and Peter L. Bergen, *The Osama bin Laden I Know: An Oral History of al Qaeda's Leader* (New York: Free Press, 2006), 352, 354.

57. The definitive account of the Ramadi ambush and pursuit is Sean Naylor, "Closing in on Zarqawi," *Army Times,* May 8, 2006.

58. Naylor, "Closing in on Zarqawi."

59. Peter Grier and Faye Bowers, "U.S. at Least Seizes Zarqawi's Laptop," *Christian Science Monitor,* April 27, 2005.

60. See John F. Burns and Richard A. Oppel Jr., "Internet Posting Says Zarqawi, America's Most Wanted Man in Iraq, Has Been Wounded," *New York Times,* May 25, 2005; and John Hendren, "Rumsfeld Tells Nations Not to Help Zarqawi," *Los Angeles Times,* June 2, 2005.

61. See Hala Jaber, Sarah Baxter, and Michael Smith, "How Iraq's Ghost of Death was cornered," *Sunday Times* (London), June 11, 2006; and Sarah Baxter and Michael Smith, "Zarqawi Gunfight Kept from U.S. Hero's Widow," *Sunday Times* (London), June 25, 2006.

62. Zawahiri quoted in Susan B. Glasser and Walter Pincus, "Seized Letter Outlines Al Qaeda Goals in Iraq," *Washington Post,* October 12, 2005; Maqdisi quoted in Stephen Ulph, "Zarqawi's War on the Shia," *Jane's Terrorism and Insurgency Centre,* December 16, 2005.

63. On Zarqawi's demotion, see Weaver, "Inventing al-Zarqawi," 100.

64. See Matthew Alexander, *How to Break a Terrorist: The U.S. Interrogators Who Used Brains, Not Brutality, to Take Down the Deadliest Man in Iraq* (New York: Free Press, 2008), 204; and Dan Murphy, "Zarqawi Message: 'I'm still here,'" *Christian Science Monitor,* April 27, 2006.

65. Alexander, *How to Break a Terrorist,* 203.

66. Alexander, 15, 16. For statistics on violence in Iraq, see Michael O'Hanlon and Jason Campbell, "Iraq Index: Tracking Variables of Reconstruction & Security in Post-Saddam Iraq," February 26, 2007, 10, 11. Available at http://www.brookings.edu/fp/saban/iraq/index20070226.pdf.

67. Mark Bowden, "The Ploy," *Atlantic Monthly,* May 2007, 60; Alexander, 85.

68. Naylor, "Closing in on Zarqawi"; Alexander, 84–89.

69. Alexander, 275.

70. Alexander, 276.

71. Alexander, 277–78; Dexter Filkins, "His Long War," *New York Times Magazine,* October 18, 2009, 44.

72. See Ellen Knickmeyer, "Zarqawi's Hideout Was Secret Till Last Minute," *Washington Post,* June 11, 2006; and Bowden, "The Ploy," 66.

73. Bowden, "The Ploy," 66–67; Evan Thomas and Rod Nordland, "Death of a Terrorist," *Newsweek,* June 19, 2006.

74. Zarqawi quoted in Hala Jaber, "Zarqawi 'Sleeps in Suicide Belt,'" *Sunday Times* (London), January 22, 2006; Jaber, Baxter, and Smith, "How Iraq's Ghost of Death Was Cornered."

75. Solomon Moore, "Autopsy Details How Zarqawi Died," *Los Angeles Times,* June 13, 2006; Bowden, 67.

76. Quoted in Bowden, 67. See also John Burns, "After Long Hunt, U.S. Bombs Kill Al Qaeda Leader in Iraq," *New York Times,* June 9, 2006. Yet Zarqawi's death may have contributed to the achievement of strategic success in Iraq in a little-noticed way over the long term. Unbeknownst to US commanders at the time, internal fissures prevented al-Qaeda from appointing a successor to Zarqawi for three months. During this time, US forces began forming an alliance against al-Qaeda with the Sunni tribes around Ramadi, which led to the formation of the Anbar Salvation Council in September. This alliance marked the foundation upon which the 2007 "Surge" would build upon to secure Iraq. As JSOC Commander Lieutenant General Stanley McChrystal noted, despite the frighteningly high levels of killing, as early as the fall of 2006 it looked like al-Qaeda was falling apart. "We sensed that Al Qaeda was going to implode," he said. "We could just feel it. We were watching it and feeling it and seeing it." Thus, it is possible that Zarqawi's death had the secondary effect of facilitating the "Anbar Awakening" that helped earn a strategic victory in Iraq. But because the counterfactual of what would have happened had Zarqawi survived is unknowable, unless the few surviving AQI jihadists from that period were to write honest memoirs, the impact of Zarqawi's death in June 2006 may never be fully understood. See Filkins, "His Long War," 43.

CHAPTER EIGHT: THE HUNT FOR OSAMA BIN LADEN, PART II:
TORA BORA RECONSIDERED, ABBOTTABAD,
AND MANHUNTING LESSONS LEARNED

1. Myers quoted in Bergen, "The Long Hunt for Osama," 94. Ironically, it was General Ralston who first advised General Myers after September 11 not to make

the killing or capturing bin Laden the measure of success. Author interview with General (Ret.) Joseph Ralston, March 22, 2010.

2. President George W. Bush, press conference, Washington, DC, March 13, 2002.

3. McNeill quoted in Smucker, *Al Qaeda's Great Escape,* 203.

4. See Tommy Franks, "War of Words," *New York Times,* October 19, 2004.

5. President-elect Barack Obama, interview by Katie Couric, *CBS Evening News,* CBS, January 14, 2009, transcript available at http://www.cbsnews.com/stories/2009/01/14/eveningnews/main4722185.shtml.

6. See Kimberly Dozier, "AS Sources: Raiders Knew Mission a One-Shot Deal," Associated Press, May 17, 2011, http://news.yahoo.com/s/ap/20010517/ap_on_re_us/us_bin_laden_raid.

7. On the Escobar manhunt, see Mark Bowden, *Killing Pablo: The Hunt for the World's Greatest Outlaw* (New York: Penguin, 2001).

8. See Isby, 266; and Casper, 135.

9. See Jack Kelley, "High-Tech Tools Used to Hunt Saddam," *USA Today,* July 31, 2003; and Marie Colvin and Tony Allen-Mills, "Target Saddam—Life on the Run," *Sunday Times* (London), December 21, 2003.

10. Dexter Filkins, Mark Mazzetti, and Richard A. Oppel Jr., "How Surveillance and Betrayal Led to a Hunt's End," *New York Times,* June 9, 2006.

11. See Reeve, *The New Jackals,* 206, 264; and Jacquard, *In the Name of Osama Bin Laden,* 91.

12. Benjamin Lambeth, *Air Power Against Terror: America's Conduct of Operation Enduring Freedom* (Santa Monica, CA: RAND, 2005), 138.

13. See Fury, 289–90; and Peter John Paul Krause, "The Last Good Chance: A Reassessment of US Operations at Tora Bora," *Security Studies* 17, no. 4 (2005), 651.

14. Berntsen recalled, "Day and night, I kept thinking, *We need US soldiers on the ground! We need them to do the fighting! We need them to block a possible al-Qaeda escape into Pakistan!*" and that "the biggest and most important failure of CENTCOM leadership came at Tora Bora when they turned down my request for a battalion of US Rangers to block bin Laden's escape." See Berntsen, 290, 306, 314; Mary Anne Weaver, "Lost at Tora Bora," *New York Times Magazine,* September 11, 2005; and Bergen, *The Osama I Know,* 336.

15. Senate Foreign Relations Committee Majority Staff, *Tora Bora Revisited: How We Failed to Get Bin Laden and Why It Matters Today* (Washington, DC: US Government Printing Office, 2009), 2.

16. Joseph Collins, "From the Ground Up," *Armed Forces Journal,* October 2006, 46.

17. Lieutenant General Michael DeLong, *Inside CentCom: The Unvarnished Truth About the Wars in Afghanistan and Iraq* (Washington, DC: Regnery Publishing, 2004), 55.

18. Krause, "The Last Good Chance," 676, 677.

19. General Tommy Franks to the Senate Armed Services Committee, July 31, 2002, quoted in Berntsen, 314.

20. See DeLong, *Inside CentCom,* 55; Smucker, *Al Qaeda's Great Escape,* 88; and Fury, 293.

21. Franks told PBS's *Frontline:* "The Afghans themselves wanted to get in to Tora Bora. They wanted to do it very quickly. At that time, our Special Forces troopers were not yet in large numbers, even with those forces that we were providing support to. So rather than taking a decision that said, 'Let's take a break for some prolonged period of time and try to introduce large numbers of non-Afghani coalition forces,' the determination was made." See PBS *Frontline* interview with

General Tommy Franks, June 12, 2002, available at http://www.pbs.org/wgbh/pages/frontline/shows/campaign/interviews/franks.html. See also Tenet, 226.

22. Tenet, 227, emphasis added. The Democratic staff of the Senate Foreign Relations Committee cites journalist Ron Suskind's account of this meeting as evidence that President Bush was personally complicit in the decision not to send sufficient US troops to Tora Bora. But Suskind chooses to cut off the scene rather than include Crumpton's complete response, and the Democratic staffers chose not to cite Tenet's account of the meeting despite citing Tenet elsewhere in their report. See Ron Suskind, *The One Percent Doctrine: Deep Inside America's Pursuit of Its Enemies Since 9/11* (New York: Simon & Schuster, 2006), 56–59; and Senate Foreign Relations Committee Majority Staff, *Tora Bora Revisited,* 13.

23. Michael O'Hanlon estimates that it would have taken only 1,000 to 3,000 troops to close the 100 to 150 escape routes out of Tora Bora, but offers no explanation for this number. See Michael O'Hanlon, *Defense Strategy for the Post-Saddam Era* (Washington, DC: Brookings, 2005), 32–33. On the Operation Anaconda planning estimates, see Sean Naylor, *Not a Good Day to Die: The Untold Story of Operation Anaconda,* (New York: Berkeley Books, 2005), 62.

24. Author interview with "Dalton Fury," April 22, 2010; and Fury, 293. Fury suggests, however, that had the Marines been committed to the Pakistani side of the border to assist the Frontier Forces in blocking the passageways out of the Tora Bora mountains, "or at least to keep those new allies honest," more fleeing al-Qaeda would have been killed or captured. See Fury, 294.

25. Justin Huggler, "They Seek Him Here, They Seek Him There," *The Independent,* August 4, 2004, http://independent.co.uk/news/world/asia/they-seek-him-here-they-seek-him-there-555313.html.

26. Naylor, *Not a Good Day to Die,* 375. Also see Paul L. Hastert, "Operation Anaconda: Perception Meets Reality in the Hills of Afghanistan," *Studies in Conflict & Terrorism* 28: 11–20

27. See Milan Hauner, "One Man against the Empire: The Faqir of Ipi and the British in Central Asia on the Eve of and during the Second World War," *Journal of Contemporary History* 16, no. 1 (January 1981), 183–212. Gunaratna quoted in Huggler, "They Seek Him Here, They Seek Him There."

28. See Terrell, *Apache Chronicle,* 383.

29. Smith et al., 30.

30. Atkinson, "The Raid That Went Wrong."

31. "Elite Officer Recalls Bin Laden Hunt," CBS's *60 Minutes,* episode aired October 5, 2008, transcript available at http://www.cbsnews.com/stories/2008/10/02/60minutes/main4494937.shtml.

32. Quoted in Smucker, *Al Qaeda's Great Escape,* 195.

33. Hayden quoted in Jason Ryan and Brian Ross, "CIA Chief: Bin Laden Alive, Worried About 'Own Security,'" *ABC News,* November 13, 2008. See also Bergen, "The Long Hunt for Osama," 95.

34. In October 1919, the Marines occupying Haiti targeted Charlemagne Péralte, the leader of roughly five thousand guerrillas who for six months had been subjecting US forces to hit-and-run attacks. Herman Hanneken, a Marine sergeant serving as a captain in the Haitian gendarmerie, drew the insurgents into a trap on October 31, 1919, by establishing a fake guerrilla unit that would attack an American outpost. Similar to Funston, Hanneken than snuck behind enemy lines with twenty Haitians disguised as rebels, located Peralte's camp, and shot and killed the rebel leader. See Max Boot, *The Savage Wars of Peace: Small Wars and the Rise of American Power* (New York: Basic Books, 2002), 172–74. This case stretches the

definition of strategic manhunts, however, as no new forces were deployed for the operation, only forces already in Haiti on occupation duty.

35. Zahid Hussain and Jeremy Page, "Widow Says Home Was Base for 5 Years," *Wall Street Journal*, May 6, 2011, 8.

36. See Isby, 354. Baram quoted in Thomas and Nordland, "Death of a Terrorist."

37. John J. Pershing to Funston, March 25, 1916, PP 372, quoted in Smythe, 277.

38. Tompkins, 100. Pershing similarly wrote a friend: "From the very first, from the time we crossed the line, we were met by nothing but misinformation and subtle maneuvers to lead us off on wrong trails. And throughout the pursuit we *never* received a bit of correct information till it was too late." See John J. Pershing to James Hopper, July 11, 1916, PP 372, quoted in Smythe, 269.

39. Mason, 83.

40. Hoar quoted in Isby, 298. Also see Baumann, Yates, and Washington, 5, 132. Moreover, the intelligence collection effort in the Aideed manhunt was crippled by bureaucracy and poor resource allocation. UNOSOM II's intelligence staff suffered from an acute shortage of resources. Most of the CENTCOM Intelligence Support Element (CISE) departed with UNITAF, causing presence in the streets to shrivel from several dozen agents to only a few collectors. The remaining CISE in Mogadishu experienced 100 percent turnover in the third week of September, at the height of the Aideed manhunt. JSOC intelligence officers later reported that CISE support to Task Force Ranger was "minimal," with a poor focus on HUMINT. Additionally, the CIA sent all information collected in Mogadishu back to its headquarters in Langley, Virginia, where decisions were made about what could be disseminated. "Many times they got good and correct information," a Somali involved in the intelligence effort said, "but they didn't do an operation because they kept the info too long." See James T. Faust, *Task Force Ranger in Somalia* (Carlisle, PA: US Army War College Personal Experience Monograph, March 1999), 13. See also Baumann, Yates, and Washington, 103–04, 121; and Peterson, 103.

41. Author interview with General (Ret.) Joseph Ralston, March 22, 2010. See also Tenet, 120; and Coll, *Ghost Wars*, 520.

42. Roger Cressey quoted in Bergen, "The Long Hunt for Osama," 99.

43. Abdel Bari Atwan, editor of *Al Quds al Arabi* newspaper, quoted in Bergen, *The Osama bin Laden I Know*, 380–81.

44. Bearden quoted in *PBS Frontline: Hunting Bin Laden*, 2001, available at http://www.pbs.org/wgbh/pages/frontline/shows/binladen/interviews/bearden.html. See also Bergen, "The Long Hunt for Osama," 92; Smucker, *Al Qaeda's Great Escape*, 46, 48.

45. Smucker, *Al Qaeda's Great Escape*, 50–51, 52, 57, 122. Even in these areas, Pakistani journalist Hamid Mir observed, bin Laden was "more popular than any political leader in Pakistan." Mir quoted in Bergen, *Holy War, Inc.*, 151.

46. Kenneth Finlayson, "The 2nd Ranger Battalion and the Capture of Che Guevara," *Veritas: Journal of Army Special Operations History* 4, no. 4 (2008), 94–97; Gary Prado Salmon, *The Defeat of Che Guevara: Military Response to Guerrilla Challenge in Bolivia* (Westport, CT: Praeger, 1987); and Felix I. Rodriguez and John Weisman, *Shadow Warrior: The CIA Hero of a Hundred Unknown Battles* (New York: Simon and Schuster, 1989).

47. See Bowden, *Killing Pablo*.

48. Abdul Hakim Mujahid and Hamid Mir quoted in Bergen, *The Osama bin Laden I Know*, 232, 236.

49. See Sydney J. Freedberg Jr., "Special, Short, and Stealthy: The United States Military Actually Has Some Successes Under Its Belt in Snatch-and-Grab Expeditionary Missions," *National Journal* 33, no. 39 (September 29, 2001), 298.

50. Fury, 190.

51. Mohammed Musa quoted in Smucker, *Al Qaeda's Great Escape,* 110–11. See also ibid., 45.

52. Fury, 287.

53. See Musicant, 352; Hoffman, 80; and Millett, 259.

54. See Musicant, 352; Hoffman, 80; and Millett, 259.

55. Munro to Assistant Secretary Francis White, June 28, 1928, Francis White papers in the National Archives, box 14, as quoted in Kamman, 134.

56. See Neil Macauley, *The Sandino Affair* (Micanopy, FL: Wacahoota Press, 1967), 142–43.

57. Pershing Manuscript, Chapter 23, p. 5. Before the Punitive Expedition entered Mexico, the Carranza government made clear it would not allow the US Army to use Mexican railroads, which prevented Pershing from flanking Villa to the south in the initial phase of the campaign. On March 16 the retreating Villistas encountered a large Carrancista force only two miles away. The government troops simply rode on and did not engage the Villistas.

58. Personal message from commanding general, Tenth Mountain Division, to the Army Chief of Staff, September 15, 1993, as quoted in Hooker, 132. Similarly, one American NCO wrote: "The contingents that stick out most in my mind in regard to these safe passage agreements were the Italians and Saudis. They both drove around Mogadishu without a care in the world." See Baumann, Yates, and Washington, 133. Italian units in Mogadishu refused to participate in operations against the SNA and were publicly accused by some UN and US officials of collaborating with Aideed's forces. Some in Task Force Ranger believed they were flashing signals with their headlights out into Mogadishu whenever the helicopters took off at night, and the UN eventually requested the Italian contingent relieve its commander.

59. See Douglas Jehl, "Captured Official Is Said to Tell U.S. Hussein Survived," *New York Times,* June 21, 2003.

60. NSC email, Clarke to Berger, February 11, 1999, quoted in *The 9/11 Commission Report,* 134. Roland Jacquard claims bin Laden spent more than $60 million from 1997 to 2001 to subvert Pakistani nuclear scientists and to ensure the collusion of Pakistani generals and members of the secret services. See Jacquard, 158.

61. Tenet, 139–40.

62. Smucker, *Al Qaeda's Great Escape,* 89, 112.

63. *The 9/11 Commission Report,* 368.

64. Quoted in Bergen, *The Osama bin Laden I Know,* 366.

65. See Bill Roggio and Alexander Mayer, "Senior al Qaeda and Taliban leaders killed in US airstrikes in Pakistan, 2004–2011," *The Long War Journal,* http://www.longwarjournal.org/pakistan-strikes-hvts.php; see also Peter Bergen and Katherine Tiedemann, "The Drone War: Are Predators Our Best Weapon or Worst Enemy?" *New Republic,* June 3, 2009, pp. 22–25.

66. See for example Adam Entous and Matthew Rosenberg, "Pakistan Tells U.S. to Halt Drones," *Wall Street Journal,* April 12, 2011; Jane Perlez and Ismail Khan, "Pakistan Tells U.S. It Must Sharply Cut C.I.A. Activities," *New York Times,* April 12, 2011, p. 1; and Greg Miller and Karen DeYoung, "Pakistan Threatens to Restrict CIA Strikes," *Washington Post,* April 12, 2011, p. 1.

67. Leon Panetta, interviewed by *Time* magazine, May 3, 2011, http://www.time .com/time/quotes/0,26174,2069357,00.html.

68. Wright, 332.

69. Barrett quoted in Neil MacFarquhar, "Bin Laden's Likely Heir Is Viewed as Organizer, Not as Inspiring Figure," *New York Times,* May 3, 2011, p. F4.

70. Ismail quoted in Bergen, *The Osama bin Laden I Know,* 386. See also ibid., xxvi.

71. See Eli Lake, "How bin Laden Led Operations," *Washington Times,* May 4, 2011, p.1; and Mark Mazzetti and Scott Shane, "Data Show Bin Laden Plots," *New York Times,* May 6, 2011, p.1.

72. According to a Pew Research survey, confidence in bin Laden in Jordan fell from 56 percent in 2003 to 13 percent in 2011, and in Lebanon from 19 to 1 percent.

73. Peter Finn, "Terrorist Threat May Be at Most 'Heightened State' since 9/11, Napolitano Says," *Washington Post,* February 9, 2011, http://www.washingtonpost. com/wp-dyn/content/article/2011/02/09/AR2011020906648.html.

CONCLUSION: BEYOND BIN LADEN:
THE FUTURE OF STRATEGIC MANHUNTS

1. This is not to say, of course, that al-Qaeda does not remain a threat, especially that posed by affiliated organizations such as al-Qaeda in the Arabian Peninsula, which was responsible for the failed "underwear bomber" attack in 2009 and the October 2010 attempted bombing of UPS planes flying from Yemen to the United States.

2. Colin Powell, *My American Journey* (New York: Ballantine Books, 1995), 414.

3. David Isby, *Leave No Man Behind: Liberation and Capture Missions* (London: Weidenfeld & Nicolson, 2004), 292.

4. Colin H. Kahl, "In the Crossfire or the Crosshairs? Norms, Civilian Casualties, and U.S. Conduct in Iraq," *International Security* 32, no. 1 (Summer 2007), 9, 39.

5. Harvey M. Sapolsky and Jeremy Shapiro, "Casualties, Technology, and America's Future Wars," *Parameters,* Summer 1996, 119–27.

6. Lawrence Freedman and Efraim Karsh, "How Kuwait Was Won: Strategy in the Gulf War," *International Security* 16 (Fall 1991), 39.

7. See Kenneth Waltz, *Theory of International Politics* (New York: McGraw-Hill, 1979), 60–68, 91–101. For a first cut at developing a theory of how individuals affect international security, see Daniel L. Byman and Kenneth M. Pollack, "Let Us Now Praise Great Men: Bringing the Statesman Back In," *International Security* 25, no. 4 (Spring 2001), 107–46.

8. Steven R. David, "Deposing Dictators," unpublished paper, Johns Hopkins University, January 1994, 2, 3.

9. Ralph Peters, "A Revolution in Military Ethics?" *Parameters,* Summer 1996, 102–08. Also see Bruce A. Ross, "The Case for Targeting Leadership in War," *Naval War College Review* 46 (Winter 1993), 90.

10. Editorial, "Targeting Mr. Gaddafi," *Washington Post,* May 3, 2011, 16.

11. Peters, "A Revolution in Military Ethics?"

12. Rupert Smith, *The Utility of Force: The Art of War in the Modern World* (New York: Alfred Knopf, 2007), 286.

13. Powell, *My American Journey,* 505.

14. See Max Boot, "Israel's Tragic Gaza Dilemma," *Wall Street Journal,* January 5, 2009. Boot applies this argument to contemporary Israeli operations.

15. Kahl, "In the Crossfire or the Crosshairs?" 15–18, 21.

16. Paul Leventhal and Yonah Alexander, *Preventing Nuclear Terrorism* (Lexington, MA: Lexington Books, 1987), 9, 58.

17. See Jessica Stern, *The Ultimate Terrorists* (Cambridge, MA: Harvard University Press, 1999), 59, 65.

18. See Glenn Reynolds, *An Army of Davids: How Markets and Technology Empower Ordinary People to Beat Big Media, Big Government and Other Goliaths* (Nashville, TN: Nelson Current, 2006), 206, 265.

19. Bruce Hoffman, "Responding to Terrorism Across the Technological Spectrum," in John Arquilla and David Ronfeldt, *In Athena's Camp: Preparing for Conflict in the Information Age* (Santa Monica, CA: RAND, 1997), 349, 353–54.

20. Qiao Lian and Wang Xiangsui, *Unrestricted Warfare: China's Master Plan to Destroy America* (Beijing: PLA Literature and Arts Publishing House, 1999).

21. See Gregory D. Kutz, "Military and Dual-Use Technology: Covert Testing Shows Continuing Vulnerability of Domestic Sales for Illegal Export," Testimony before the Subcommittee on Oversight and Investigations, Committee on Energy and Commerce, House of Representatives, June 4, 2009.

22. Thomas X. Hammes, *The Sling and the Stone: On War in the 21st Century* (St. Paul, MN: Zenith Press, 2004), 194, 198.

23. Hoffman, "Responding to Terrorism Across the Technological Spectrum," 350.

24. Martin C. Libicki, "The Small and the Many," in Arquilla and Ronfeldt, *In Athena's Camp*, 192, 193, 195.

25. Peters, "A Revolution in Military Ethics?"

26. Annual report of Aircraft Squadrons, Second Brigade, July 1, 1927, to June 20, 1928, in "Professional Notes," *Marine Corps Gazette* 13, no. 4 (December 1928), 248–57.

27. "Information from a Deserter . . . Who Has Been with Sandino's Forces for Almost a Year," in Second Brigade, B-2 Report, February 12, 1929, MCHA, Nicaragua: Reel 14, as quoted in Macauley, 121.

28. Quoted in P. W. Singer, *Wired for War: The Robotics Revolution and Conflict in the 21st Century* (New York: Penguin, 2009), 268.

29. Smith, *The Utility of Force*, 228–229.

30. Pete Blaber, *The Mission, The Men, and Me: Lessons from a Former Delta Force Commander* (New York: Penguin, 2008), 140.

31. See Katz, 605–06; Mason, 228.

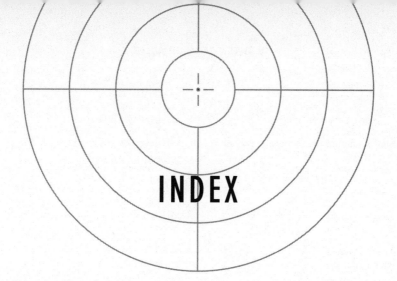

INDEX